PUBLIC NUISANCE

In *Public Nuisance*, Linda Mullenix describes the landscape of 21st century mass tort litigation involving public harms – including lead paint, opioids, firearms, e-cigarettes, climate change, and environmental pollution – and the novel theory of public nuisance that lawyers and local governments have used to receive compensation from those who have created public nuisances. The book surveys conflicting judicial decisions rooted in common law and statutory interpretation and evaluates the competing arguments for and against the expansion of public nuisance law. Mullenix argues that that the development of public nuisance theory is part of the historical arc of mass tort litigation and suggests a middle approach to new public nuisance law, namely, that we should embrace the common law and legislated public nuisance statutes.

Linda S. Mullenix is the Rita and Morris Atlas Chair in Advocacy at the University of Texas School of Law. She holds a Ph.D. in political theory from Columbia University and a J.D. from Georgetown University Law Center. Professor Mullenix has served as a U.S. Supreme Court Fellow; a scholar-in-residence at the Rockefeller Foundation Bellagio, Italy; and the Fulbright Senior Distinguished Chair in Law, in Trento, Italy. She is an elected Life Member of the American Law Institute, the Texas Bar Foundation, and the American Bar Foundation.

Public Nuisance

THE NEW MASS TORT FRONTIER

LINDA S. MULLENIX

The University of Texas at Austin

CAMBRIDGE
UNIVERSITY PRESS

CAMBRIDGE
UNIVERSITY PRESS

Shaftesbury Road, Cambridge CB2 8EA, United Kingdom

One Liberty Plaza, 20th Floor, New York, NY 10006, USA

477 Williamstown Road, Port Melbourne, VIC 3207, Australia

314–321, 3rd Floor, Plot 3, Splendor Forum, Jasola District Centre, New Delhi – 110025, India

103 Penang Road, #05–06/07, Visioncrest Commercial, Singapore 238467

Cambridge University Press is part of Cambridge University Press & Assessment, a department of the University of Cambridge.

We share the University's mission to contribute to society through the pursuit of education, learning and research at the highest international levels of excellence.

www.cambridge.org
Information on this title: www.cambridge.org/9781009334921

DOI: 10.1017/9781009334907

First published 2024

A catalogue record for this publication is available from the British Library

A Cataloging-in-Publication data record for this book is available from the Library of Congress

ISBN 978-1-009-33492-1 Hardback
ISBN 978-1-009-33491-4 Paperback

For my next generations, children and grandchildren

Robert, Joyce, Jack, Laura, William, Amy, Chris, Ben, Ned, Oliver, and Sophie

Contents

Acknowledgements

I have revised and repurposed portions of one book chapter and an article authored by me for use in this book. I am indebted to the copyright holders identified below for permission to reprint excerpts from the following materials:

Exposition in Chapter 2 uses material from my book chapter, Linda S. Mullenix, "Aggregationists at the Barricades: Assessing the Impact of the ALI Principles of the Law of Aggregate Litigation," in *The ALI at 100: Essays on Its Centennial* (American Law Institute, Andrew Gold and Robert W. Gordon, eds. 2023), copyright @ 2023 by the American Law Institute. Reprinted with a license to reproduce materials.

Exposition in Chapter 9 is based on materials from my article, Linda S. Mullenix, "Outgunned No More? Reviving the Prospect of A Firearms Mass Tort Litigation," 49 *Sw. L. Rev.* 390 (2020), copyright @ 2020 by the Southwestern University Law School. Reprinted with the permission of the Southwestern University Law Review.

I also wish to thank the Cambridge University Press editors and the anonymous reviewers of this manuscript for their help and comments.

Austin, Texas   Professor Linda S. Mullenix
May 2023

Introduction

On July 6, 2021, Governor Andrew Cuomo signed Senate Bill S7196 amending the New York state public nuisance law to subject gun sellers and gun manufacturers to liability for public nuisance if they failed to implement reasonable controls to prevent the unlawful sale, possession, or use of firearms in New York.[1] The statute allows gun manufacturers and distributors to be held liable for actions that harm public safety. The public nuisance statute specifically regulates the marketing, distribution, and sale of firearms. The legislation reflected a carefully crafted state workaround of the federal Protection of Lawful Commerce in Arms Act (2005),[2] in a bold and innovative state attempt to end the firearms industry's immunity from liability for criminal misuse of firearms. In January 2022, California followed New York's lead and introduced AB 1594 declaring that gun manufacturers have created a public nuisance if their failure to follow state and local gun laws result in injury or death.[3]

In August 2021, Mexico filed a $10 billion lawsuit in Massachusetts federal district court against gun manufacturers Smith & Wesson, Sturm, Ruger & Co., Beretta USA, Barrett Firearms Manufacturing, Colt's Manufacturing Co., and Glock Inc.[4] The lawsuit accuses major U.S. gun makers of facilitating weapons trafficking to drug cartels, leading to thousands of deaths. The complaint set forth several claims alleging that the defendants' conduct created and contributed to a public nuisance by unreasonably interfering

---

[1] N.Y. S7196, An Act to Amend the General Business Law, in Relation to the Dangers to Safety and Health and Creation of a Public Nuisance Cause by the Sale, Manufacturing, Distribution, Importing and Marketing of Firearms, Art.39-DDDD.

[2] Pub. L. 109-92, 119 Stat. 2095, codified at 15 U.S.C. §§ 7901–7903.

[3] Cal. Assembly Bill AB 1594 (June 27, 2022); Cal Civ. Code Div. 3, Part 4, Title 20: Firearms Industry Responsibility Act.

[4] Estados Unidos Mexicanos v. Smith & Wesson Brands, Inc., et al., Case 1:21-cv-11269-FDS (D. Mass 2021).

with public safety and health and undermining Mexico's gun laws, resulting in specific and particularized injuries suffered by the government. The complaint further alleged that the Mexican government and its residents had the right to be free from conduct that created an unreasonable risk to the public health, welfare, and safety, and to be free from conduct that created a disturbance and reasonable apprehension to person and property. Thirteen states and three Latin American and Caribbean countries filed amicus briefs in support of Mexico.

Climate change has been at the forefront of recent public nuisance litigation, leading to conflicting federal and state decisions concerning the viability of using public nuisance law to remedy problems relating to climate change. In 2018 and 2019, in a second wave of climate change litigation, plaintiffs filed a spate of state lawsuits against fossil fuel companies asserting public nuisance claims for producing and distributing fuels that generate greenhouse gases that unreasonably interfere with a public right by contributing to the climate change crisis.

These lawsuits followed a series of similar public nuisance litigation against power companies allegedly responsible for creating a public nuisance through their carbon dioxide emissions exacerbating climate change. However, climate change public nuisance lawsuits have encountered numerous challenges, including a Supreme Court ruling that the federal Clean Air Act displaced federal common law public nuisance claims against power companies.[5] On April 1, 2021, a Court of Appeals for the Second Circuit upheld the dismissal of a New York municipal lawsuit against oil company defendants that sought to hold the defendants legally liable for climate change under public nuisance law.[6]

Beginning in 2020 with the advent of the COVID-19 pandemic and consequent transmission of the virus and resulting illnesses, attorneys sued employers invoking public nuisance doctrine in a series of workplace safety lawsuits. These lawsuits alleged that the company defendants, by failing to follow public health protocols, created a COVID transmission hazard that not only threatened workers but also unreasonably interfered with the public's right to health and safety. As a common law tort, workers could sue under a private right of action and avoid federal preemption based on an express common law exemption under the Occupational Health Act. These lawsuits have met with mixed results.

In 2020 an Illinois state court granted McDonald employees a preliminary injunction requiring multiple McDonald locations to enforce statewide

---

[5] American Power Co., Inc. v. Connecticut, 564 U.S. (2011).
[6] New York v. Chevron Corp., No. 18-2188, 2021 WL 1216541 (2d Cir. Apr. 1, 2021).

mask-wearing and social distancing protocols.[7] The court cited the company's failure to abide by state health guidelines, concluding that the company's practices constituted a substantial interference with the public health in a pandemic. Other courts have deferred COVID-related public nuisance suits under the primary jurisdiction doctrine to allow a relevant administrative agency to act first. Some courts have rejected COVID public nuisance lawsuits for the failure of plaintiffs to show the "special injury" necessary for standing under public nuisance law.

The emergence of the role of public nuisance claims is the newest frontier and battleground in resolving mass tort litigation. But courts are split concerning the viability of public nuisance claims and the theories underlying these claims, which conflict is amply illustrated by inconsistent rulings in the state as well as national opioid litigation and other attempted public nuisance lawsuits concerning opioid harms. Beginning in 2017, plaintiffs filed more than 2,500 public nuisance opioid cases in federal and state courts. On November 9, 2021, the Oklahoma Supreme Court overturned a $465 million opioid public nuisance judgment following a bench trial in which the judge found facts in favor of Oklahoma against opioid manufacturers.[8] The state had sued Johnson & Johnson, Purdue Pharma, and Teva Pharmaceuticals alleging they created a public nuisance when they manufactured, marketed, and sold opioids as an effective painkiller, that they were or should have been aware of the dangers associated with opioid abuse and addiction, and that they should have warned the public about these dangers.

In overturning the verdict, the Oklahoma Supreme Court stated that while the state's nuisance statutes had been applied to unreasonable conduct that interfered with and endangered the public's health and safety, the application of those statutes was limited to criminal conduct that affected public property. In a similar vein, a California Superior Court judge ruled against several local governments and in favor of four large pharmaceutical companies, concluding that the governments failed to prove how many medically unnecessary prescriptions had been written because of the manufacturers' alleged misleading marketing efforts, and whether and how much such prescriptions had contributed to a public nuisance.[9] On the other hand, on November 22, 2021, a federal jury in Cleveland, Ohio, after a six-week trial before Judge Dan Polster, found that CVS Health, Walmart, and Walgreens created a public

---

[7]   Massey v. McDonald's Corp., Case No. 2020-CH-04247 (Ill. Cir. Ct. 2020).

[8]   State *ex. rel.* Hunter v. Johnson & Johnson, 499 P.3d 719 (Okla. 2021).

[9]   California v. Purdue Pharma, No. 30-2014-00725287-CU-BT-CXC), 2021 WL 5227329 (Cal. App. Supp. Nov. 1, 2021).

nuisance that contributed to the opioid crises in two northeastern Ohio counties when the pharmacies overlooked the so-called red flags when filling certain opioid subscriptions.[10]

The advent of public nuisance claims has generated a battle between plaintiff and defense counsel concerning the legitimacy of public nuisance doctrine to remediate mass tort litigation. Whether modern public nuisance claims in mass tort litigation are viable remains to be seen. But there is evidence that the threat of a public nuisance claim has served to encourage mass tort settlements before trial. Thus, in Oklahoma, Purdue Pharma and Teva settled with the state agreeing to pay $270 million and $85 million, respectively. In summer 2021, Walgreens, Rite Aid, CVS, and Walmart settled with two New York counties for a combined $26 million. In Ohio, Rite Aid and Giant Eagle, a regional chain, settled before trial for an undisclosed amount. Johnson & Johnson and three large drug distributors (McKesson, Cardinal Health, and AmerisourceBergen) entered into a $26 billion settlement to resolve several states' claims, although the Washington state attorney general characterized this settlement as "not nearly good enough for Washington" and the case has gone to trial in Seattle.

To understand the revolutionary contemporary use of public nuisance law as the new frontier in mass tort litigation, this book begins with an historical overview of traditional concepts that distinguished private and public nuisance. Earliest private nuisance law involved harms arising from interference with another person's enjoyment and use of land. The law has long recognized that a person with rightful possession had rights to occupancy and unimpaired condition in reasonable comfort and convenience.

Historically, public nuisance interfered with group rights and was considered a criminal wrong. A public nuisance was defined as an act or omission that obstructed, damaged, or inconvenienced community rights. Public nuisance covered a wide variety of minor crimes that threatened the health, morals, safety, comfort, convenience, or community welfare. Examples of the same included shooting fireworks in the streets, gaming, houses of prostitution, keeping diseased animals, or harboring a vicious dog. A person or entity that created a public nuisance might be punished by a criminal sentence, a fine, or both.

Public nuisances were subject to injunctions or abatement remedies, and violators might be charged with the costs of a cleanup. There was no civil remedy for an individual harmed by a public nuisance, except for a specific tort injury limited to damages that were the direct result of the public nuisance.

---

[10] Meryl Kornfield & Lenny Bernstein, CVS, Walgreens and Walmart are Responsible for Flooding Ohio Countries with Pain Pills, Jury Says, Wash. Post (Nov. 23, 2021).

After surveying historical concepts of nuisance, the book discusses the emergence of public nuisance as a claim asserted in mass tort litigation beginning in the twenty-first century. This discussion sets forth the theoretical basis for public nuisance claims in mass tort cases, the relationship to traditional tort theories, and the introduction of public nuisance statutes. This analysis concludes with a roadmap for ensuing chapters, tracing the historical public nuisance jurisprudence, initial rejection in the 1990s of public nuisance claims, and the expansion of public nuisance to products cases. Chapters explore issues relating to litigating public nuisance claims including pleading, defenses, and remedies. In addition, the new public nuisance litigation has encountered many challenges, including standing, federal preemption, separation of powers, Commerce Clause, and the constitutionality of public nuisance statutes.

After setting out the framework for understanding the new public nuisance law, the book examines public nuisance claims in five illustrative mass torts: lead paint, environmental pollution, opioids, firearms, and e-cigarettes. These chapters assess the fate of public nuisance claims in the mass tort context. The book evaluates the competing arguments for expansion of public nuisance, balanced against arguments of the illegitimacy of public nuisance claims in mass tort cases. The book concludes with observations on evolving public nuisance jurisprudence in the new legal landscape of mass tort litigation, suggesting that shaping public nuisance law legislatively, as a matter of public policy, may be used in tandem with common law development.

Considering the inroads accomplished by the new public nuisance claims, the common law has evolved to expand the nature of public nuisance claims, the parties who may pursue such claims, the elements and defenses to such claims, and available remedies, including compensatory damages. In addition to common law developments, some states have enacted targeted public nuisance statues that have created new claims, complementing common law public nuisance jurisprudence.

The recent emergence of public nuisance claims as the basis for remediation in mass tort litigation has ignited controversy concerning the judicial expansion of vague concepts of common law public nuisance doctrine as a workaround of traditional products liability law. Courts are split concerning whether public nuisance law may be a proper avenue for vindicating mass tort harms. The debate centers on whether courts in their role to create and interpret common law may expand and rewrite public nuisance jurisprudence to advance claims that otherwise would not be actionable as products liability cases.

Critics have suggested that applying common law nuisance principles and state statutes to lawful products creates unlimited and unprincipled liability for product manufacturers. These critics argue that gun manufacturers and pharmaceutical companies have no control over those who sell (in the case of guns) or prescribe (in the case of opioids) their products and whether those who obtain them use them properly. Other commentators have urged that the solution to the emerging use of public nuisance theories to resolve mass tort litigation should lie with the political branches of government as a matter of public policy, not with the courts through unwarranted expansion of the law of public nuisance.

The debate over the legitimacy of emerging public nuisance in mass tort products litigation need not be reduced to a binary choice between competing approaches. The existing terrain of public nuisance law, embracing common law and statutory approaches, can co-exist to accommodate the traditional role of common law development as well as institutional preferences for legislative policy enactments. The theoretical underpinning of public nuisance jurisprudence might expansively focus on social goals and distributive justice, as contrasted to private nuisance law, which focuses on prioritizing individual property rights and corrective justice. As a basis for mass tort litigation, public nuisance jurisprudence might rightly focus on harms to the public health or welfare and on the police powers of the state, or on individuals, to enforce and redress societal harms.

It has always been the nature of common law to adapt to changed circumstances. We may anticipate that common public nuisance law will continue to develop to embrace more flexible standards of public rights, harm, and remediation. The element of public nuisance law that requires an individual to plead and prove a "special injury" to obtain monetary damages has proved difficult for courts to unpack from the societal harm giving rise to the public nuisance. Thus, evolving public nuisance jurisprudence legitimately might relax the special injury requirement to enable claimants harmed by a public nuisance to obtain monetary relief.

In the same vein, courts engaged in refining public nuisance jurisprudence might take the opportunity to clarify the plaintiff's requirement to prove that the defendant's conduct amounted to an unreasonable interference with a public right. In nuisance cases, judicial standards for reasonableness are vague and inconsistently applied. This does not mean that a common law reasonableness standard is unworkable or unmanageable. At any rate, public nuisance violations might be considered a strict liability offense. In addressing the reasonableness standard, some state public nuisance statutes adopted this approach to eliminate the reasonableness requirement altogether.

Apart from potential evolution of common law doctrine, a model public nuisance statute, based on the state's police power to protect the general health and welfare of its citizens, might cover behavior that threatened or harmed a community's health, safety, comfort, convenience, or a right common to the public. Conceptually, a public nuisance interferes with the public as a class, not merely one person or a group of persons. The right to sue for and recover monetary damages should be available to individuals as well as public authorities responsible for protecting the rights of the public, including federal and state agencies.

Public nuisance jurisprudence law was developed chiefly in the era before the emergence of widespread mass tort harms to entire communities, in the context of property and environmental contamination litigation. Public nuisance law might evolve to adapt to the changing legal landscape of mass tort product cases, as a function of common law development as well as legislative enactment. The fact that these lawsuits arise from events relating to harmful products does not lessen the fundamental communitywide harmful consequences to public health and welfare, nor the police powers to protect citizens.

Public nuisance claims have emerged as a novel, innovative approach to pursuing and resolving mass tort litigation in the twenty-first century. The development of public nuisance claims as a basis for group remediation is likely to be the focus of mass tort litigation in the next decades. With successful litigation and settlement of public nuisance claims, parties and courts will increasingly make recourse to public nuisance as a viable legal theory in mass products litigation. Federal and state courts have been cautiously receptive to public nuisance claims, and attorneys have successfully leveraged these claims to encourage massive settlements in tobacco, opioid, lead paint, PCBs, e-cigarettes, and other mass tort lawsuits. Analysis of unsuccessful public nuisance mass torts, however, illustrates the limitations on judicial reception to the new wave of public nuisance litigation.

This book is the first to survey, discuss, and analyze the emergence of public nuisance law as the newest approach to the resolution of mass tort cases. The book argues that conceiving the new public nuisance debate as a binary choice is not useful. The legal system is expansive enough to embrace both the common law approach along with new public nuisance statutory initiatives. Thus, the existing regime of evolving common law, coupled with statutory enactments reflecting carefully crafted public policy, provides a middle ground approach that accommodates the historical role of judicial common law development as well as institutional preferences for legislatively enacted public policy choices.

1

Historical Context of Private and Public
Nuisance at Law and Equity

1.1 DISTINGUISHING PRIVATE AND PUBLIC NUISANCE

A brief examination of the jurisprudential development of nuisance law helps provide a context for understanding the evolution of public nuisance law into the contemporary mass tort litigation landscape. The English jurisprudence surrounding private and public nuisance law was transplanted in the United States in the seventeenth century, with the immigration of colonists who brought with them the English common law system. Over time, nuisance law began to subsume elements of criminal, property, and tort laws. The historical evolution of nuisance law suggests three significant points.

First, nuisance law historically has been plagued with vague and fuzzy conceptualization, which has contributed to imprecise, inconsistent common law interpretations. In response, some jurisdictions turned to legislatively codifying nuisance principles. Such statutory nuisance law, however, has not been without its own controversies concerning statutory construction of nuisance laws. Additionally, the general fuzziness of nuisance common law principles – especially public nuisance law – has contributed to the modern controversies over the applicability of public nuisance law to contemporary mass tort litigation.

Second, the history of nuisance law presents a jurisprudential terrain constantly in a flux, often expanding to meet the challenges of new legal problems or retracting in resistance to novel approaches.[1] This understanding provides a basis for current advocates, who champion the new application of public nuisance theories to twenty-first century mass tort litigation, or detractors who resist the expansion of public nuisance in the mass tort arena. In the same

[1] For a comprehensive discussion of the development of modern nuisance law, *see* Donald G. Gifford, Public Nuisance as a Mass Products Liability Tort, 71 U. Cin. L. Rev. 741 (2003).

way that courts and litigants, spanning five decades of mass tort litigation, embraced novel theories of substantive and procedural justice, the expanding notions of public nuisance law represent the evolving nature of contemporary mass tort litigation.

Third, an understanding of the history of nuisance law illustrates how long-standing doctrinal precepts relating to public nuisance continue to bedevil the judicial reception of public nuisance claims in mass tort litigation. While the assertion of public nuisance claims has attempted to create a novel approach to thinking about mass harms and remediation, conventional common law defenses impair parties' ability to assert public nuisance theories. Public nuisance defenses, supplemented with other contemporary challenges to public nuisance claims, remain an obstacle to judicial embrace of this new frontier of mass tort litigation.

The torts scholar William L. Prosser described the law of nuisance as an "impenetrable jungle."[2] Historically, the word nuisance had its general origins in the French word for harm, but the term came to describe legal liability for two types of legal harms.[3] Nuisance law has been confused by colloquial understandings; sometimes, courts loosely applied nuisance to an array of legally inappropriate contexts, such as alarming advertisements or a cockroach baked into a pie.[4] Contemporary commentators have suggested that older decisions relating to nuisance claims were based on "broad, almost meaningless definitions and terminology that can now be largely discarded."[5] In addition, the concepts of private and public nuisance often were not carefully distinguished. Thus, nuisance has come to mean more than mere hurt, annoyance, or inconvenience but instead denotes invasions of different plaintiff interests, with a focus on the defendant's conduct.[6]

1.2 PRIVATE NUISANCE

From the twelfth century forward, common law nuisance recognized two branches: private and public nuisance. Private nuisance was narrowly concerned with a defendant's invasion of another person's use or enjoyment of their land. A private nuisance constituted a civil right with a remedy at law,

---

[2] W. Page Keeton, Dan B. Dobbs, Robert E. Keeton, & David G. Owen, *Prosser and Keeton on the Law of Torts* § 86 at 616 (5th ed. 1984).

[3] *Restatement (Second) of Torts* ch. 10, Intro. note (Am. L. Inst. 1979).

[4] Keeton, *supra* note 2.

[5] Daniel B. Dobbs, Paul T. Hayden, & Ellen M. Bublick, *Hornbook on Torts* § 30.1 at 733 (2d ed. 2015).

[6] *Id.*

limited to interference with the use or enjoyment of land.[7] Any form of property ownership was sufficient to be characterized as a property interest to support a private nuisance claim.[8] In recent eras, private nuisance law has been heavily supplemented with regulations, zoning statutes, land-use ordinances, and the law of unconstitutional takings.[9] Legislatures that desire to end a land use may enact statutes to declare a property use as a nuisance.[10]

At common law, a person who owned or rightfully possessed land was entitled to its unimpaired condition and occupancy in reasonable comfort and convenience. The defendant's interference might cause physical or tangible harm to a plaintiff, resulting in diminution of a property's market value, or causing discomfort to a property's occupants.[11] To be actionable as a private nuisance, the disturbance or inconvenience had to be substantial, unreasonable, and offensive to a normal person. Thus, the presence of a howling dog next door was a considered private nuisance because it interfered with the undisturbed enjoyment of property.[12]

A plaintiff pursuing a claim for private nuisance at common law had to satisfy four requirements. First, the plaintiff had to show that the defendant acted intentionally to interfere with the plaintiff's use and enjoyment of the plaintiff's land.[13] Courts have construed intentionality to mean a defendant's creation and continued knowledge of a harm to the plaintiff's interests that were occurring or substantially likely to follow from the defendant's activities.[14] Second, the plaintiff had to show that the interference with the plaintiff's use and enjoyment was of the type intended.[15] Third, the plaintiff had to prove that the interference or physical harm, if any, was substantial, leading to depreciation in the value of the plaintiff's property.[16] Fourth, the plaintiff had to show that the defendant's interference was unreasonable and substantial.[17]

Courts have interpreted defendant's substantial interference as a significant harm to the plaintiff, and defendant's unreasonable conduct resulting in harm

---

[7] Keeton, *supra* note 1, § 86 at 617. *See generally* Allan Beever, *The Law of Private Nuisance* (Oxford 2013); John Murphy, *The Law of Nuisance* (Oxford 2010) § 1.04 at 5–20, §§ 2.01–6.30 at 33–131.

[8] *Id.* § 87 at 619.

[9] Dobbs, *supra* note 5.

[10] *Id.*

[11] Dobbs, § 30.2 at 735.

[12] Keeton, § 86 at 617.

[13] *Id.* at 622.

[14] *Id.* at 624–25.

[15] *Id.* at 622.

[16] *Id.* at 622–23.

[17] *Id.*

to require the defendant to compensate the plaintiff.[18] Reasonableness in contemporary nuisance law refers to the expectations of a normal person occupying their property; it does not refer to the reasonableness or unreasonableness of the defendant's conduct.[19] Contemporary applications of private nuisance permit actionable claims if the defendant created a nuisance by engaging in strict liability activity, negligence, or more broadly, intentional interference with a plaintiff's enjoyment interests in their property.[20]

Historically, private nuisance embraced disturbances or inconveniences caused by another to a property's physical condition. Examples included vibrations, blasting damage, crop destruction, flooding, raising a water table, pollution of a stream or underground water supply, noxious odors, smoke, dust or gas, loud noises, excessive light or high temperatures, repeated phone calls, and health hazards such as a mosquito infested pond as a breeding place for malaria. Some private nuisance claims consisted of a combination of disturbances or harms.[21]

A private nuisance might embrace circumstances psychologically disturbing to a property owner, such as proximity of a house of prostitution, an undertaking business, or a tuberculosis hospital. Similarly, nuisance law included fears of future disturbances or injury, such as neighboring buildings with stored explosives, inflammable structures or materials, or vicious dogs.[22] Moreover, the property depreciation caused by private nuisances might present damage and an actionable claim.[23]

Nuisance law has long been plagued with fuzzy conceptual theorizing, complicated by its relationship to trespass law. Historically, trespass referred to direct invasions of property and nuisance was characterized by indirect invasions of property. In modern jurisprudence, this distinction between direct and indirect invasions of property became murkier and uncertain. In contemporary applications, the law generally recognizes trespass as an invasion of a plaintiff's interest in exclusive possession of land, while nuisance is interference with the use and enjoyment of land.[24] Alleged nuisance claims may be confused with other tortious actions, such as negligent conduct resulting in tangible physical property damage. The two torts may, in some cases, overlap.[25]

---

[18] *Id.* at 626.
[19] Dobbs, § 30.4 at 738.
[20] *Id.* § 30.2 at 735, § 30.3 at 736.
[21] Keeton, § 87 at 620.
[22] *Id.* at 619–20.
[23] *Id.*
[24] *Id.* at 622.
[25] Dobbs, § 30.2 at 736.

The uncertainty of injury claims resulting from a defendant's release of harmful liquids that pollute property illustrates the complex relationship of nuisance theory to other branches of tort law. Thus, such activity might be actionable as a matter of trespass, nuisance, strict liability, the *Restatement (Second) of Torts* doctrine of dangerous activity, or the natural law theory.[26]

If a plaintiff established a claim for private nuisance, the plaintiff might seek three possible remedies: a legal claim for damages, equitable relief in the form of an injunction, or abatement.[27] In some egregious cases, a plaintiff might seek punitive damages.[28] Courts consistently held that the appropriate remedy for private nuisance actions was monetary damages. In cases involving either permanent or temporary nuisance, courts used various depreciation models to provide the plaintiff compensatory relief.[29]

However, a property owner might prefer an equitable injunctive remedy to require that the defendant cease or abate a nuisance. A plaintiff might seek equitable relief for a potential nuisance that had not yet occurred. A plaintiff seeking equitable relief must show that it does not have an adequate remedy at law for damages. Some courts required separate actions for injunctive relief or conditioned injunctive relief on the payment of damages.[30] A plaintiff had to exercise the privilege of abatement within a reasonable time after the plaintiff becomes aware of the nuisance.[31]

1.3 PUBLIC NUISANCE

Distinct from private nuisance, public nuisance emerged in England in tandem with private nuisance law. The two concepts have little to do with one another, except that each captures a notion of an inconvenience a defendant perpetrates on another person or persons. Public nuisance is much broader than private nuisance in that it captures conduct beyond the narrower scope of a defendant's interference with another's use or enjoyment of property.

Public nuisance generally embraced a range of conduct that interfered with community interests or the public's comfort; to be a public nuisance the defendant's activity had to affect the public's interests, rather than a particular individuals.[32] A public nuisance described a substantial and unreasonable

---

[26] Keeton, § 87 at 624.
[27] *Id.* § 89 at 637.
[28] Dobbs, § 30.7 at 747.
[29] Keeton, § 88 at 628–29.
[30] *Id.* § 87 at 623.
[31] *Id.* § 89 at 641–42.
[32] *Id.* § 90, at 643, 645. *See* John Murphy, *The Law of Nuisance, supra* note 7, §§ 7.01–8.75 at 131–87.

interference with a right that the public held in the use of public facilities, health, safety, and convenience.[33]

The doctrine of public nuisance entailed an interesting jurisprudential evolution from twelfth-century English criminal law and equity to contemporary American tort law. Although contemporary American jurisprudence now recognizes public nuisance as a branch of modern tort law, public nuisance law had its roots in criminal law and equity.

Originally, public nuisance was a creature of criminal law, limited to offenses against the sovereign. In common law in the twelfth-century England, public nuisances were an infringement of the rights of the king.[34] The earliest cases of public nuisance law involved encroachments on the royal domain or public highways; the doctrine of public nuisance was to prevent people from encroaching on the king's land or blocking a public road or waterway. Because such encroachments were infringements on the rights of the crown or the public, they constituted a crime.

By the fourteenth century, during the reign of King Edward III, the doctrine of public nuisance was enlarged to include such offenses as interference with a market or water diversion from a mill. By the end of the nineteenth century, public nuisance in England was broadly defined as an "act not warranted by law, or omission to discharge a legal duty, which inconveniences the public in the exercise of rights common to all Her Majesty's subjects."[35] Professor Keeton described public nuisance as a "species of catch-all criminal offense, consisting of an interference with the rights of the community at large."[36]

Over time, public nuisance expanded from encroachments or offenses on the crown to embrace activities constituting interferences with public health, such as keeping diseased animals, selling rotten meat, or maintaining a malarial pond; interference with public safety, such as the storage of explosives, shooting fireworks, or harboring a vicious dog; or interferences with public morals, such as maintaining houses of prostitution, gambling, lotteries, indecent exhibitions, unlicensed plays, bullfights, unlicensed prize fights, or public profanity; and interference with the public peace, such as loud and disturbing noises.[37]

Public nuisance reached activities that offended the public comfort, including noxious odors, smoke, dust, vibration; or interferences with public transportation, such as highway or navigable stream obstructions, making travel unsafe, unmanageable, or disagreeable. Public nuisance also encompassed

---

[33] Dobbs, § 30.6 at 744.
[34] Keeton., § 90 at 643.
[35] *Id.* citing Stephen, *General View of the Criminal Law of England* 105 (1890).
[36] Keeton, § 86 at 618.
[37] *Id.* § 90 at 643–45.

a range of uncategorizable activities such as embezzling public funds, eavesdropping on a jury, or being a common scold.[38]

As a crime, public nuisance was redressed as suits by the crown, prosecuted by the sheriff.[39] Until the sixteenth century, the remedy for public nuisance violations was exclusively a criminal remedy. Moreover, public nuisance claims have always been tied to state police powers, enforceable by the sheriff.

In the United States, all states enacted criminal public nuisance statutes, many defining public nuisance generally, that have been interpreted to include anything that might have been a public nuisance at common law.[40] However, to be recognized as a public nuisance, the defendant must invade some public right.[41] Public authorities might seek to abate or enjoin a public nuisance even if the activity was not recognized as a statutory crime; public nuisance law may supplement environmental statutes addressing hazardous waste and environmental contamination.[42] The notion that public nuisance entails state police powers as an enforcement mechanism has significant import for contemporary American jurisprudence, where government entities have sought to use public nuisance claims to seek remediation for their citizens.

In modern applications, public authorities might seek abatement under public nuisance theories where a tortfeasor created conditions that required public entities to expend additional funds for police, fire, health, or other public services. Although some courts have allowed municipalities to recover the cost of abatement as damages, other courts have disallowed such claims. In addition, contemporary mass tort entity litigants have sought to assert public nuisance claims against manufacturers (and others) for the costs of the public harm resulting from their products.[43]

In England and the United States, public nuisance gradually became entwined with private tort law. Thus, in the sixteenth-century England, the law held that a crime of public nuisance could give rise to an individual's private civil tort action if the plaintiff could show that because of the public nuisance, the plaintiff had sustained injuries that were different in kind from those suffered by the public generally.[44] This "specific or special injury" requirement for a private tort claim carried over into modern American public

---

[38] *Id.*

[39] *Id.* § 90 at 646.

[40] *Id. See generally* F. William Brownell, State Common Law of Public Nuisance in the Modern Administrative State, 24 *Environ. Nat. Resour. J.* 34–37 (2010).

[41] Dobbs, § 30.6 at 744. Dobbs suggests that if citizens have the right to store firearms in their homes, for example, then such storage does not invade a public right. *Id.*

[42] *Id.*

[43] *Id.* § 30.6 at 744–45.

[44] Keeton, § 90 at 646.

nuisance jurisprudence and courts uniformly have held that an individual has no action for invasion of a public right unless that individual's damages is in some way distinguishable by the injuries the public has sustained.[45]

Historically, courts have struggled with ascertaining what constituted an individual's particular damage that was sufficient to support an individual tort claim in the context of a public nuisance. Courts looked to see whether the individual's damages were different in kind, and sometimes different in degree, from damages of the public. Generally, courts upheld private tort claims where a plaintiff suffered personal injury, harm to health, or mental distress finding that those injuries constituted a different kind of damage.[46]

Laws relating to public nuisance remedies also evolved. Remedies available for a public nuisance claim overlapped with the remedies for private nuisance claims: (1) compensatory damages, (2) punitive damages in egregious cases, (3) injunctions that abate or modify the nuisance, and (4) a compensated injunction that abated a nuisance but required the defendant to pay the plaintiff the costs of abatement.[47]

Federal and state courts have long recognized private and public nuisance claims as branches of tort law. By the twenty-first century, public nuisance became a recognized branch of American tort law and federal common law embraced a concept of public nuisance. Some American courts, however, cabined public nuisance claims that have restricted the ability of twenty-first–century mass tort claimants to remedy or compensate group harms.

1.4 THE AMERICAN LAW INSTITUTE'S APPROACHES TO NUISANCE LAW

The American Law Institute (ALI) codified private and public nuisance principles in its 1979 *Restatements (Second) of the Law of Torts*, embracing more expansive concepts that generated a fair amount of controversy and confusion.

1.5 THE RESTATEMENT (SECOND) OF THE LAW TORTS

The ALI's first *Restatement of Torts*, published in 1934, did not address public nuisance at all.[48] The *Restatement (Second) of Torts*, circulated in various drafts during the 1960s and 1970s and published in 1979, set forth several

---

45 *Id.*
46 *Id.* § 90 at 648–49. *See also* Dobbs, § 30.6 at 745.
47 Dobbs, § 30.7 at 747.
48 *Restatement (Second) of Torts, supra* note 3, at § 821A Rpt.'s Note.

provisions on private and public nuisance law. Three points are salient for the subsequent development of public nuisance doctrine. First, the *Restatement's* general principles of nuisance law were not a model of clarity. The ALI Reporters, recognizing the multiple uses of the term nuisance, attempted to provide some conceptual coherence to nuisance doctrine, setting forth two types of nuisance, often eliding or combining the two: (1) human activity that was harmful or annoying to others and (2) harm caused by human conduct or physical condition that was annoying to others.[49]

For convenience, the *Restatement (Second)* combined the concepts of private and public nuisance and often resorted to the singular term nuisance "to avoid constant repetitions of cumbersome language defining both."[50] Significantly, the *Restatement (Second)* approach to nuisance did not focus on any kind of a defendant's conduct. Rather, nuisance referred to invasions of two types of interest by tortious conduct, only if the conduct fell within the usual categories of tort liability.[51]

Second, the *Restatement* recognized the possibility for tort liability for certain types of nuisance claims, distinguishing private and public nuisance claims. The *Restatement* noted that while the term nuisance was used to describe either conduct, it did not necessarily connote tort liability. For a public or private nuisance to exist, there must be a harm to another or an invasion of an interest. The *Restatement (Second)* acknowledged that there might be a public nuisance that would subject a defendant to criminal prosecution, but not tort liability. Somewhat unhelpfully, the *Restatement (Second)* explained that courts had applied tort liability arising from the two types of nuisances and concluded that a person maintaining a nuisance or engaging in harmful activity, constituting a public or private nuisance, might be legally liable, but another person might not.[52]

Third, the *Restatement (Second)* gave relatively short shrift to public nuisance law principles compared to its extensive treatment of private nuisance, despite the doctrine's lengthy lineage back to sixteenth-century England. The *Restatement's* approach to public nuisance was relatively limited compared to its treatment of private nuisance, focusing almost exclusively on an array of public harms generated by access to or interference with highways, pollution of waterways, and that holdover from English public nuisance law: the presence of a house of prostitution.[53]

---

[49] *Id.* at § 821A cmt.
[50] *Id.*
[51] *Id.*
[52] *Id.*
[53] *Id.* at § 821C, cmt. illustrations.

The *Restatement (Second)* set forth discrete provisions relating to public and private nuisance.[54] The *Restatement (Second)* defined the concept of private nuisance much more broadly than prevailing common law formulations, indicating that private nuisance encompassed not only a defendant's intentional and unreasonable interference with a plaintiff's use and enjoyment of their land, but also accidental interference actionable under liability rules for reckless, negligent, or abnormally dangerous conduct.[55] Professor Keeton has suggested that this codification of private nuisance law produced much confusion and erroneous results, eliding differences between trespass, negligence, strict liability, and nuisance law concepts.[56]

The *Restatement (Second)* set forth an entirely new section relating to public nuisance and sought to distinguish this concept from private nuisance. Thus, the *Restatement (Second)* indicated that unlike private nuisance, public nuisance may not necessarily involve interference with the use and enjoyment of land. In addition, unlike private nuisance claims generally, public nuisance claims did not afford claimants a basis for recovery in tort damages, except in limited circumstances.[57]

Generally, the *Restatement* defined a public nuisance as an unreasonable interference with a right common to the public. This section recognized actionable public nuisance claims at common law and for statutory violations. These two threads of public nuisance remediation continued through to the twenty-first century applications of common and statutory law violations in modern mass tort litigation.

The kinds of activities that might sustain a finding of public nuisance, because of unreasonable behavior, embraced whether the conduct (a) included a significant interference with the public health, safety peace, comfort, or convenience, (b) was proscribed by statute, ordinance, or administrative regulation, or (c) was of a continuous nature or had produced a long-lasting effect and the actor knew or had reason to know its significant effect upon the public right.[58]

The *Restatement (Second)* noted that at common law public nuisance had come to embrace a "miscellaneous and diversified group of minor criminal

---

[54] *Id.* at § 822 (defining and codifying principles of private nuisance), and §§ 821 (defining and codifying principles of public nuisance).

[55] *Id.* § 91 at 652, citing § 822.

[56] *Id.* § 91 at 652–53.

[57] *Id.* at § 821B cmt. h. When a harm consists of interference with the use and enjoyment of land, a public nuisance may also be a private nuisance.

[58] *Restatement (Second)* at § 821B.

offenses."[59] Although public nuisance originally was recognized as criminal offense, English jurisprudence had as long ago as the sixteenth century recognized that an individual who sustained a particular damage that differed from the public harm might have a tort remedy to recover damages for the invasion of a public right. The concept of possible tort remedies for public nuisance violations, then, had a long lineage in common law jurisprudence.

As public nuisance jurisprudence evolved over time, the criminal law's authority over public nuisance remediation receded for several reasons. In the U.S., most states eliminated common law crimes, instead enacting statutory criminal provisions. This trend generally removed the resolution of public nuisance claims from the criminal law's orbit, except for states that enacted statutes criminalizing public nuisance violations.

Thus, public nuisance law came to be governed by common law principles or statutory public nuisance law. The common law of public nuisance has persisted, along with the traditional bases for what constitutes actionable public nuisance. In addition, some states adopted statutes to provide criminal penalties for public nuisance violations, or to recognize actionable tort liability.[60] The statutes, along with municipal ordinances and administrative regulations, constituted legislative declarations that proscribed conduct was an unreasonable interference with a public right.[61]

When courts began to recognize the possibility of public nuisance tort actions, many courts resorted to jurisprudential analyses derived from the tort of private nuisance and further muddied distinctions between the doctrines. Thus, by analogy to private nuisance tort actions, a defendant might be held liable for a public nuisance if their interference with a public right was intentional or was unintentional and actionable under liability principles of negligent or reckless conduct or for abnormally dangerous activities.[62]

In borrowing from each of these traditional categories of tort liability, to hold a defendant liable for a public nuisance, the defendant's conduct interfering with the plaintiff's interest had to be intentional and unreasonable. However, courts declined to impose liability for a public nuisance that was the consequence of a pure accident and that did not fall within one of the

---

[59] *Id.* at § 821B cmts. a, b. This section noted that many states no longer recognize common law crimes, which are treated solely as statutory matters. The common law of public nuisance, however, still exists. *Id.*

[60] *Id.* § 821B cmt. e. The Reporters note that courts have construed some criminal statutes to mean that the only remedy for a public nuisance violation is criminal prosecution and that a tort action for damages is not an available remedy.

[61] *Id.* § 821B cmts. b, c.

[62] *Id.* § 821B cmt. e, referring to private nuisance tort analysis in § 822.

three traditional categories of tort liability.[63] The *Restatement (Second)* recognized that a defendant's conduct authorized by the common law, statutes, ordinances, or regulations would not subject a defendant to tort liability for an alleged public nuisance violation.[64]

The *Restatement (Second)* defined what constituted interference with a public right to constitute a public nuisance. A public right was defined as one common to all members of the public. A public nuisance did not exist merely because an actor's conduct interfered with a large number of persons' use and enjoyment of land. However, some state statutes defined public nuisance to include to include interference with "any considerable number of persons," and therefore no public right need be involved to constitute a public nuisance violation.[65]

The *Restatement (Second)* considered the types of claimants and remedies that might be available for violations of public nuisance.[66] These fell into two categories: remediation for individuals, and remediation for the benefit of the public. The *Restatement* indicated that "In order to recover damages in an individual action for public nuisance, one must have suffered harm of a kind different from that suffered by other members of the public exercising the right common to the public that was the subject of the interference."[67] The *Restatement's* formulation of an individual tort damage claim for a public nuisance violation carried over into twenty-first century mass tort litigation.

When an individual sues for remediation through tort damages the claimant's damage must be distinguished from the harm suffered by the public. Redress to an entire community was left to the community's duly appointed representatives. In addition, the *Restatement* postulated that defendants had the right not to be exposed to liability to the community complicated with individual litigation complaining of the same harms.[68] The key issues relating to individual remediation through tort damages focused on the concepts of differences in kind and degree from the harms to the public.[69]

However, when a public nuisance causes a plaintiff's personal injury or physical harm to their land or chattels, the harm was sufficiently different in

---

[63] *Id.*

[64] *Id.* at § 821B cmt. f.

[65] *Id.* § 821B cmt. g.

[66] *Id.* 821B cmt. i. Notably, the *Restatement (Second)'s* chapter on public nuisance focused on the availability of tort damages, generally not discussing other possible remedies such as injunctions or abatement. For a discussion of remedies, *see id.* § 821C.

[67] *Id.* § 821C. The RESTATEMENT noted that the first private action in tort for remediation of a public nuisance violation was in 1536. This was a tort remedy engrafted onto a crime.

[68] *Id.* § 821C, cmt. a.

[69] *Id.* § 812C, cmts. b, c.

kind from that suffered by other members of the public and a tort action might be maintained.[70] This *Restatement* view would gain special traction in twenty-first century mass tort litigation pursued as a matter of public nuisance law, combining harms to the public with individual personal injury.

In addition to individual suits for recovery of tort damages, other possible remedies for public nuisance violations included injunctions and abatement. Persons or entities entitled to seek injunctive or abatement relief for a public nuisance fell into three categories: (1) an individual with the right to recover based on differentiated injury, (2) a public official or public agency with authority to represent a state or political subdivision, and (3) an individual or entity with standing to sue as a representative of the public, as a citizen in a citizen's action, or as a member of a class action.[71] The remedies of injunctions and abatement, and the persons or entities that might seek such relief, would have salience for twenty-first century mass tort litigation where public officials, agencies, and class litigation pursued remediation based on public nuisance claims.

The *Restatement (Second)* noted, however, that the traditional rule was that if an individual had not suffered damages different in kind than the public, entitling that individual to a tort remedy for damages, then the individual had no standing to seek and maintain an action for an injunction. This rule was to prevent a multiplicity of injunctive relief actions brought by many members of the public, or to prevent individuals for pursuing relief for trivial injuries.[72] However, the *Restatement* noted that certain statutes could create citizens' actions conferring standing on individuals to represent the public for injunctive or abatement remedies.[73]

Significantly for subsequent public nuisance litigation, the *Restatement* eschewed analyzing or taking any position regarding public nuisance class litigation and the intertwined doctrines of standing. Viewing standing doctrine as a purely procedural matter, the *Restatement* indicated that standing principles were not an appropriate subject for the substantive law of torts. Therefore, it was outside the purview of the *Restatement* to set forth rules to determine when there was standing to seek an injunction or abatement of a public nuisance.[74]

---

[70] *Id.* 821C, cmt. d

[71] *Id.* § 821C.

[72] *Id.* § 821C cmt. j.

[73] *Id.*

[74] *Id.* "The purpose of the Subsection is to point out that there may be a distinction between an individual suit for damages and a suit in behalf of the public or a class action. The Subsection is worded so as to leave the courts free to proceed with developments regarding standing to sue without the restrictive effect that would be imposed by a categoric statement of the traditional rule, which is found in a limited number of cases."

1.6 THE RESTATEMENT (THIRD) OF THE LAW TORTS

In the ALI's massive effort to issue a third restatement of torts, the Reporters relocated public nuisance principles to the *Restatement of the Law Third, Torts: Liability for Economic Harm* (2020).[75] This new treatment of public nuisance law, completed forty years after the *Restatement (Second)'s* treatment of private and public nuisance, reflected a considerable sea-change in thinking about public nuisance law.

The *Restatement (Third)'s* new approach to public nuisance law reflected a narrowing of public nuisance law concepts, further cabining opportunities for public and individual remediation. The legal landscape between 1979 and 2020 had changed dramatically; mass tort litigation emerged in the late 1970s. Essentially, the *Restatement (Second)* missed the emergence plaintiffs' attempts to utilize public nuisance in mass tort litigation.

By the time of the ALI's drafting of the *Restatement Liability for Economic Harms*, the Reporters were already reflecting on a legal landscape characterized by numerous attempts to pursue mass tort litigation using public nuisance claims. The limitation of public nuisance concepts in the *Restatement (Third)* reflected a considerable influence of corporate and defense interests to further restrict common law public nuisance claims and divert judicial embrace of novel public nuisance theories.

Three salient points emerge from consideration of the *Restatement (Third)'s* exposition of public nuisance law. First, to the extent that private and public nuisance law had always been something of a confused, messy backwater of tort law, the *Restatement (Third)* elected to further diminish its importance by devoting relatively scant analysis in the overall *Restatement* project. The placement of public nuisance law in the economic loss volume reflected the ALI's attitude to the relative unimportance of public nuisance in tort law.

Second, the *Restatement (Third)'s* treatment of public nuisance law significantly dismissed leveraging public nuisance doctrine as a basis for asserting claims in mass tort products litigation. By the time the ALI was engaged in drafting a new section on public nuisance law, plaintiffs' attorneys in state and federal courts were attempting to accomplish just that, with mixed results. The corporate and defense bars were solidly opposed to the expansion of public nuisance law to provide individual, governmental, and group entities with an ALI-sanctioned public nuisance approach to products' mass torts. The *Restatement (Third)*, then, endeavored to undercut the possible use of the doctrine by mass tort lawyers.

---

[75] *Restatement of the Law of Torts (Third): Liab. for Econ. Harm* (Am. L. Inst. 2020).

Third, the new chapter acknowledged that public nuisance was a matter of common and statutory law – an important framing convention for the current debate over the use of public nuisance in mass tort litigation. Contemporary advocates and adversaries of public nuisance theories endorse either common law or statutory approaches. The ALI *Restatement (Third)* elected a narrow common law construct of public nuisance claims and remediation. Nonetheless, it acknowledged that extant statutes tended to define public nuisance law more broadly than common law. The section noted that public nuisance statutes also might provide individuals with rights of recovery that were more expansive than recognized by the common law.

The *Restatement (Third)* approach to public nuisance limited the doctrine's purview to cases that solely would produce tort liability for economic loss.[76] The chapter recast public nuisance exclusively with reference to resulting economic harm; it was not intended to restate the law of public nuisance generally. The Reporter noted that many examples of public nuisance did not give rise to tort liability for economic damage, such as when a plaintiff collided with an obstruction the defendant negligently left in a roadway, or when a defendant's conduct polluted the plaintiff's land. These types of nuisance cases were outside the scope of the new public nuisance provision.[77]

The *Restatement (Third)* definition of public nuisance generally reflected prior common law formulations but imported tort theories into the determination of public nuisance violations. Thus, "a public nuisance arises when a defendant's wrongful act causes harm to a public right; a right held by all member of the community."[78] A wrongful act could be the result of a statutory violation (constituting a public nuisance "per se"). In addition, under common law principles, a plaintiff could demonstrate a defendant's wrongful conduct if the actor's actions were unreasonable, intentional, unprivileged, or subject to strict liability.[79]

The new chapter on public nuisance did not frame its consideration of the doctrine in terms of community harm and redress but instead recast public law more narrowly with a focus on an individual plaintiff's specific entitlement to relief. Thus, "an actor whose wrongful conduct harms or obstructs a public resource or public property is subject to liability for resulting economic loss if the court concludes that the claimant's losses are distinct in

---

[76] *Id.* § 8.
[77] *Id.* 8, cmt. a.
[78] *Id.* § 8, cmt. b.
[79] *Id.*

kind from those suffered by member of the affected community in general."[80] In so doing, the *Restatement (Third)* embraced the old common law principle that an individual claimant could recover for loss only if the claimant's losses were distinct in kind from those suffered by the public; the individual's reme- diation was narrowed to economic loss.

Significantly, the *Restatement (Third)* issued several warnings about recourse to common law or statutory principles of public nuisance. It noted that the principles tended to be stated at a high level of generality, which caused confu- sion about the scope of those principles and led to occasional unsound claims of public nuisance "to be brought on facts outside the traditional ambit of the tort."[81] Thus, "the actual scope of tort liability for economic loss caused by public nuisance has generally and appropriately been confined to the more limited circumstances stated in the black letter of this Section and discussed in the comments."[82]

The *Restatement (Third)* devoted an entire section to public nuisance claims it deemed especially inappropriate: namely, products cases. Here, the *Restatement* noted that plaintiffs' lawyers had filed tort suits seeking recovery for public nuisance against product manufacturers that caused harm, such as tobacco, firearms, and lead paint. The cases involved various damage theories, but also claims for economic loss suffered by plaintiffs as a consequence of defendants' activities, such as the costs of removing lead paint or providing medical health services for plaintiff harmed by smoking.[83]

The *Restatement (Third)* noted that most courts rejected such public nui- sance theories as applied to mass tort products litigation. The ALI position on public nuisance law, then, excluded consideration of claims based on prod- ucts as harm to the public and suggested that common law public nuisance principles were an inapt vehicle to address manufacturers' conduct. Instead, mass harms caused by dangerous products were better addressed through products liability law, "which has been developed and refined with sensitivity to the various policies at stake."[84]

Further deflecting the possible application of public nuisance claims in mass tort litigation, the *Restatement (Third)* additionally suggested that the reimbursement of plaintiffs' expenses in such mass products cases might be

---

[80] *Id.* § 8.
[81] *Id.* § 8, cmt. b.
[82] *Id.*
[83] *Id.* § 8, cmt. g.
[84] *Id.*

addressed by warranty law or restitution. Lastly, the *Restatement (Third)* suggested that if these possible legal sources were inadequate to provide relief, a better course of action to supply adequate remedies or deterrence was through legislation that could account for all the interested issues.[85]

The *Restatement (Third)'s* approach to public nuisance law, then, was to narrow the doctrine endeavoring to clarify the concepts of "special injury" to an individual plaintiff, what constituted a harm to public resources, the categories of cases embraced by obstructions of public property, and when an individual plaintiff might seek abatement of a public nuisance.[86] But the most significant portion of the ALI's revised public nuisance codification was its outright rejection of public nuisance law as a legal basis for mass tort litigation claims, a special discussion not included in the *Restatement (Second)*. While dangerous products might once have seemed a matter for public nuisance law because the term was loosely defined in such broad language as to reach anything injurious to public health and safety, the *Restatement (Third)* eschewed this conclusion. "The traditional office of the tort, however, has been narrower than those formulations suggest, and contemporary case law has made clear that its reach remains more modest."[87]

The *Restatement (Third)'s* position on public nuisance law was anything but a neutral statement of principles. Instead, the ALI's new public nuisance position that excluded products liability cases from the purview of public nuisance law was congruent with corporate and defense interests, including those of the U.S. Chamber of Commerce. These corporate and defense interests squarely aligned in resisting expansion of public nuisance law to encompass mass product defect cases, especially in the evolving mass tort litigation arena.

Centrally, the ALI's position on public nuisance law in the realm of mass products harms eschewed judicial power to develop public nuisance law as a matter of common law development. This resistance to judicial common law development of mass tort public nuisance would have especial salience in jurisdictions without statutory public nuisance provisions, because then courts would default to common law principles to determine the scope of public nuisance law as applied products cases causing mass harms.

The contemporary debate over the use of public nuisance law as a basis for remediation in mass tort litigation, then, is an evolving story about the tension between the role of the common law in expansively developing old doctrines

---

[85] *Id.*

[86] *Id.* § 8 cmts. c-f.

[87] *Id.* § 8 cmt. g. "The rules stated in this Section and Comment reflect this modesty."

pitted against an insistence on narrowly drawn statutes to exclude such public nuisance claims. This has been the emerging dispute between the plaintiffs' mass tort litigation bar, which encourages judicial common law developments, opposed by defense-side interests resisting expansion of the common law and insisting, instead, on statutory public nuisance law.

2

Shifting Mass Tort Theories in the 1990s and the Judicial Resistance to the Expansion of Public Nuisance Liability

By the time of the publication of the *Restatement Torts (Third)* in 2020, the fact that mass tort attorneys had been and were continuing to assert public nuisance claims in mass products cases caused the American Law Institute (ALI) to pay attention and exclude these cases from the domain of public nuisance law. Prior to the emergence of mass tort litigation, public nuisance cases concerned paradigmatic interference with property lawsuits based on generations of public nuisance common law principles.

Public nuisance law in mass products cases, it will be seen, evolved with the development of mass tort litigation over five decades. During the first generation of mass tort cases that emerged in the 1970s, attorneys typically based their lawsuits on conventional tort theories. As plaintiffs' attorneys experienced judicial resistance towards aggregating mass tort claimants, they regrouped and creatively sought new grounds to hold bad-actor defendants liable for harms to large numbers of individuals.

The development of public nuisance law evinces a gradual doctrinal evolution beginning in the 1990s, when mass tort attorneys first attempted to allege that products causing harm to large numbers of people might be pursued under public nuisance theories. The emergence of public nuisance in mass products cases is a testament to the trial lawyers' continuing resourcefulness in advocating novel theories in mass tort cases. However, in the same fashion that courts resisted aggregating mass tort claims under traditional tort theories, the judiciary at first did not enthusiastically embrace the novel assertion of public nuisance claims in mass products cases. Not until the twenty-first century did public nuisance claims begin to gain acceptance in some judicial quarters.

2.1 PARADIGMATIC PUBLIC NUISANCE
LAWSUITS BEFORE THE MASS TORT ERA

Prior to the emergence of mass tort litigation in the late 1970s, public nuisance lawsuits typically involved a substantial and unreasonable interference with a public right held in common, often pertaining to property rights or other community offenses.[1] The *Restatement (Second) of Torts* enumerated eight categories of public nuisance.[2] These included interference with the public right of passage on a highway, interference with use of a public place, interference with navigation of streams, and interferences with public health, public safety, public morals, public peace, or public comfort.[3] Many of these paradigmatic public nuisance cases had long lineages to the seventeenth century England. Nonetheless, these traditional categories of public nuisance persisted well into the twentieth century throughout American federal and state jurisdictions.

A New York lawsuit illustrated a mundane public nuisance caused by a defendant's interference with the public's use and access of a public highway.[4] The court concluded that a defendant's erection of a lumber advertising sign surrounded by mounded earth, supported by boulders and railway ties, constituted a public nuisance. The sign was located within the right-of-way of a county road and interfered with the public's free and unobstructed use of a public highway. The sign was not a mere name post or temporary structure to fulfil a short, reasonable necessity; it was an unlawful encroachment on a county highway. The court quoted the common law understanding of a public nuisance: "It is elementary law that the public is entitled to the free and unobstructed use of the city streets and that any obstruction of such streets for private use interferes with the public right, constitutes a nuisance and may be removed."[5]

Another New York state court permanently enjoined a stockcar raceway's weekly operation as a public nuisance, characterizing the cumulative effect of the raceway's excessive noise and dust, as well as other safety dangers related to its operation, as an assault on the community as a whole.[6] The court defined a public nuisance as an offense to the public of a neighborhood or a community in the enjoyment of common rights, as distinguished from an activity that results in injury even to large numbers of persons in the enjoyment of public rights.[7]

---

[1] Daniel B. Dobbs, Paul T. Hayden, & Ellen M. Bublick, *Hornbook on Torts* § 30.6 at 745 (2d ed. 2015).

[2] *Restatement (Second) of Torts* § 821B Rptr.'s Note (Am. L. Inst. 1979).

[3] *Id.*

[4] Erie County v. Marjorie's Grove & Catering Serv., 97 Misc.3d 329, 411 N.Y.S.2d 501 (1978).

[5] *Id.* at 331, quoting People *ex. rel.* Hofeller v. Buck, 193 App. Div. 262, 264, aff'd N.Y. 608.

[6] State v. Waterloo Stock Car Raceway, Inc., 96 Misc.2d 350, 357, 409 N.Y.S. 2d 40 (1978).

[7] *Id.*

Quoting Justice Cardozo, the court indicated that a "public nuisance is the nuisance whereby a 'public right or privilege common to every person in the community is interrupted or interfered with,'" … "Public also is the nuisance committed in such place and in such manner that the aggregation of private injuries becomes so great and extensive as to constitute a public annoyance and inconvenience, and a wrong against the community, which may be properly be the subject of a public prosecution."[8]

Other traditional twentieth century public nuisance lawsuits resonated with allegations of community interference with property rights.[9] Thus, a Maryland federal court upheld a public nuisance action brought by property owners in a residential development project, who sued the builders who built and marketed their homes. The owners alleged that the homes had been constructed on a solid waste dump, giving rise to a heightened risk of methane gas explosions evidenced by the elevated levels of methane detected in their basements. The court held that the homeowners sufficiently stated a private right of action for public nuisance because they had alleged an unreasonable interference with a right common to the public: injuries to their properties from the public nuisance.[10]

Similarly, a Massachusetts federal court concluded that a homeowner stated a viable claim for public nuisance where she alleged that the defendant's long-time practice of dumping PCB contaminates in the surrounding area resulted in her inability to sell her property as well as anxiety concerning health risks to her children. The complaint sufficiently set forth a public nuisance claim because the facts alleged an interference with public health and the environment.[11] In a similar vein, a Pennsylvania federal court upheld a property purchaser's right to sue a seller for private and public nuisance claims arising from waste materials that the seller deposited and left on the property. The court held that the seller's disposal of waste at the site constituted a continuing trespass as well as a private and public nuisance.[12]

A defendant's interference with navigable or communal waters traditionally constituted another significant category of public nuisance claims throughout the twentieth century. A defendant could be sued for a public nuisance violation if the defendant contaminated public waters by a chemical spill or

---

[8] *Id.* at 356, quoting People v. Rubenfeld, 254 N.Y. 245, 247.
[9] Adams v. NVR Homes, Inc., 193 F.R.D. 243, 251 (D. Md. 2000).
[10] *Id.*
[11] Lewis v. General Electric Co., 37 F. Supp.2d 55, 60 (D. Mass. 1999).
[12] In re Joshua Hill, Inc., 199 B.R. 298, 322 (E.D. Pa. 1996).

continuous discharge of noxious substances into communal waters.[13] A New Jersey federal court upheld a public nuisance crossclaim against a lessee for contamination of water supply wells, holding that the landowner alleged interference with a public right of the public aquifer located beneath its property.[14]

A federal appellate court upheld a nonprofit corporation's public nuisance action against the federal government for the government's operation of a flood control project. The plaintiffs alleged that the government's unnecessary use of water pumps, failure to use a sump area, lateral drainage during high water, and lack of maintenance caused high amounts of sediment to be deposited downstream in a watercourse, damaging a recreational area. The court concluded that the government's various operational failures gave rise to a public nuisance action.[15]

Finally, federal and state courts during the twentieth century continued to recognize public nuisance lawsuits based on the general categories of interferences with public health, public safety, public morals, public peace, or public comfort. Thus, a Pennsylvania state court issued an injunction barring the continued operation of an adult bookstore that contained video viewing booths and dancing areas, finding that sexual conduct occurring in the booths and dance areas could lead to the spread of HIV. The court concluded that those areas could be considered public nuisances.[16] A Hawaii state court upheld a finding of criminal public nuisance for a defendant's nude sunbathing at a beach that was a popular location for fishermen and used by the public.[17] State courts in Pennsylvania and Virginia found defendants liable for public nuisance violations for the sheltering an excessive number of dogs, or of excessive and continuous dog-barking in violation of city ordinances.[18]

Courts also upheld statutory public nuisance claims. Thus, in 1970, the Georgia Supreme Court upheld a plaintiff's public nuisance lawsuit brought under the state's public nuisance statute, against a defendant's plant that rendered animal material into bone meal and other products. Plaintiffs

---

[13] Dobbs, *supra* note 1, § 30.6 at 745–46. *See* Leo v. Genera; Elec. Co., 145 A.D.2d 291, 538 N.Y.S.2d 844, 846 (N.Y. Sup. Ct. App. Div. 1989) (viable public nuisance claim by commercial fishermen and their associations against company that recklessly and negligently polluted a river and caused statewide ban on sale of striped bass).

[14] Mayor and Council v. Klockner & Klockner, 811 F. Supp. 1039, 1056 (D.N.J. 1993).

[15] Taylor Bay Protective Assoc. v. Adm'r., U.S. E.P.A., 884 F.2d 1073, 1077 (8th Cir. 1989).

[16] Com. *ex rel.* Preate v. Danny's New Adam & Eve Bookstore, 155 Pa. Commw. Ct. 281, 285, 625 A.2d 119, 122 (1993).

[17] Hawaii v. Rocker, 52 Haw. 336, 475 P.2d 684 (Hawai'i 1970).

[18] Patterson v. City of Richmond, 39 Va. App. 706, 715, 576 S.E.2d 759, 763 (Va. App. 2003); Muehlieb v. City of Philadelphia, 133 Pa. Commw. Ct. 133, 574 A.2d 1208, 1211, 1212 (Pa. Commw. Ct. 1993).

complained of malodorous scents emanating from the rendering plant onto their properties. The court concluded that the plaintiffs stated a viable public nuisance claim within the Georgia public nuisance statute, which stated that a public nuisance existed "if the act complained of affects rights which are common to all within a particular area."[19]

2.2 THE EMERGENCE OF MASS PRODUCTS LITIGATION PURSUANT TO CONVENTIONAL TORT THEORIES

The fact that public nuisance emerged in the 1990s as an innovative legal theory for mass tort remediation is part of the evolving narrative of the resourcefulness of the trial attorneys' bar in seeking remediation in mass tort cases. Beginning in the 1970s, plaintiffs' attorneys pursued an array of conventional tort theories in suing corporate defendants in mass products cases. Many, if not most, of these early mass tort cases failed to gain judicial approval to proceed as class litigation under conventional tort theories, due to the differences among claimants, specific causation requirements, affirmative defenses, damages, applicable law, and the consequent failure of these proposed classes to satisfy Rule 23 class certification requirements.

For example, in *Yandle v. PPG Industries, Inc.*,[20] 570 employees of a refinery in Tyler, Texas, suffering from various stages of asbestosis, lung cancer, and various pulmonary and other diseases sued multiple asbestos manufacturing and distributing defendants. Their class action complaint alleged claims for negligence, failure to warn of hazards, gross negligence, strict liability, and exemplary damages under Texas Workmen's Compensation Act.[21]

Characteristic for federal courts in the 1970s, the Texas federal district court declined to certify this proposed class. The court articulated policy reasons as well as technical rule-based grounds for repudiating this proposed class remediation effort. As a policy matter, the court noted that the Advisory Committee on Civil Rules specifically eschewed use of Rule 23 damage class actions in tort cases.[22] Moreover, the court indicated that each claimant should have a

---

[19] Atlanta Processing Co. v. Brown, 227 Ga. 203 (Ga. 1971). *See* Ga. Code §§ 72-101, 72-102, 72-202.

[20] 65 F.R.D. 566 (E.D. Tex. 1974).

[21] *Id.* at 567–68.

[22] *Id.* at 568, quoting the Advisory Committee Note to Fed. R. Civ. P. 23(b)(3): "… A mass accident's resulting in injuries to numerous persons is ordinarily not appropriate for a class action because of the likelihood that significant questions, not only of damages but of liability and defenses to liability, would be present, affecting individuals in different ways. In these circumstances an action conducted nominally as a class action would degenerate in practice into multiple lawsuits separately tried…"

personal right to prosecute their own claim, apart from the group. The court further expressed concern that permitting a class action based on these tort theories might encourage attorney solicitation of business.[23]

The court concluded that the proposed class could not satisfy the Rule 23(b)(3) predominance requirement. Evaluating this proposed class action, the court suggested that individual issues might predominate in the litigation, especially any affirmative tort defense that was unique to individual class members.[24] Construing the alleged tort theories in the plaintiffs' complaint, the court concluded that common questions among the refinery workers did not predominate and that there existed too many individualized facts and issues; therefore, the litigation would likely "degenerate into multiple lawsuits separately tried."[25]

In support of this conclusion, the court noted that the employees were engaged at the refinery in various positions – the nine defendants had acted differently over time – the court would have to take into account individual employees' knowledge of the danger of breathing asbestos, and the fact that not a single act of negligence or proximate cause applied to each class member.[26]

Finally, the court noted that attempted mass tort cases were different than single mass accident cases that allowed class proceedings in limited circumstances, and that a class action was not superior means for resolving case. Pursuing mass tort relief under conventional tort theories would be time consuming, involve expensive notice, and render vulnerable exposure-only claimants who neglected to opt-out of the litigation. Finally, the court suggested that individual claimants had a significant interest in controlling own litigation.[27]

Like the *Yandle* asbestos litigation, plaintiffs' attorneys in almost all first-generation mass tort litigation through the middle of the 1990s based their lawsuits on conventional tort theories. Thus, plaintiffs in the 1975 Dalkon Shield litigation, alleging various injuries and harm to women's reproductive capacities, based their lawsuits on claims for negligence, negligent design, strict products liability, breach of express and implied warranty, wanton and reckless conduct, conspiracy, and fraud.[28] For reasons similar to those explained by the *Yandle* court, a federal appellate court repudiated class certification of

---

[23] *Id.* at 568.
[24] *Id.* at 570–71.
[25] *Id.*
[26] *Id.*
[27] *Id.* at 572.
[28] In re Northern Dist. Cal., Dalkon Shield IUD Prods. Liab. Litig., 693 F.2d 847, 849 (9th Cir. 1982).

the proposed Dalkon Shield California state class for compensatory damages as well as a national class for punitive damages.[29]

Similarly, plaintiffs in the penile implant litigation brought against the American Medical Systems, Inc. for injuries allegedly resulting from use of the defendant's medical device, alleged claims for strict products liability, negligence, breach of implied and express warranties, fraud, and punitive damages.[30] A federal appellate court reversed class certification, finding that the proposed class of penile impact claimants failed the class certification requirements for commonality, typicality, adequacy, predominance, and superiority.[31]

Through the mid-1990s, numerous examples abound of trial lawyers' pursuit of mass tort remediation premised on conventional tort theories. The *Agent Orange* litigation, brought by Vietnam war veterans and their spouses against defendants for injuries arising from the veterans' exposure to the chemical defoliant Agent Orange, was based on claims for strict products liability, negligence, breach of warranty, and intentional tort.[32] The nationwide *School Asbestos Litigation*, brought by plaintiffs seeking compensation for the costs of asbestos abatement, was based on claims for negligence, strict liability in tort, intentional tort, breach of warranty, concert of action, and common law conspiracy.[33] Breast implant litigation, pursued by women alleging various injuries from silicone breast implants, sought remediation against the product manufacturers and physicians under Colorado law for strict liability, negligence, and breach of warranty.[34]

By the mid-1990s, partially because of judicial resistance to class certification of mass tort products cases under conventional tort theories, the mass tort trial lawyers retreated and regrouped. An agile and creative plaintiffs' bar learned from the judicial lessons advanced for the failure of mass tort products class actions. The plaintiffs' bar understood that courts were not inclined to certify mass tort products cases based on personal injury tort theories that would involve individualized enquiries into claimants' injuries and damages, as well as individualized defenses.

In the face of these doctrinal impediments, the plaintiffs' bar determined to pursue mass tort remediation by recasting litigation in other than conventional tort theories. By the mid-1990s the plaintiffs' bar understood

[29] *Id.* at 850–57.
[30] In re Am. Med. Sys., Inc., 75 F.3d 1069, 1074 (6th Cir. 1996).
[31] *Id.* at 1080–86.
[32] In re "Agent Orange" Prods. Liab. Litig., 506 F. Supp. 762, 769 (E.D.N.Y. 1980).
[33] In re Asbestos School Litig., 104 F.R.D. 422, 425 (E.D. Pa. 1984).
[34] In re Breast Implant Litig., 11 F. Supp.2d 1217, 1221 (D. Colo. 1998).

that seeking class action status for personal injury torts was not viable; to accomplish remediation, the attorneys would have to pursue work-around approaches to aggregate litigation.

This change in plaintiff's litigation strategy gave rise to several signal pleading innovations: recasting mass tort injuries based on fraud and misrepresentation, creation of the novel medical monitoring claim, and pursuit of punitive-damages only classes. The plaintiffs' assertion of these inventive claims shared the common theme of avoidance of aggregation under conventional personal injury claims. Much less recognized, the plaintiffs' bar also began to assert public nuisance theories in support of claims for remediation of mass tort injuries.

2.3 A 1990S PARADIGM SHIFT: RECASTING MASS TORT LITIGATION AS FRAUD, MISREPRESENTATION, AND BREACH OF CONTRACT CLAIMS

A prominent example of the plaintiffs' bar recasting theories other than conventional personal injury tort claims occurred in the *Castano* tobacco litigation.[35] For forty years tobacco industry defendants pursued a "no settlement" strategy in which the companies successfully defended against plaintiffs' individual lawsuits alleging personal injuries as a consequence of smoking. Alternatively, tobacco defendants encouraged voluntary dismissal by making litigation excessively expensive and burdensome. For many years tobacco defendants effectively defeated attempts to hold the industry accountable for tobacco-related harms.[36]

By the early 1990s, however, a skilled, knowledgeable cadre of mass tort plaintiffs' lawyers emerged with two decades of experience honed on the first generation of mass torts: asbestos, DES, Dalkon Shield, breast implants, Agent Orange, and diet drugs. The lucrative settlement of many mass torts encouraged proliferation of a plaintiffs' mass tort bar, fueled by an expanding war chest of financial resources obtained through mass tort settlements. In addition, plaintiffs' attorneys realized the benefits of coordinating resources and strategies.[37]

The tobacco industry became the next big target. Experienced mass tort attorneys formed a consortium to sue the tobacco industry in the largest ever

---

[35] Castano v. American Tobacco Co., 160 F.R.D. 544 (E.D. La. 1995), rev'd Castano v. American Tobacco Co., 84 F.3d 734 (5th Cir. 1996).

[36] Howard M. Erichson, The End of the Defendant Advantage in Tobacco Litigation, 26 Wm. & Mary Envtl. L. & Pol'y Rev. 123, 126 (2001).

[37] *Id.* at 129.

class action pursued.[38] The plaintiffs' attorneys had learned from the failure of personal injury mass tort class litigation. Thus, the plaintiffs' *Castano* tobacco strategy was to recraft their tobacco litigation as anything other than a personal injury mass tort, and to forum-shop for a federal judge willing to certify the recast class action.

In 1994, plaintiffs sued seven tobacco company defendants in federal district court in Louisiana in a class action complaint.[39] The plaintiffs alleged claims were for fraud and deceit, negligent misrepresentation, intentional infliction of emotion distress, violation of consumer protection statutes under state law, breach of express warranty, breach of implied warranty, strict product liability, and redhibition under Louisiana law.[40] The plaintiff's litigation theory rested upon their contention that the tobacco company defendants had fraudulently failed to inform smokers that nicotine was addictive, despite the defendants' possession of knowledge that tobacco products were addictive.[41] The plaintiffs' attorneys, then, advanced a novel "nicotine addiction as harm" theory of litigation.

The plaintiffs' attorneys carefully crafted their complaint not to seek damages for personal injury claims. Instead, the class sought a declaratory judgment holding the defendants financially responsible for notifying all class members of the addictive nature of tobacco products, along with restitution and refunds of money class members paid for cigarette purchases. The plaintiffs also sought disgorgement of the defendants' profits made from the sale of cigarettes, with restitution to class members.[42]

What was striking about the *Castano* class action complaint was its deliberate avoidance of alleging personal injury claims or seeking compensatory damages to class members. In certifying the proposed class action, the court specifically noted that "Plaintiffs do not seek recovery of personal injury damages in the form of physical pain and suffering or any related damages."[43] Instead, this *Castano* tobacco litigation focused on the defendants' actions, rather than on injuries to individual claimants, and the litigation sought an array of equitable remedies capable of classwide award.

By focusing on the defendants' conduct, the plaintiffs successfully convinced the trial court that the proposed *Castano* class was suitable for class

---

[38] At the time, commentators estimated that the *Castano* class embraced some fifty million claimants.

[39] Castano, *supra* note 35, at n.1.

[40] *Id.* at 548.

[41] *Id.*

[42] *Id.*

[43] *Id.*

certification under the Rule 23(a) threshold requirements of commonality, typicality, and adequacy, as well as the Rule 23(b)(3) requirements for predominance of common questions and superiority. By cloaking what might have been personal injury claims in other legal garb, the plaintiffs successfully convinced the court that common factual issues predominated over individual issues. These common issues included whether the defendants knew that cigarette smoking was addictive, and failed to inform cigarette smokers of such and took actions to addict cigarette smokers. In addition, the court found predominant legal issues common to the class in the defendants' fraud, negligence, breach of express or implied warranty, strict liability, and violation of consumer protective statutes.[44]

A federal appellate court swiftly repudiated the district court's certification of the *Castano* class action for reasons that resonated in earlier federal jurisprudence rejecting class certification of mass tort litigation.[45] The *Castano* litigation represented a significant paradigm shift in the historical arc of mass tort litigation. The *Castano* complaint was a first attempt by the mass tort lawyers to pursue relief for aggregate tort claimants by recasting the claims and theories for relief to avoid class certification barriers. As such, the *Castano* litigation presented a template for a new way of thinking about the pursuit of mass tort remediation.

2.4 INVENTING NEW TORT THEORIES

Contemporaneous with the *Castano* litigation, mass tort lawyers forged ahead with a nationwide class action on behalf of hemophiliacs who received tainted blood product transfusions resulting in HIV infections or death from AIDS.[46] The defendants were manufacturers who extracted certain factors from donated blood. The plaintiffs asserted claims for negligence, negligent failure to warn of the dangers involved in the use of the defendants' products, strict products liability, breach of implied warranty, conspiracy, and breach of fiduciary duty.

The plaintiffs' core negligence claim was that the defendants knew in the 1970s that viruses which cause certain diseases (such as hepatitis) were blood-borne and, therefore, they should have taken precautions to prevent or reduce viral contamination of their products. The plaintiffs alleged that the defendants knew they used plasma collected from paid donors, a group that

---

44 *Id.* at 553.
45 Castano v. Am. Tobacco Co., 84 F.3d 734 (5th Cir. 1996).
46 Wadleigh v. Rhone-Poulenc Rorer, Inc., 157 F.R.D. 410, 413–14 (N.D. Ill. 1994).

included many persons at high risk for viral infection, such as intravenous drug users. The plaintiffs alleged defendant's negligence in failing to use the then-available technology to sterilize blood products despite their knowledge that a high percentage of the patients who would use their blood products were being infected with hepatitis and other serious viral disease.[47]

An Illinois federal judge certified the hemophiliac's class with reference to predominant common issues of the defendants' negligence. Eliding differences among state tort law, the court instead concluded that the definition of ordinary negligence was substantially identical in all jurisdictions.[48]

On appeal, the appellate court reversed the class certification for reasons independent of Rule 23 class certification requirements.[49] The court acknowledged that the plaintiffs asserted a conventional negligence theory, alleging that the defendants dragged their heels in screening donors and taking other measures to prevent contamination of the blood products.[50] But the court expressed some scepticism over what the plaintiffs characterized as their "serendipity" theory of tort liability, a newly created theory of tort liability. Under this theory, the defendants had a duty of due care with respect to the risk of Hepatitis B infection so as to require the defendants to take measures to purge their blood products of the hepatitis virus from their blood products. Had the defendants not been negligent in purging the Hepatitis B virus, hemophiliacs would have been protected not only against Hepatitis B but also, fortuitously, against HIV.[51]

The appellate court rejected the district court's finding that state laws of negligence were universally the same to support certification of a nationwide class action.[52] The court suggested that it doubted it was true that negligence law was identical, "… and we greatly doubt that it is true in a case such as this in which one of the theories presented by the plaintiffs, the 'serendipity' theory, is novel."[53] The court further suggested the plaintiffs' novel serendipity tort theory dispensed, rightly or wrongly, with proof of foreseeability, even though a number of states incorporated foreseeability of risk into their tests for negligence.[54]

Commentators primarily recognize the appellate decision in *Rhone-Poulenc* for its compelling articulation of reasons for repudiating nationwide mass tort

---

[47] *Id.* at 414.

[48] *Id.* at 419.

[49] In the Matter of Rhone-Poulenc Rorer Inc., 51 F.3d 1293 (7th Cir. 1995).

[50] *Id.* at 1296.

[51] *Id.*

[52] *Id.* at 1300. "One is put in the mind of the concept of 'general' common law that prevailed in the era of *Swift v. Tyson*."

[53] Rhone-Poulenc, at 1300.

[54] *Id.* at 1301.

class litigation.[55] But the hemophiliac litigation is instructive in another way. The underlying complaint provides another illustration of how mass tort attorneys, by the mid-1990s, were crafting mass tort class actions alleging both conventional tort theories and asserting novel claims where ordinary tort theories might not expansively cover the grounds for relief.

2.5 EMERGENCE OF MEDICAL MONITORING IN MASS TORT CLAIMS

Perhaps the most striking mass tort innovation in the mid-1990s was the creative pleading of medical monitoring claims and remedies. While it was possible to find antecedent requests for medical monitoring in prior litigation,[56] precedents for medical monitoring were scarce and largely undeveloped and underutilized. Initially, there was considerable doctrinal confusion concerning whether medical monitoring for mass tort injuries constituted a claim for relief or an equitable remedy as a part of damages.[57] Moreover, as late as 1994 a federal district court struggled with "squaring" the plaintiffs' request for medical monitoring relief with traditional tort law.[58]

The plaintiffs' requests for medical monitoring was very much part of the shifting mass tort litigation landscape in the mid-1990s. Like the repackaging of the tobacco personal injury mass torts under fraud or misrepresentation theories, the creative use of medical monitoring represented another example of trial lawyers' repackaging personal injury mass tort litigation under another guise.

The plaintiffs' innovative advocacy of medical monitoring solved many of the plaintiffs' difficulties in pursuing aggregate personal injury mass tort litigation on a classwide basis. Significantly, plaintiffs attempted to craft pleading requests for medical monitoring as an equitable remedy under Federal Rule of Civil 23(b)(2). Thus, pleading medical monitoring as a form of equitable relief allowed attorneys to avoid the Rule 23(b)(3) requirements of predominance and superiority that otherwise defeated attempts to certify mass tort personal injury claims. And, in latent injury mass torts where the harm to

---

[55] *See generally*, Laurie C. Uustal, Casenote, In the Matter of Rhone-Poulenc Rorer: Shielding Defendants Under Rule 23, 51 U. Miami L. Rev. 1247 (1997).

[56] *See e.g.*, Day v. NLO, 851 F. Supp. 869 (S.D. Ohio 1994).

[57] Pankaj Venugopal, Note, The Class Certification of Medical Monitoring Claims, 102 Colum. L. Rev. 1659, 1660 (2002); George W.C. McCarter, Medical Sue-Veillance: A History and Critique of the Medical Monitoring Remedy in Toxic Tort Litigation, 45 Rutgers L. Rev. 227, 231 (1993).

[58] *Id.* at 879–80.

claimants might not manifest for many years, the request for medical monitoring captured the problematic subset of future mass tort claimants with exposure-only injuries.

Initially, the novelty of medical monitoring in the mass tort arena was evidenced by uncertainty of how to plead medical monitoring and the courts' concomitant uncertainty whether to permit or deny such requests. This doctrinal confusion was no better illustrated than the approach to medical monitoring in the 1997 *Atrial "J" Leads Products Liability Litigation*,[59] where the lawyers sought certification for a nationwide subclass of all medical monitoring claims under Rule 23(b)(1)(A), (b)(1)(B), and (b)(3).[60] Not only did the court find that the proposed medical monitoring class satisfied all the threshold requirements of Rule 23(a) (numerosity, commonality, typicality, and adequacy), but the court also further approved certification of the proposed medical monitoring class under Rule 23(b)(1)(A), (b)(1)(B), and Rule 23(b)(3).

This judicial approval of a medical monitoring class was short-lived, however. That courts might approve a request for a medical monitoring class under various Rule 23 provisions did not go unnoticed by mass tort attorneys seeking to hold the tobacco companies accountable. Following on their class defeat in *Castano*, plaintiffs' attorneys regrouped and sought certification of a medical monitoring class of smokers under Rule 23(b)(2) and (b)(3) in Pennsylvania federal court.[61] In this instance, the district court rejected certification of a medical monitoring class under either provision and sought to clarify medical monitoring jurisprudence.

The court looked to underlying Pennsylvania law and concluded that a request for medical monitoring constituted a claim for relief, rather than an element of damages.[62] Construing state law, the federal circuit court had concluded that four elements were required for plaintiffs to maintain a class for medical monitoring.[63] Over the next two decades, many (but not all) states legislatively adopted medical monitoring statutes with enumerated elements constituting the claims.[64]

The Pennsylvania court did not outrightly reject the possibility of certifying a Rule 23(b)(2) medical monitoring class but indicated that the dispositive factor was the type of relief the plaintiffs sought. If the plaintiffs' request was

[59] In re Telectronics Pacing Sys., Inc., Accufix Atrial "J" Leads Prods. Liab. Litig., 172 F.R.D. 271 (S.D. Ohio 1997).

[60] *Id.* at 284–87.

[61] Arch v. Am. Tobacco Co., Inc., 175 F.R.D. 469 (E.D. Pa. 1997).

[62] *Id.* at 481.

[63] *Id.*

[64] *See* In re Welding Fumes Prod. Liab. Litig., 245 F.R.D. 279 (N.D.Ohio 2007).

"a disguised request for compensatory damages," then the medical monitoring claim could only be characterized as a claim for monetary relief not certifiable under Rule 23(b)(2). But if the plaintiffs sought establishment of a court-supervised medical monitoring program through which plaintiffs would receive periodic examinations, then the plaintiffs' request could be properly characterized as seeking injunctive relief.[65] Reviewing the plaintiffs' formulation of its medical monitoring request, the court concluded it failed as a disguised request that predominantly was for compensatory damages.[66] The court further concluded that the medical monitoring request was not suitable for class certification under Rule 23(b)(3) because of lack of predominant common questions and superiority.[67]

The jurisprudential distinction drawn between permissible and impermissible Rule 23(b)(2) medical monitoring classes encouraged plaintiffs' attorneys to engage in tightly crafted artful pleading of medical monitoring requests. When the Pennsylvania attorneys redrafted their medical monitoring proposal to request only the establishment of a court-supervised medical monitoring program, the appellate court again rebuffed this creative attempt, imposing a new "cohesion" requirement for proposed (b)(2) medical monitoring classes.[68]

Notwithstanding the doctrinal disarray and occasional setbacks, the trial lawyers' mass tort bar has continued to pursue medical monitoring claims unabated in hundreds of lawsuits throughout the twenty-first century, in both state and federal courts.[69] In 2007 a federal district judge summarized the state of medical monitoring jurisprudence: "The law of medical monitoring varies from state to state. Some states recognize medical monitoring as an element of damages when liability is otherwise established, while other states recognize medical monitoring as an independent cause of action; some states require proof of a present, physical injury to obtain medical monitoring, and some do not; and some states do not provide for medical monitoring at all."[70]

The increasing receptivity of courts towards approving medical monitoring classes continues to have great appeal to mass tort plaintiffs' lawyers as a surrogate pleading mechanism rather than personal injury mass tort claims.[71]

---

[65] *Arch, supra* note 61, at 483.

[66] *Id.* at 483–84.

[67] *Id.* at 485–96.

[68] Barnes v. Am. Tobacco Co., 161 F.3d 127, 143 (3d Cir. 1998).

[69] *See* Welding Fume Prods., *supra* note 64.

[70] *Id.* at 291–92.

[71] *See e.g,* In re Nat'l Football League Players Concussion Injury Litig., 2016 WL 1552205 (3d Cir. 2016); In re Nat'l Collegiate Athletic Ass'n Student-Athlete Concussion Injury Litig., 314 F.R.D. 580 (N.D. Ill. 2016).

Moreover, the presence of a medical monitoring claim coupled with the likelihood of judicial approval exerts hydraulic pressure on defendants to settle
what otherwise might be viewed as a personal injury mass tort. Thus, the creative development of medical monitoring claims provides an example of flexible, innovative lawyering by the mass tort plaintiffs' bar.

2.6 THE PUNITIVE DAMAGE CLASS

Another example of the plaintiffs' mass tort bar's adaptability and resilience
is illustrated by its pursuit of a mass tort punitive damage class. The punitive
damage class represented yet another creative work-around of the personal
injury mass tort damage class action. The history of the punitive damage class
illustrates the plaintiffs' refusal abandon a novel approach to resolving mass
tort claims, in the context of repeated failure. The punitive damage class is a
narrative about the plaintiffs' repeated retreating, regrouping, and rethinking
legal theory.

The idea for a punitive damage class made intuitive sense: the theory
focused on a defendant's conduct rather than on an individual claimants'
injuries, and punitive damage relief would apply classwide, thereby evading
problematic Rule 23(b)(3) predominance requirements. The plaintiffs' attorneys quickly recognized the benefits of class certification of a punitive damage
class under Rule 23's provision for a limited fund action,[72] which would easily satisfy threshold certification requirements for commonality and typicality
and not be subject to additional Rule 23(b)(3) requirements.

From the 1980s through the end of the twentieth century, attorneys repeatedly sought to certify punitive damage classes and courts repeatedly repudiated these efforts. Nationwide proposed punitive damage classes failed for
differences among state punitive damage laws,[73] under-inclusiveness,[74] but
most often for the proponents' failure to prove up the existence of a defendant's limited fund.[75] Despite repeated setbacks, the plaintiffs' attorneys kept
pursuing the same limited fund template for a punitive damage class, thereby
attempting to leverage settlement advantage against defendants through the
sheer threat of a massive punitive class certification and award.

---

[72] Fed. R. Civ. P. 23(b)(1)(B).
[73] In re Northern Dist. Of California, Dalkon Shield IUD Prods. Liab. Litig., 693 F.2d 847, 850
     (9th Cir. 1982).
[74] In re School Asbestos Litig., 789 F.2d 996, 1005 (3d Cir.1986).
[75] In re School Asbestos Litig., *supra* note 74, at 1003; In re Northern Dist. of California, *supra*
     note 73, at 851–52; *In re* Agent Orange Prod. Liab. Litig, 506 F. Supp. 762, 789–90 (E.D.N.Y.
     1980); Payton v. Abbott Labs, 83 F.R.D. 382, 389 (D. Mass 1979).

At the end of the twentieth century, the plaintiffs resuscitated the mass tort punitive damage class with the aid of several Supreme Court decisions effectively capping the size of punitive awards based on constitutional due process constraints.[76] The due process constraints on punitive damage awards had been raised but laid dormant in prior mass tort cases,[77] but the theory was given new life with the Court's imprimatur.

Hence, in 2000, the ever-adaptive mass tort plaintiffs' attorneys, in yet another attempt to hold the tobacco industry accountable for smoking harms, seized on the Court's constitutional cap on punitive damage awards to seek certification of a nationwide Rule 23(b)(1)(B) punitive damage class based on the theory that the constitutional cap created the limited fund necessary for class certification. The lack of proof of a limited fund previously had been the primary barrier to certification of a punitive damage class. The plaintiffs' bar creatively seized on the Court's reconsideration of constitutional punitive damages, spotting an opportunity to revitalize the mass tort punitive damage class. The attorneys successfully sold this novel limited fund theory to federal Judge Jack Weinstein, who in 2002 agreed with the theory and certified the punitive damage class.[78] Three years later the appellate court reversed the class certification.[79]

Although the fate of the revitalized punitive damage class was another failure, the chronicle of this effort was part of the plaintiffs' shift in the 1990s towards exploring novel legal theories and innovative lawyering to pursue mass tort litigation. The punitive damage initiative was another example of the plaintiffs' attorneys recasting personal injury mass tort under claims of fraud, misrepresentation, contract law, made-up serendipity tort theory, and medical monitoring. Amid this era of creative lawyering, some plaintiffs' attorneys began to venture the first mass tort litigation based on public nuisance law.

2.7 THE SHIFT TO NOVEL PUBLIC NUISANCE THEORIES IN MASS TORT LITIGATION

Plaintiffs' attorneys during the first two decades of mass tort litigation were adept at learning from their successes and failures in convincing courts to

[76] *See generally* State Farm Mutual Automobile Ins. Co. v. Campbell, 538 U.S. 408 (2003); BMW v. Gore, 517 U.S. 559 (1996); Honda Motor Co. v. Oberg, 512 U.S. 415 (1994): TXO Prod. Corp. v. Alliance Res. Corp., 509 U.S. 443 (1966); Pac. Mutual Life Ins. Co. v. Haslip, 499 U.S. 1 (1991).

[77] School Asbestos Litig., *supra* note 74 at 1004–05.

[78] In re Simon II Litig., 211 F.R.D. 86 (E.D.N.Y. 2002).

[79] In re Simon II Litig., 407 F.3d 125 (2d Cir. 2005).

permit mass tort products cases to proceed as class litigation. Thus, the plaintiffs' bar became skilled at reconfiguring mass harm cases under evolving or new theories. The plaintiffs' bar demonstrated a resilient ability to rebound after suffering setbacks or defeats in state and federal court, and to regroup by reconfiguring mass tort litigation pursuant to an array of different legal theories. The more apparent it became that courts were unwilling to certify class litigation under conventional tort theories, the more inventive plaintiffs' attorneys became in exploring new avenues for pursuing mass tort litigation. In a sense, the plaintiffs' bar pointedly challenged the judiciary to reject their novel forays into mass harm remediation.

As part of this lawyering evolution some plaintiffs' attorneys in the 1980s and 1990s began to include public nuisance claims in their class complaints against defendant corporations. Like the introduction of other novel mass tort theories, courts did not initially receive these initial forays into public nuisance theory with favor. Instead, courts typically defaulted to a narrow view of nuisance law grounded in property theories.

Thus, courts in asbestos, tobacco, and gun litigation initially declined to recognize public nuisance claims, refusing to accept plaintiff's invitations to expand public nuisance beyond its historical grounding in property concepts. Several courts declined to permit public nuisance claims to proceed, noting that traditional nuisance cases typically concerned the use of property, not products. Other courts reasoned that lawsuits alleging harms from products sounded in causes of action for products liability, not public nuisance, and the law of public nuisance had never been applied to products, however harmful they may have been.

Examples of judicial rejection of public nuisance for products tort recovery appeared early in the 1980s. During the heyday of asbestos litigation, an appellate court rejected a plaintiff's attempt to recover from an asbestos manufacturer the costs of abating asbestos from North Dakota school buildings. In its lawsuit, the plaintiff pleaded an array of conventional tort claims with an additional claim for violation of North Dakota's public nuisance statute.[80] After a favorable jury verdict for the plaintiff, the defendant appealed challenging the court's submission of the public nuisance claim to the jury.[81] The appellate decision catalogued a full array of reasons for rejecting public nuisance claims in products cases and served as a template for similar judicial assessment of public nuisance claims.

---

[80] Tioga Pub. Sch. Dist. $15 of Williams Cty., North Dakota v. United Gypsum Co., 984 F.2d 915, 917 (8th Cir. 1993).

[81] *Id.*

The appellate court agreed with the defendant that the trial court had erred in sending the public nuisance claim to the jury;[82] the decision was based on two provisions of North Dakota's nuisance statute, which provided: "A nuisance consisted in unlawfully doing an act or omitting to perform a duty, which act or omission: 1. Annoys, injures, or endangers the comfort, repose, health, or safety of others; … or 4. In any way renders other persons insecure in life or the use of property."

The appellate court held that all federal courts agreed that nuisance law was not a remedy against an asbestos manufacturing product to an owner whose building was contaminated by asbestos. "All courts that have considered the issue have rejected nuisance as a theory of recovery in such cases."[83] The court further noted that all North Dakota cases applying the state's nuisance statute had arisen in the classic context of a landowner or other person in control of property conducting an activity on his land in such manner so as to interfere with the property rights of a neighbor.[84]

The plaintiff had failed to present the court with any precedent extending application of the state's nuisance statute to situations where one party sold a product to another party that later was alleged to constitute a nuisance. The court observed that North Dakota's nuisance statute was more than 100 years old and "the absence of analogous cases supports an inference that the statute was neither intended nor has it been understood to extend to cases" such as the asbestos litigation.[85]

Finally, the court concluded that the state's statute had not wholly changed or replaced the common law of nuisance, noting that the North Dakota Supreme Court at the time of the statute's enactment viewed the provisions as "but a continuation of the common law to be construed therewith."[86] Were the court to interpret the statute espoused by the plaintiff "would in effect totally rewrite North Dakota tort law."[87]

In other asbestos abatement litigation, a Michigan appellate court agreed that manufacturers, sellers, or installers of defective products may not be held liable on public nuisance theories caused by a product defect.[88] The court noted that the law of nuisance almost universally concerned the use or

---

[82] *Id.* at 920–21. *See* N.D. Cent. Code § 42-01-01 (1983).
[83] Tioga Pub. Sch. Dist., *supra* note 80, at 920.
[84] *Id.*
[85] *Id.*
[86] *Id.* at 921, citing Reeves v. Russell, 28 N.D. 265, 148 N.W. 654, 659 (1914).
[87] Tioga Pub. Sch. Dist., *supra* note 80, at 921.
[88] Detroit Bd. of Educ. v. Celotex Corp., 493 N.W.2d 513, 520–22, 196 Mich. App. 694 (Mich. App. 1992).

condition of property, not products.[89] In so concluding, the Michigan court expressed concerns about expansion of public nuisance doctrine in products cases beyond the litigation before it: "To hold otherwise would significantly expand, with unpredictable consequences, the remedies already available to persons injured by products, and not merely asbestos."[90]

The plaintiffs' mass tort bar regrouped and reconfigured their legal attacks against the tobacco industry several times during the 1990s, including initial forays into public nuisance law. Nonetheless, courts similarly rejected plaintiffs' recourse to public nuisance theory for recovery of damages against tobacco company defendants.[91] In a multi-claim assault against tobacco company defendants, Texas sought to recoup damages for the state costs for medical treatment for tobacco-related injuries.[92] The state pleaded that the tobacco company defendants had intentionally interfered with the public's right to be free from unwarranted injury, disease, and sickness and had caused damage to the public health, safety and general welfare of Texas citizens.[93] In essence, this type of litigation was a precursor of the twenty-first century actions state and municipal governments brought in the opioid litigation.

The Texas federal court rejected the plaintiffs' attempt to seek recovery for abatement of a public nuisance or recovery of damages. Taking the narrowest possible view of the Texas public nuisance statute, the court noted that only the Texas Attorney General was authorized to seek abatement of a public nuisance. A public nuisance, described in the statute, was the use of any place for certain, specific proscribed activities such as gambling, prostitution, and the manufacture of obscene materials. Because the plaintiffs' allegations did not concern proscribed conduct in the public nuisance statute, the State could not maintain an action for an injunction.[94]

The Texas federal court further held that the plaintiff could not maintain an action for damages under a public nuisance theory, because the plaintiff had failed to properly plead the elements of a claim under Texas public nuisance law. "Specifically, the State failed to plead that defendants improperly used their own property, or that the State itself had been injured in its use or employment of its property."[95] Similar to the Michigan court, the Texas court indicated that the "overly broad definition of the elements of public nuisance

---

[89] *Id.* at 521.
[90] *Id.*
[91] Texas v. Am. Tobacco Co., 14 F. Supp.2d 956 (E.D. Tx. 1997).
[92] *Id.* at 965, 969–72.
[93] *Id.* at 972.
[94] *Id.* at 972–73, citing Tex. Civ. Prac. & Rem. § 125.021.
[95] *Id.* at 973.

urged by the State is simply not found in Texas case law and the Court is unwilling to accept the state's invitation to expand a claim for public nuisance beyond its ground in real property."[96]

By the late 1990s, the prospect of holding the firearms industry accountable for gun-related harms presented a new, significant, and ripe target for mass tort lawyers. Attorneys attempting to sue gun manufacturers and distributors, however, faced daunting obstacles, not the least of which were federal and state statutes immunizing these prospective defendants from suit. In the late 1990s Philadelphia and certain civic organizations sued the gun industry alleging that the defendants' methods for distributing guns was negligent and a constituted a public nuisance.[97]

The plaintiffs alleged that the defendants' marketing and distribution schemes were responsible for placing guns in the hands of persons who caused damage to Philadelphia residents. The plaintiffs alleged that the defendants knew or wilfully avoided knowing that their distribution channels allowed guns to fall into the hands of criminals and children. They alleged that the defendants failed to monitor and supervise federal firearms' licensing provisions, and that their marketing schemes were tailored to appeal to criminals.[98]

Assessing the public nuisance claim as a question of first impression, the federal judge framed the issue: "Does Pennsylvania law recognize a public nuisance tort for distribution practices of a legal, non-defective product which causes harm to individuals after the product has left the defendant manufacturers' control?"[99]

The federal district court dismissed the case, holding that the plaintiffs lacked standing to sue and could not recover under any theory they asserted.[100] The court observed that the public nuisance claim sought to exert traditional state power, noting that the first public nuisance suits were encroachments on the royal domain or public highways.[101] The right to sue for public nuisance had passed to the states and their surrogates. But neither the plaintiffs nor the defendants cited cases in support of or discounting the novel theory of public nuisance asserted in the litigation.[102]

The court acknowledged that Pennsylvania law adopted the *Restatement (Second)* approach to public nuisance.[103] In construing the scope of public

---

[96] *Id.*
[97] Philadelphia v. Beretta U.S.A., Corp., 126 F. Supp.2d 882 (E.D. Pa. 2000).
[98] *Id.* at 888.
[99] *Id.* at 906.
[100] *Id.* at 886.
[101] *Id.* at 893, quoting the *Restatement (Second) of Torts* § 821B cmt. a (1979).
[102] Philadelphia, *supra* note 97, at 906.
[103] *Id.* at 907:

(1) A public nuisance is an unreasonable interference with a right common to the public.

nuisance law, the court rested heavily on defendants' interferences with property or property rights. Nuisance law served two purposes: (1) providing a remedy for interference with the use or enjoyment of land, and (2) providing a basis for the prosecution of those who infringed the rights of the crown or the public. Drawing heavily on the Prosser and Keeton treatise, the court explained that the leading examples of public nuisance included encroachments on the royal domain or public highways.[104]

The district court noted that the Pennsylvania Supreme Court had explained that "nuisance was the use of property or a course of conduct which transgressed the just restrictions on use or conduct which the proximity of other persons or property in civilized communities imposes upon what would otherwise be rightful freedom."[105] Nuisances were wrongs that arose from unreasonable, unwarranted, or unlawful use of one's real or personal property that obstructed the right of the public such that it produced material harm that the law presumed a consequent damage.[106] Pennsylvania courts had found public nuisance violations for acid drainage from an abandoned mineshaft into a nearby waterway, the manufacture of fireworks in a populated area, sexual conduct on premises that could lead to the transmission of HIV, and keeping twenty purebred huskies on a residential street.[107]

The plaintiffs' assertion of a public nuisance claim against the firearms' defendants failed because the plaintiffs could only cite cases where Pennsylvania courts had applied public nuisance law in this traditional fashion. Plaintiffs' cases were of little use because they involved either traditional land-based nuisances or violations of ordinances.[108] The court further rejected the plaintiffs' suggestion that the court follow an expansive approach to public nuisance law ascribed to Professors Prosser and Keeton. Instead, the court asserted that the treatise writers viewed the "amorphous expansion of public nuisance as an alarming development, not a welcome one."[109]

(2) Circumstances that may sustain a holding that an interference with a public right is unreasonable include the following:
  (a) Whether the conduct involves a significant interference with the public health, the public safety, the public peace, the public comfort or the public convenience;
  (b) Whether the conduct is proscribed by statute, ordinance, or administrative regulation; or
  (c) Whether the conduct is of a continuing nature or had produced a permanent or long-lasting effect, and, as the actor knows or has reason to know, has a significant effect on the public right.

[104] Philadelphia, *supra* note 97, at 907.
[105] *Id.* citing Kramer v. Pittsburgh Coal Co., 341 Pa. 379, 19 A.2d 362, 363 (1941).
[106] Philadelphia, *supra* note 97, at 907–08.
[107] *Id.* at 908.
[108] *Id.* at 908–09.
[109] *Id.* at 909.

Finally, the federal court contended the concept of public nuisance law had been restricted since 1985 with judicial refusal to apply the public nuisance tort in the context of personal injuries caused by product defect design and distribution. The only appellate court to have considered a public nuisance claim by a municipality against the gun industry had refused to apply public nuisance law.[110] The Pennsylvania federal court concluded that judicial refusal to apply public nuisance law to the manufacturing, marketing, and distribution of firearms products conformed with the elements of public nuisance law. The defendants did not create the injurious acts with their harmful consequences, but rather by criminals and others unlawfully in possession of firearms. Gun manufacturers did not wrongfully use their products and their distribution practices, and their actions could not be said to be unreasonable, unwarranted, or unlawful use of their personal property.[111]

Finally, the Pennsylvania federal court sounded a negative, cautionary note against the plaintiffs' attempt to obtain remediation in gun litigation through the pursuit of novel theories:

> Even assuming, for present purposes, that the City could sue and that the organizational plaintiffs do have standing, they still could not prevail in this action as a matter of law. To lend credence to their novel legal theories, plaintiffs categorize their claims for negligence and public nuisance as traditional state causes of action. But current negligence and public nuisance law are not nearly as malleable as they suggest. Trial courts should be circumspect before creating rights ex nihilo. Judge Learned Hand once observed, it is "not desirable for a lower court to embrace the exhilarating opportunity of anticipating a doctrine which may be in the womb of time but whose birth is distant."[112]

---

[110] *Id.* at 910, citing Cincinnati v. Beretta U.S.A. Corp., 2000 WL 1133078, at *9-10 (Ohio Ct. App. Aug. 11, 2000).

[111] Philadelphia, *supra* note 97, at 910.

[112] *Id.* at 898, quoting Spector Motor Service v. Walsh, 139 F.2d 809, 823 (2d Cir. 1943) (Hand, J., dissenting).

3

Expanding Public Nuisance Doctrine

Inroads and Retreats, the Lead Paint Mass Tort Litigation

Notwithstanding the resistance of many state and federal courts in the late twentieth century to expand public nuisance jurisprudence to mass tort products litigation, a minority of courts began to accomplish inroads into applying public nuisance theory to mass tort events in the early twenty-first century. The persistent judicial attachment to traditional property-based views of public nuisance law inhibited development of a more expansive view of public interest theories applied to products cases.

In the early twenty-first century, the most significant judicial breach in resistance to mass tort public nuisance claims occurred in lead paint litigation. The arc of lead paint litigation presents an object lesson in how plaintiffs' attorneys achieved significant success in advancing novel public nuisance claims against the paint industry, only to experience a judicial backlash rejecting expansion of public nuisance doctrine. In many respects, the narrative of public nuisance lead paint litigation paralleled the experience of medical monitoring claims, with initial success followed by judicial restraint, leaving the litigation landscape in disarray.

Federal and state statutes enacted to address the lead paint crisis enabled the development of public nuisance law in lead paint cases. Plaintiffs in Rhode Island led the country in the first successful lead paint assault again the paint industry. Wisconsin, New Jersey, and California courts followed quickly, upholding public nuisance claims in lead paint litigation, relying both on traditional common law and statutory bases.

The lead paint cases presented a new paradigm for pursuing mass tort relief in products cases through public nuisance law. In the same way that mass tort attorneys had to develop and invent legal theories that circumvented Rule 23 class certification requirements, twenty-first century mass tort attorneys had to learn how to circumvent traditional property paradigms for public nuisance claims. Moreover, the lead paint litigation again demonstrates the persistence and ingenuity of the plaintiffs' mass tort bar in using the lessons from other mass tort litigation to adapt to new circumstances and learn to craft pleadings to conform to statutory and common law requirements.

3.1 THE LEAD PAINT LITIGATION CRISIS

Commentators have well documented the events giving rise to the lead paint mass litigation.[1] In the early twentieth century the Environmental Protection Agency forecast that that nearly one million children under the age of six suffered from lead poisoning because of exposure to lead-based paint found in an estimated thirty million older houses.[2] Studies of lead paint poisoning concluded that the undeveloped neurological systems of young children were especially vulnerable to the toxic, damaging effects of lead poisoning.

The presence of lead-based paint in older residential homes presented compelling risks, as the older paint aged and cracked, releasing both chips and lead dust particles into the air and ground. Lead-based paint chips and dust presented the greatest risk to young children because of the common and normal hand-to-mouth activities of young children, increasing the likelihood that they would ingest harmful lead-based paint residue. One study estimated that that approximately 3.8 million children had blood lead levels high enough to cause health problems.[3]

Lead-based paints were widely used in residential buildings until the mid-1970s.[4] As a consequence of the advance of scientific understanding of the harmful effects of lead-based paint, Congress enacted the Lead-Based Paint Poisoning Prevention Act (LPPPA) in 1971,[5] which recognized the need for federal action to combat the growing hazard of lead paint exposure to young children. The Act recommended studying the effects of childhood exposure to

---

[1] *See generally* Shana R. Cappell, Lead Paint Poisoning and the Resource Conservation and Recovery Act: A New Partnership for the 21st Century, 35 Colum. J.L. & Soc. Probs. 175 (2001); Mark P. Gagliardi, Note and Comment, Stirring the Debate in Rhode Island: Should Lead Paint Manufacturers Be Held Liable for the Harm Caused by Lead Paint?, 7 Roger Williams U.L. Rev. 314 (2002); Frederick C. Schaefer & Christine Nykiel, Lead Paint: Mass Tort Litigation and Public Nuisance Trends in America, 74 Def. Couns. J. 153 (2007); Lisa A. Perillo, Note, Scraping Beneath the Surface: Finally Holding Lead-Based Paint Manufacturers Liable by Applying Public Nuisance and Market-Share Liability Theories?, 32 Hofstra L. Rev. 1039 (2004).

[2] Cappell, *id.* at 175–78; Perillo, *id.* at 1039.

[3] Cappell, *supra* note 1, at 175.

[4] Rhode Island v. Lead Paint Industries Ass'n, 951 A.2d 428, 437 (R.I. 2008).

[5] Pub. L. No. 91-659, 84 Stat. 2078 (1971) (formerly codified at 42 U.S.C.A.) §§ 4801–46 (1971).

lead paint and eliminating lead-based paint from federally owned or financed housing.[6] At the same time, the Secretary of Housing and Development was authorized to promulgate regulations to eliminate the harms of lead-based paint in federally owned or funded housing.[7] Through amendments to the LPPPA and government regulations, the federal government effectively moved to ban the sale or use of lead-based paint in federal housing.[8] And, in 1978, the Consumer Product Safety Commission banned the sale of residential paint containing more than 0.06 percent lead.[9]

Although the federal government first began in the 1970s to address the problem of lead paint contamination, it was not until the 1990s that the government began an exerted effort to deal with lead paint poisoning.[10] Pursuant to HUD disclosure rules and regulations, landlords were now required to inform renters of the status of lead paint in rental units. The law provided for civil and criminal penalties for landlords' failure to disclose lead paint hazards.[11] These initiatives, however, only applied to federally owned or funded housing; they did not extend to the private housing market.

Following the federal initiatives to address the burgeoning lead exposure health crisis in young children, many states investigated the depth of child lead poisoning exposure in their states. In response to findings of widespread presence of lead paint in older housing stock, state legislatures enacted statutes dealing with lead poisoning prevention and abatement.[12] Many of the state statutes were modeled after federal law and guidelines; many states issued laws and regulations requiring the disclosure of lead paint hazards in housing.

A commentator noted that state legislative programs relating to lead paint hazards varied widely, due to "budgetary constraints, concern for the impact of lead liabilities on affordable housing, and inadequate lead-related insurance provisions for property owners."[13] The state regulations ranged from

---

[6]   *Id.*

[7]   Ashton v. Pierce, 716 F.2d 56, 58–59 (D.C. Cir. 1983).

[8]   Rhode Island, *supra* note 4, at 491. *See also* the Residential Lead-Based Paint Hazard Reduction Act (RLPHRA), Pub. L. No. 102-550, 106 Stat. 3897 (1992) (codified at 42 U.S.C.A. §§ 4851–56 (1992).

[9]   Ban of Lead-Containing Paint and Certain Consumer Products Bearing Lead-Containing Paints, 16 C.F.R. § 1303.1 (2008); Office of Lead-Based Paint Abatement and Poisoning Prevention, 61 Fed. Reg. at 29171.

[10] Cappell, *supra* note 1, at 179–80.

[11] *Id.*

[12] *See e.g.,* New Jersey, Lead Paint Act, L. 1971, c.366 (originally codified at N.J.S.A. 24:14A-1 to 12); Rhode Island, Lead Poisoning Prevention Act (LPPA), (P.L. 1991, ch. 355, § 1 (1991), Title 23, Chap. 24.6; Rhode Island, Lead Hazard Mitigation Act (LHMA) P.L. 2002, ch. 187, § 3), G.L. Title 42, 1956 chap. 128.1. *See also* Cappell, *supra* note 1, at 180.

[13] Cappell, at 180.

comprehensive abatement projects to programs merely providing public information concerning the dangers of residential lead paint poisoning.

3.2 INITIAL FAILURE OF LEAD PAINT TORT LITIGATION

By the end of the twentieth century, the ability of a plaintiff to pursue relief for children poisoned by lead paint exposure under conventional contract or tort theories was incredibly difficult. Various federal statutes presented potential claimants with a legal conundrum, whereby plaintiffs were prevented from pursing tort claims, but were doctrinally defeated in pursuing breach of contract claims and remedies.[14] Title X on the Lead-Based Paint Poisoning Prevention Act restricted plaintiffs from bringing a personal injury claim and limited a plaintiff to contract remedies rather than tort damages. However, careful contract language often excluded the ability of a property lessee to bring a claim on behalf of the child victim of lead poisoning; the child would never be the purchaser or lessee of the property.[15]

It also was problematic for plaintiffs to pursue various common law tort claims against a landlord for damages to a child resulting from lead poisoning. Common law negligence was not the only tort theory upon which plaintiffs could seek relief in lead paint litigation. In individual lawsuits, plaintiffs also sued paint manufacturers and trade associations for claims sounding in strict liability, product liability, failure to warn, engaging in an abnormally dangerous activity, fraud, misrepresentation, conspiracy, concealment, and concert of action.[16] Courts routinely rejected or dismissed individual lawsuits asserting these various theories for recovery.[17]

Judicial reception of negligence tort claims illustrates the barriers that plaintiffs' attorneys encountered in pursuing individual lead paint tort litigation. To prove negligence a plaintiff would have to show that a landlord breached a duty to maintain the tenant's property in a safe and sanitary condition. The plaintiff would have to show that the landlord knew of, or should have known, that the property conditions when the landlord rented the property to the plaintiff's family posed a health risk.

Lead paint tort litigation in New York provides an example of the difficulty of plaintiffs' recovery in these cases. In New York, personal injury negligence cases against landlords were routinely dismissed if a tenant was unable to

---

[14] Cappell, *id.* at 181–82.
[15] *Id.*
[16] Perillo, *supra* note 1, at 1063–73.
[17] *Id.*

prove that the landlord had actual notice that there was lead-based paint in the apartment. If the landlord did not test for lead and didn't know lead was present, the landlord could not be held liable.[18] A Maryland court dismissed a case against paint manufacturers because the plaintiffs failed to adduce evidence that the industry hid information concerning the hazardous nature of lead in paint.[19] Moreover, any number of landlord defendants disincentivized plaintiffs' negligence actions by counterclaiming against the litigating parents, alleging that the parents failed to prevent their children from ingesting lead paint, and therefore, the parents' failure was the proximate cause of the child's injuries.[20]

Through the end of the twentieth century, then, the fact that individual litigation for injuries resulting from lead poisoning was difficult to pursue rendered the likelihood of a mass tort litigation against the paint industry equally unlikely.[21] For a mass tort to be viable, several factors needed to coalesce. There needed to be a large class of victims. There needed to be a cohort of experienced mass tort litigators who were willing to undertake a novel, costly, and difficult mass tort litigation. The plaintiffs needed to identify deep pocket defendants such as the major paint manufacturers or their trade association, such as the Lead Industries Association. A problem was that the paint manufacturing business was fluid, with many companies coming into and going out of business over the years. Wrongdoing would be hard to prove when paint had been applied many years in the past from a possibly unknowable source.[22]

The plaintiffs needed to represent the defendants in a bad light, for example, through evidence showing that the companies lied about paint being safe around children. Finally, for the plaintiffs to prevail in ordinary negligence cases, they needed at a minimum to satisfy that the paint defendants were the proximate cause of the plaintiffs' injuries, which had been the major obstacle to plaintiffs' prevailing in individual litigation. In addition, the proof of causation issue was complicated by the fact that paint was not the only possible source of lead contamination in home environments.[23]

The trial lawyers' chief solution to the problem of defendant identification was advocacy of the relatively new theory of market-share liability where the plaintiff could not specify the particular paint manufacturer of the lead particles their child had ingested. In a 1997 Pennsylvania case, the plaintiffs joined

---

[18] Cappell, *supra* note 1, at 181–82.
[19] Perillo, *supra* note 1, at 1048.
[20] Cappell, *supra* note 1, at 183.
[21] Perillo, *supra* note 1, at 1048–49.
[22] *Id.* at 1054–55.
[23] *Id.* at 1048–50.

all the manufacturers of lead paint from 1870 through 1997 (which was when the U.S. government banned lead-based paint). The plaintiffs' alleged claims sounding in collective liability, market-share liability, alternative liability, concert of action, and civil conspiracy. The court rejected all these theories. The court refused to apply market-share liability, holding that it was too great a departure from the traditional tort requirement that a plaintiff show that the defendant's negligence proximately caused the plaintiffs' injuries.[24] The court further rejected all the plaintiffs' alternative theories for collective liability.[25]

Thus, at the end of the twentieth century, lead paint litigation presented a forbidding landscape; the prospect of potential cases failed to offer an especially inviting opportunity for plaintiffs' attorneys considering the record of judicial defeat. Perhaps, the most startling statistic was that, as of 2004, the paint industry had never lost an individual lead-poisoning case.[26] Not only were individual lawsuits unavailing, but the numerous obstacles inherent in individual tort litigation made the pursuit of collective redress through mass class litigation equally unattractive. Against this background of failure, in 1999, the State of Rhode Island led the nation in breaking through the legal logjam in lead paint litigation. It did so by recourse to the novel theory of public nuisance. And, as Rhode Island went, so did other states follow.

3.3 RHODE ISLAND LEADS THE NATION IN PUBLIC NUISANCE LEAD PAINT LITIGATION

Rhode Island presented an opportune forum for attempting to stage the first mass tort litigation against lead paint manufacturers and their trade associations. The state contained a very large stock of aging housing and by the time the state attorney general filed a lawsuit against the paint defendants in 1999, it was estimated that approximately 25 percent of Providence, Rhode Island, children were attending school with elevated blood-lead levels.[27]

The Rhode Island legislature had undertaken several initiatives to investigate the problem of childhood lead poisoning in the early 1990s and was on record as identifying the lead paint problem as a danger to the public health, safety, and general welfare. As a result of its study, the General Assembly found that "[e]nvironmental exposure [] to even low levels of lead increase[s] a child's [health] risk," and that "[t]he most significant sources of

---

[24] Skipworth v. Lead Industries Ass'n., Inc., 690 A.2d 169, 171 (Pa. 1997).
[25] Cappell, *supra* note 1, at 172.
[26] Perillo, *supra* note 1, at 1058.
[27] *See* Margaret Cronin Fisk, R.I. to Try First State Suit Over Lead Paint, Nat'l L.J. Aug. 19, 2002, at A1, A14.

environmental lead are lead-based paint in older housing and house dust and soil contaminated by this paint."[28] It found that "tens of thousands of Rhode Island's children are poisoned by lead at levels believed to be harmful," and that "[c]hildhood lead poisoning is dangerous to the public health, safety, and general welfare of the people and necessitates excessive and disproportionate expenditure of public funds for health care and special education, causing a drain upon public revenue."[29]

In response to these findings, the General Assembly in 1991 enacted the Lead Poisoning Prevention Act (LPPA).[30] Characterizing lead poisoning as the most severe environmental health hazard in Rhode Island, the stated purpose of the legislation was to establish a comprehensive program to reduce exposure to environmental lead and prevent childhood lead poisoning. The statute required the Rhode Island Department of Health to implement various programs, including statewide blood-screening, lead prevention programs, and educational programs.[31]

The convergence of several events inspired Rhode Island's decision to sue the paint industry for lead-based harms in 1999.[32] A coalition of state attorneys' general, in cooperation with private outside counsel, accomplished a massive state settlement with tobacco industry defendants in 1998.[33] After decades of unsuccessful litigation against the tobacco industry, the 1998 multistate tobacco Master Settlement Agreement represented an enormous victory for state attorneys generals in cooperation with the plaintiffs' private mass tort bar. The settlement also represented a new paradigm for resolving mass tort claims; namely, the coordinated litigation strategy among public entities and private plaintiffs' lawyers.

Observing that the novel 1998 multistate tobacco settlement represented a new mass tort paradigm, commentators immediately began speculating as to which potential mass tort litigation would be the next likely candidate for similar joint public-private resolution.[34] The speculation focused on

---

[28]   State v. Lead Industries Ass'n., *supra* note 4, at 438, citing Section 23-24.6-2(1)-(2).

[29]   *Id.* citing Section 23-24.6-2(4), (5).

[30]   P.L. 1991, ch.355, § 1, Title 23 chap. 24.6.

[31]   State v. Lead Industries Ass'n., *supra* note 4, at 438.

[32]   *Id.* at 1081.

[33]   *See* A New Tobacco Deal, N.Y. Times, Nov. 22, 1998, at 2, § 4.

[34]   *See generally* Andrew M. Dansicker, The Next Big Thing for Litigators, 37 Md. B.J. No. 4, July–Aug. 2004, at 12–17; Molly McDonough, Lawyers, Guns and Lead, 89 A.B.A.J. No. 2, Feb. 2003, at 22–23; Allan Rostron, Shooting Stories: The Creation of Narrative and Melodrama in Real and Fictional Litigation Against the Gun Industry, 73 U.M.K.C.L. Rev. 1047 (2005); John J. Zefutie, Jr., From Butts to Big Macs – Can Tobacco and Nationwide Settlement with States' Attorneys General Serve as a Model for the Fast Food Industry?, 34 Seton Hall L. Rev. 1383 (2004) (possible mass tort litigation against the fast food industry).

three likely targets: the fast-food industry, the firearms industry, and the lead paint industry.[35]

In determining to take on the paint industry, the Rhode Island state attorney general blamed the industry of knowing that "lead was toxic as far back as 1904 yet profited from by that use. [The paint industry] wilfully made the mess that had endangered the health of many children and imposed great burdens on Rhode Island families and the state."[36]

On October 12, 1999, the attorney general filed a complaint against nine named lead pigment manufacturers and John Doe corporations, collectively designated as the lead paint industry.[37] The state retained two private law firms, which had extensive mass tort litigation experience in asbestos and tobacco litigation.[38] The Rhode Island complaint would become a template for future mass tort litigation by public entities, in coordination with private counsel, suing industry-wide defendants for harm to state citizens.

The complaint alleged that the extensive history of the defendants' conduct consisted of their continued misrepresentations and concealment of lead hazards. The state alleged that it had been harmed by the defendants' conduct because the state incurred and continued to incur substantial costs relating to discovering and abating lead, detecting lead poisoning, providing medical or other care to lead-poisoned state residents, and providing educational programs for children suffering from lead exposure injuries.[39] The plaintiffs alleged ten causes of action, including a public nuisance claim. The plaintiffs sought compensatory and punitive damages, and injunctive and other equitable relief.[40]

In 2001, the defendants moved to dismiss the complaint for failure to state any cause of action cognizable under Rhode Island law. The court dismissed several of the plaintiffs' claims but permitted others to proceed, including the plaintiffs' public nuisance claim.[41] Eventually, only the state's public nuisance claim was permitted to proceed to trial.[42] The plaintiffs' complaint asserted

---

[35] *Id. See* Richard L. Cupp, Jr., State Medical Reimbursement Lawsuits After Tobacco: Is the Domino Effect for Lead Paint Manufacturers and Others Fair Game?, 27 Pepp. L. Rev. 685 (2000); Amber E. Dean, Comment, Lead Paint Public Entity Suits: Has the Broad Stroke of Tobacco and Firearms Litigation Painted a Troubling Picture for Lead Paint Manufacturers?, 28 Pepp. L. Rev. 915 (2001).

[36] Perillio, *supra* note 1, at 1082.

[37] Rhode Island v. Lead Industries Ass'n., Inc., 2001 WL 345830, *1 (Super Ct. R.I. Apr. 2, 2001).

[38] The state retained Ness, Motley, Rice, a South Carolina law firm that had negotiated asbestos and tobacco mass tort settlements on contingency fee agreements.

[39] *Id.*

[40] Rhode Island, *supra* note 37, at *1.

[41] *Id.* at **6–8.

[42] Rhode Island, *supra* note 4, at 440.

that the paint defendants created an environmental hazard that continued and would continue to unreasonably interfere with the health, safety, peace, comfort, or convenience of state residents, constituting a public nuisance.[43]

The Rhode Island trial court relied on common law rationales in permitting the public nuisance claim to proceed, which would become a jurisprudential model for subsequent decisions allowing mass tort public nuisance claims. Rhode Island law granted the attorney general equitable power and jurisdiction to abate a public nuisance.[44] The trial court was aided by a 1998 Rhode Island Supreme Court decision affirming a trial court's grant to the attorney general of a preliminary injunction seeking abatement of lead paint from premises.[45] That court had indicated, "it would rule as a matter of law based on the evidence ... [that] the premises are a public nuisance."[46] The Rhode Island Supreme Court affirmed that the "persistence of the continuing hazard of lead paint presents immediate and irreparable harm to the public so long as that hazard remains unabated."[47]

Citing Rhode Island precedents and the *Restatement (Second)* §§ 821B(1), (2)(a), the trial court in the 1999 lawsuit held that public nuisance was "an unreasonable interference with a right common to the public: it is behavior that unreasonably interferes with the health, safety, peace, comfort or convenience of the general community."[48] The court relied heavily on the *Restatement (Second)* for the common law principles of public nuisance. Thus, the plaintiff carried the burden to show the existence of an injury caused by the public nuisance. One was subject to liability for causing or participating in an activity resulting in a public nuisance.

The defendants opposed the public nuisance claim on two grounds. First, they alleged that a public right had not been infringed because the defendants' lead did not cause the harm while within their control as product manufacturers or promoters. Second, the plaintiffs' allegations failed to satisfy the requirement regarding enjoining the person(s) "maintaining the nuisance and any and all persons owing any legal or equitable interest in the place from further maintaining or permitting the nuisance."[49]

The State countered that the defendants were responsible for the presence of lead, a product the courts and legislature had recognized as constituting

---

[43]   Rhode Island, *supra* note 37, at *6.

[44]   *Id.* citing G.L. 1956 § 10-1-1 *et seq.*

[45]   Rhode Island, *supra* note 37, at *7, citing Pine v. Kalian, 723 A.2d 804, 805 (R.I. 1998).

[46]   Rhode Island, *supra* note 37, at *7.

[47]   *Id.* citing Kalian, at 805.

[48]   Rhode Island, *supra* note 37, at *7.

[49]   *Id.* at *8.

a potential severe health hazard in public and private properties throughout the state. In addition, the defendants' misconduct – including a conspiracy to mislead the government and public of the dangers of lead exposure – had unreasonably interfered with the public health, including the public's right to be free from the hazards of unabated lead.[50]

The court reviewed legislative findings in Rhode Island's Lead Poisoning Prevention Act of 1991 and concluded in light of those findings, the Rhode Island case law, and the Supreme Court's decision, that the attorney general adequately stated an action for public nuisance.[51] In the first jury trial the jury declared that lead paint was a public nuisance and required three paint manufacturers to pay for cleanup of contaminated buildings.[52] Plaintiffs' attorneys greeted this victory, observing that it might inspire other cities plagued by lead paint harms to take action against paint manufacturers.[53]

A few days after the Rhode Island trial verdict, a California appellate court reinstated a class action against former paint manufacturers and other state courts revived litigation against paint company defendants.[54] "The tide has finally changed against the lead paint industry, which has escaped liability for the last few decades," said Jack McConnell, a Providence lawyer who was co-lead counsel at the trial. "Beginning with the Rhode Island jury verdict and including California, New Jersey, and Wisconsin decisions, the industry is finally going to be held liable for its past misconduct."[55]

3.4 WISCONSIN PUBLIC NUISANCE LEAD PAINT LITIGATION

Almost contemporaneously with the Rhode Island litigation, attorneys for Milwaukee filed suit on April 9, 2001, against a national manufacturer of lead pigment and residential lead paint and also a Wisconsin manufacturer and seller of residential lead paint.[56] The city alleged that childhood lead-paint poisoning and residential lead-paint hazards in Milwaukee were a public nuisance. The plaintiffs contended that the defendants' sale of lead-based paint products and their conduct were a substantial contributing factor in the

---

[50] *Id.*

[51] *Id.*

[52] Rhode Island v. Lead Indus, Ass'n., No 99-5226 (R.I. Prov. Cty. Super Ct. Feb. 22, 2006).

[53] Karen Ertel, Rhode Island Lead Paint Victory May Be First of Many, Lawyers Say, 42 Trial (May 2006).

[54] *Id.*

[55] *Id.*

[56] Brief of Appellant, City of Milwaukee v. NL Industries, Inc., No. 03-2786, 2003 WL 25257400, *2 (Wis. App. I Dist 2003).

contamination of Milwaukee housing and the lead poisoning of children in the community.

The complaint pointed to facts relating to childhood lead poisoning in Milwaukee. The city alleged that one in five children tested in 1998 showed blood levels at or above the Center for Disease Control's threshold for lead poisoning. The alleged source of the lead poisoning was dust and chips on old wood windows in homes where children lived. In response, the city had undertaken an abatement program in two target areas. The complaint estimated that the potential abatement cost could exceed one hundred million dollars.[57]

Milwaukee alleged claims sounding in both public nuisance, equity, conspiracy, and conventional tort theories. The city asked that the defendants pay for the costs associated with the abatement program. They requested compensatory and equitable relief for abatement of the toxic lead-paint hazards in Milwaukee homes, restitution for amounts the city expended for abatement, and punitive damages.

The trial court dismissed several claims but permitted the public nuisance claim to proceed. The trial court ruled that lead products could constitute a public nuisance, the city had standing to sue for abatement damages, and that the city was not required to provide notice in a creation of a public nuisance case. Nonetheless, the court granted the defendants' summary judgment motion holding that the city could not prove that these defendants caused the particular lead hazard in any location.[58]

The Wisconsin appellate court reversed the summary judgment and held that genuine issues of material fact existed concerning the causation element of the city's public nuisance claim.[59] The court's summary judgment reversal provided another illustration of judicial support for a public nuisance claim for lead paint harms based on common law principles. Relying on a series of Wisconsin precedents dealing with public nuisance, the court held that "a public nuisance is a condition or activity which substantially or unduly interferes with the use of a public place or with the activities of an entire community."[60] The court noted that although numerous Wisconsin cases discussed the concept of public nuisance, no case had explicitly listed the elements that a plaintiff had to prove to prevail on a claim for public nuisance when alleging the defendant created, rather than maintained, a public nuisance.

---

[57] Milwaukee v. NL Industries, 278 Wis.2d 313, 318, 691 N.W.888, 2005 WI App. 7 (2004).

[58] Brief of Appellant, *supra* note 58, at **2–4.

[59] Milwaukee, *supra* note 59.

[60] *Id.* at 320, citing Physicians Plus Ins. Corp. v. Midwest Mut. Ins. Co., 2002 WI 80, ¶ 21, 254 Wis. 77, 646 N.W.2d 777.

Surveying Wisconsin precedents, the court concluded that the same legal standards should apply regarding a defendant's causing or maintaining a public nuisance.[61] Agreeing with the city, the court indicated that a plaintiff had to establish three elements: (1) harm occurred to the public, (2) defendants were a substantial factor in causing the harm, and (3) abatement of the cause of harm was reasonable.[62] Finally, citing Wisconsin common law precedent, the court indicated that a defendant's liability for a public nuisance could be limited on public policy grounds.[63]

Applying these principles, the court concluded that there existed genuine issues of material fact regarding the cause of childhood lead poisoning in Milwaukee, the extent of the defendants' promotion and sale of paint in Milwaukee, whether those sales were a substantial cause of the alleged public nuisance, and whether the defendants participated in the creation of a public nuisance of childhood lead poisoning in Milwaukee.[64]

The court concluded that at trial the jury would have the opportunity to determine whether a public nuisance existed, whether the defendants' conduct in promoting the use and sale of lead paint were substantial factors causing the nuisance, and whether the public nuisance, if found, resulted in the city's damages. The court declined to address the defendants' contention that public policy considerations precluded their liability.[65]

The 2001 Wisconsin lead paint lawsuit illustrates appellate approval of a triable public nuisance claim based on the plaintiffs' assertion that childhood lead poisoning was a community-wide public nuisance in Milwaukee. In upholding the public nuisance claim's viability for trial, the court relied on its common law precedents setting forth legal standards for creating a public nuisance. These included the defendant's conduct as a substantial cause of the existence of the public nuisance and a substantial factor in causing injury to the public.

3.5 NEW JERSEY PAINT LITIGATION

Following the Rhode Island lead paint lawsuit, and citing judicial approval of the public nuisance claim, numerous New Jersey governmental entities sued defendant former manufacturers and promoters of lead pigments used

---

[61] Milwaukee, *id*. at 321–22.

[62] *Id*. at 320–21.

[63] *Id*. at 322, citing Physicians Plus, *supra* note 62.

[64] *Id*. at 323–26.

[65] *Id*. at 326–28.

throughout New Jersey houses and buildings. In February 2002, all the lead paint litigation was assigned to the Superior Court of New Jersey.[66]

The plaintiffs alleged that the defendants had actual knowledge of the severe adverse effects caused by human exposure to lead for nearly a century. The plaintiffs alleged that the industry's conduct (1) publicly misrepresented lead as safe, (2) promoted lead for use in areas accessible to children, (3) suppressed studies and research supporting problems with lead, (4) opposed all governmental initiatives to mitigate or solve lead problems, and (5) favored increased profits over ensuring citizens' health.[67]

The plaintiffs sought damages for the costs the governments incurred to detect lead poisoning and provide medical monitoring and preventive screening for residents, as well as to provide public health and education programs concerning lead poisoning prevention. In addition, the plaintiffs sought an order of abatement, pursuant to the court's equitable powers, sufficient to remove lead paint from private homes and public and private buildings within specified geographic boundaries.[68] The governmental entities contended that they had inherent police powers to abate public nuisances in absence of any statutory constraints. The plaintiffs asserted their lawsuit was a matter of public interest law and to fulfil the New Jersey's legislative intent which recognized lead paint poisoning as a public nuisance and public health crisis.[69]

The defendants opposed the lawsuit based on four grounds: remoteness; the fact that the allegations were not conduct based, but product based under New Jersey's Products Liability Act; infringement on separation of powers principles; and failure to state a claim of common law upon which relief could be granted.[70]

The trial court granted the defendants' motion to dismiss, agreeing on all grounds. The court observed: "Plaintiffs seek an unwarranted and impermissible expansion of their role as local government entities to act on behalf of the public. Unlike the Attorney General or other appropriate executive branches of the state government, these plaintiffs overstep their role and authority by bringing suit against the defendants under the guise of public interest litigation. Such actions violate the constitutional doctrine of separation of powers and fail under the doctrine of remoteness and existing New Jersey case law."[71]

---

[66] In re Lead Paint, 2002 WL 31474528, *4 (N.J. Super. Ct. Nov. 4, 2002).
[67] *Id.* at *5.
[68] *Id.*
[69] *Id.*
[70] *Id.* at *6.
[71] *Id.* at *8.

The court indicated that New Jersey precedents had defined public nuisance as "an unreasonable interference with a right common to the public." Courts traditionally recognized two types of public nuisance actions: interference with specific real property, and violation of a specific statute that infringed public rights.[72] The court rejected the plaintiffs' reliance on New Jersey's Lead Paint Statute, which stated that "[t]he presence of lead paint upon the interior of any dwelling ... is hereby declared to be a public nuisance."[73]

The trial court held that there simply was no case law that allowed the plaintiffs to bring an action for public nuisance. Cities could not recover for service costs in absence of explicit legislation authorizing such recovery. Municipalities could not recover the costs of tax-supported services provided as part of governmental functions, and numerous state courts cited this doctrine for dismissing municipal public nuisance lawsuits against gun manufacturers.[74]

Moreover, the court rejected the plaintiffs' action because they had masked their lawsuit in common law public nuisance claims "rather than revealing their true nature as products liability cases." Citing the *American Law of Products Liability (Third)*, the court noted, "A product which caused injury cannot be classified as a nuisance to hold liable the manufacturer or seller for the products injurious effects."[75] Consistent with the *Products Liability (Third)*, New Jersey courts expressed their intent to confine public nuisance law to property claims rather than public nuisance claims against manufacturers for lawful products lawfully placed in the stream of commerce.[76] The defendants had no control over their instrumentality (lead paint) after it was sold; the lead paint did not flow with the land; and the plaintiffs' remedy for the alleged harms was not sought within the Products Liability Act.[77]

Finally, the trial court rejected the plaintiffs' attempt to seek remediation through a public nuisance claim, opining that they were asking the court to act as a super-legislature; the plaintiffs were seeking to utilize public nuisance to effectuate public policy through the court rather than through the legislature. "The governmental entities here seek to obtain through this judicial forum what must be obtained through the State Legislature. This is impermissible and the plaintiffs' claim for public nuisance must therefore be dismissed."[78]

---

[72] *Id.* at *14, citing New Jersey cases.
[73] *Id.* citing N.J.S.A. 24:14A4-5.
[74] *Id.* citing cases from Pennsylvania, Connecticut, Florida, and Ohio.
[75] *Id.* at *15, citing Am. L. Prod. Liab. 3d § 27:3.
[76] *Id.* at *16.
[77] *Id.*
[78] *Id.* at **15–16.

The plaintiffs appealed dismissal of their lawsuit.[79] The appellate court held that the trial court erred in ruling that the proposed action violated the constitutional principle of separation of powers,[80] and that the Commerce Clause should not bar their complaint.[81] The court further concluded that the trial court erred in dismissing the plaintiffs' public nuisance claim.[82] Citing the *Restatement (Second) of Torts*, § 821B(1), the court held: "A public nuisance is an unreasonable interference with a right common to the public." To recover for public nuisance a plaintiff had to allege that the defendant had control over the nuisance, or substantially participated in it, and establish proximate cause.[83]

The appellate court rejected the notion that New Jersey courts had limited public nuisance claims only to cases involving impairment of real property usage, as opposed to harms caused to persons by products. Rather, New Jersey courts had adopted the *Restatement (Second)* view that "unlike private nuisance, a public nuisance does not necessarily involve interference with use and enjoyment of land."[84] In response to the trial court's conclusion that the public nuisance claim was a masked products lawsuit subject to the Products Liability Act, the appellate court disagreed holding that the plaintiffs' proposed action qualified as an environmental tort; the claim sounded in exposure to toxic chemicals or substances. The Products Liability Act expressly did not apply because it excluded from its purview any environmental tort action. Cases involving harmful environmental exposure such as asbestos litigation probably were excluded from the Products Liability Act, and lead paint hazards fell into the same category.[85]

The appellate court further rejected the conclusion that the public nuisance claim could not proceed because of remoteness and proximate causation concerns. The court noted that the expenditure of public funds to provide medical diagnostic and treatment services, particularly to citizens with no access to health coverage or insufficient resources, was hardly remote. Moreover, the municipal cost-recovery bar should not preclude a claim where a defendant's repeated course of conduct created a public nuisance that necessitated the expenditure of public funds to abate the nuisance.[86]

---

[79]   In re Lead Paint Litig., 2005 WL 1994172 (N.J. Super Ct. Aug. 17, 2005).
[80]   *Id.* at **3–6.
[81]   *Id.* at **6–7.
[82]   *Id.* at *14, *21.
[83]   *Id.* at *11.
[84]   *Id.* at *9, citing *Restatement (Second) of Torts*, § 821B, cmt. h (1979).
[85]   *Id.* at *11.
[86]   *Id.*

3.6 CALIFORNIA LEAD PAINT LITIGATION

Beginning in March 2000 several California governmental entities, on behalf California citizens, filed a class action against a group of lead manufacturers. Over the course of six years and four amended complaints, the plaintiffs pursued claims for strict liability, negligence, fraud and concealment, unjust enrichment, and unfair business practices.[87] The plaintiffs alleged their damages to include (1) costs incurred to educate the public about the hazards of lead and the steps to take to minimize the risk, (2) costs incurred to inspect and test property and the environment for the presence of lead, (3) costs incurred to train and fund staff to investigate and respond to lead-contaminated properties and lead-exposed children, and (4) costs incurred for property damage: abatement, removal, replacement and/or remediation of lead in private, county, and city-owned, managed, leased, controlled, and/or maintained properties.[88]

In the plaintiffs' second amended complaint, they alleged two separate public nuisance causes of action: one on behalf of the people seeking abatement, and one brought by the class alleging a special injury to individual class members.[89] The trial court granted the defendants' demurrer to the public nuisance claims with leave to amend. In the plaintiffs' third amended complaint they amended the public nuisance claim on behalf of the California citizens but omitted the other claim by class plaintiffs.[90] During pretrial proceedings, the trial court granted the defendants' demurrers to the two public nuisance claims and summary judgment on all the causes of action, dismissing the case.[91]

On appeal, the court reversed the grant of the defendants' demurrer to the representative public nuisance claim, but upheld dismissal of the private class action nuisance claim. Like the New Jersey litigation, the nub of the California appellate decision centered on an analysis of whether a public nuisance claim was a masked products litigation. The defendants had contended that even where facts might constitute a public nuisance, a cause of action could not lie where the underlying cause of action was a product for which only a products liability cause of action would lie.[92] The California appellate court, consistent with the New Jersey appellate ruling, held that lead paint public nuisance claims were not products case and, therefore, such claims could proceed.

---

[87] Santa Clara v. Atlantic Richfield Company, 137 Cal. App. 4th 292, 40 Cal. Rptr. 313 (2006).
[88] *Id.* at 300.
[89] *Id.* at 304.
[90] *Id.*
[91] *Id.* at 298.
[92] *Id.* at 305.

The appellate court repeated the general common law principles of public nuisance: "Public nuisances are offenses against, or interferences with, the exercise of rights common to the public." To qualify as a public nuisance and be subject to an injunction or abatement, the interference must be substantial and unreasonable. A public nuisance was substantial if it caused significant harm and unreasonable if its social utility is outweighed by the gravity of the harm inflicted.[93] Moreover, a defendant's liability did not hinge on whether the defendant owned, possessed, or controlled the property nor on whether the defendant was in a position to abate the nuisance. The critical question was whether the defendant created or assisted in the creation of the nuisance.[94]

The court held that a representative public nuisance cause of action seeking abatement of a hazard by a defendant's knowing promotion of a product for a hazardous use was not essentially a products liability action "in the guise of a nuisance action" and "does not threaten to permit public nuisance 'to become a monster that would devour in one gulp the entire of tort law.'"[95]

A public nuisance cause of action was not premised on a product defect or failure to warn, but on the defendant's affirmative conduct that assisted in the defendant's creation of the hazardous condition. In this litigation, the defendants' alleged liability for the public nuisance was their affirmative promotion of lead paint for interior use, not the mere manufacture and distribution of lead paint or their failure to warn of its hazards.[96]

In contrast, a plaintiff who suffered a physical injury to their person or property could bring a products liability case limited to recovering for damages because of their injury. A products liability action did not provide a means to prevent future harm from a hazardous condition and could not permit a public entity to act on behalf of a community subjected to a widespread public health hazard.[97]

Finally, while the appellate court held that the trial court erred in granting the defendant's demurrer to the governmental entities' public nuisance class action, the court upheld dismissal of the individual class plaintiffs' public nuisance action.[98] The court distinguished this second effort, characterizing it as basically an action on behalf of individuals to recover damages for special injury rather than abatement. The core of the entities' lawsuit was for remediation of a health hazard. This second public nuisance action, in

---

[93] *Id.* citing California cases.
[94] *Id.* at 306, citing California cases.
[95] *Id.* at 309.
[96] *Id.* at 309–10.
[97] *Id.* at 310.
[98] *Id.* at 311–13.

contrast, was brought on behalf of individuals, rather than the community, and was much more like a products liability cause of action. Hence, the court concluded, "We are reluctant to extend liability for damages under a public nuisance theory to an arena that is otherwise fully encompassed by products liability law."[99]

3.7 REPUDIATION, RETRENCHMENT, AND RETREAT

While judicial decisions in the early 2000s upholding public nuisance claims in lead paint litigation inspired the plaintiffs' bar, these early victories were short-lived. Further, appellate litigation in Rhode Island, New Jersey, and Wisconsin repudiated public nuisance as a theory to resolve lead paint lawsuits, or demonstrated the difficulties in litigating a public nuisance claim if permitted to proceed. Collectively, these decisions led to a retrenchment and retreat of public nuisance lead paint litigation.

The appellate decisions clearly articulated the rationales for rejecting public nuisance as applied to mass tort claims, which portended the jurisprudential struggle in the ensuing decade concerning the plaintiffs' ability to make inroads using public nuisance as applied to other widespread community harms. And the Wisconsin jury trial of a lead paint public nuisance claim signaled the unhappy denouement of public nuisance litigation in the lead paint arena.

In 2008 the Rhode Island Supreme Court issued a lengthy opinion repudiating the lower courts' determination that the state's public nuisance claim against lead paint defendants could proceed.[100] The Rhode Island first trial had ended in mistrial, and a second trial – the longest in the state's history – resulted in a jury verdict imposing liability on lead pigment manufacturers for creating a public nuisance. On appeal, the defendants argued that the trial judge erred by misapplying the law of public nuisance.[101]

Agreeing with the defendants, the Rhode Island Supreme Court generally held that the state had failed to allege an infringement of a public right sufficient to state a cause of action for public nuisance. The trial court erred in denying the defendants' motion to dismiss. The Supreme Court concluded that the state had not and could not allege any set of facts to support its public nuisance claim that established the defendants interfered with a public right, or that the defendants were in control of the lead pigment that they,

---

[99] *Id.* at 313.
[100] *See* discussion *supra* at notes 37–57.
[101] Rhode Island v. Lead Industries Ass'n., Inc., 951 A.2d 428, 434–35 (2008).

or their predecessors, manufactured at the time it caused harm to Rhode Island children.[102]

Addressing broad policy concerns, the court noted that it was bound by the law and could provide justice only to the extent allowed by law. Courts were powerless to fashion independently a cause of action that would achieve justice for the children. Articulating its philosophy of the judicial role, the court indicated that it consistently had adhered to "principle of judicial restraint [that] prevent [courts] from creating a cause of action for damages in all but the most extreme circumstances." Thus, the courts had long held that the creation of new causes of action was a legislative function, and the judiciary's function was to determine the law, not to make the law.[103]

After an extensive review of the history of public nuisance law, the court indicated that Rhode Island had long recognized public nuisance as a legally viable cause of action. The state attorney general was authorized by statute to bring actions to abate public nuisances. Rhode Island's definition of a public nuisance was consistent with that of the *Restatement (Second)*, many other jurisdictions, and scholarly commentary. Common law principles established that a public nuisance was an unreasonable interference with a right common to the public. It was a behavior that unreasonably interfered with the health, safety, peace, comfort, or convenience of the general community.[104]

Rhode Island jurisprudence recognized three principal elements essential to establish a claim for public nuisance: (1) an unreasonable interference, (2) with a right common to the public, (3) by a person or people with control over the instrumentality alleged to have created the nuisance when the damage occurred. If the plaintiffs could establish these elements of public nuisance they then must determine whether the defendant caused the public nuisance.[105]

Reviewing the plaintiff's complaint, the court determined that it could not ascertain allegations to support each of the elements of a public nuisance claim. The state's complaint failed to allege that the defendants had interfered with a public right. Equally problematic was the absence of any allegations that defendants had control over the lead pigment at the time it caused harm to children.[106] The court held that the state's allegation that defendants interfered with the health, safety, peace, comfort or convenience of state residents was insufficient, alone, to constitute an allegation of interference with a public right.[107]

[102] *Id.* at 435, 443, 455.
[103] *Id.* at 436.
[104] *Id.* at 443–46.
[105] *Id.* at 446–47.
[106] *Id.* at 453.
[107] *Id.*

Moreover, the trial judge erred in departing from traditional require-ments of common law public nuisance. The Supreme Court indicated that the *Restatement (Second)* warned against such departures, noting that "[i]f a defendant's conduct in interfering with a public right does not come within one of the traditional categories of the common law crime of public nuisance or is not prohibited by legislative act, the court is acting without an established and recognized standard."[108]

Returning to its theme of judicial restraint the court suggested that expand-ing the definition of public right based on the plaintiff's allegations "would be antithetical to the common law and would lead to a widespread expansion of public nuisance law that was never intended."[109] Thus, "the enormous leap that the state urges us to take is wholly inconsistent with the widely recognized principle that the evolution of the common law should occur gradually, pre-dictably, and incrementally. Were we to hold otherwise, we would change the meaning of public right to encompass all behavior that causes a widespread interference with the private rights of numerous individuals."[110]

Lastly, the Rhode Island Supreme Court suggested that the proper means for suing manufacturers of lead pigments for the sale of an unsafe product was a products liability action. The law of public nuisance had never before been applied to products, however harmful. Other state courts consistently rejected product-based public nuisance lawsuits against lead pigment manu-facturers, expressing the concern that allowing such lawsuits would circum-vent the basic requirements of products liability law. Public nuisance focused on abatement of annoying or bothersome activities. Products liability law was designed to hold manufacturers liable for harmful products that manufactur-ers had caused to enter the stream of commerce.[111]

* * *

In 2007, the New Jersey Supreme Court articulated similar rationales and themes in repudiating the local governmental entities' litigation against lead paint defendants.[112] The New Jersey Supreme Court's reaction to the lead paint litigation was to doctrinally limit and narrowly define public nuisance. The court agreed with an oft-cited conclusion by other courts that had rejected novel, expansive public nuisance claims: "[W]ere we to find a cause of action

---

[108] *Id.* at 455, citing *Restatement (Second) of Torts*, § 821B. cmt. e at 90.
[109] *Id.* at 453.
[110] *Id.* at 454.
[111] *Id.* at 456, citing cases.
[112] In re Lead Paint Litig., 191 N.J. 405, 924 A.2d 484 (N.J. 2007).

here, 'nuisance law would become a monster that would devour in one gulp the entire law of tort.'"[113]

After reviewing the historical development of public nuisance, the New Jersey Supreme Court fixed on the concept's historical antecedents in criminal law to inform the court's understanding of modern tort principles.[114] In addition, the court indicated that it was equally essential to the modern public nuisance tort that it historically was linked to the use of land by the one creating the nuisance.[115] The court further noted that the development of modern public nuisance law was closely tied to environmental pollution litigation.[116]

The court articulated three core concepts of modern public nuisance law. First, public nuisance is related to the conduct performed in a location within the actor's control which had an adverse effect on a common right. Second, a private party who has suffered a special injury may seek to recover damages to the extent of the special injury and by extension, may also seek to abate the nuisance. Third, a public entity which proceeds against the one in control of the nuisance may only seek to abate, at the expense of the one in control.[117]

Construing the meaning of the state's Lead Paint Act that declared the presence of lead paint a public nuisance, the court concluded that the legislature intended the term "public nuisance" in it strict historical sense.[118] The legislature had attached to the activity a criminal penalty; it directed local boards of health to effect an abatement of the nuisance; and it directed that premise owners where a public nuisance was found would be liable for abatement costs. Thus, the legislature's approach "remained tethered to the historical bases that have defined public nuisance dating back centuries."[119] The court concluded that there was no basis that the legislature, in using the term "public nuisance," expected that it would be the springboard for expansive reading that the plaintiffs suggested.[120]

The court further rejected the plaintiffs' public nuisance theory objecting that their expansive view trenched on ordinary products liability claims. In this litigation, the court was addressing an unregulated consumer product sold in the ordinary course of commerce. Thus, if the court determined that the

---

[113] *Id.* at 440, citing cases.

[114] *Id.* at 422–23.

[115] *Id.* at 423. "…public nuisance has historically been tied to conduct on one's own land or property as it affects the rights of the general public."

[116] *Id.* at 424–25.

[117] *Id.* at 429.

[118] *Id.* at 429–30. *See* N.J.S.A. 24:14A-5,-8.

[119] *Id.* at 430–31.

[120] *Id.* at 431.

plaintiffs stated a public nuisance claim, "we would necessarily be concluding that the conduct of merely offering an everyday household product for sale can suffice for the purpose of interfering with a common right as we understand it. Such an interpretation would far exceed any cognizable cause of action."[121] The court suggested that allowing the plaintiffs to proceed on this public nuisance theory would stretch the theory "to the point of creating strict liability to be imposed on manufacturers of ordinary consumer products which, when sold ... have become dangerous through deterioration and poor maintenance by purchasers."[122]

The New Jersey Supreme Court further elaborated that the plaintiffs' lead paint claims could only be cognizable as products liability claims. Citing New Jersey's Product Liability Act, the court noted that the Act was both expansive and inclusive. The harms that the plaintiffs sought to vindicate in their lead paint litigation were and should be addressed in the context of a products liability claim.[123] Construing the statute the court held that nothing in the statute's language suggested that lead paint sold for use in homes and buildings was intended to be excluded from the Product Liability Act as an environmental tort. To recognize the plaintiffs' public nuisance claim would create a cause of action entirely inconsistent with the Product Liability Act's comprehensive legislative scheme.[124]

* * *

The fate of the Wisconsin lead paint litigation presents an objective lesson in the perils of actually prosecuting a public nuisance claim. After Milwaukee won a significant victory in reversing the defendant's summary judgment, the litigation proceeded to trial on the public nuisance claim. At trial, the jury had to find two fundamentals: (1) that the defendant created a public nuisance, and (2) that the defendant manufacturer knew the public nuisance resulted or was substantially certain to result from its conduct. The jury entered a verdict for the defendants and the plaintiffs appealed.[125]

The appellate court upheld the defendants' jury's verdict, which challenged the verdict and numerous jury instructions. The appellate court held that the jury had found sufficient evidence to conclude that there was a public nuisance. The public nuisance was not the presence of lead painting on

---

[121] *Id.* at 433–34.
[122] *Id.* at 434.
[123] *Id.* at 436–37, citing N.J.S.A. 2A:58C-1 through -7.
[124] *Id.* at 438–40.
[125] Milwaukee v. NL Industries, 315 Wis.2d 443, 762 N.W.2d 757, 2008 WI App 181 (2008).

the dwellings' walls, but rather the hazardous childhood lead exposure.[126] To establish liability for public nuisance, the city was required to establish a causal connection between the nuisance and the underlying tortious acts attributable to the defendants.

The jury found that the defendant did not intentionally cause the public nuisance.[127] The appellate court upheld that there was sufficient evidence to support the jury's finding that the defendant did not know that the public nuisance resulted or was substantially certain to result from its conduct, where the dangers associated with lead dust were unknown during the time the defendant sold lead pigment and paint.[128] The appellate court rejected all other plaintiffs' challenges to the trial judge's jury instructions.[129]

---

[126] *Id.* at 464.
[127] *Id.* at 452.
[128] *Id.* at 471.
[129] *Id.* at 451, 466–85.

4

Litigating Public Nuisance Claims

Burdens on Plaintiffs

Pursuing a public nuisance claim in the twenty-first century has not been an easy task for plaintiffs' attorneys who have sought to expand the doctrine to mass tort harms. Plaintiffs carry considerable burdens in convincing courts that their litigation presents a viable, triable public nuisance claim. In addition, plaintiffs may plausibly plead a public nuisance claim, a jury may find that a public nuisance existed, but then absolve the defendants of liability for the public nuisance.

Common law doctrines and statutory requirements set forth plaintiffs' burdens in alleging and establishing a public nuisance claim. While many jurisdictions refer to the *Restatement (Second) of Torts* as a source for the pleading and proof requirements of a public nuisance claim, many jurisdictions superimpose additional common law glosses on the *Restatement* standards. Statutory public nuisance, in contrast, typically set forth specific requirements for alleging public nuisance claims. Moreover, governmental entities or private persons may pursue public nuisance suits, in which cases different standards apply to evaluate whether a public nuisance claim can proceed.

Most states following the *Restatement (Second)* define public nuisance as an unreasonable interference with a right that is common to the public. Courts have recognized that a plaintiff carries the burden of showing: (1) a right held in common by the public, in the use of public facilities, health, safety, and convenience, (2) a defendant caused or maintained a substantial and unreasonable interference with the right held in common, (3) a defendant's conduct was intentional, unreasonable, or subject to strict liability, or (4) a defendant's conduct violated a statute (public nuisance "per se"). Courts have interpreted these elements in conflicting ways, particularly regarding what constitutes a public right and an unreasonable interference with that right. In addition, once a plaintiff successfully establishes a public nuisance, a private plaintiff can only sue to redress a special injury that is distinct in kind from the harm suffered by all affected members of the community.

4.1 RIGHT HELD IN COMMON BY THE PUBLIC

Courts have disagreed concerning what constitutes a right held in common by the public. Often this question becomes intertwined with the plaintiff's status seeking remediation pursuant to a public nuisance theory. Thus, courts have distinguished between cases in which public or governmental entities are seeking relief on behalf of the public, or private persons are seeking relief based on a public nuisance theory. In the former instances, courts are more likely to entertain a public nuisance lawsuit; in the latter instance, courts are more discerning whether to allow a private litigant to pursue relief by the individual on behalf of a common right.

In entity lawsuits, a public nuisance claim will not be cognizable if the plaintiff fails to show a violation of a public right. Several courts have declined to permit public nuisance claims to proceed holding that the plaintiffs failed to carry their burden of identifying a right held in common to the public. Other courts have permitted public nuisance claims on very expansive understandings of what constitutes a public nuisance.

Some courts have narrowly construed the concept of public nuisance in construing state statutory provisions. For example, in the Oklahoma opioid litigation brought against Johnson & Johnson as the manufacturer, marketer, and seller of prescription opioids, the Oklahoma Supreme Court, construing its public nuisance statute, determined not to extend public nuisance law to reach Johnson & Johnson's conduct.[1] The court identified three reasons: (1) the manufacture and distribution of products rarely caused a violation of a public right, (2) a manufacturer does not generally have control of its product once it is sold, and (3) a manufacturer could be held perpetually liable for its products under a nuisance theory.[2]

Addressing the violation of a public right, the court indicated that a public right is a right to a public good, such as "an indivisible resource shared by the public at large, like air, water, or public rights-of-way."[3] The court disagreed with the plaintiffs' characterization of the lawsuit as involving an interference of the public right of health, holding that "[t]his case does not involve a comparable incident to those in which we have anticipated that an injury to public health would occur, e.g., diseased animals, pollution in drinking water, or the discharge of sewer on property."[4]

---

[1]   Oklahoma *ex rel.* Hunter v. Johnson & Johnson, 499 P.3d 719, 726 (2021). *See* 50 O.S.2011, §§ 1 & 2.
[2]   *Id.*
[3]   *Id.* citing cases.
[4]   *Id.* at 727, citing cases.

Similarly, the Illinois Supreme Court upheld a trial court's dismissal of the public nuisance claim brought by Chicago against firearms manufacturers, distributors, and dealers of handguns.[5] The city alleged that the defendants oversupplied the market with their products and marketed their products to appeal to persons who intended to use them for criminal purposes. The city sought abatement of the nuisance, including costs for medical services, law enforcement efforts, and cost for prosecutions of gun ordinance violations. The Illinois Supreme Court agreed that the plaintiffs failed to show an unreasonable interference with a public right. The alleged public right to be free from the threat of others "may defy [criminal] laws [and] would permit nuisance liability to be imposed on an endless list of manufacturers, distributors, and retailers of manufactured products."[6]

In the lead paint litigation, the Rhode Island Supreme Court also rejected expansion of the concept of a public nuisance cause of action. The court indicated that a cause of action for public nuisance involved three elements: (1) an unreasonable interference, (2) with a right common to the public, (3) by a person or people with control over the instrumentality alleged to have created the nuisance when the damage occurred.[7] In defining what constituted a right common to the public, the court looked to common law precedents. The court indicated that an alleged nuisance must affect an interest common to the public, rather than peculiar to one individual. Public nuisance occurring on private property was actionable as long as the nuisance affected public rights.[8]

In its complaint, the state alleged that the defendant had infringed the public's right to be free from the hazards of unabated lead, which constituted the public nuisance. The Rhode Island Supreme Court held that, standing alone, this allegation did not constitute an interference with a public right. The plaintiffs failed to allege that the defendants had interfered with a public right "as that term long has been understood in the law of public nuisance."[9] Thus, the term "public nuisance" was reserved more appropriately for indivisible resources shared by the public, such as air, water, or rights of way.[10]

In contrast to the cases in which courts determined that the plaintiffs failed to allege violation of a common public right based on narrow constructions, California courts have been especially willing to entertain broader understandings of public nuisance. For example, a California appellate court took

---

[5] Chicago v. Beretta U.S.A. Corp., 213 Ill.2d 351, 290 Ill. Dec. 525, 821 N.E.2d 1099 (2024).
[6] 821 N.E.2d at 1116.
[7] Rhode Island v. Lead Indus. Ass'n, Inc., 951 A.2d 428 (R.I. 2008).
[8] *Id.* at 447–48.
[9] *Id.* at 453.
[10] *Id.*

a much more liberal approach to construing a common public right, based on its statutory law.[11] The court upheld a trial court's determination that a manufacturer's interior lead paint promotion interfered with a public right that could be considered a public nuisance.[12] The plaintiffs alleged that the defendant's affirmative promotion of lead paint for interior use, not their mere manufacture and distribution of lead paint or their failure to warn, constituted public nuisance.[13]

Citing California law, the court stated that "anything which is injurious to health ... or is indecent or offensive to the senses, or an obstruction to the free use of property, so as to interfere with the comfortable enjoyment of life or property ... is a nuisance."[14] Further, "[A] public nuisance is one which affects at the same time an entire community or neighborhood, or any considerable number of persons, although the extent of the annoyance or damage inflicted upon individual may be unequal."[15]

The defendants argued that any possible lead exposure inside a private home could not involve the exercise of any public right and that unlike streets, residential housing was not a shared community resource. The appellate court disagreed, holding that most members of the public resided in residential housing which, like water, electricity, natural gas, and sewer services was an essential community resource.[16] The court held that pervasive lead exposure in residential housing threatened the public right to essential community resources.[17]

Similarly, a California federal court held that plaintiffs successfully pleaded a public nuisance claim under state law in alleging physical injury to their property. Los Angeles governmental entities, including its County Flood Control District, sued defendant Monsanto Company for pollution of the county's stormwater drainage system with toxic PCBs. The plaintiffs relied on the California civil code provision, to the effect that a public nuisance was "anything which was injurious to health ... or is an obstruction to the free use of property, so as to interfere with the comfortable enjoyment of life or property ... or unlawfully obstructs the free passage or use of a water body or public property."[18]

---

[11]   People v. Conagra Grocery Prods. Co., 17 Cal. App. 5th 51, 227 Cal. Rptr.3d 499 (2017).
[12]   *Id.*
[13]   *Id.*, 17 Cal. App. 5th at 91, citing Santa Clara v. Atlantic Richfield Co., 137 Cal. App.4th 292, 389–10, 40 Cal. Rptr.3d 313 (2006) (*Santa Clara I*).
[14]   Civ. Code § 3479.
[15]   Civ. Code § 3480.
[16]   Conagra, *supra* note 11, at 112.
[17]   *Id.*
[18]   Los Angeles v. Monsanto Company, 2019 WL 13064885, at *11 (C.D. Cal. Nov. 21, 2019), citing Cal. Civ. Code § 3479.

The court held that the plaintiffs had a property interest in stormwater that the defendants injured by its conduct. Municipalities can obtain a usufructuary right to stormwater they capture. The plaintiffs claimed such a usufructuary interest because they had adopted plans for the capture and beneficial uses of stormwater and runoff. For millions of people the county provided water quality, flood protection, water conservation services, and recreational opportunities: collectively, a public interest in clean water. The defendants' PCB contamination activities resulted in fish consumption advisories at system parks and reservoirs. Thus, the court held that the plaintiffs had adequately pleaded a public nuisance claim through their allegations of the loss of enjoyment of their water bodies because of the defendants' PCB contamination.[19]

Consistent with California's broad understanding of permissible public nuisance claims, a California federal court approved a public nuisance claim in litigation concerning electronic nicotine delivery systems devices, commonly known as e-cigarettes. In this litigation, consumers and governmental entities in several states filed a class action, suing defendants that created, sold, distributed, or sold supplies for these electronic smoking devices.[20] The plaintiffs' alleged that the defendants created a public nuisance by producing, promoting, distributing, and marketing e-cigarette products for underage use in school districts and counties, in violation of states' public nuisance laws.[21]

The plaintiffs alleged that the defendants' activities created a highly addictive product that they deceptively targeted and marketed to attract a youth market. This successful marketing and distribution campaign resulted in costly use of school resources to address the vaping crisis. The local governmental plaintiffs sought to recover the costs incurred in responding to the crisis.[22]

A threshold question concerned whether the plaintiffs had adequately pleaded a public nuisance claim. The defendant contended that the plaintiffs failed to sufficiently allege that the defendant's activities and conduct interfered with a public right. They argued that the governmental entities should not be allowed to expand public nuisance law beyond its traditional bounds.[23] The defendant argued that the plaintiffs' claims should be dismissed because they were essentially product liability claims for economic damages under the guise of nuisance law.[24]

---

[19] *Id.* at *11.
[20] In re JUUL Labs, Inc., Marketing, Sales Practices, and Prod. Liab. Litig., 497 F.Supp.3d 552, 575–78 (N.D. Cal. 2020).
[21] *Id.* at 645.
[22] *Id.* at 577–78.
[23] *Id.* at 645.
[24] *Id.* at 645–46.

The court disagreed with the defendants' arguments, instead upholding the plaintiffs' public nuisance claim. The court noted that California plaintiffs had been permitted to bring public nuisance claims against product manufacturers and distributors as long as their claims were not predicated on product liability theories.[25] The plaintiffs' claim, the court explained, did not sound in products liability, nor was the plaintiffs' claim as novel as the defendant characterized it. The governmental public nuisance claims did not stretch into products liability law.[26] The plaintiffs' claim did not concern itself with the e-cigarette product itself, but rather with the alleged consequence of the defendants' conduct. The public nuisance claims were premised on the defendant's aggressive promotion of its e-cigarette to teenagers and its efforts to create and maintain an e-cigarette market based on youth sales, not on any alleged defect with the e-cigarette product.[27]

4.2 SUBSTANTIAL AND UNREASONABLE INTERFERENCE WITH COMMON RIGHT; PROXIMATE CAUSATION

If a plaintiff successfully identifies a public nuisance, some courts additionally require the plaintiff to allege that the defendant's activities constituted a substantial and unreasonable interference with a common right. Some courts have required an allegation and showing of affirmative conduct on the defendant's part in creating and/or maintaining the nuisance. In addition, many courts have imposed requirements that the plaintiff allege and prove that the defendant's conduct was the cause-in-fact and proximate cause of the plaintiff's harm.

Courts have defined these elements of a public nuisance cause of action in different ways and reached different conclusions regarding the plaintiffs' success in alleging or proving these elements. In some instances, courts have found that plaintiffs adequately pleaded defendant's substantial and unreasonable interference, affirmative conduct, and causation of the public nuisance; but in other cases courts have concluded that plaintiffs failed to carry these burdens.

Many California courts have interpreted these elements liberally. For example, in the California lead paint litigation an appellate court upheld the trial court's finding of a public nuisance. The court reviewed the standards for holding a defendant liable for public nuisance, which included an element of causation based on a defendant's affirmative conduct.[28] The court indicated that

---

[25] *Id.* at 646, citing cases.
[26] *Id,.* at 647.
[27] *Id.* at 646.
[28] Conagra, *supra* note 11, at 111–12.

the critical question was whether the defendant created or assisted in creation of the nuisance. A public nuisance claim was not premised on a product defect or failure to warn, but on affirmative conduct that assisted in the creation of a hazardous condition.[29] Causation was an element of a cause of action for public nuisance; "a connecting element to the prohibited harm must be shown."[30]

The causation element can be satisfied if the defendant's activities were a substantial factor causing the nuisance the plaintiff sought to abate.[31] The court indicated that to qualify as a public nuisance subject to injunction and abatement, the defendant's interference with the public right had to be both substantial and unreasonable.[32] An interference was substantial if it caused significant harm and was unreasonable if its social utility was outweighed by the gravity of the harm inflicted.[33]

The court held that the "substantial factor" standard was relatively broad, requiring only that the contribution of cause be more than negligible or theoretical. A force that played only an infinitesimal of theoretical part in causing an injury, damage, or loss was not a substantial factor. However, a minor force that did cause harm was a substantial factor.[34] Reviewing the evidence, the court concluded that there was substantial proof that the defendants' affirmative promotions of lead paint for interior residential use played at least a minor role in creating the nuisance.[35]

Similarly, in the California federal opioid litigation against opioid manufacturers, distributors, and pharmacies, the district court held that the elements of an action for public nuisance included causation. The plaintiffs pleaded that the defendant manufacturers' marketing tactics substantially increased the supply of prescription opioids which proximately caused harm to the city and that the distributors and pharmacies failed to maintain effective controls against diversion of the drugs. Collectively, the defendants' conduct was a substantial factor in producing the plaintiffs' alleged harm.[36]

The court held that to establish causation, in fact, the plaintiff had to prove that the defendants' conduct was a substantial factor in bringing about the result.[37] Additionally, the plaintiff had to establish proximate cause, that is, the

---

[29] *Id.*
[30] *Id.* at 101–02.
[31] *Id.*
[32] *Id.* at 112.
[33] *Id.*
[34] *Id.* at 102.
[35] *Id.*
[36] San Francisco v. Purdue Pharma L.P., 491 F.Supp.3d 610, 676 (N.D. Cal. 2020), citing Conagra, *supra* note 11, at 101.
[37] San Francisco, *id.*

defendant's wrongful conduct was not too remote from the current hazard to be its legal cause.[38]

The court concluded that the plaintiffs had plausibly alleged a public nuisance claim in that the defendants engaged in affirmative conduct, which was a substantial factor and proximate cause of the San Francisco opioid epidemic.[39]

Like the California courts addressing the opioid litigation, an Ohio federal district court sustained the plaintiffs' pleading of a public nuisance claim brought by several counties against several manufacturers, distributors, and pharmacies. The court held that the aggregate evidence of massive increases in the supply of prescription opioids, and the defendants' failure to maintain effective controls against diversion of the drugs to illicit markets, supported a reasonable inference that the defendants' conduct was a substantial factor in creating the nuisance of a danger to the public health and safety.[40] The trial judge had instructed the jury that "[A] defendant's conduct is substantial if a reasonable person would regard that conduct as the cause, or one of the material, meaningful, or considerable causes, of the nuisance. If you find that the conduct of any defendant proximately caused a public nuisance, it is not a defense to liability that some other entity may also be to blame."[41]

In the California e-cigarette litigation, a federal court upheld the plaintiffs' public nuisance claim, concluding that the defendants' activities interfered with a common public right.[42] Citing the *Restatement (Second)*, the court noted that courts following the *Restatement* characterized an unreasonable interference with a right common to the public as conduct that involved a significant interference with public health.[43] All jurisdictions involved in the e-cigarette class action had public nuisance law that prohibited conduct that interfered with public health. The governmental entities had sufficiently alleged that the defendant interfered with public health, impacting their schools and communities.[44]

Other courts, however, have taken narrow views of these requirements and not sustained public nuisance claims where plaintiffs failed to allege a substantial or unreasonable interference with a public right, affirmative conduct, or a causal relationship between the defendant's conduct and the plaintiff's

---

[38] *Id.*

[39] *Id.* at 676–84.

[40] In re Nat'l Prescription Opiate Litig., 589 F. Supp.3d 790, 805, 809 (E.D. Ohio 2022).

[41] *Id.* at 810.

[42] In re JUUL Labs, Inc., *supra* note 20 at 647–48.

[43] *Id.* at 647, citing *Restatement (Second) of Torts* § 821B (1979).

[44] *Id.* at 648.

harm. In the lead paint litigation, for example, the Rhode Island Supreme Court indicated that in a cause of action for public nuisance the plaintiff carried the burden to allege and prove that a defendant's legal activities were an unreasonable interference with a right common to the public.[45] The court indicated that whether an interference was unreasonable depended on the magnitude of the interference.

A defendant's activities that violated state laws or municipal ordinances could be unreasonable if the conduct interfered with a public right. Moreover, a defendant's activities were unreasonable if the defendant's conduct did not violate statutory law but instead created a substantial and continuing interference with a public right.[46] While a public nuisance claim was characterized by an unreasonable interference with a common right, basic fairness dictated that a defendant must have *caused* the interference.[47] Finding that the plaintiffs' complaint failed to support the causation elements for a public nuisance claim, the Rhode Island Supreme Court reversed the lower court's judgment sustaining a public nuisance claim.[48]

A federal appellate court rejected litigation by public hospitals in Washington against several tobacco company defendants, to recover their unreimbursed costs for treating patients suffering from tobacco-related illnesses.[49] The appellate court held that the district court properly dismissed the plaintiffs' state common law claims, including their public nuisance claim. Under Washington law, proximate causation was an element of public nuisance.

Washington courts defined proximate cause consistent with the common law requirement of directness; that is, a cause "which, in a direct sequence unbroken by any new independent cause, produces the injury complained of, and without which such injury would not have happened."[50] Applying the state common law standards, the appellate court upheld the trial court's dismissal of the public nuisance claim. The appellate court held that the plaintiffs' common law public nuisance claim failed because the tobacco companies' unlawful conduct was not the proximate cause of the plaintiffs' injuries.[51]

[45] Rhode Island, *supra* note 7, at 447.
[46] *Id.*
[47] *Id.* at 452.
[48] *Id.* at 453.
[49] Ass'n of Washington Pub. Hosp. Districts v. Philip Morris Inc., 241 F.3d 696, 700 (9th Cir. 2001).
[50] *Id.* at 707.
[51] *Id.*

4.3 ACTUAL KNOWLEDGE; INTENTIONAL
OR UNREASONABLE CONDUCT

In determining whether a defendant's conduct is actionable under a public nuisance theory, several courts have imposed requirements that the defendant's conduct in causing or maintaining the nuisance be intentional or made with actual knowledge. Many courts subsume these elements under a generalized requirement that the plaintiffs allege the defendant's causation of the public nuisance. Courts have expressed varying views concerning what constitutes requisite intentional conduct, or whether defendants had actual knowledge of their conduct.

California courts have taken broad views of the requirements of a defendant's intentional conduct and actual knowledge. In the California opioid litigation, a federal court held that San Francisco sufficiently pleaded a cause of action for public nuisance against the Purdue Pharma LLC, including the actual knowledge element of the claim.[52] The actual knowledge element required that the defendant engage in conduct with knowledge of the hazard such that the product's use would create the hazard.[53] The court held that the plaintiffs pleaded sufficient allegations to demonstrate that the defendant manufacturers' had actual knowledge that their marketing and promotional tactics of prescription opioids would increase the manufacture, distribution, and prescription of opioids, thereby creating and furthering the opioid epidemic.

In the Ohio national opioid litigation several counties sued pharmacy company defendants, alleging the defendants' unlawful and intentional conduct in dispensing opioids substantially contributed to an oversupply of legal prescription opioids and diversion into illicit markets outside appropriate medical channels, thereby endangering public health or safety and creating a public nuisance.[54] After an eight-week trial the jury returned a verdict favorable to the counties on the liability issue. Nonetheless, the defendants moved for a judgment as a matter of law to overturn the jury's verdict.

The trial judge upheld the jury verdict and denied the defendants' request. The court indicated there was sufficient proof at trial that the defendants engaged in intentional and culpable conduct. The court instructed the jury that to find a person had engaged in intentional conduct "it [was] enough that the person intended to act and knew, or was substantially certain, that the

[52] San Francisco v. Purdue Pharma L.P., *supra* note 36, at 673. *See* discussion *supra* at notes 36–39.

[53] *Id.* citing Conagra, *supra* note 11, at 84; Santa Clara v. Atl. Richfield Co., 137 Cal. App. 4th 292, 309–10 (2006).

[54] In re Nat'l Prescription Opiate Litig., *supra* note 40, at 795.

circumstances resulting from the act would interfere with the public health or safety."[55] If a defendant learned that circumstances resulting from their conduct interfered with the public health or safety, and the defendant continued with that conduct, then the subsequent conduct was intentional.[56]

The trial evidence showed that the defendants knew that prescription opioids were highly addictive and had a high potential for abuse that could lead to significant community harms. Despite that knowledge the defendants dispensed copious quantities of opioids without taking the necessary steps to avoid diversion of the drugs. Based on this evidence the jury reasonably concluded that each defendant intentionally dispensed opioids, which it knew or were substantially certain would interfere with the public health and safety.[57]

Similarly, in a California environmental pollution litigation, a federal district court upheld a public nuisance claim based on an affirmative conduct standard. The court indicated that in order to plead a viable nuisance claim in California, a plaintiff had to plead affirmative conduct by a manufacturer defendant that directly contributed to the creation of a nuisance.[58] Los Angeles County and the Los Angeles County Flood District sued Monsanto Company alleging that the defendant had contaminated and continued to contaminate the storm water and their stormwater drainage system with polychlorinated biphenyls (PCBs).[59] Citing California case law, the court noted that a defendant could be liable for assisting in the creation of a nuisance if it either affirmatively instructed the polluting entity to dispose of the hazardous substances in an improper or unlawful manner, or manufactured or installed the disposal system.[60] This standard required actual knowledge, not constructive knowledge of the hazard that the defendant's affirmative conduct would create.[61]

The court indicated that a defendant could not be said to create a public nuisance unless it more actively or knowingly generated or permitted the specific nuisance condition. Thus, "[s]uch actions, however, must amount to more than simply the manufacture or distribution of the defective product – rather, the defendant must take other 'affirmative acts' that contribute directly to the nuisance."[62] Moreover, evidence might give rise to a reasonable

---

[55] *Id.* at 805.
[56] *Id.*
[57] *Id.* at 805–06.
[58] Los Angeles v. Monsanto Company, 2019 WL 13064885, at *9 (C.D. Cal. Nov. 21, 2019).
[59] *Id.* at *1.
[60] *Id.* at *9.
[61] *Id.* citing People v. ConAgra Grocery Prods., Co., 17 Cal. App. 5th 51, 83 (2017) (Santa Clara III).
[62] Los Angeles, *supra* note 58, at *9.

inference that a defendant must have known by the early twentieth century that a product posed serious harm to the plaintiffs.[63]

The court held that the defendant engaged in affirmative acts that contributed to the nuisance by instructing their customers to dispose of PCBs directly into landfills. The plaintiff alleged that the defendants knew that PCBs were toxic as early as the 1930s and certainly by the 1950s. This case was distinguished from others wherein the defendant merely did not alert users to the proper methods for disposal; here, the defendant actively encouraged the harmful activity by encouraging users to dispose of PCBs in harmful ways.[64]

In contrast to the courts upholding a public nuisance claim based on sufficient pleading and proof of causation, several courts have rejected nuisance claims for the plaintiffs' failure to sufficiently allege this element of a nuisance claim. In the California firearms litigation, brought by the city attorneys of several jurisdiction, the plaintiffs sued several handgun manufacturers, distributors, and trade associations, alleging a claim for public nuisance. The public nuisance claim alleged the defendants marketed, distributed, promoted, and designed handguns in a manner that facilitated the use of the guns in violent crimes. The plaintiffs alleged the defendants created and maintained a public nuisance in failing to incorporate safety features in the firearms, deceiving the public about the dangers of firearms, and circumventing federal, state, and local laws.[65]

Citing the California Code, the court noted that a public nuisance was one that affected an entire community neighborhood, or any considerable number of persons.[66] Relying on the *Restatement (Second)*, the court determined that the plaintiff carried the burden of showing defendant's causation of the public nuisance. The *Restatement's* examples of actionable public nuisance claims illustrated that a defendant's action must not only create a risk of some harm, but also that the actions were likely to lead to the invasion of the public right.[67] It was not necessary that plaintiffs needed to show that harm actually occurred, but the plaintiff "must show that the defendant's acts were likely to cause a significant invasion of a public right."[68]

The court determined: "If a plaintiff could obtain an injunction absent a showing of causation of an interference with a public right, the plaintiff could enjoin the manufacturing of a firearm solely because the mere existence of

---

[63] *Id.*

[64] *Id.* at *10.

[65] In re Firearms Cases, 126 Cal. App.4th 959, 967–68, 24 Cal. Rptr.3d 659 (2005).

[66] *Id.* at 987, citing Cal. Civ. Code § 3480.

[67] *Id.* at 987–88.

[68] *Id.* at 988.

the firearm, creates a risk of harm. A connecting element to the prohibited harm must be shown."[69] Thus, merely engaging in what plaintiffs characterized as a risky practice, without a connection to a threatened harm, was not a public nuisance.

The appellate court held that the trial court properly rejected the plaintiffs' public nuisance theory, which failed for a lack of any evidence of causation. The plaintiffs failed to carry their burden of demonstrating a causal connection between any of the defendants' conduct and any incident of illegal acquisition of firearms, criminal acts, or accidental injury by a firearm.[70] The court found that the plaintiffs' complaint attempted to reach back too far in the chain of distribution when it targeted the manufacturer of a legal, nondefective product that it lawfully distributed only to buyers licensed by the federal government.[71]

The Rhode Island Supreme Court, in its lead paint litigation, also addressed the causation element of a public nuisance claim.[72] The court noted that the plaintiff alleging a public nuisance must not only demonstrate the existence of the nuisance, but also must demonstrate that the nuisance caused the injury. A defendant could be held liable only if the defendant's conduct actually caused the interference with a public right. In addition to proving that the defendant's conduct was the cause-in-fact of the plaintiff's injury, the plaintiff also had to demonstrate proximate causation, a more exacting standard than simple "but for causation."[73]

The court indicated that the proper inquiry regarding causation involved an assessment of foreseeability: that is, whether a reasonable person would foresee the injury as a likely consequence of its conduct. A defendant's liability could not be predicated on a prior remote cause that merely furnished the condition for an injury resulting from an intervening unrelated cause. A plaintiff did not need to exclude every other possible cause for its injury but had to demonstrate proximate cause by reasonable inferences from facts.[74]

Moreover, a defendant's liability in a public nuisance action was dependent upon whether the defendant had control over the instrumentality causing the alleged nuisance when the damage occurred. Control over the instrumentality at that time was crucial in public nuisance claims because the remedy for the harm was abatement. As the party in control of the instrumentality that

[69] *Id.*
[70] *Id.* at 988–89.
[71] *Id.* at 991.
[72] Rhode Island, *supra* note 7, at 450–52.
[73] *Id.* at 451.
[74] *Id.*

alleged caused the nuisance, the defendant was best positioned to abate it.[75] The Rhode Island Supreme Court concluded that it was problematic that the plaintiffs had failed to allege any allegation that defendants had control over the lead pigment at the time it caused harm to children.[76]

4.4 VIOLATION OF A STATUTE

Some courts have evaluated whether a public nuisance claim is viable based on statutory construction of a state's public nuisance law. Thus, the Oklahoma Supreme Court, construing the state's public nuisance statute, determined that an action brought by the state against an opioid manufacturer for its manufacturing, marketing, and selling prescription opioids did not create a public nuisance.[77] The Oklahoma public nuisance statute provides a good example of a narrowly draw statement of what constitutes public nuisance, imposing a legal duty on defendants.

The court noted that Oklahoma's nuisance statute codified the common law, and that public nuisance evolved from its criminal origins into a common law tort. Nonetheless, public nuisance historically was linked to the use of land by the person creating the nuisance, and courts had limited public nuisance claims to these traditional bounds. Assessing the plaintiffs' claim presented an exercise in statutory construction that posed a question of law.[78]

The statute stated that: "A nuisance consists in unlawfully doing an act, or omitting to perform a duty, which act or omission either: (1) annoys, injures or endangers the comfort, repose, health, or safety of others; or (2) offends decency; or (3) unlawfully interferes with, obstructs or tends to obstruct, or renders dangerous for passage, any lake or navigable river, stream, canal or basin, or any public park, square, street or highway; or (4) in any way renders other person insecure in life, or in the use of property, provided, this section shall not apply to preexisting agricultural activities."[79] The Oklahoma legislature defined public nuisance as a nuisance that contemporaneously affects an entire community or large group of people, but need not damage or annoy equally to all.[80]

The court concluded that the plaintiffs' allegations relating to the defendant opioid manufacturer did not fit within the Oklahoma public nuisance statute.

---

[75] *Id.* at 449.

[76] *Id.* at 453.

[77] Oklahoma *ex rel.* Hunter, *supra* note 1. *See* 50 O.S.2011, §§ 1 & 2.

[78] *Id.* at 723–24.

[79] 50 O.S.2011, § 1.

[80] 50 O.S.2011, § 2.

The court noted that for the past hundred years, in applying the statute, courts had limited their application to defendants committing crimes constituting a nuisance, or causing physical injury to property or participating in an offensive activity that rendered the property uninhabitable.[81]

The court rejected the plaintiffs' proposal to expand public nuisance to the manufacturing, marketing, and selling of lawful products. Public nuisance and product-related liability, the court explained, were two distinct causes of action, each with boundaries not intended to overlap. The classic articulation of tort duties to warn of or make safe products, sounded in product-related liability. "Applying nuisance statutes to lawful products as the State requests would create unlimited and unprincipled liability for product manufacturers…."[82] The Oklahoma Supreme Court cited the Rhode Island Supreme Court, in its lead paint litigation, and the *Restatement (Third) of Torts*, for the proposition that mass harms caused by dangerous products are better addressed through products liability law.[83]

A Texas federal district court similarly rejected a public nuisance claim brought by the state against tobacco companies seeking to recover costs in providing medical treatment for tobacco-related injuries.[84] The state alleged that the tobacco companies intentionally interfered with the public's right to be free from unwarranted injury, disease, and sickness and had caused damage to the public health, safety and general welfare.

Relying on the Texas public nuisance statute, the court indicated that a public nuisance was defined as the use of any place for certain, specific prescribed activities such as gambling, prostitution, and the manufacture of obscene materials.[85] The state attorney general was authorized to sue to enjoin or abate a public nuisance. However, the court concluded, "Where an action to enjoin a nuisance is brought under statutory authority, the case is limited to the provisions of the statute."[86] Thus, because the litigation did not involve any of the proscribed activities defined in the statute, the state could not maintain a public nuisance action for an injunction.

In addition, the state could not maintain an action for damages under a public nuisance theory. The state failed to plead a proper nuisance claim in that it failed to allege that the defendants had improperly used their property,

---

[81] State ex rel. Hunter, *supra* note 1, at 724.

[82] *Id.* at 725.

[83] *Id.* citing State v. Lead Paint Indus. Ass'n., Inc., 951 A.2d 428, 456 (R.I. 2008), and *Restatement (Third) of Torts: Liab. For Econ. Harm* § 8 cmt. g (Am. Law. Inst. 2020).

[84] Texas v. Am. Tobacco Co., 14 F. Supp.2d 956, 972 (E.D. Tex. 1997).

[85] Tex. Civ. Prac. & Rem. § 125.022.

[86] Texas, *supra* note 84, at 972, citing cases.

or that the state itself had been injured in its use or enjoyment of its property. Thus, the court held that "the overly broad definition of the elements of public nuisance urged by the State is simply not found in Texas case law and the Court is unwilling to accept the state's invitation to expand a claim for public nuisance beyond its ground in real property." The court dismissed the plaintiff's claim for public nuisance.[87]

In addition to recourse to state public nuisance statutes, plaintiffs have attempted to bootstrap common law public nuisance claims onto legislation dealing with the protection of the health and safety of citizens. Various New York municipalities attempted just such a strategy in litigation arising out of the plaintiffs' claims that the governmental entities were deprived of tax revenues by the out-of-state defendants' business of illegal marketing and selling of cigarettes over the internet and shipping the cigarettes into New York. The plaintiffs asserted a common law public nuisance claim based on New York's Public Health Law.[88]

The Public Health Law made it unlawful for any person engaged in the business of selling cigarettes to ship cigarettes to any person in state not licensed as a cigarette tax agent, wholesale dealer, registered retail dealer, or other person who was a government agent or employee acting in an official capacity. The statute included several provisions prohibiting the transport or shipment of cigarettes.[89] The plaintiffs claimed that the legislative findings accompanying the Public Health Law permitted the plaintiffs to bring an action to abate their "newly characterized" public nuisance claim.[90]

Viewing the issue as one of pure statutory construction, the appellate court determined that the plaintiffs could not assert a common law public nuisance claim by reference to the Public Health Law. The legislature did not contemplate that the statute would be used as a predicate for public nuisance actions in litigation that primarily involved claims of tax evasion.[91] The court determined that the public health thrust of the statute was related to the prevention of underage smoking; the legislature did not intend its findings to authorize a public nuisance claim based primarily on alleged tax evasion.[92] Thus, permitting the plaintiffs' claims to proceed under a public nuisance theory would not have been consistent with the legislative scheme. The injury

---

[87] *Id.* at 973.
[88] New York v. Smoke-Spirits.com, Inc., 12 N.Y.3d 616, 911 N.E.2d 834, 883 N.Y.S.2d 772, N.Y. Slip. Op. 04699 (N.Y. Ct. App. 2009). *See* Public Health Law § 1399-*ll*.
[89] New York, *id.* at 625.
[90] *Id.* at 624.
[91] *Id.* at 624–25.
[92] *Id.* at 629.

that the plaintiffs' alleged, namely lost revenue, was a harm that was subject to regulation by other laws.[93]

The Idaho Supreme Court, construing the state's nuisance statute, concluded that the plaintiff failed to establish an existing nuisance in a lawsuit against a county's operation of a gun range on property adjacent to the plaintiff's property.[94] Consequently, the plaintiff was not entitled to injunctive relief.[95] The Idaho statute defined a nuisance as: "Anything which is injurious to health or morals, or is indecent, or offensive to the senses, or an obstruction to the free use of property, so as to interfere with the comfortable enjoyment of life or property, or unlawfully obstructs the free passage or use, in the customary manner, of any navigable lake, or river, stream, canal, or basin, or any public park, square, street, or highway, is a nuisance."[96]

The defendant challenged the claim, contending that there was no continuing and ongoing nuisance because the incidents the plaintiffs alleged as constituting the nuisance occurred years before the gun range made improvements, effectively abating the nuisance. The Supreme Court agreed to the trial court's dismissal of the nuisance claim because the defendant had abated the nuisance.[97]

Construing its public nuisance statute, the Idaho Supreme Court indicated that a party may pursue a private nuisance action that is neither a public nor moral nuisance. Neither the Idaho Code or the *Restatement (Second)* expressly defined a nuisance as being ongoing and continuous. However, earlier Idaho cases indicated that nuisances had an element of persistence. Once a party established the existence of a nuisance, the defendant had an opportunity to show that the nuisance had been abated.[98]

4.5 SPECIAL INJURY FOR PRIVATE PLAINTIFF RECOVERY

Both common law principles as well as statutory provisions have indicated that a private person may maintain an action for public nuisance if it is especially injurious to the individual, but not otherwise. If the individual has a harm in common with the public, then the individual may not pursue a public nuisance claim. This proposition is known as the special injury requirement for individual assertion of a public nuisance claim and for individual recovery.

---

[93] *Id.*
[94] Spirit Ridge Mineral Springs, LLC v. Franklin County, 157 Idaho 424, 337 P.3d 583 (2014).
[95] *Id.* at 428.
[96] I.C. § 52–101.
[97] Spirit Ridge Mineral Springs, LLC, *supra* note 94, at 428.
[98] *Id.* at 427.

Courts have variously both recognized and rejected public nuisance suits brought by private parties under the special injury doctrine. In a consumer class action against General Mills corporation alleging that boxed baking mixes containing trans fats, the plaintiff alleged that the defendant's conduct constituted a public nuisance under California law.[99] California statutory law defined a public nuisance as "anything which is injurious to health ... so as to interfere with the comfortable enjoyment of life or property ... which affects at the same time an entire community or neighborhood, or any considerable number of persons."[100] In addition, "a private person may maintain an action for public nuisance, if it is specially injurious to himself, but not otherwise."[101]

The court indicated that a plaintiff suing on an individual basis had to demonstrate a special injury to himself of a character different in kind – not merely in degree – from that suffered by the public. Applying this standard, the court determined that many courts in trans-fat litigation found that individual plaintiffs did not suffer injuries that were different in kind from the public. Trans fats were not uniquely harmful to the plaintiff, but rather constituted a general health hazard to anyone who consumed them. Consequently, the court dismissed the plaintiff's public nuisance claim.[102]

Similarly, in litigation brought by hospitals seeking reimbursement for unreimbursed medical care to nonpaying patients suffering from tobacco-related diseases, a federal appellate court upheld a trial court's determination that the hospitals could not state a public nuisance claim.[103] The court recited the proposition that in order to recover for damages in a private action for public nuisance, a plaintiff must have suffered a harm of greater magnitude and of a different kind than that which the public suffered.[104] Relying on the *Restatement (Second)*, the court indicated the reasons for the special injury rule in private actions: (1) the difficulty in drawing a satisfactory line for any public nuisance, and (2) to avoid multiplicity of actions, invasions of common public rights should be remedied by public action by officials.[105]

The court agreed that the plaintiff hospitals had not sufficiently alleged they suffered a harm different from and of a greater magnitude than the public harm. The hospitals' injuries were derivative of the nonpaying patients' injuries, and the hospitals were one of numerous parties affected by the

---

[99] Backus v. General Mills, Inc., 122 F. Supp.3d 909, 930 (N.D. 2015).
[100] Cal. Civ. Code §§ 3479–80.
[101] *Id.* at § 3493.
[102] Backus, *supra* note 99, at 931.
[103] Allegheny General Hosp. v. Phillip Morris, Inc., 228 F.3d 429 (3d Cir. 2000).
[104] *Id.* at 446, citing cases.
[105] *Id.* citing *Restatement (Second) of Torts* § 821C cmt. b (1979).

defendants' activities. In these circumstances, remedying the source of the public nuisance was more properly a task for public officials.[106]

Pleading a special injury that would entitle an individual plaintiff to recover has proven to be difficult in most contemporary public nuisance litigation. However, some litigants have been successful in pleading the special injury requirement. Thus, in the California e-cigarette litigation, a federal court concluded that the plaintiff school districts had provided sufficient detail in their complaints about the kinds of harm caused by the defendant's conduct that was different in kind from that suffered by their community.[107] The plaintiffs adequately alleged that the defendant's conduct – including a targeted marketing campaign on social media, flavored products, and other actions targeting school-aged youth – created and maintained an illicit market of school-aged youth addicted to nicotine. This consequently caused extreme disruption in classrooms and unique harms to schools, that was different in kind to the community at large.[108]

---

[106] Allegheny Gen. Hosp., *supra* note 103, at 446.
[107] In Re JUUL Labs, Inc., *supra* note 20, at 649.
[108] *Id.* at 650.

5

Expanding Public Nuisance Doctrine: Defenses

Defendants responding to common law or statutory public nuisance claims have an array of traditional defenses centered on whether the plaintiffs have successfully pleaded or proved the elements of a public nuisance claim. Thus, defendants may contest the plaintiffs' allegations or proof of the definition of a public right – whether the defendant's conduct was substantial, unreasonable, affirmative, or intentional; whether the defendant's conduct was the cause-in-fact or proximate cause of the nuisance giving rise to plaintiffs' injuries; or whether an individual plaintiff's injuries were special and different in kind than the groups, so as to afford an individual a right of recovery for a public nuisance. Defendants have experienced mixed success in challenging public nuisance claims by contesting the plaintiff's fulfillment of the elements of a public nuisance claim.

In the developing jurisprudence of the twenty-first century public nuisance litigation, defendants have expanded the possible array of defenses against public nuisance claims. These defenses include the doctrines of remoteness and statutes of limitation; control over the instrumentality causing the nuisance; standing; regulated conduct and statutory compliance; no private right of action; primary jurisdiction; federal preemption; penalizing lawful conduct; economic loss doctrine; municipal cost recovery doctrine; ongoing nuisance; unconstitutional vagueness; the dormant Commerce Clause; and the First, Eleventh, and Fourteenth Amendments. Broadly, defendants have challenged mass tort public nuisance claims on public policy grounds.

Defense attorneys have succeeded in advancing some of these defense theories, while being rebuffed in other litigation. Nonetheless, many of the plaintiff and defense attorneys have succeeded in framing the public policy debate over contemporary mass harms pursued under a public nuisance concept. These litigants have pressed the debate concerning whether the public nuisance should be expanded to address current mass tort public harms, or whether expansion of public nuisance doctrine is properly left to legislative bodies.

5.1 REMOTENESS AND STATUTES OF LIMITATION

A favored defense to plaintiffs' public nuisance claims has been the defendants' invocation of a remoteness argument. The essence of this argument posits that a defendant should be absolved of responsibility for a current hazard because their conduct in creating the nuisance was too remote or attenuated to hold a defendant liable for a continuing public nuisance. In addition, defendants frequently contend that they cannot be held accountable for a current hazard when the intervening actions of others occurred since the defendant's original conduct.

Unsurprisingly, defendants in the lead paint, firearms, and opioid litigation – where the defendants' products have circulated through a chain of actors resulting in a continuous nuisance – have invoked this remoteness argument as a defense against defendant's accountability for current hazards. The remoteness defense has met with mixed judicial reception in these public nuisance products cases.

For example, the firearms manufacturers, distributors, and dealers successfully raised the remoteness defense in Chicago's lawsuit to recover compensation for law enforcement and medical services incurred as a result of gun violence.[1] The defendants contended that any public nuisance that resulted from the possession and use of firearms was not caused by their conduct, but by the criminal acts of independent, third-parties. The defendants' sale of firearms, they argued, merely furnished a condition that enabled the criminal acts of others and, therefore, was too remote to be the legal cause of a public nuisance that was the aggregate effect of many such criminal acts.[2] The criminal misuse of a firearm was not a foreseeable consequence of the legal sale of firearms to the public.

The Illinois Supreme Court focused on whether the defendants' conduct in selling firearms was the legal cause of the public nuisance, assuming arguendo that the presence and use of illegal firearms constituted a public nuisance. The court held that the legal cause of a nuisance could be found only if reasonable persons in the firearms retail business would have foreseen the creation of a nuisance in Chicago. The court further held that legal cause for a nuisance would not be found where the criminal acts of third parties broke the causal connection. Moreover, individuals in Chicago who illegally possessed and used firearms were not under the control of the defendant dealers.[3]

---

[1] Chicago v. Beretta U.S.A. Corp., 213 Ill.2d 351, 821 N.E.2d 1099, 1132 (Ill. 2004).
[2] *Id.*
[3] *Id.* at 1134.

Applying these standards, the court concluded that the defendants could not reasonably foresee that the guns they legally sold would be illegally taken into the city in substantial numbers and used in such a manner as to create a public nuisance. A defendant's lawful commercial activity could not be considered the proximate of harm to a person or property where the injury was caused principally by the criminal activities of intervening third parties.[4]

Applying the remoteness doctrine, a New York court adopted a similar view concerning the liability of handgun manufacturers, wholesalers, and retailers in a public nuisance litigation by New York state.[5] The plaintiff's complaint failed because the harm that the plaintiff alleged was far too remote from the defendants' otherwise lawful activity to fairly hold the defendants accountable for common law public nuisance. In addition, the defendants' lawful commercial activity, followed by harm caused directly by the criminal activity of intervening third parties, could not be considered a proximate cause of the harm.[6] The court noted that several other jurisdictions had reached the same conclusion barring firearms public nuisance claims, based on the remoteness doctrine.[7]

The court observed that judicial rejection of firearms public nuisance lawsuits represented a judicial resistance to the expansion of the defendant's duty to control the conduct of third persons so as to prevent them from harming others. This resistance grew out of the practical concerns about defendants' potentially limitless liability and the unfairness of imposing liability for the actions of others.[8]

The court rejected the plaintiff's contention that to advance a cognizable public nuisance claim, it only had to allege and prove that the defendants' business practices caused or contributed to the maintenance of a public nuisance. Instead, the court determined that it could not conclude that, no matter how far removed from the defendants' lawful business practices the harm was felt, the defendants nonetheless remained liable under a public nuisance theory.[9]

The Oklahoma Supreme Court similarly approved the opioid manufacturers' remoteness argument against the plaintiffs' public nuisance lawsuit. In rejecting the public nuisance claim against opioid manufacturer Johnson & Johnson, the Oklahoma Supreme Court noted that nuisance claims against

---

[4] *Id.* at 1136.

[5] New York v. Sturm, Ruger & Co., Inc., 309 A.D.2d 91, 761 N.Y.2d 192 (Sup. Ct. App. Div. 2003).

[6] *Id.* at 103.

[7] *Id.* at 93, citing Philadelphia v. Beretta U.S.A. Corp., 277 F.3d 415 (3d Cir. 2002); Camden County Bd. of Chosen Freeholders v. Beretta, U.S.A., Corp., 273 F.3d 536 (3d Cir. 2001); Ganim v. Smith & Wesson Corp., 258 Conn. 313, 780 A.2d 98 (2001).

[8] New York, *supra* note 5, at 95.

[9] *Id.* at 103.

product manufacturers sidestepped any statute of limitations.[10] The Oklahoma court observed that the trial court had held Johnson & Johnson responsible for products that entered the stream of commerce more than 20 years ago and thereby shifted the wrong from the manufacturing, marketing, and selling of its product to their continuing presence in the marketplace. The Supreme Court resisted this conclusion, holding that Oklahoma law had rejected endless liability in all other traditional tort theories. Thus, product manufacturers could not be held perpetually liable for their products pursuant to a public nuisance theory.[11]

In contrast to those courts endorsing and approving the remoteness defense, other courts have rejected its application in public nuisance lawsuits. Thus, a California state appellate court rejected defendants' remoteness challenge in a public nuisance litigation against manufacturers of lead paint used in residential interiors.[12] The defendants argued that their alleged wrongful conduct in marketing and promoting their paint products was too remote and attenuated to hold them responsible for the current lead paint hazard in residential properties.[13]

In rejecting this challenge, the court noted that the question of remoteness was a fact question for a jury. Nonetheless, the court opined that a reasonable jury could conclude that the defendants' wrongful promotion of their paint products was not unduly remote from the presence of interior residential use during the period of the defendants' wrongful promotions and within a reasonable period after that. The court concluded that the connection between the defendants' long ago promotion and the current presence of lead paint in residences was not particularly attenuated. Moreover, the court determined that the defendants who initially marketed and promoted their paint could be held accountable, even though the actions of others or owner neglect played a role in the current hazard.[14]

Although different from the various remoteness theories, defendants also have raised related ordinary statutes of limitations defenses. In the Ohio national opioid litigation, for example, the pharmacy defendants contended that the plaintiffs' suits were based on conduct that had ceased more than four years prior to the litigation, and therefore, the claims were timed-barred. The defendants argued that the plaintiffs' time to file was not extended by the discovery rule, fraudulent

---

[10] Oklahoma *ex rel.* Hunter v. Johnson & Johnson, 499 P.3d 719, 729 (Okla. 2021), citing Detroit Bd. of Educ. v. Celotex Corp., 196 Mich. App. 694, 493 N.W.2d 513, 521 (1992).

[11] *Id.*

[12] People v. Conagra Grocery Prods. Co., 17 Cal. App.5th 51, 104, 227 Cal. Rptr.3d 499 (2017).

[13] *Id.*

[14] *Id.*

concealment, or the continuing violations doctrine. Applying ordinary statute of limitations principles, the court disagreed. The court held that accrual dates and tolling doctrines for filing were irrelevant, because "absolute and statutory public nuisance claims [were] exempt from a statute of limitations."[15]

5.2 CONTROL OVER THE INSTRUMENTALITY OF CAUSING NUISANCE

Defendants frequently invoke the defense that they cannot be held liable for public nuisance harms that occur after they effectively lose control over the instrumentality allegedly causing harm. Several courts have indicated that an additional prerequisite to imposing liability on defendants for public nuisance is that the defendants must have control over the instrumentality causing the alleged nuisance at the time the damage occurred.[16]

This element is crucial to a public nuisance claim, according to some courts, because the principal remedy for a public nuisance harm is abatement. Therefore, if defendants are no longer in control of the instrumentality at the time of the injury, defendants lack the power to abate the nuisance and the plaintiffs cannot succeed on this theory for relief.[17] Not surprisingly, defendants involved in public nuisance litigation dealing with lead paint, firearms, and opioids have favored the argument based on lack of control over the instrumentality because of the attenuated connection between the manufacture, marketing, and distribution of their products and the ultimate harms to the communities from these products.

Critics of the expansion of public nuisance law have argued that is it impossible for manufacturers or distributors who have relinquished possession of a product by selling or distributing it to end the harmful conduct.[18] In addition, "[f]urnishing a product or instrumentality – whether it be chemicals, asbestos, guns, lead paint, or other product – is not the same as having control over that instrumentality."[19]

The New Jersey Supreme Court, in its lead paint litigation, concluded that the defendants could not be liable under a public nuisance theory. The court

---

[15] In re Nat'l Prescription Opiate Litig., 589 F.Supp.3d 790, 825 (N.D. Ohio 2022).

[16] Rhode Island v. Lead Indus. Ass'n, Inc., 951 A.2d 428, 449 (2008), citing cases.

[17] *Id.*

[18] Donald G. Gifford, Public Nuisance as a Mass Products Liability Tort, 71 U. Cin. L. Rev. 741, 829 (2003).

[19] Victor E. Schwartz & Phil Goldberg, The Law of Public Nuisance: Maintaining Rational Boundaries in a Rational Tort, 45 Washburn L.J. 541, 548 (2006). *See also* Mark G. Gagliardi, Note, Stirring Up the Debate in Rhode Island: Should Lead Paint Manufacturers Be Held Liable for the Harms Caused by Lead Paint?, 7 Roger Williams U.L. Rev. 341, 376 (2002).

indicated that the defendants' control over the instrumentality at the time the damage occurred was a time-honor element of a public nuisance claim. The court stated that "a public nuisance, by definition, is related to conduct, performed in a location within the actors' control...." The court repudiated the plaintiffs' public nuisance claim based on lack of control of the lead paint at the time the consequences of lead paint in residential buildings caused harm, years after marketing, distribution, and selling the product.[20]

However, the Chief Justice of the New Jersey Supreme Court dissented, claiming that the defendants' control over the instrumentality that gave rise to the nuisance was not a necessary element of a common law public nuisance claim. The justice agreed with other courts holding that it was enough the defendants contributed to the creation of an unreasonable interference with a common right, and it was immaterial whether defendants continued to exercise control over the instrumentality of the nuisance.[21]

In public nuisance firearms litigation, courts have reached conflicting conclusions concerning whether defendants cannot be held liable for a public nuisance because they did not have control over the instrumentality at the time of the injury. The Illinois Supreme Court concluded that the firearms defendants could not be held accountable under a public nuisance theory because they lacked control over their firearms after the manufacture, distribution, and sale of the guns to consumers. In reaching this conclusion, the court defaulted to the narrowest conception of public nuisance doctrine: that it traditionally had been tied to harms resulting from the use of land. In this context, the question of control most frequently occurred when the defendant had completely divested himself of any connection with the property involved.[22]

Reviewing precedential property public nuisance decisions, the court concluded that those cases stood for the unremarkable proposition that a court would not issue an injunction ordering a defendant to abate a nuisance upon land if he had no authority by ownership or possession to enter on the land. Therefore, by analogy, these cases did not support the imposition of a separate control requirement in public nuisance litigation that was not predicated on the defendant's use of land.[23]

Following the Illinois Supreme Court, the Oklahoma Supreme Court held that Johnson & Johnson, as an opioid manufacturer, could not be held liable for public nuisance because it did not control the instrumentality alleged to

---

[20] In re Lead Paint Litig., 191 N.J. 405, 924 A.2d 484, 499 (2007).
[21] *Id.* at 510 (Zazzali, C.J., dissenting).
[22] Chicago v. Beretta, *supra* note 1, at 1130.
[23] *Id.* at 1128–31.

have caused the nuisance at the time it occurred.[24] The court held that a product manufacturer's responsibility was to put a non-defective product into the market, but there was no common law duty to monitor how a consumer used or misused the product after it was sold. And, without having control over the product after it was sold, the manufacturer could not remove or abate the nuisance.[25]

In so concluding, the court relied on the authority of the Illinois Supreme Court's *Beretta* decision in Chicago's public nuisance litigation against firearms manufacturers, distributors, and handgun dealers.[26] The Oklahoma Supreme Court noted that just as in *Beretta*, the alleged nuisance in the opioid litigation was several times removed from the initial manufacture and distribution of the product. Like the firearms defendants, Johnson & Johnson had no control of its products through multiple distribution levels, "including after it sold the opioids to distributors and wholesalers, which were then disbursed to pharmacies, hospitals, and physicians' officers, and then prescribed by doctors to patients."[27]

In contrast to the Oklahoma Supreme Court's reliance on the defendant's lack of control defense to defeat a public nuisance opioid litigation against Johnson & Johnson, several courts in opioid lawsuits have rejected the defense. For example, in the national opioid litigation, the defendant opioid manufacturers and pharmacies contended that once the opioids were dispensed by pharmacies, they lacked control of the physical opioid pills, and therefore, they were unable to prevent the alleged nuisance.[28]

The federal court rejected this defense. The court indicated that the defendant's arguments rested on the false premise that the instrumentality of the nuisance was the opioid medication. The court countered that the plaintiffs' claims did not stem from the products themselves, but from the way in which the defendants dispensed the products. Regarding this conduct, the court concluded that the defendants failed to provide effective controls to detect red flags and prevent diversion of their medications to the community.[29]

A California federal court similarly rejected this defense invoked by the JUUL defendant in the e-cigarette litigation. The court held that plaintiffs had plausibly pleaded the defendant's control of the instrumentality, which

---

[24] Oklahoma *supra* note 10, at 727–28.
[25] *Id.*
[26] Chicago v. Beretta, *supra* note 1 (2004).
[27] Oklahoma, *supra* note 10, at 727–28.
[28] In re Nat'l Prescription Opiate Litig., *supra* note 15, at 817.
[29] *Id.* at 816–17.

was their conduct in creating and maintaining the youth e-cigarette crisis.[30] Like the defendants in the opioid litigation, the JUUL defendant's contention rested on the false premise that the instrumentality of the nuisance was the JUUL product itself. The court disagreed that finding the level of the defendant's requisite control over their marketing and distribution practices was plausibly pleaded to permit the public nuisance claim to proceed.[31]

5.3 STANDING

Defendants sometimes challenge the plaintiffs' lack of standing to bring public nuisance claim. Often challenges to plaintiffs' standing are tied to factual arguments concerning the remoteness or attenuated connection between the defendants' past conduct or actions and the current public nuisance hazard.

Defendants in an early Connecticut firearms public nuisance litigation raised a standing defense.[32] The Connecticut Supreme Court noted that it was axiomatic that a party must have standing to assert a claim for a court to have valid subject matter jurisdiction. Standing jurisprudence consistently entailed that a plaintiff, in an individual or representative capacity, must have a colorable claim of direct injury traceable to the defendant's conduct. Where the plaintiff's claimed injuries were remote, indirect, or derivative to the defendant's conduct, then the plaintiff was not a proper party to assert their claims and lacked standing to do so.[33]

In assessing whether the plaintiff's harms were the direct, indirect, remote, or derivative conduct of the defendant, a court is simply not tasked with applying a set of labels. Federal courts have recognized that the question of a defendants' proximate cause of the harm and the plaintiffs' standing "are part and parcel of the same inquiry."[34] Moreover, the standing inquiry embraces a policy consideration whether the defendant's responsibility should extend to conferring standing on a plaintiff.[35] The Connecticut Supreme Court concluded that the municipality and its mayor, joined by the state's attorney general, lacked standing to bring a public nuisance firearms action.[36]

---

[30] In re JUUL Labs, Inc., Marketing, Sales Practices, and Prod. Liab. Litig., 497 F.Supp.3d 552, 648–49 (N.D. Ohio 2020).

[31] *Id.* at 649.

[32] Ganim v. Smith and Wesson Corp., *supra* note 6, at 119–30.

[33] *Id.* at 119–20.

[34] *Id.* at 121.

[35] *Id.* at 120.

[36] *Id.* at 121–30, 133.

The Connecticut Supreme Court rejected the plaintiffs' contention that they had standing to sue under the state's Home Rule Act.[37] Provisions of the statute provided that any municipality had the power to sue and be sued; other provisions gave municipalities the power to "[p]rovide for the health of inhabitants and all things necessary or desirable to secure and promote the public health."[38] Construing the statutory scheme, the court determined that the statute's primary purpose was to relieve the state attorney general of the burden of handling and enacting special legislation of local municipal concern.[39]

Moreover, it was settled that municipalities had no inherent powers of their own, and only had powers the state expressly granted them that were necessary to discharge its duties. The court concluded that the general provisions of the Home Rule Act did not provide the plaintiffs with standing. The general power to sue or be sued, and the provisions relating to protection of the health and safety of citizens, did not mean that municipalities could bring suit.[40]

Defendants in the national opioid litigation attempted to challenge the plaintiffs' standing based on the Supreme Court's 2021 decision in *TransUnion LLC v. Ramirez*.[41] The defendants contended that under *TransUnion*, plaintiffs could not base their Article III standing "on regulatory noncompliance or an allegedly increased risk of harm stemming from regulatory noncompliance."[42] The trial court disagreed with the defendants' reliance on *TransUnion*, holding that the defendants failed to persuade the court that *TransUnion* applied to strip the plaintiffs of their standing to sue.

The court read the *TransUnion* decision to deny standing to uninjured plaintiffs who were not seeking to remedy any harm but instead were merely seeking to ensure a defendant's compliance with regulatory law. In addition, a plaintiffs' suit for damages with an unmaterialized risk of future harm was insufficient to confer Article III jurisdiction. The court rejected the defendants' invocation of the *TransUnion* decision, holding that the plaintiffs lawsuit was not based solely on statutory violation or a hypothetical risk of future harm.[43]

The Monsanto Company unsuccessfully asserted a standing challenge against the Los Angeles entity plaintiffs in litigation over stormwater contamination by defendants' PCBs. The defendants argued that the plaintiffs lacked

---

[37] *Id.* 130–33; *see* General Statutes §§ 7-148(c)(1)(A) and (7)(H)(ix).

[38] *Id.* at 130.

[39] *Id.*

[40] *Id.* at 131.

[41] In re Nat'l Prescription Opiate Litig., *supra* note 15, at 823, citing TransUnion LLC v. Ramirez, __U.S. __, 141 S.Ct. 2190, 210 L.Ed.2d 568 (2021).

[42] *Id.* at 823.

[43] *Id.*

standing to assert a non-representative public nuisance claim for property they did not own or had not been injured by PCBs.[44] The defendants contended that this failure was because there were multiple separately incorporated municipalities on the same permit to manage the area's stormwater, and that the failure to identify which specific property interests belonged to them was fatal to their public nuisance claim.

The court indicated that California recognized two types of claims: (1) actions for damages or abatement by one whose property was injuriously affected, or (2) an action brought in the name of the people of California to abate a public nuisance.[45] The court noted that the plaintiffs' claims were not sought on behalf of the people of California. Therefore, to have standing the plaintiffs needed to show that their property was injuriously affected by the defendants' alleged public nuisance. The court agreed that the plaintiffs could not bring non-representative nuisance claims for property they did not actually own. Nonetheless, on the facts, the court concluded that the plaintiffs had properly identified the properties that they owned and sustained the public nuisance claim as against the standing challenge.[46]

5.4 REGULATED CONDUCT AND STATUTORY COMPLIANCE

Defendants often raise the defense that they have engaged in conduct that does not violate any statutory provision, and in absence of a law prohibiting their conduct, the defendants cannot be held liable for a current nuisance. As a corollary, defendants contend that they cannot be held accountable for the manufacture, marketing, or distribution of a lawful product that complies with regulatory standards when placed in the stream of commerce. Like other defenses, courts have had mixed responses to defendants' objection that they have complied with regulatory provisions and have not violated a statutory duty.

A California appellate court rejected this compliance defense in its lead paint litigation. The defendants argued that residential lead paint could not be a public nuisance because it did not violate any regulatory standards and the court was required to follow state regulations declaring that intact lead paint was not a hazard.[47] In rejecting this argument, the court noted that the state health and safety code did not declare that intact lead paint was not a hazard.[48] Construing

---

[44] Los Angeles v. Monsanto Company, 2019 WL 13064885, at *10 (C.D. Cal. Nov. 21, 2019).
[45] *Id.* citing Cal. Code Civ. P. § 731.
[46] *Id.*
[47] Conagra, *supra* note 12, at 113.
[48] *Id.* citing California Health and Safety Code § 17920.10.

the statutory lead paint scheme, the court determined that nowhere in the statute had the legislature declared *any other type* of lead paint in buildings was not a hazard, was lawful, or was authorized by statute. In addition, the absence of a regulation or statute declaring lead paint to be unlawful did not bar a court from declaring it to be a public nuisance.[49]

In the Ohio national opioid litigation, defendants contended that the Ohio legislature comprehensively regulated the field of controlled substance dispensing and provided specific remedies that conflicted with the plaintiffs' common law public nuisance claim. The defendants argued that the controlled substances statute provided the exclusive avenue for relief for public nuisance claims.[50] The court concluded that the Ohio statute did not preclude the plaintiff's common law public nuisance claims.[51]

The court indicated that the Ohio legislature had not codified the law or provided a comprehensive statutory or regulatory scheme that precluded the plaintiffs' ability to seek public nuisance remedies at common law. The statute authorized the state attorney general, county prosecutors, and the state pharmacy board to bring actions to enjoin certain conduct mandated by federal or state law, which these actors declared to be a public nuisance. This statutory scheme did not indicate a legislative intent to preclude different entities from seeking common law relief based on the same conduct.[52]

The defendants argued as they were duly authorized to dispense controlled substances, federal and state law extensively regulated their conduct, and therefore, they could not be held liable for undertaking those activities. The court rejected this defense. The court held that safe harbor immunity from absolute nuisance liability was available only to persons or entities that performed their jobs in accordance with applicable licensing regulatory obligations. The court determined that the plaintiffs' evidence tended to show the defendants' material non-compliance with the Controlled Substance Act, which raised a triable issue of fact for the jury.[53]

Other courts have found that where federal and state laws regulated defendants' conduct, and defendants reasonably complied with those statutes, this precluded common law public nuisance claims based on the defendants' activities. Thus, the firearms defendants in the Chicago public nuisance

---

[49] Conagra, *supra* note 12, at 113.
[50] In re Nat'l Prescription Opiate Litig., *supra* note 15, at 814, citing ORC § 4729.35 (controlled substances act).
[51] *Id.* at 815.
[52] *Id.* at 814.
[53] *Id.* at 816.

litigation contended that their business practices could not be deemed unreasonable if the defendants complied with state and federal regulations.[54]

The Supreme Court of Illinois agreed with the gun manufacturer defendants. The court indicated that it was possible to create a public nuisance by conducting a lawful enterprise in an unreasonable manner. However, if federal and state law highly regulated an enterprise, then the proper framework for addressing unreasonableness required showing that (1) the defendant violated the applicable statutes or regulations, (2) the defendant was otherwise negligent in carrying out the enterprise, or (3) the law regulating the defendant was invalid.[55] The court determined that there was no suggestion that the federal or state regulations regarding firearms were invalid; that there were no allegations that the defendants had violated any applicable statutes; and that the plaintiffs failed to state a cause of action for public nuisance based on negligence. Hence, there could be no finding that the firearms defendants had acted unreasonably in carrying out their enterprise in compliance with statutory law and regulations.[56]

Similarly, in rejecting the state's opioid public nuisance claim against Johnson & Johnson as an opioid manufacturer, the Oklahoma Supreme Court noted that the regulation of prescription opioids belonged to federal and state legislatures and their agencies. For example, Oklahoma had enacted an Anti-Drug Diversion Act that required all dispensers of controlled dangerous substances to send information to a central depository controlled by the Oklahoma State Bureau of Narcotics and Dangerous Drug Control.[57] Therefore, the Johnson & Johnson defendants could not be subjected to a public nuisance claim for conduct regulated by statutory law.

5.5 NO PRIVATE RIGHT OF ACTION

Some defendants have challenged plaintiffs' public nuisance claims by alleging that a federal or state statute confers an exclusive private right of action on the plaintiffs to pursue relief for violations of the statutory law. The defendants in the Ohio national opioid litigation raised this defense, contending that the plaintiffs had a private right of action under the Federal Controlled Substances Act. According to the defendants, the Drug Enforcement Agency had the exclusive authority to enforce the provisions of the Controlled Substances Act,

---

[54] Chicago v. Beretta, *supra* note 1, at 1121.
[55] *Id.* at 1124.
[56] *Id.* at 1121–27.
[57] Oklahoma, *supra* note 10, at 728.

and therefore, the plaintiffs had no right to enforce the defendants' alleged failure to maintain effective controls over the diversion of opioid medication, by asserting a common law public nuisance claim.[58]

The trial court rejected this defense, holding that the plaintiffs were not seeking to enforce the defendants' statutory and regulatory duties. Therefore, the plaintiffs' nuisance claims did not rest on a private right of action under the Controlled Substances Act.[59]

In New York litigation aimed at the defendants' alleged illegal marketing and shipment of cigarettes over the internet, thereby depriving the city of tax revenues, the court held that the city could not assert a common law public nuisance claim predicated on a provision of the Public Health Law.[60] The court held that the public health law statute did not create an implied right of action.[61] To determine whether a plaintiff had an implied right of action, the court considered (1) whether the plaintiff was one of a class for whose particular benefit the statute was enacted, (2) whether recognition of a private right of action would promote the legislative purpose, and (3) whether creation of such a right would be consistent with the legislative scheme.[62]

Reviewing the legislative scheme relating to the regulation of cigarettes in the public health law statute, the court concluded that the legislature's clear intent regarding public health concerns were related to the prevention of underage smoking, and therefore, the legislature did not intend to authorize a public nuisance claim expressly or impliedly based on primarily on the defendants' alleged tax evasion.[63]

5.6 PRIMARY JURISDICTION; SEPARATION OF POWERS

The primary jurisdiction doctrine is a discretionary doctrine that permits courts to refer matters for administrative agency determination "whenever enforcement of the claim requires the resolution of issues which, under a regulatory scheme, have been placed within the special competence of an administrative body."[64] The doctrine is intended to promote the proper relationship of courts and administrative agencies charged with regulatory duties.

---

[58] In re Nat'l Prescription Opiate Litig., *supra* note 15, at 820.

[59] *Id.*

[60] New York. v. Smokes-Spirits.com, Inc., 12 N.Y.S.3d 616, 911 N.E.2d 834, N.Y.S.2d 772 (2009). *See* N.Y. Public Health Law § 1399-ll.

[61] *Id.* at 627–28.

[62] *Id.* at 627.

[63] *Id.* at 628.

[64] Nat'l Prescription Opiate Litig., *supra* note 15, at 821, quoting U.S. v. W. Pac. R.R. Co., 352 U.S. 59 (1956).

The U.S. Supreme Court has indicated that there is no fixed formula for the exercise of this discretion, but that several factors may inform a court's determination to confer primary jurisdiction on an administrative agency and make a referral: (1) to advance regulatory uniformity, (2) to answer a question within an agency's discretion, and (3) to benefit from technical or policy considerations within the agency's expertise.[65]

In the Ohio national opioid litigation, the defendants raised the primary jurisdiction argument and urged the court to refrain from adjudicating the plaintiffs' public nuisance claim, arguing that the plaintiffs' claims required the resolution of issues that fell within the special competence of the federal Drug Enforcement Agency. In particular, the defendants contended that the court should leave for the DEA's determination whether or not the defendants had complied with the Controlled Substances Act. The defendants argued, "The Court should stay its hand until [the] DEA has had the opportunity to pass upon the Plaintiffs' novel theory of the duties that the CSA imposes on the Defendants."[66] The defendants indicated that the plaintiffs' novel question of a pharmacy's corporate-level CSA dispensing obligations required the DEA's "expertise within a complicated statutory and regulatory framework."[67]

The trial court rejected the defendant's request for a discretionary referral to the DEA. The court indicated that the DEA had already provided guidance on the issue of which registrant entities had to provide effective controls and procedures concerning diversion of medications, and this included the defendant pharmacies. Moreover, the court was well-equipped and fully capable to apply established standards to the defendants' alleged conduct. Finally, the defendants failed to show that an agency referral would efficiently aid in resolving the plaintiffs' claims.[68]

Defendants also have raised arguments that a trial court's endorsement of a public nuisance claim violated separation of powers doctrine where, in so deciding, courts have breached or invaded the legitimate jurisdiction of legislative bodies. For example, defendants in the early lead paint litigation advanced this defense, arguing that the constitutional principle of separation of powers would be violated if the plaintiffs were permitted to sue outside the statutory framework of New Jersey's Lead Paint Statute, which imposed on property owners the responsibility of abating any lead paint

---

[65] In re Nat'l Prescription Opiate Litig., *supra* note 15, at 821, quoting Charvat v. EchoStar Satellite, LLC, 630 F.3d 459, 466 (6th Cir. 2010).

[66] In re Nat'l Prescription Opiate Litig., *supra* note 15, at 820–21.

[67] *Id.* at 821.

[68] *Id.* at 821–22.

hazards.[69] The defendants contended that the statute did not impose such responsibility on the paint manufacturers or distributors. Moreover, the statute conferred enforcement powers on the local health boards and not municipalities. Thus, to permit the plaintiffs' public nuisance claim to proceed would severely dislocate the remedial structure the legislature had enacted.[70]

The New Jersey appellate court disagreed with the trial court's holding that the plaintiffs' lead paint public nuisance lawsuit violated the separation of powers doctrine. The court suggested that the fundamental issue was whether the legislature, in enacting the Lead Paint Statute, demonstrated an intention that no other remedies than those in the statute might be pursued. Construing that statute, the appellate court concluded that nothing in the law purported to limit remedies to those specified in the statute.

The relief that the plaintiffs demanded – funding for future programs and compensation for municipal abatement and health care expenses – would not interfere with the municipalities' ongoing enforcement actions under the Lead Paint Statute. Therefore, the trial court erred in ruling that to permit the plaintiffs public nuisance claim to proceed would offend the constitutional principle of separation of powers by sanctioning a remedial process that was independent of the scheme the legislature created.[71]

Similarly, defendants in the California lead paint litigation interposed a separation of powers argument on appeal from a trial court's order requiring abatement of deteriorated interior lead paint, contending that the court's order violated the separation of powers doctrine.[72] The defendants argued that the state legislature had rejected a bill that would have declared the presence of lead in a residence to be a public nuisance and instead had enacted a statute that permitted owners to maintain intact lead-based paint in their residence.[73] Therefore, the court's order had violated the separation of powers doctrine by countermanding what the statute legislature intended through statutory enactment.

The California appellate court rejected this separation of powers argument, holding that the defendants misrepresented the legislative history of lead paint legislation by grounding their argument on a proposed bill that the legislature declined to enact. Instead, the court observed, the enacted bill was directed towards lead paint hazard abatement. The legislature's rejection of the proposed statute was "therefore not a rejection of the potential for a court to

---

[69] In re Lead Paint, 2002 WL 31474528, **4, 7-12 (N.J. Sup. Ct. Nov. 4, 2002) (Law Div.); In re Lead Paint Litig., 2005 WL 1994172, at *5 (Aug. 17, 2005).

[70] *Id.*

[71] *Id.* at 5–6.

[72] Conagra, *supra* note 12, at 115.

[73] *Id.*

concluded that certain conditions created by lead paint in the interiors of residences and posing imminent danger to children were public nuisances."[74]

5.7 PENALIZING LAWFUL CONDUCT

Defendants often raise the objection that they may not be held liable in a public nuisance lawsuit for the lawful production and sale of a non-defective product. This contention is typically based on the defendants' argument that plaintiffs' public nuisance claims actually are product liability claims repackaged as a public nuisance. Firearms and opioid defendants frequently have raised this defense when sued for public nuisance because of the harmful community effects of their activities.

The Supreme Court of Illinois declined to extend public nuisance liability to gun manufacturers based on this theory.[75] The court held that a products liability claim against a defendant who lawfully manufactured and sold a non-defective product must fail. The court further admitted that although the legislature had enacted various statutes declaring practices and conduct to constitute a public nuisance, "We have no indication from the legislature that it would be inclined to impose public nuisance liability for the sale of a product that may be possessed by legally by some persons in some parts of the state."[76]

In contrast, defendants in the Ohio national opioid litigation failed in their efforts to challenge the public nuisance claim against them on the grounds that defendants could not be held liable for the lawful sale of a non-defective product. The defendants contended that the plaintiffs were seeking to penalize them for lawful conduct, in violation of preemption and due process principles. The defendants argued that they could not be held liable for dispensing activities that the federal Drug Enforcement Agency had authorized.[77]

The court rejected this defense, holding that the defendant's argument rested on a false premise; to wit, that the plaintiffs' claim was based on the defendants' lawful conduct. Instead, the court pointed out, the plaintiffs' allegations were premised on the defendant's alleged unlawful conduct in violating their obligations to provide effective measures to detect illicit distribution and diversion of the medications, and/or intentionally contributing to an oversupply of the highly addictive drugs in the community. The defendants' arguments, then, could not apply to public nuisance claims based on unlawful conduct.[78]

[74] *Id.* at 115–16.
[75] Chicago v. Beretta, *supra* note 1, at 1119.
[76] *Id.* at 1121.
[77] In re Nat'l Prescription Opiate Litig., *supra* note 15, at 820.
[78] *Id.* at 820.

5.8 ECONOMIC LOSS DOCTRINE

Defendants have raised the economic loss doctrine as a bar to plaintiffs' claims for damages in public nuisance litigation. Twenty-eight states have adopted the majority view of the economic loss doctrine, which posits that a purchaser of a defendant's product cannot recover in a tort action against the manufacturer for solely economic loss due to a product defect, or when the negligence of others results in purely economic loss. To subject a product manufacturer for economic losses resulting from a product malfunction would make the manufacturer a guarantor that its products would continue to function satisfactorily throughout its productive life. These claims are better handled by contract law, rather than tort law.

In contrast, seventeen states have adopted a minority view of the economic loss doctrine, which permits recovery in tort actions for purely economic losses. Because various jurisdictions have adopted different approaches to the economic loss doctrine, this split in authority has resonated in judicial reception to the invocation of the economic loss doctrine in public nuisance litigation.

Defendants in the Chicago firearms litigation successfully raised the economic loss doctrine as a bar to the plaintiffs' entity public nuisance claims.[79] Citing the *Restatement (Second)*, the Illinois Supreme Court noted that the *Restatement* appeared to limit the recovery of economic damages in public nuisance suits to individual plaintiffs so affected by a public nuisance that they had standing to bring an action.[80] The court further noted that Illinois precedent concluded that there was no reason to treat private nuisance claims differently from other torts – in which case, the economic loss doctrine would apply even to bar claims brought by individuals alleging a public nuisance cause of action. But because Chicago's governmental entities brought the public nuisance lawsuit on behalf of their citizens, the court held that the economic loss doctrine did not permit an award of solely economic damages to the public entities in their public nuisance action.[81]

In contrast, other courts have declined to recognize defendants' invocation of the economic loss doctrine as a bar to public nuisance litigation. For example, the defendants in the national opioid litigation raised the economic loss doctrine as a bar to the plaintiffs' public nuisance claims, relying on the *Restatement (Third) or Torts: Liability for Economic Harm*.[82] The court

---

[79] Chicago v. Beretta, *supra* note 1, at 1139–43.

[80] *Id.* at 1143, citing *Restatement (Third) of Torts* § 821C(1) (1979). Standing would need to be conferred under the special injury rule.

[81] Chicago v. Beretta, *supra* note 1 at 1043.

[82] In re Nat'l Prescription Opiate Litig., *supra* note 15, at 824. In particular, the defendants relied on § 8 cmt. g.

rejected the defendants' invocation of the economic loss doctrine, holding that their reliance on the *Restatement (Third)* was misplaced. The court noted that § 8 of the *Restatement* applied only to claims for economic loss brought by a private party who had suffered an injury distinct in kind from those suffered by the general community. Moreover, § 8 expressly recognized the authority of governmental entities to pursue public nuisance claims.[83] Ohio case law clearly and uniformly limited the economic loss doctrine to negligence-based nuisance claims and did not apply it to intentional torts, such as the intentional conduct alleged by the plaintiffs in the opioid litigation.[84]

5.9 MUNICIPAL COST RECOVERY DOCTRINE

Defendants often invoke the municipal cost recovery doctrine as another bar to plaintiffs' remediation under a public nuisance theory. The rule sometimes is referred to as the "free public services doctrine." The municipal cost recovery rule is a common law doctrine that generally posits that plaintiffs may not recover, as damages, for municipal costs and expenditures a municipality ordinarily expends as part of its ongoing governmental functions, budgeted by the municipality.

Thus, defendants frequently argue that the rule bars recovery of municipal expenses incurred, not by reason of an accident or emergency necessitating the normal provision of police, fire, and emergency services, but to remedy public harm caused by a defendants' intentional persistent course of deceptive conduct. Like all other defenses raised in the twenty-first century public nuisance litigation, this defense has met with mixed judicial reception.

The Illinois Supreme Court, in the Chicago firearms litigation, concluded that the municipal cost recovery doctrine served as a bar to the governmental entities' public nuisance claim. The court indicated that the result it reached concerning the economic loss doctrine applied with equal force to the municipal cost recovery rule. Thus, public expenditures made in the performance of governmental functions were not recoverable in tort.

The court further observed that jurisdictions that had adopted this rule based it, in part, on the constitutional doctrine of separation of powers.[85] The court explained that governmental entities had allocation schemes of liability for damages resulting from the costs of municipal emergency services, in response to communal disasters. Where the government provided such services and the costs were spread by taxes, the tortfeasor did not expect a

---

[83] *Id.* citing *Restatement (Third) of Torts: Liability for Economic Harm*, § 8 cmt. a.
[84] *Id.*
[85] Chicago v. Beretta, *supra* note 1, at 1143–44.

demand for reimbursement.[86] Hence, defendants' expectations of potential business would be upset if an entirely new scheme of liability were imposed when a new tort doctrine emerged. The court concluded that a fair and sensible system for spreading costs already existed regarding municipal services.[87]

The municipal cost recovery rule has proven to be a relatively weak defense to public nuisance claims since the early twenty-first century when defendants began to assert this challenge. In 2002, the Ohio Supreme Court determined that the municipal recovery rule did not bar plaintiffs' recovery of governmental costs resulting from the firearms defendants ongoing conduct in manufacturing, marketing, selling, and distributing firearms. The court held that the costs of the plaintiffs' governmental services were recoverable to the extent that they exceeded the ordinary costs of providing those services and evidence established that these excessive costs were incurred due to the defendants' violation of state law.[88]

In 2005, in the New Jersey lead paint litigation, an appellate court similarly concluded that a trial court erred in holding that the plaintiffs' public nuisance claim was barred by the municipal cost recovery doctrine.[89] Citing New Jersey precedent, the court opined that the municipal cost recovery rule should not apply to claims alleging an ongoing nuisance where defendants' repeated course of conduct required a municipality to expend substantial governmental funds on a continuous basis. In addition, there was authority that the municipal cost recovery rule had no application where the governmental entity sought to recover damages for the costs of abating the nuisance.[90] The court endorsed criticism of the municipal cost recover rule, "given the economic realities faced by cities, and the unfairness of the notion that taxpayers must subsidize the conduct of tortfeasors."[91]

In the Ohio national opioid litigation, the opioid defendants challenged the plaintiffs' public nuisance claims based on the municipal cost recovery doctrine.[92] The trial judge determined that the municipal cost recover rule did not bar the plaintiff tribes and counties from recovering costs and expenses incurred in dealing with the opioid crisis in their communities. The plaintiffs alleged misconduct by the opioid manufacturers, distributors, and pharmacies

---

[86] *Id.* at 1144, citing Flagstaff v. Atchison, Topeka & Santa Fe Ry. Co., 719 F.2d 322, 323 (9th Cir. 1983).

[87] *Id.*

[88] Cincinnati v. Beretta U.S.A. Corp., 95 Ohio St.3d 416, 768 N.E.2d 1136, 1149–50 (2002).

[89] In re Lead Paint, *supra* note 69, at **14–15.

[90] *Id.* at *8, citing James v. Arms Technology, Inc., 359 N.J. Super. 291, 326–27 (App. Div. 2003).

[91] *Id.*

[92] In re Nat'l Prescription Opiate Litig., *supra* note 15, at 825.

had created and maintained an opioid epidemic. The plaintiffs sought damages attributable to the defendants' misconduct, including costs of emergency, law enforcement, and criminal justice services.[93]

The court declined to bar public nuisance claims based on this defense. In holding that the municipal cost recovery rule did not bar the plaintiffs' public nuisance claim for damages relief, the judge indicated: "The current trend among state court judges' ruling in opioid-related cases around the country is that the municipal recovery cost rule does not apply when, as alleged here, an ongoing and persistent course of intentional misconduct creates an unprecedented, man-made crisis that a governmental entity plaintiffs could not have reasonably anticipated as part of its normal operating budget for municipal, county, or in this case, tribal services."[94]

Other courts involved in opioid public nuisance litigation similarly declined to apply the municipal cost recovery rule to deny plaintiffs the opportunity to recover costs and expenses incurred in addressing the consequences of the opioid epidemic in their communities. In New York state, for example, multiple counties sued opioid defendants alleging that the defendants' deceptive marketing campaign fueled the opioid crisis, causing the municipalities to spend millions of dollars for employees' and Medicaid beneficiaries' prescriptions, as well as forcing the counties to pay the costs of implementing opioid treatment programs, purchasing naloxone to treat overdoses, and combating opiate-related criminal activities. The court held that the municipal cost recovery rule did not bar the counties' public nuisance claims, concluding that to hold otherwise "would distort the doctrine beyond recognition."[95]

A federal appellate court held that "the cost of public services for protection from fire or safety hazards is to be borne by the public as a whole, not assessed against the tortfeasor who negligence creates the need for the service."[96] However, the court further indicated that recovery of damages was permitted where the acts of a private party created a public nuisance which the government sought to abate.[97]

---

[93] In re Nat'l Prescription Opiate Litig. – Muscogee (Creek) Nation, 2019 WL 2468267, at *8 (N.D. Ohio Apr. 1, 2019), report and recommendation adopted in part, rejected in part, 2019 WL 3737023 (N.D. Ohio June 13, 2019); *see also* In re Nat'l Prescription Opiate Litig. – Summit County, 2018 WL 4895856, at *10 (N.D. Ohio Oct. 5, 2018), report and recommendation adopted in part, and rejected in part, 2018 WL 6628898 (N.D. Ohio Dec. 19, 2018).

[94] In re Nat'l Prescription Opiate Litig. – Muscogee (Creek) Nation, *supra* note 93, at *1.

[95] In re Opioid Litig., 2018 WL 3115102, at *10. (N.Y. Sup. June 18, 2018).

[96] In re JUUL Labs, *supra* note 30, at 643, citing Flagstaff v. Atchison, Topeka & Santa Fe., *supra* note 86, at 323.

[97] *Id.*

In 2020, following the opioid decisions disallowing a municipal cost recovery defense, a California federal district ruled likewise; the court held that the municipal cost recovery rule did not bar seven government entities from seeking monetary damages from the JUUL defendants for recovery of their expenses in addressing the e-cigarette vaping crisis in schools.[98] The court held that the plaintiffs had plausibly alleged damages that were not a result of a single, discrete incident that a government could reasonably expect to incur.

Rather, the damages were a result of an ongoing and persistent deceptive campaign and intentional targeting of youth that led to expenses that the municipalities and school boards could not reasonably have anticipated to incur.[99] The court held that JUUL's misconduct forced school districts to devote and divert resources to deal with the e-cigarette crisis. The plaintiffs incurred costs for counseling, training, educating, and disciplining students, as well as physical modifications to school properties to deal with disposing of hazardous waste.[100]

5.10 ONGOING NUISANCE

Several defendants have sought dismissal of plaintiffs' public nuisance litigation on the grounds that the plaintiffs must demonstrate an *ongoing* public nuisance, and the failure to do so mandates dismissal of the claim. The defendants in the Ohio national opioid litigation advanced this argument. The defendants contended that the plaintiffs alleged a current illicit opioid crisis, but all that the defendants had ever done was to dispense FDA-approved prescription opioids. Thus, having ceased the alleged misconduct, the defendants were not responsible for the subsequent consequences of an over-supply and diversion of the drugs into illegitimate markets.[101]

Citing the *Restatement (Second)*, the court disagreed. The court held that "a nuisance may result either from harm caused by human activity or by a physical condition that results from the activity and continues after the conduct leading to the condition ceases."[102] The plaintiffs' assertion that the public nuisance was continuing fit within the *Restatement* definition.[103] The court concluded that even if, as the defendants contended, they discontinued the conduct that led to the creation and existence of the nuisance, they were still subject to liability for abatement of any ongoing consequential effects of the nuisance they created.[104]

---

[98] In re JUUL Labs, *supra* note 30, at 645.
[99] *Id.*
[100] *Id.*
[101] In re Nat'l Prescription Opiate Litig., *supra* note 15, at 826.
[102] *Id.* citing *Restatement (Second of Torts)*, § 821(A), cmt. b.
[103] *Id. See also Restatement (Second of Torts)*, § 821(A), cmt. e.
[104] In re Nat'l Prescription Opiate Litig., *supra* note 15, at 826.

5.11 UNCONSTITUTIONAL VAGUENESS

The Oklahoma Supreme Court, in rejecting expansion of public nuisance doctrine to embrace litigation against the opioid manufacturer Johnson & Johnson, noted that the state plaintiff had presented the courts with a novel theory of public nuisance liability for the marketing and selling of a legal product, based on the acts not of one manufacturer, but of an entire industry.[105] The court was unconvinced that such actions amounted to public nuisance under Oklahoma law. The court suggested that Oklahoma public nuisance claims addressed "discrete, localized problems, not policy problems." Thus, "erasing the traditional limits on nuisance liability leaves Oklahoma's public nuisance statute impermissibly vague."[106]

5.12 THE COMMERCE CLAUSE

Some defendants sued in public nuisance actions have alleged sweeping constitutional Commerce Clause challenges, arguing that Article I, § 8, clause 3 of the U.S. Constitution grants exclusive power to Congress "[t]o regulate Commerce ... among the several states," and judicial decisions upholding nuisance claims violated this provision.

In the early lead paint litigation, a trial court held that the plaintiffs' lawsuit wrongfully sought to regulate lawful conduct occurring outside New Jersey's borders.[107] "The Commerce Clause ... precludes the application of a state statute to commerce that takes place wholly outside of the States borders, whether or not the commerce had effects within the State."[108] "Only Congress can enact a policy for the entire nation, and it is clear that no state can do so, even to impose its policies on neighboring states. Thus, the governmental entities may not reach out to other states and impose their policy choices on them ... the court must respect the balance between the branches of government. It cannot act as a superlegislature."[109]

A New Jersey appellate court rejected this defensive Commerce Clause theory. The court noted that courts had rejected the Commerce Clause theory in gun manufacturer cases in which governmental entities or private persons asserted public nuisance claims. In an early firearms lawsuit, an appellate court rejected the defendants' Commerce Clause argument, holding it meritless.[110]

---

[105] Oklahoma, *supra* note 10, at 731.
[106] *Id.*
[107] *See* In re Lead Paint, *supra* note 69, at *13.
[108] *Id.*
[109] In re Lead Paint Litig, supra note 69, at *6.
[110] Ileto v. Glock, Inc., 349 F.3d 1191, 1217 (9th Cir. 2003).

The court held that the state's interest in protecting the health and safety of its residents was clearly legitimate and whatever indirect burden an award of damages to the plaintiffs might have on the defendants, this did not approximate the public interest in protecting Californians' health and safety.[111] Moreover, the Commerce Clause was not designed to prevent states from protecting state citizens from the tortious activity of those engaged in interstate commerce whose products or activities put the state's citizens at risk.[112]

5.13 PUBLIC POLICY GROUNDS

The developing state and federal opioid decisions have framed the competing public policy issues involved in the emerging doctrine of public nuisance law, with conflicting opinions concerning the expansion of public nuisance law to embrace mass tort claims. Some courts have emphatically rejected the expansion of public nuisance law to encompass mass tort claims; other courts have been willing to exercise a flexible approach to extending the public nuisance doctrine to reach these types of group harms.

In 2021, the Oklahoma Supreme Court, in a lawsuit against Johnson & Johnson for the manufacturing, marketing, and selling of prescription opioids, concluded that the state could not assert a public nuisance claim against the opioid manufacturers under Oklahoma law.[113] The court surveyed 100 years of public nuisance litigation and determined that courts had limited Oklahoma's public nuisance statute to defendants' commission of crimes constituting a public nuisance, causing physical injury to property, or participating in offensive activity that rendered property uninhabitable.[114] The court contended that to permit public nuisance claims to address policy problems such as the opioid epidemic would render Oklahoma's nuisance statute impermissibly vague.[115]

Furthermore, the Supreme Court deferred policymaking to the legislative and executive branches and rejected the trial court's unprecedented expansion of public nuisance law. The court noted that expansion of public nuisance law allowed courts to manage public policy matters that legislative and executive branches should handle; "these branches of government were more

---

[111] *Id.* at *7.
[112] *Id.* citing N.A.A.C.P. v. AcuSport, Inc., 271 F. Supp. 435, 464 (E.D.N.Y. 2003); Cincinnati v. Beretta, *supra* note 88, at 1150.
[113] Hunter v. Johnson & Johnson, 499 P.3d 719, 723–31 (Okla. 2021).
[114] *Id.* at 724.
[115] *Id.* at 731. The court noted that North Dakota and South Dakota courts had rejected public nuisance claims against the same defendants for the same conduct complained of in the Oklahoma opioid litigation. *See Id.* at 730, citing cases.

capable than courts to balance the competing interests at play in societal problems."[116] The court indicated that the district court had gone too far in step-
ping into the shoes of the legislature in creating and funding government
programs designed to address social and health issues.[117]

In a similar vein, Federal Judge Alex Kozinski dissented on public policy
grounds in an appeal from a California federal firearms litigation that permitted a public nuisance claim to proceed against gun manufacturers and
distributors by individual victims and survivors of a gunman's assault.[118] He
delineated several policy reasons for not extending public nuisance liability in
the context of the underlying gun litigation:

> Imposing novel tort theories on economic activity significantly affects the
> risks of engaging in that activity, and thus alters the costs and availability of
> the activity within the forum jurisdiction. In effect, it is a form of regulation
> administered through the courts rather than state regulatory agencies. It is,
> moreover, a peculiarly blunt and capricious method of regulation, depend-
> ing as it does on the vicissitudes of the legal system, which makes results
> highly unpredictable in probability and magnitude. Courts should therefore
> be chary of adopting new broad theories of liability, lest they undermine the
> democratic process through which the people normally decide whether, and
> to what degree, activities should be fostered or discouraged within the state.[119]

Other courts, however, have endorsed or reached the opposite conclusion,
embracing an expansive view of public nuisance theory to reach defendants'
interference and consequent harm against communities resulting from the
defendants' activities. Thus, the Ohio court overseeing the national opioid litigation indicated that Ohio's Supreme Court recognized that public nuisance
law was broad enough to include public nuisance claims against gun manufacturers. Citing Cincinnati's litigation against the Beretta corporation, the
Ohio court determined that "although we have often applied public nuisance
law to actions connected to real property or statutory or regulatory violations
involving public health or safety, we have never held that public nuisance law
is strictly limited to these types of actions."[120] The federal court in the national
opioid litigation – applying Ohio precedent – concluded that Oklahoma law
was different and inapplicable.

---

[116] *Id.* at 724.
[117] *Id.*
[118] Ileto v. Glock, Inc., *supra* note 110, at 868 (9th Cir. 2004) (Kozinski, J., dissenting from denial of rehg. en banc).
[119] *Id.*
[120] In re Nat'l Prescription Opiate Litig., *supra* note15, at 815, citing Cincinnati v. Beretta, *supra* note 88, at 1142 (2002).

6

Expanding Public Nuisance

Remedies beyond Injunctions and
Abatement to Monetary Damages

As some courts in the twenty-first century embraced an expanded concept of public nuisance law, the remedies available to plaintiffs and their attorneys have proved problematic. In typical mass tort class action litigation that counsel pursue under conventional tort, contract, and statutory theories, plaintiffs may seek compensatory and punitive damages, injunctive and declaratory relief, attorney fees, and any other relief a court deems appropriate. As mass tort litigation evolved, courts have approved new forms of relief such as medical monitoring.

In the new era of emerging public nuisance mass tort claims, courts have limited remedies to existing narrow doctrines of relief. Traditionally, at common law, public officials asserting public nuisance claims typically were limited to equitable remedies of an abatement or injunction of the nuisance.[1] It was difficult for public entities to seek legal remedies of compensatory or punitive damages. As public nuisance law developed, courts carved out a complicated exception for individuals asserting public nuisance seeking a damage remedy for themselves.

The narrow scope of remedies for public nuisance claims, then, have presented challenges for governmental entities seeking reimbursement for the costs in addressing the effects of public nuisance harms on their communities. Many governmental entities have pursued public nuisance claims that request payment to recoup not only past costs and expenses, but to provide funds for ongoing public education initiatives, as well as the costs of municipal services to maintain the public health and safety. In addition, to the extent that private attorneys ally with state attorneys in pursuing such litigation, private counsel have an expectation of receiving attorney fees.

Public nuisance remedies, then, focus on two distinct problems and claimants: (1) public officials seeking municipal remediation on behalf of their

---

[1] *Restatement (Second) of Torts* § 821C (1979).

citizens, and (2) individuals seeking compensation for harms resulting from a public nuisance.[2] The historical limitation on individual's ability to obtain damages in the context of a public nuisance action focused on the special injury requirement; the special injury requirement foreclosed public nuisance actions by product users who were unable to claim distinctive injuries.

Courts have followed the *Restatement (Second)* approach to the role of remedies in public nuisance litigation, focusing on the status of the plaintiff seeking relief. Thus, courts have recognized that remedies for public nuisance vary between the public and an individual plaintiff. Public officials who are authorized to pursue public nuisance litigation to vindicate communal rights may seek criminal penalties or civil actions to abate the nuisance. A private plaintiff, on the contrary, may not necessarily sue to vindicate a public right, but to seek compensation of a special injury the individual has sustained, apart from the interference with a public right.[3]

The plaintiffs' inappropriate pleading of its public nuisance remedy may result in a failure to state a public nuisance claim. For example, in the New Jersey lead paint litigation the New Jersey Supreme Court concluded that the governmental plaintiffs failed to state a public nuisance claim in part because their complaint sought damages rather than an abatement remedy. As such, they fell outside the scope of remedies available to a public entity plaintiff. The municipal entities could only proceed in the manner of private plaintiffs.[4] As such, the governmental entities would have to identify a special injury to which an award of damages could attach, but they failed to do so. All the injuries the plaintiffs identified were general to the public.[5]

Perhaps the most significant development in mass tort public nuisance litigation has been judicial recognition of a broader concept of abatement funds that allows governmental entities to obtain monetary payments to remedy harms experienced by their municipalities. In embracing this expanded concept of remediation, courts have indicated that they may consider social utility when considering public nuisance remedies.

6.1 COMMUNAL REMEDIES OF ABATEMENT AND INJUNCTIVE RELIEF

The traditional remedy for liability for a public nuisance is abatement of the nuisance or an injunction, and plaintiffs commonly have pleaded this relief

---

[2] In re Lead Paint Litig., 191 N.J. 405, 502, 924 A.2d 484 (N.J. 2007).
[3] *Restatement (Second) of Torts* § 821C(2) cmt. a.
[4] In re Lead Paint Litig., *supra* note 2, at 502.
[5] *Id.* at 503.

in their public nuisance actions. The controversy in seeking an abatement remedy centers on whether plaintiffs may seek and are entitled to monetary damages in an abatement remedy. The manner in which plaintiffs plead their public nuisance action and request for relief may determine whether a court will sustain the public nuisance claim.

A California lead paint public nuisance suit illustrates the difficulties courts encounter in interpreting the nature of a plaintiffs' request for an abatement remedy. Several California municipalities brought a representative public nuisance claim against lead paint manufacturers. The remedy the plaintiffs sought was abatement "from all public and private homes and property so affected throughout the State of California."[6]

The defendants argued that the plaintiffs could not plead a public nuisance claim against product manufacturers that created health hazards because such harms were remediable only through a products liability action. The plaintiffs could not obtain the abatement remedy they sought.[7] The defendants contended that California's general nuisance statute expressly permitted an individual to recover damages in a public nuisance suit, but did not grant a damage remedy in a representative action to abate a public nuisance. Thus, the plaintiffs in this representative action could not avoid the rule by seeking damages in the form of the costs of the abatement. The trial court agreed and granted defendants' demurrer to the public nuisance claim.

On appeal, the California appellate court reversed the demurrer, noting that the plaintiffs' representative action was not seeking damages for injury or the cost of remediating their property. Because the plaintiffs did not seek damages but rather abatement, they could obtain relief before the hazards caused any physical injury or physical damage to property.[8] While the municipalities could not recover damages or reimbursement for past remediation of lead paint hazards, the representative action seeking future abatement did not suffer from any apparent infirmity.[9]

The appellate court rejected the defendants' contention that they lacked the ability to abate the hazard because they did not own or control the buildings in which the lead paint was located. The court noted that the defendants could cite to no authority for the proposition that a complaint alleging facts that stated an abatement claim for public nuisance was demurrable on that ground. Abatement was accomplished by an injunction that was proper and

---

[6] Santa Clara v. Atlantic Richfield Co., 137 Cal. App.4th 292, 137 Cal. App.4th 292, 304–05 (2006).
[7] *Id.* at 324.
[8] *Id.* at 309–10.
[9] *Id.* at 329.

suitable based on the facts of each case. There was no authority for the proposition that the plaintiffs carried a burden of affirmatively pleading that the defendants had the ability to abate.[10]

Several courts, however, have taken a narrower view of the availability of abatement as a remedy for public nuisance, rejecting the claim where defendants are unable to accomplish the requested abatement. Thus, some courts have declined to afford this remedy where the defendant is no longer in control of the instrumentality allegedly causing the harm, and hence, lacks the ability to effectuate a meaningful abatement.

Relatively early in the history of asbestos litigation, a Michigan appellate court held that the trial court should have been granted a summary judgment dismissal of the plaintiffs' public nuisance claim by the Detroit Board of Education against various asbestos manufacturers.[11] In addition to holding that manufacturers, sellers, or installers of defective products could not be held liable on a nuisance theory for injuries caused by a product defect, the court further held that nuisance cases almost universally concerned the use or condition of property, not products.[12]

A defendant's liability for a nuisance could not extend to where an object constituting part of the nuisance or the hazardous condition was out of the defendants' control. To be actionable, the defendants must have control over the nuisance at the time of the injury. This was not true for the Detroit Board of Education's lawsuit; the defendants gave up ownership and control of their products when they were sold to the plaintiffs. Thus, the defendants presently lacked the legal right to abate whatever hazards their products might pose; ownership and possession lay exclusively with the plaintiffs. The plaintiffs' proper remedies were product liability actions for negligence or breach of warranty.[13]

The Supreme Court of Rhode Island reached this conclusion in the state's lead paint litigation.[14] The Rhode Island court recognized that the principal remedy for the harm caused by a nuisance was abatement or an injunction, but the defendant's control over the instrumentality at the time the damage occurred was critical. Where defendants, at the time of manufacture and sale, no longer had the power to abate the nuisance a basic element of the public nuisance tort was absent, and the plaintiffs could not succeed on this theory of relief.[15] The court rejected the plaintiffs' public nuisance claim based in part

[10] *Id.* at 330.
[11] Detroit Bd. of Educ. v. Celotex Corp., 196 Mich. App. 694, 494 N.W.2d 513 (Mich. App. 1992).
[12] *Id.* at 521.
[13] *Id.*
[14] Rhode Island v. Lead Industries Ass'n, Inc., 951 A.2d 428 (R.I. 2008).
[15] *Id.* at 449.

on the impracticability of an abatement remedy, a conclusion reached by the New Jersey Supreme Court in a parallel lead paint public nuisance litigation.[16]

In some cases where plaintiffs have acknowledged that an abatement remedy would not be feasible, they have instead simply pleaded for compensatory relief. In litigation brought by Illinois cities and counties against firearms manufacturers, distributors, and dealers, the plaintiffs claimed more than $433 million in operating expenses attributable to the alleged public nuisance between 1994–98.[17] This amount included expenses for emergency communications, emergency response, health care provided to victims of gun violence, police investigations, and the prosecution and defense of persons accused of illegal possession and use of firearms. The plaintiffs also sought punitive damages against each defendant.[18] The plaintiffs contended that because abatement of the alleged firearms nuisance was not feasible, they were entitled to recover damages "representing the cost of providing governmental services made necessary by the widespread unlawful possession and use of firearms."[19]

The Supreme Court of Illinois rejected plaintiffs' damage efforts. The court first noted that it was generally conceded that a nuisance was remediable by an injunction or a suit for damages. But, citing the *Restatement (Second)* on nuisance remedies, the court noted that no mention was made of the ability of public officials or entities to recover damages in an action for public nuisance brought on behalf of the public.[20]

The court further rejected the plaintiffs' claims to compensatory damage based on the economic loss doctrine, analogizing the purpose of that doctrine to the special injury requirement for recovery of damages in public nuisance litigation.[21] The court concluded that the damages the plaintiffs sought were solely economic damages and, as such, were not permitted to be awarded to the public entities in their public nuisance action.[22] The court further concluded that this result was consistent with the outcome mandated by the municipal recover rule, which held that public expenditures in the performance of governmental functions were not recoverable in tort.[23]

The court concluded that even if the plaintiffs properly pleaded a cause of action in public nuisance, money damages would not be available to them

---

[16]   In re Lead Paint Litig., *supra* note 2, at 499.

[17]   *Id.* at 1138.

[18]   *Id.* at 1139.

[19]   Chicago v. Beretta, 213 Ill.2d 351, 821 N.E.2d 1099, 1139 (Ill. 2004).

[20]   *Id.* citing *Restatement (Second) of Torts* § 821C and comments.

[21]   *Id.* at 1141.

[22]   Chicago, *supra* note 19, at 1143.

[23]   *Id.* at 1144.

because the claimed damages did not represent the actual cost of abatement of the nuisance or for compensation for actual harm to the city's or county's property.[24]

Finally, the court suggested that if the state legislature concluded that the costs of public services should be borne by the defendants whose conduct necessitated those services, rather than the taxpayer, then the legislature had the ability to enact a statute expressly authorizing the recovery from the defendants causing the nuisance.[25] In absence of statutory authorization, courts lacked the ability to impose these costs on defendants in municipal public nuisance litigation.

An Ohio federal district court similarly invoked the economic loss rule to disallow damages in a public nuisance litigation brought by Cleveland against numerous firms involved in securitizing subprime loans into mortgage-backed securities. The plaintiffs' theory of the case was that the defendants' activities resulted in increased property foreclosures, thereby creating a public nuisance. The plaintiffs sought the cost of monitoring, maintaining, and demolishing foreclosed properties, as well as the diminution in the city's property tax revenues. The court dismissed the plaintiffs' lawsuit holding that the economic loss rule applied to public nuisance actions under Ohio law, barring Cleveland's claim. The damages that Cleveland sought were purely economic, and the city failed to allege any injury to persons or property in which it had an interest.[26]

6.2 CONSTITUTIONAL CHALLENGES TO STATUTORY REMEDY SCHEMES

Defendants have challenged the ability of plaintiffs to seek remedies in addition to those provided by a statutory scheme for remediation of a public nuisance. A New Jersey appellate court upheld a trial court's approval of a remedial process that was independent of a legislative scheme for a public nuisance, holding that approval of additional remedies did not violate the constitutional principal of separation of powers.[27]

The New Jersey legislature enacted a lead paint statute that conferred on municipal health boards the power to abate public nuisances and to seek an injunction against continuance of a nuisance.[28] The statute authorized municipal health boards to detect and remediate any public nuisance caused

---

[24] *Id.* at 1147.
[25] *Id.*
[26] Cleveland v. Ameriquest Mortg. Securities, Inc., 621 F.Supp.2d 513, 522–24 (N.D. Ohio 2009).
[27] In re Lead Paint Litig., 2005 WL 1994172, *6 (Aug. 17, 2005).
[28] N.J.S.A. 26:3-46, 50, and 54.

by lead paint on surfaces accessible to children.[29] The health boards had the authority to investigate violations and enforce the Act, including ordering property owners to remove or cover up the paint. If the property owner failed to do so, the board had the power to abate the hazard itself and then recover the costs in a civil action against the property owner.[30]

Another statute, the Hotel and Multiple Dwelling Law, imposed a duty on property owners – but not on the local government – to abate nuisances in multiple dwellings.[31] In the context of this legislative scheme, the state attorney general had the power to sue to abate a public nuisance where the public interest was at stake.

Twenty-six governmental entities sued various lead paint manufacturers and distributors, seeking to recover the costs of detecting and removing lead paint, to provide care to lead-paint-poisoned residents, and to develop programs to educate residents of the hazards of lead paint.[32] The plaintiffs sought funding of future programs and compensating municipalities for their abatement and health care expenses. The trial court granted the defendants' motion to dismiss, concluding that the plaintiffs sought an "unwarranted and impermissible" expansion of their role as local governments acting on behalf of the public, by bringing a suit against the defendants "cloaked under the guise of public interest litigation."[33]

The defendants contended that the plaintiffs' action subverted New Jersey's statutory scheme for nuisance remediation if plaintiffs were allowed to sue and recover relief outside the lead paint statutory scheme. Such an action violated the constitutional doctrine of separation of powers between the legislative and judicial branches.[34] To permit the plaintiffs' lawsuit to continue would "severely dislocate" the remedial structure that the state legislature enacted to deal with lead paint hazards in dwellings.[35]

The New Jersey appellate court rejected the argument that the municipalities' public nuisance lawsuit violated separation of power doctrine. The court held that nothing in the lead paint statute limited lead paint remedies to those specified in the statute. Without any such express limitation, courts were required to assume that the lead paint statute was not intended to bar any common law remedy that was not inconsistent with the remedies authorized in the Act.[36]

---

[29] N.J.S.A 24:14A-5.
[30] N.J.S.A. 24:14-6-10.
[31] N.J.S.A. 55:13A-1 to 28.
[32] In re Lead Paint Litig., *supra* note 27, at *1-2.
[33] *Id.* at *1.
[34] *Id.*
[35] *Id.* at *5.
[36] *Id.*

The appellate court distinguished the plaintiffs' action from the statute's requirements, noting that different remedial tools looked to different responsible parties. The lead paint statute imposed an abatement duty on property owners, while the municipal plaintiffs' lawsuit demanded that the paint industry defendants compensate the cities for their expenditures caused by the defendants' creation of a public nuisance. Thus, the "civil lawsuit can proceed on a parallel track that need not ever intersect with the mechanisms set forth in the [l]ead [p]aint statute."[37]

The appellate court concluded that the plaintiffs' requested relief would not interfere with the municipalities' ongoing enforcement efforts under the lead paint statute, and their health boards remained free to sue property owners for the costs of removal. None of the statute's enforcement tools could be used against manufacturers or distributors. Therefore, the two remedial methods were complementary and not conflicting or duplicative.[38]

6.3 EXPANDING COMMUNAL REMEDIES: ABATEMENT FUNDS

Perhaps the most dramatic innovation in public nuisance litigation has been judicial recognition of abatement funds as an equitable remedy in mass tort public nuisance litigation. This endorsement of abatement funds and the possibility of large financial awards to governmental entities that may extend over several years and support an array of activities, has increased the attractiveness of such litigation to entity plaintiffs and trial attorneys.

In approving abatement funds, these decisions resonate in the gradual judicial acceptance of medical monitoring funds pursued under class action procedure. In the mass tort litigation arena, courts initially were unwilling to permit the creation of medical monitoring actions that were thinly disguised damage class actions. Instead, courts were willing to accept medical monitoring class actions pleaded as a form of equitable relief, characterized by court-sponsored and court-supervised medical monitoring funds. Courts approved medical monitoring class actions so long as moneys invested in these funds were not utilized to pay direct compensation to injured claimants. The concept of abatement funds for public nuisance claims appears to be developing along very similar conceptual lines.

The California Supreme Court in 2011 presaged the concept of an abatement fund in an early lead paint decision dealing with contingent fee arrangements in public nuisance litigation.[39] In analyzing the competing constitutional rights implicated in public nuisance representation, the court

---

[37] *Id.*
[38] *Id.*
[39] Santa Clara v. Superior Court, 50 Cal.4th 35, 112 Cal. Rptr.3d 697, 235 P.3d 21 (2011).

distinguished between cases involving only past acts, as opposed to litigation addressing ongoing nuisance.

Characterizing the lead paint litigation as involving ongoing marketing interests, the Supreme Court suggested that the trial court would be asked to determine whether the defendants should be held liable for the nuisance, and if so, how the nuisance should be abated. The Supreme Court indicated that the case would result, at most, in the defendants having to expend resources to abate the lead-paint nuisance they allegedly created, either by paying into a fund dedicated to that abatement purpose, or by undertaking the abatement themselves.[40]

In 2017, a California appellate court led the country in upholding and approving the imposition of an abatement fund on defendants found liable in a lead paint public nuisance litigation, citing with approval the California Supreme Court's earlier referral to the possibility of an abatement fund.[41] After a lengthy trial by ten California counties against the Conagra Grocery Products Company and other paint manufacturer defendants, the trial court found the defendants liable and ordered the defendants to pay $1.5 billion into a fund to be used to abate the public nuisance created by interior residential lead paint in those jurisdictions.[42]

The trial court's order required "abatement through the establishment of a fund, in the name of the People, dedicated to abating the public nuisance," that would be administered by the State of California "unless the State was 'unwilling or unable to do so.'"[43] The court ordered those defendants deposit funds into a specifically designated, dedicated, and restricted abatement fund.

The order did not contemplate or require or permit the deposit of those funds into the state treasury.[44] The defendants were held jointly and severally liable to pay into the fund, to be disbursed to the ten plaintiff jurisdictions. The remediation program was to last four years from the date of total payment by the defendants. The Superior Court of California, Santa Clara County, was to have continuing jurisdiction over the plan and its implementation.

On appeal, the defendants contended that the trial court's abatement order was invalid because it actually was a thinly disguised damage award to plaintiffs for unattributed past harm to private homes over which the defendants had no control.[45] In the defendants' view, the plaintiffs were barred from obtaining compensatory damages in a public nuisance lawsuit.

---

[40] *Id.* at 55–56.
[41] People v. Conagra Grocery Products Co., 227 Cal. Rptr.3d 499, 570, 17 Cal. App.5th 51 (2017).
[42] *Id.* at 514.
[43] *Id.*
[44] *Id.* at 570–71.
[45] *Id.* at 568.

In rejecting the defendants' challenge to the court-ordered abatement fund, the California appellate court rehearsed an array of common law propositions relating to remedies for public nuisance claims. Thus, a court of equity accomplished abatement of a public nuisance by means of an injunction suitable to the facts of each case. A public entity might not recover, in a public nuisance action, funds already expended to remediate a public nuisance. However, a court might order defendants to deposit funds in an abatement fund to be utilized to prospectively fund remediation of the public nuisance.[46]

The trial court's order directing the abatement fund was not a thinly disguised damages award. The court indicated that the distinction between an abatement order and a damages award was stark. Thus, an abatement order was an equitable remedy, while damages were a legal remedy. Generally, continuing nuisances were subject to abatement, while permanent nuisances were subject to damages. The sole purpose of an equitable remedy was to eliminate the hazard causing prospective harm to a plaintiff. An equitable remedy provided no compensation to a plaintiff for prior harm. Damages, in contrast, were directed at compensating a plaintiff for prior accrued harm resulting from a defendant's wrongful conduct.[47]

In the plaintiffs' lead paint litigation, the plaintiffs were not seeking damages to recover for any past accrued harm, or compensation of any kind. Rather, the plaintiffs were seeking the equitable remedy of abatement because the hazard created by the defendant was continuing to cause harm to children. The deposits into the abatement fund that the court required would not be utilized to pay anyone compensation for accrued harm, but solely to pay for the prospective removal of the hazards the defendants created.[48]

The appellate court concluded that the trial court made a reasonable decision to create a remediation fund that would be overseen by a knowledgeable receiver, and ultimately by the court. The term of the fund was limited to four years and the abatement funds that were not utilized would be returned to the defendants. The court could have chosen to have the defendants handle the remediation by themselves, "but such an order would have been difficult for the court to oversee and for the defendants to undertake."[49]

The California federal district court in the e-cigarette litigation expanded the concept of an abatement fund to extend to liability to a defendant's officers and directors.[50] After concluding that officers and directors could be held

---

[46] *Id.* at 568–69.
[47] *Id.* at 569.
[48] *Id.*
[49] *Id.*
[50] In re JUUL Labs., Inc, Marketing, Sales Practices, Prods. Liab. Litig., 497 F.Supp. 3d 552, 651–53 (N.D. 2020).

liable for a public nuisance, the court further indicated that an abatement order could include a requirement that defendants expend the money necessary to abate the nuisance.[51] The court noted that was exactly the relief that the governmental entities – school districts – sought: equitable relief to fund prevention education and addiction relief. If they were found liable, officers and directors would contribute to the abatement fund, which would be used to support various measures relating to the youth e-vaping epidemic.

Citing the California *Conagra Grocery* decision, the court noted that an abatement fund was not a thinly disguised damage award, but rather an equitable remedy designed to eliminate the nuisance.[52] Furthermore, the court indicated that even if the governmental entities could not seek injunctive relief from the defendants' officers and directors, the plaintiffs could seek equitable relief in the form of an abatement fund.[53]

While the California courts have led the way with upholding creation of monetary funds to abate public nuisance claims, other courts have simply rejected such approaches. In the Oklahoma state opioid litigation, after a thirty-three day trial, the court held the defendant Johnson & Johnson liable under Oklahoma's public nuisance statute for conducting a false, misleading, and dangerous marketing campaign about prescription opioids. The court ordered Johnson & Johnson to pay $465 million to fund one year of the state's abatement plan, appropriating money to twenty-one government programs to combat opioid abuse. When Johnson and Johnson appealed, the State cross-appealed arguing the Johnson & Johnson should be responsible to pay 20 years of the state's abatement plan, or approximately $9.3 billion to fund governmental programs.[54]

The Oklahoma Supreme Court held that public nuisance law did not provide a remedy for the harm of opioid addiction in Oklahoma. Addressing the lower court's imposition of its financial remedy on Johnson & Johnson, the Supreme Court indicated that the defendant could not abate the alleged nuisance. The condition – opioid use and addiction – would not cease to exist even if Johnson & Johnson paid for the state's abatement plan. The court held that "the State's Abatement Plan is not an abatement in that it does not stop the act or omission that constitutes a nuisance. The abatement is not the opioids themselves."[55] In addition, the Supreme Court held that the state's abatement plan was not an injunction to halt Johnson & Johnson's promotion and marketing of opioids; the defendant had ceased promoting opioids for several years.

---

[51] *Id.*
[52] *Id.* at 653, citing Conagra, *supra* note 41.
[53] *Id.*
[54] Oklahoma *ex rel.* Hunter, 499 P.3d 719, 722–23 (2021).
[55] *Id.* at 729.

Instead, the lower court's award to the state was to fund activities over which Johnson & Johnson had no control, such as multiple governmental programs for medical treatment, preventative services, investigatory and regulatory activities, and prosecutions for violation of Oklahoma laws on opioid distribution. The Supreme Court noted: "Our Court, over the past 100 years in deciding nuisance cases, has never allowed the State to collect a cash payment from a defendant that the district court line-item apportioned to address social, health, and criminal issues arising from conduct alleged to be a nuisance."[56]

6.4 INDIVIDUAL REMEDIES FOR DAMAGES: THE SPECIAL INJURY RULE

While some courts notably have made inroads on the possibility that governmental entities may recover compensatory or monetary damages as relief for a public nuisance, the twenty-first century judicial approach to individual monetary compensation has received a mixed reception from state and federal courts. The problem of individual relief for public nuisance is significant for mass tort public nuisance cases, where governmental actors may be remediated, but individuals suffering from the communal harm may or may not accomplish monetary relief. The primary reason for judicial resistance to awarding individual monetary relief in public nuisance actions is grounded in adherence to *Restatement (Second)* principles that govern awards to individuals seeking damages.

The *Restatement (Second)* sets forth the fundamental common law principles that a person seeking individual damages for a public nuisance must satisfy to obtain relief. In all twenty-first century public nuisance litigation where plaintiffs individually have sought compensatory relief, courts invariably cite and rely on the *Restatement (Second)* principles.[57]

English courts recognized the right of an individual to maintain a tort action in the context of a public nuisance as far back as the sixteenth century.[58] A person seeking individual relief had to show that the person suffered a particular harm distinguished from the harm caused to the public or public members exercising the same public right. The rationale for this rule was to protect the defendant from a multiplicity of actions that might result if every individual was free to sue for a common wrong.[59]

---

[56] *Id.*
[57] *Restatement (Second) of Torts* § 821C.
[58] *Id.* cmt. a.
[59] *Id.*

In defining the concept of a different harm, it is not enough for an individual to contend that he or she has suffered the same kind of harm or interference as the public, but to a greater extent or degree. Courts generally have refused to consider differences in degree of harm because of the difficulty or impossibility of drawing a satisfactory line concerning gradations of degrees of harm. Nonetheless, in determining whether there is a difference in the kind of harm, courts must consider the degree of interference as an important factor.[60]

The *Restatement (Second)* further indicates that when a public nuisance causes personal injury to the plaintiff or physical harm to his land or chattels, this harm normally is different in kind from that suffered by the public, and an individual may maintain a tort action.[61] Moreover, if a plaintiff suffers a pecuniary loss resulting from a public nuisance, that normally is considered a different kind of harm than that suffered by the public. However, if the pecuniary loss is common to an entire community and the plaintiff suffers the loss only in a greater degree than others, this is not a different kind of harm and the plaintiff cannot recover for the invasion of a public right.[62]

Generally, a public official may bring a public nuisance action if the government authorizes the official to sue for abatement or injunction of a public nuisance. In addition, a person who has suffered damages that are different from the public may not only bring an action for the individual's tort damage but may also seek an injunction against the public nuisance. Conversely, if an individual has not suffered an injury that is different, that person lacks standing to maintain an injunctive action. The reason for this rule is to prevent a multiplicity of lawsuits by members of the public, and to prevent a multiplicity of actions for trivial injuries.[63]

The possibility for individuals to seek damages in a public nuisance lawsuit is one of the most frequently litigated questions raised in public nuisance actions. Courts grappling with the special injury rule have determined, in almost equal measure, that plaintiffs satisfy or fail to satisfy the requirement of pleading a special injury. There is no common thread among these rulings; the cases largely are decided by a court's fact-bound interpretation and application of the rule. Prospective litigants, then, have a difficult time in crafting their pleadings or predicting judicial receptivity to the request for individual damages.

---

[60] *Id.* at cmts. b and c.
[61] *Id.* at cmt. d.
[62] *Id.* at cmt. H.
[63] *Id.* at cmt. subsection (2).

6.5 SATISFACTION OF THE SPECIAL INJURY RULE

Some plaintiffs have successfully convinced courts that they have alleged a sufficient special injury to proceed with public nuisance litigation. For example, relying on the *Restatement (Second)* provisions concerning the allegation of special injury, the a California federal court in an e-cigarette lawsuit, upheld the right of school districts to pursue public nuisance litigation under a special injury finding.[64] The defendant argued that the government entities' public nuisance claims failed because the school districts had not alleged an injury that was cognizable through a public nuisance claim for damages.

The court held that the school districts had provided sufficient detail in their complaints about the defendants' conduct that was unique to the school and different from that suffered by the general community. Thus, the school districts had to undertake numerous actions to combat widespread youth vaping, diverting resources to create educational materials, installing e-cigarette detectors and cameras, and managing hazardous waste disposal of e-cigarette devices and pods on school grounds. The defendant's marketing plan and other actions targeting the school-age market caused an extreme disruption in classrooms: a unique harm to schools that was different in kind than the community at large.[65]

Similarly, in the national opioid litigation, the federal district court held that a hospital plaintiff had plausibly pleaded concrete economic losses that differed in kind from the generalized injury to health suffered by the public. These concrete economic losses included increased operational costs to train hospital staff, provide diagnostic tools to identify pill seekers, and hire additional personnel to keep the hospital's opioid inventory secure.[66]

Corn farmers successfully alleged the requisite special injury in a public nuisance lawsuit against the manufacturer and distributor of genetically modified corn. The plaintiffs alleged that the defendants disseminated a product that contaminated the entire U.S. corn supply, and that this contamination created a public nuisance. An Illinois federal district court denied in part the defendants' motion to dismiss the case, holding that the plaintiffs stated a public nuisance claim, and that they could establish special harm. The court concluded that the commercial farmers, as a group, were affected differently than the public; they showed both physical harm to chattels and pecuniary business losses.[67]

---

[64] In re JUUL Labs., Inc., *supra* note 50.
[65] *Id.* at 649–50.
[66] In re Nat'l Prescription Opiate Litig. – West Boca, 452 F.Supp.3d at 774 (N.D. Ohio 2021).
[67] In re Starlink Corn Prods. Liab. Litig., 212 F.Supp.2d 828, 848 (N.D. Ill. 2002).

A plaintiff alleging injury from exposure to secondhand smoke convinced a California appellate court that the plaintiff pleaded a cause of action sufficient to allege a public nuisance claim. The plaintiff, a minor child, sued an apartment complex where she lived, contending that the complex's management company failed to limit secondhand smoke that aggravated her childhood asthma and chronic allergies. The appellate court reversed a demurrer in the defendant's favor, holding that the plaintiff had pleaded a sufficient cause of action for a public nuisance and that her harm – increased risks of heart disease and lung cancer – were different than the harm suffered by the public from breathing secondhand smoke.[68]

6.6 FAILURE TO ALLEGE A SPECIAL INJURY

Other litigants have been less successful in alleging a special injury sufficient to support public nuisance claim. For example, a consumer who purchased boxed baking mixes containing trans fats in the form of partially hydrogenated vegetable oils sued General Mills in a class action claiming a public nuisance, among other claims.[69] The court held that the class representative had not alleged an injury that was different in kind to the public.[70]

In rejecting the public nuisance claim, the court relied on provisions of the California Code of Civil Procedure which provided that "a private person may maintain an action for public nuisance, if it is specially injurious to himself, but not otherwise."[71] In construing this provision, and tracking the language of the *Restatement (Second)*, the court noted that a plaintiff suing on this basis was required to show special injury to himself that was of a character different in kind, and not merely different in degree, than that suffered by the public.

The plaintiff argued that his alleged injuries were different in kind than those of the public because his own injuries were physical and emotional harm and loss of money, whereas the harm to the public was a violation of the public's right to a safe food supply and interest in ensuring that only safe food products were allowed for sale.

The court rejected the plaintiff's contention, holding that the public's interest in a safe food supply was only a more generalized version of the plaintiff's interest in eating safe food. Surveying California precedents, the

---

[68] Birke v. Oakwood Worldwide, 169 Cal. App.4th 1540, 1550, 87 Cal. Rptr.3d 602, 610 (Cal. App. 2009).

[69] Backus v. General Mills, Inc., 122 F.Supp.3d 909 (N.D. Cal.2015).

[70] *Id.* at 931.

[71] Cal. Civ. Code § 3494.

court held that the multiple courts that heard trans fats challenges concluded that the plaintiffs did not allege injuries that were different in kind than the public. The only harm to the public was the risk of harm due to the consumption of artificial trans fats. No California court had sustained a public nuisance claim for interference with the public's right to a safe food supply by selling products with unhealthy ingredients. Trans fats were not uniquely harmful to plaintiffs, but constituted a general health hazard to anyone who consumed them.[72]

In the California lead paint litigation, the appellate court reached a similar conclusion. In that litigation, the plaintiffs pleaded two different actions: a public nuisance cause of action by three municipalities on behalf of the people seeking abatement, and a class action on their own behalf, seeking damages for a special injury rather than abatement. The court, without characterizing whether the plaintiffs successfully pleaded a special injury, nonetheless rejected the plaintiffs' public nuisance claim. The court concluded that this class action was an action for damages for injuries caused to the plaintiffs' property by a product, while the core of the representative action was for remediation of a health hazard.[73]

A federal appellate court upheld a district court's dismissal of a public nuisance lawsuit for the plaintiffs' failure to appropriately allege a special injury entitling them to pursue a public nuisance claim. Sixteen Pennsylvania hospitals sued various tobacco companies and their trade associations to recover the costs to the hospitals for unreimbursed health care costs provided to nonpaying patients suffering from tobacco-related illnesses.[74]

In rejecting the hospitals' public nuisance claim, the court cited the *Restatement (Second)* for the proposition that a plaintiff must have suffered a harm of greater magnitude and of a different kind than that suffered by the public. The court noted the *Restatement's* rationales for the special injury rule, which was to avoid a multiplicity of actions and the difficulty of drawing a satisfactory line for any public nuisance.[75]

The appellate court upheld the trial court's conclusion that the hospitals failed to sufficiently allege they suffered a harm different from and of greater magnitude than the harm suffered by the public. Instead, the hospital's injuries were derivative of the nonpaying patients' injuries, and the hospitals were

---

[72] Backus, *supra* note 71, at 930–31. (N.D. Cal.2015), citing Guttmann v. Nissin Foods (U.S.A.), Inc., 2015 WL 4309427, at *5 (N.D. Cal. July 15, 2015), and Simpson v. California Pizza Kitchen, Inc., 989 F.Supp.2d 1015, 1025 (S.D. Cal. 2013).
[73] Santa Clara, *supra* note 6, at 304–05.
[74] Allegheny Gen. Hosp. v. Philip Morris, Inc., 228 F.3d 429, 430 (3d Cir. 2000).
[75] *Id.* at 446, citing *Restatement (Second) of Torts* § 821C cmt. b (1979).

only one of numerous parties harmed by the defendants' alleged conspiratorial behavior. In these circumstances, the court observed, remedying the source of the tobacco conspiracy was more properly a task for public officials.[76]

Plaintiffs' efforts to pursue public nuisance claims for alleged injuries from asbestos exposure similarly have been rejected by courts for failure of plaintiffs to successfully plead a special injury. In a Massachusetts litigation brought by courthouse employees, the plaintiffs sued the manager alleging that asbestos located throughout the building had been improperly maintained and constituted an unabated public nuisance. The plaintiffs alleged that because of the manager's unreasonable conduct to properly maintain the courthouse asbestos, they were exposed to the highly toxic substance that placed the employees at greater risk of developing mesothelioma. The court held that the plaintiffs failed to allege a special injury other than what the public shared who were exposed to the environmental conditions at the courthouse.[77]

---

[76] *Id.* at 446.
[77] Sullivan v. Chief Justice, 448 Mass. 15, 858 N.E.2d 699, 716 (Mass. 2006).

7

Environmental Contamination, PCBs, and Climate Change as Public Nuisance Harms

The largest universe of modern public nuisance litigation relates to environmental pollution lawsuits, although environmental litigation has a long historical lineage. The largest number of public nuisance claims arise from contamination of common resources such as water supplies or ground soil, or the emission of noxious odors or toxic chemical plumes into surrounding communities. In contemporary practice, claims associated with the industrial effects on climate change represent the newest landscape of environmental public nuisance litigation.

The prevalence of public nuisance environmental litigation is perhaps best understood as most closely relating to interference and enjoyment of property rights. Thus, it has been relatively easier for plaintiffs in environmental litigation to identify the common property interest that is the predicate for asserting a public nuisance claim. Unlike litigation that sounds in mass tort products claims, environmental nuisance litigation typically is grounded in assertion of common property interests.

Plaintiffs have pursued environmental public nuisance litigation in federal and state courts. Since the 1960s when Congress actively began regulating environmental concerns, environmental public nuisance claims have been governed by a complex array of federal and state statutes and regulatory administrative provisions. The federal statutes governing environmental regulation include the Resource Conservation and Recovery Act (RCRA),[1] the Clean Air Act (CAA),[2] the Clean Water Act (CWA),[3] and the Comprehensive Environmental Response, Compensation, and Liability Act (CERCLA).[4]

---

[1] 42 U.S.C. § 6901 et seq.
[2] 42 U.S.C. § 7401 et seq.
[3] 33 U.S.C. § 1251 et seq.
[4] 42 U.S.C. 9601 et seq.

In construing federal environmental public nuisance claims, federal courts have articulated the contours and limitations of a federal common law of nuisance.

Most states have enacted local versions of environmental protection statutes, which may impose different or more stringent requirements than federal law. The existence of parallel federal and state regulation of environmental law has implicated questions of federal preemption and displacement of law regarding public nuisance claims. In addition, federal and state environmental statutes define who may pursue public nuisance litigation, as well as available remedies. Both governmental entities and private citizens may pursue environmental public nuisance litigation on behalf of communities harmed by a defendant's actions. And, like all other public nuisance litigation, a private citizen typically must show a special injury that is different in kind and degree from the community harms to bring an environmental public nuisance lawsuit.

The most litigated environmental public nuisance claims fall into three discrete categories: (1) contamination of water supplies, (2) noxious odors and toxic plumes emanating from chemical and manufacturing facilities or waste dumps, and (3) industrial actions affecting climate change. Litigation resulting from contamination of waterways and the emission of noxious odors illustrate traditional approaches to public nuisance claims. Thus, courts may uphold a public nuisance claim arising from an oil spill as it affected an entire community but deny lost profits or damages for reduced incomes that constitute a common misfortune. On the contrary, courts have awarded damages to commercial fisheries holding that they suffered special injuries distinct from the community. Courts determine satisfaction of the special injury requirement on a case-by-case factual basis.

Recent climate change litigation illustrates the intersection of the federal common law of public nuisance and its displacement by federal statutes. The Supreme Court in 2011, in *American Electric Power* determined that the Clean Air Act, which authorized the Environmental Protection Agency to regulate carbon dioxide levels, displaced any asserted federal common law public nuisance claim against electric power companies emissions.[5] In the aftermath of the Court's *American Electric Power* decision, plaintiffs pursued a second wave of climate change public nuisance litigation based on state law, which may entail federal preemption issues.

Contemporary mass tort litigation relating to PCBs illustrate how plaintiffs' attorneys can successfully pursue environmental public nuisance claims to induce massive settlements years after federal courts and an international pollution convention banned a toxic substance. Monsanto corporation was

---

[5]   American Elec. Power Co., Inc. v. Connecticut, 564 U.S. 410 (2011).

the sole company manufacturing polychlorinated biphenyls (PCBs) from the 1930s to the 1970s. Federal law banned PCB production in 1978, as did the 2001 Stockholm Convention on Persistent Organic Pollutants.

Various businesses widely used PCBs as coolants and insulating fluids for electrical transformers, pigments in carbonless copy paper, and to increase plasticity in paints and caulk. State and local governments are required to address contaminated bodies of water and spend millions of dollars to reduce PCBs discharged through stormwater. Attorneys asserted a public nuisance claim because PCB contamination in water bodies across the U.S. contaminated fish that humans then consumed. A federal court declined to dismiss the lawsuit based on a statute of limitations defense, holding that the court was inclined to find the plaintiffs' injuries as continuing. The PCB public nuisance lawsuit never went to trial and resulted in multimillion-dollar settlements.

7.1 HISTORICAL ROOTS OF ENVIRONMENTAL LAWS IN PUBLIC NUISANCE THEORY

Courts have noted that common law public nuisance principles formed the core doctrinal concepts in modern environmental statutes.[6] Thus, in assessing the applicability of RCRA provisions to alleged contamination arising from two open garbage dumps in Dallas, Texas, the court rehearsed the common law public nuisance roots of RCRA.[7] The court noted that nuisance laws originated in England in the twelfth century and that public nuisance began to be recognized in the sixteenth century. Thus, a defendant's improper operation of a landfill was recognized as a public nuisance even by the early public law.[8]

The *Restatement (Second)* codified the principle of public nuisance: conduct that involved a significant interference with public health, safety, peace comfort, and convenience.[9] Public nuisance theory lent itself naturally to combating the harms created by environmental problems because most environmental harms related to interference with property rights, or property rights held in common. Private and public nuisances were not set in mutually rigid categories, but environmental harms such as polluted air and water could be both a public and private nuisance.

---

[6] Cox v. City of Dallas, 256 F.3d 281, 289, 291 (5th Cir. 2001), citing William H. Rodgers, Jr., *Handbook on Environmental Law* § 2.1, at 100 (1977).

[7] Cox., *id.* at 289–91.

[8] *Id.* at 291, citing Geo-Tech Reclamation Indus., Inc., v. Hamrick, 886 F.2d 662, 665 (4th Cir. 1989).

[9] *Restatement (Second) of Torts* § 821B.

A leading environmental treatise author noted that: "Nuisance actions have involved pollution of all physical media – air, water, and land – by a variety of means…. Nuisance actions have challenged virtually every major industrial and municipal activity which is today the subject of comprehensive environmental regulation…. Nuisance theory is the common law backbone of modern environmental and energy law."[10]

In legislating environmental protection statutes, Congress has acknowledged that the statutes embody common law concepts of public nuisance law. For example, Congress indicated that "[The RCRA] is essentially a codification of common law public nuisance remedies … [and], therefore, incorporates the legal theories used for centuries to assess liability for creating a public nuisance (including [the theories of] intentional tort, negligence, and strict liability) to determine appropriate remedies…."[11] Similarly, a court noted that the Clean Air Act protected interests that overlapped "to a great extent with the interests that nuisance law protects."[12]

While acknowledging that contemporary environmental statutes are grounded in ancient public nuisance principles, courts have indicated that Congress intended some statutory terms to be more liberally interpreted than their common law counterparts.[13] Thus, federal courts in some instances have embraced more elastic interpretations of statutory provisions in environmental litigation, rather adhering to narrower statutory constructions.

For example, a federal court was called upon to interpret RCRA's statutory language allowing commencement of an action for liability "against any past or present operator of a treatment, storage or disposal facility *who has contributed or who is contributing* to the past or present handling, storage, treatment, transportation, or disposal of any solid or hazardous that might present an imminent and substantial endangerment to health or the environment."[14] In construing the "contributing to" language, the court adopted a broader interpretation of the provision to mean "have a part or share in producing an effect."[15]

The court cited a federal appellate court's reasoning for adopting a liberal approach to environmental statutory construction based on common law precedents:

> [Congress] has mandated that the former common law of nuisance, as applied to situations in which a risk of harm from solid or hazardous waste

---

[10] Rodgers, *supra* note 6.

[11] S. Rep. No. 96-172, at 5 (1979), *reprinted in* 1980 (U.S.C.C.A.N. 5019, 5023).

[12] Solid Waste Agency v. U.S. Army Corps. of Eng'rs., 101 F3d 503, 505 (7th Cir. 1996).

[13] Cox, *supra* note 6, at 292.

[14] *Id.*, citing 42 U.S.C.A. § 6972(a)(1)(B).

[15] *Id.* at 295.

exists, shall include new terms and concepts which shall be developed in a liberal, not restrictive manner. This ensures that problems that Congress could not have anticipated when passing the [RCRA] will be dealt with in a way minimizing the risk of harm to the environment and the public.[16]

7.2 FEDERAL DISPLACEMENT OF FEDERAL COMMON LAW OF NUISANCE

The possibility of interstate pollution raised questions concerning states' ability to pursue federal litigation under common law public nuisance theories, seeking to abate or otherwise remedy environmental harms emanating from one state and causing harm in another. The diversity basis of such lawsuits raised the fundamental question of applicable law; the U.S. Supreme Court famously announced in *Erie Railroad v. Tompkins* that there was "no federal general common law."[17]

However, in a series of Supreme Court decisions the Court nonetheless determined that there was a federal common law to deal "with air and water in their ambient or interstate aspects."[18] Judicial recognition of interstate pollution litigation even pre-dated the Court's *Erie* decision where the Court approved the application of federal common law brought by one state to abate pollution emanating from another state.[19]

Although the Supreme Court long recognized the existence of federal common law to govern interstate environmental pollution litigation, Congressional enactment of federal statutes implicated judicial authority to create controlling law in the presence of federal statutes governing environmental concerns. Thus, the question arose whether federal environmental statutes displaced federal common law, and otherwise controlled. The Supreme Court answered affirmatively: "[W]hen Congress addresses a question previously governed by a decision rested on federal common law the need for such an unusual exercise of law-making by federal courts disappears."[20]

The Supreme Court determined that the test for whether a federal environmental statute displaced federal common law asked whether the statute spoke directly to the question at issue in the litigation.[21] Legislative displacement did not require the same sort of clear and manifest Congressional intention

---

[16]   *Id.* citing U.S. v. Waste Indust., Inc., 734 F.2d 159, 167 (4th Cir. 1984).
[17]   Erie R. Co. v. Tompkins, 304 U.S. 64, 78 (1938).
[18]   Illinois v. Milwaukee, 406 U.S. 91 (1972) (Milwaukee I).
[19]   American Elec., *supra* note 5, at 421, citing Missouri v. Illinois, 180 U.S. 208 (1901).
[20]   American Elec., at 423, citing Milwaukee v. Illinois, 451 U.S. 304, 314 (1981) (Milwaukee II).
[21]   American Elec., at 424, citing Mobil Oil Corp. v. Higginbotham, 436 U.S. 618, 625 (1978).

needed for federal preemption of state law.[22] Moreover, the relevant question for federal displacement of common law was whether the statute occupied the field, and not whether it was occupied in a particular manner.[23]

In 2011, in *American Elec. Power Co., Inc. v. Connecticut*, the Court issued its leading decision recognizing federal displacement of the common law of public nuisance.[24] The litigation began in 2004, when eight states, New York City, and three land trusts brought federal common law nuisance claims against four private power companies and the federal Tennessee Valley Authority. The plaintiffs alleged that the defendants owned and operated fossil-fuel-fired power plants in twenty states that were emitting carbon dioxide and other greenhouse gases contributing to the public nuisance of global warming. The complaint stated that the defendants' carbon dioxide emissions created "a substantial and unreasonable interference with public rights," in violation of the federal common law of interstate nuisance, or, in the alternative, of state tort law.[25]

The plaintiffs contended that because of the defendants' emissions, public lands, infrastructures, and health were at risk from climate change. The trust plaintiffs alleged that the defendants' emissions would destroy animal habitats and rare species of plants and trees. The plaintiffs sought a decree that would cap carbon dioxide emissions for each defendant, to be reduced annually.[26]

The Court held that the Clean Air Act and the Environmental Protection Agency actions authorized by the CAA displaced the plaintiffs' federal common law nuisance claims.[27] In reaching this conclusion the Court analyzed the Clean Air Act. The court noted that the CAA authorized federal regulation of carbon dioxide and other greenhouse gas emissions, which qualified as air pollutants. As such, regulation of greenhouse gases was within the regulatory authority of the Environmental Protection Agency. In 2010 the EPA, recognizing the deleterious effects of greenhouse gases on the environment, issued a rulemaking regulating emissions from light-duty vehicles. The EPA also began a rulemaking to set limits on greenhouse gas emissions emanating from new, modified, and existing fossil-fuel-fired powerplants.

The Court held that the CAA and the EPA actions to regulate carbon dioxide emissions displaced any federal common law nuisance claims seeking abatement of carbon-dioxide emissions from fossil-fuel-fired powerplants. The Court previously had determined that carbon dioxide emissions qualified as

---

[22] American Elec., at 423, citing Milwaukee II, *supra* note 20, at 317.
[23] American Elec., at 426, citing Milwaukee II, at 324.
[24] American Elec., *supra* note 5.
[25] *Id.* 564 U.S. at 418.
[26] *Id.* at 415–16, 418–19.
[27] *Id.* at 415.

air pollution subject to regulation under the CAA. Moreover, the CAA spoke directly to carbon dioxide emissions from the defendants' plants.[28]

The CAA directed the EPA Administrator to list categories of stationary sources of greenhouse gas emissions that caused or significantly contributed to air pollution that might reasonably be anticipated to endanger public health or welfare. Once listed, the EPA had authority to establish performance standards for emission pollutants. Even though the EPA had not issued regulatory standards governing carbon emissions from fossil-fuel-fired powerplants at the time of the litigation, the Court nonetheless held that the statutory scheme displaced the federal common law of public nuisance.[29] Even if the EPA never exercised its authority at the conclusion of its rulemaking, the federal courts could not employ the federal common law of public nuisance to upset the EPA's expert determinations. In addition, the CAA provided multiple means for public and private enforcement.[30]

The Supreme Court resisted allowing federal courts judges to set emission standards by judicial decree. The EPA, as the expert administrative agency, was the first decider concerning environmental air pollution standards under the CAA. The critical point was that Congress delegated to the EPA the decision whether and how to regulate carbon dioxide emissions from powerplants; this delegation was what displaced federal common law, not when the EPA exercised the delegation.[31] The EPA was better equipped and suited to serve as the primary regulator of greenhouse gas emissions rather than individual federal district judges on an ad hoc, case-by-case basis. Federal judges lacked the scientific, economic, and technological resources that the EPA could utilize in issuing orders relating to standards for greenhouse gas emissions.[32]

Setting environmental emissions standards involved a complex balancing problem of competing interests, made in combination with state regulators. "As with other questions of national or international policy, informed assessment of competing interests [was] required. Along with the environmental benefit potentially achievable, our Nation's energy needs, and the possibility of economic disruption must weigh in the balance."[33]

The Court noted that the CAA envisioned extensive cooperation between federal and state authorities that permitted states to first determine how to achieve emission standards.[34] The litigation thus implicated the question

---

[28] *Id.* at 424.
[29] *Id.* at 426.
[30] *Id.* at 424–25.
[31] *Id.*
[32] *Id.* at 428.
[33] *Id.* at 427.
[34] *Id.* at 428, citing 42 U.S.C.A. §§ 7401(a), (b); 7411(c)(1).

whether plaintiffs could pursue relief under the state law where defendant operated powerplants. The appellate court did not address this issue because it determined that federal common law governed. In reversing, the Supreme Court indicated that considering its holding that statutory law displaced federal common law, the availability of a lawsuit under state nuisance law depended on the preemptive effect of the CAA. Because none of the parties had briefed this issue, the Court left the preemption issue open for consideration on remand.[35]

7.3 FEDERAL PREEMPTION OF ENVIRONMENTAL PUBLIC NUISANCE CLAIMS

The Supreme Court in *American Electric Power* did not address the question of the preemptive effect of the CAA on plaintiffs' ability to assert state common law public nuisance claims in environmental litigation. State supreme courts, however, that have addressed the federal preemption issue have reached contrary conclusions concerning the intersection of federal and state environmental regulation and common public nuisance litigation.

The Connecticut Supreme Court determined that federal law preempted a state plaintiff's public nuisance claim in litigation against a nuclear plant operator.[36] The plaintiff sought a temporary restraining order and injunctive relief against Dominion Nuclear Connecticut, Inc., which owned and operated a nuclear power station. The purpose of the injunctive relief was to restrain the defendant from increasing its electric power generating capacity, which allegedly would cause unreasonable pollution by significantly increasing the discharge of radioactive waste. In addition, the plaintiff contended that increased generating capacity would raise the temperature of cooling water (a thermal plume) released into the Long Island Sound.[37] The plaintiff generally alleged the deleterious effects of global warming on wildlife and marine life.

The trial court dismissed the plaintiff's claims based on the plaintiff's lack of standing under various state statutes and the common law of public nuisance, and alternatively, on federal preemption grounds. The Connecticut Supreme Court agreed, holding that federal law preempted the plaintiff's claim regarding an increase in the discharge of radioactive waste. In addition, the court held that the plaintiff's claim regarding the thermal plume was properly dismissed for a lack of standing.[38]

---

[35] *Id.* at 429.
[36] Burton v. Dominion Nuclear Conn., Inc., 300 Conn. 542, 23 Atl. Rprt.3d 1176 (2011).
[37] *Id.* at 544, 546.
[38] *Id.* at 549.

The court noted that Congress created two types of federal preemption: field preemption and conflict preemption. Field preemption embodied the concept of federal displacement of state law where Congress intended federal law to occupy the field of regulation. Thus, courts had established that within constitutional limits Congress could preempt state authority in express terms, or impliedly by manifesting an intent to supersede state law based on the presence of a comprehensive scheme of federal regulation.

Thus, where a federal regulatory scheme "was so pervasive as to make reasonable the inference that Congress left no room for the [s]tates to supplement it, because the [a]ct of Congress may touch a field in which the federal interest is so dominant that the federal system will be presumed to preclude enforcement of state laws on the same subject, or because the object sought to be obtained by the federal law and the character of the obligations imposed may reveal the same purpose."[39]

Where Congress did not displace state law by field preemption, state law could be preempted to the extent that it conflicted with federal law. "Such a conflict arises when compliance with both federal and state regulations is a physical impossibility ... or when state law stands as an obstacle to the accomplishment of the full purposes and objectives of Congress."[40]

The relevant statute governing the plaintiff's lawsuit was the Atomic Energy Act of 1954.[41] The U.S. Supreme Court had determined that in enacting the Atomic Energy Act, the Congress intended that the federal government would regulate the radiological effects of nuclear plant construction and operation, leaving to states the ability to regulate electrical utilities for questions relating to the need, reliability, costs, and other state concerns.[42] The Court indicated that "the [f]ederal [g]overnment maintains complete control of the safety and 'nuclear' aspects of energy generation."[43]

Based on the Supreme Court precedent, the Connecticut Supreme Court determined that the Atomic Energy Act preempted the plaintiff's state claims and that the trial court properly dismissed these. The court held that the trial court had no jurisdiction to consider the plaintiff's claim regarding the increase in radioactive waste because the federal government had exclusive authority over radiation hazards and safety, as well as radioactive discharges

---

[39] *Id.* at 551, citing Pacific Gas & Electric Co. v. Energy Resources Conservation & Development Comm., 461 U.S. 190, 203–04 (1983).
[40] Burton, *supra* note 36, at 551–52, citing Pacific Gas, *id.*
[41] 42 U.S.C. §§ 2011-2021, 2022-2286i, 2296-2297H-13.
[42] Burton, *supra* note 36, at 552, citing Pacific Gas, at 205.
[43] *Id.*

from nuclear plants.[44] Although the Connecticut Supreme Court held that the Atomic Energy Act preempted a plaintiff's state public nuisance claim, the Iowa Supreme Court came to the oppose conclusion concerning the preemptive effect of the Clean Air Act on a state public nuisance claim.[45] In this litigation, eight Iowa residents brought a class action lawsuit against the Grain Processing Corporation, which operated a local corn wet milling facility. The plaintiffs alleged that the defendant's milling activities caused harmful pollutants and noxious odors to invade their land, diminishing the full use and enjoyment of their property. The milling operation created hazardous by-products and harmful chemicals which were released directly into the air, including volatile organic compounds such as acetaldehyde, sulfur dioxide, starch, and hydrochloric acid.[46]

The plaintiffs contended that the dispersion of these chemical particulates onto their properties and yards caused them to suffer from persistent irritations, discomforts, annoyances, inconveniences, and put them at serious risk for other health effects. The plaintiffs alleged claims for common law and statutory nuisance, trespass, and negligence. They alleged that the defendant's use of its facility constituted a nuisance under the common law and the Iowa Code statutory framework for nuisance claims.[47] The manner in which the defendant operated its facility unreasonably interfered with the reasonable use and enjoyment of their properties.[48] They sought damages for the lost use and enjoyment of their property, punitive damages, and injunctive relief.[49]

The defendant moved for summary judgment asserting that the CAA preempted the plaintiffs' common law nuisance and other common law claims. Alternatively, the defendant argued that the Iowa Code, which was the state companion to the CAA, preempted the plaintiffs' common law public nuisance claim.[50] The district court concluded that the CAA preempted the plaintiffs' assertion of a common law public nuisance claim, citing various federal precedents holding that the CAA preempted state law claims.[51] And, for the same reasons, the district court concluded that the Iowa statutory nuisance provisions preempted the plaintiffs' common law public nuisance claim.[52]

---

[44] Burton, *id.* at 552–53.
[45] Freeman v. Grain Processing Corp., 848 N.W.2d 58 (Iowa 2014).
[46] *Id.* at 63–64.
[47] *See* Iowa Code § 657.1 (statutory nuisance).
[48] Freeman, *supra* note 45, at 64.
[49] *Id.* at 63.
[50] *Id.*
[51] *Id.* at 64–65, citing cases.
[52] *Id.*

The Iowa Supreme Court ultimately determined that the CAA did not preempt the plaintiffs' common law public nuisance claim in a lengthy decision analyzing the history of common law public nuisance claims, the advent of statutes regulating environmental concerns, the legislative history of the CAA, its implementation by federal and state governments, and litigation to protect the public interest under the statutory and common law.[53] The court noted that Iowa courts had recognized nuisance claims for decades and that plaintiffs had utilized nuisance claims to address environmental harms.[54]

The court further noted that courts had drawn a clear distinction between statutory and common law regimes. Thus, a party seeking to establish a statutory violation did not need to demonstrate the presence of a nuisance, while a party seeking to show a nuisance did not need to show a violation of some other law.[55] Moreover, remedies differed among the regimes: the CAA provided for civil monetary penalties for law violations but did not provide for damages to harmed individuals. In contrast, the common law focused on special harms to property owners caused by pollution to property at a specific location. Thus, through common law nuisance a plaintiff might obtain damages, punitive damages, and injunctive relief to address environmental harms.[56]

The court indicated that a property owner seeking full compensation for harm relating to the use and enjoyment of property, therefore, must resort to common law or state theories to receive full recovery. "In addition, the common law offers the prospect of creative remedies, such as paying for clean-up costs or creation of a common law fund for compensation or restoration."[57]

The Iowa Supreme Court observed that the U.S. Supreme Court had been reluctant to find federal preemption of state laws in areas where states traditionally exercised their police powers.[58] The existence of common law public nuisance to address pollution had been part of the historic state police powers, and prior to the 1970s, the Supreme Court had held that federal common nuisance law governed the use and misuse of interstate waterways.[59] With Congressional enactment of the Clean Water Act in 1972, the Court determined that where a federal statute pervasively occupied a field, then federal common law relating to pollution of interstate waterways displaced and

---

[53] *Id.* at 66–70.
[54] *Id.* at 67.
[55] *Id.* at 70.
[56] *Id.* at 67.
[57] *Id.* at 70.
[58] *Id.* at 75.
[59] *Id.* at 76, citing Hinderlider v. La Plata River & Cherry Creek Ditch Co., 304 U.S. 92, 110 (1938) and Missouri v. Illinois, *supra* note 19, at 518–20.

preempted federal common law.[60] However, the Court declined to consider whether the CWA preempted a public nuisance claim under state common law.[61]

In 1987, the Supreme Court partially answered the question concerning CWA preemption of state common law claims.[62] The Court held that the CWA preempted state nuisance actions to the extent that state law applied to an out-of-state polluter; Vermont plaintiffs, for example, could not impose Vermont law on an out-of-state polluter.[63] However, the Court further concluded that nothing in the CWA barred aggrieved individuals from bringing a nuisance claim pursuant to the law of the polluter's source state law.[64]

Summarizing federal jurisprudence, the Iowa Supreme Court concluded that the question of federal common law displacement was different than the question of preemption of state law actions. In addition, state common law nuisance actions had a different purpose than the regulatory regime the CAA established. The purpose of state public nuisance claims was to protect the use and enjoyment of property, not to achieve a regulatory purpose. Moreover, an activity might be entirely lawful yet constitute a nuisance because of the impairment to the use and enjoyment of property.[65]

Moreover, the standards for displacement of federal common law were different than preemption of state common law.[66] The U.S. Supreme Court's jurisprudence in CWA litigation evinced a clear pattern of holdings. First, the CWA preempted federal common law over pollution of interstate waterways considering the CWA's comprehensive scheme and the expertise vested in the EPA and state agencies. Second, preemption applied to state law claims against out-of-state pollution sources because this would be inconsistent with the CWA's regulatory framework and would create chaos by imposing multiple regulatory schemes on a single source. Third, state law claims against in-state sources of pollution were not preempted, and the CWA permitted states and citizens to sue polluters under the statutory citizens' and states' rights saving clauses.[67]

Turning to the CAA, the Iowa Supreme Court determined that nothing in the CAA expressly or impliedly preempted the plaintiffs' common law nuisance claims; Congress did not impliedly oust state law actions against the

---

[60] Freeman, *supra* note 45, at 77, citing Milwaukee II, *supra* note 20, at 317–19. The Supreme Court would similarly hold that the Clean Air Act displaced the federal common law regarding air pollutants. Freeman at 81, citing American Electric Power, *supra* note 5, at 2537.

[61] Freeman, *supra* note 45, at 78, citing Milwaukee II, *supra* note 20, at 310 n.4.

[62] Freeman at 79; Int'l Paper Co. v. Ouellettte, 479 U.S. 481 (1987).

[63] Ouellette, at 497.

[64] *Id.*

[65] Freeman, *supra* note 45, at 84.

[66] *Id.* at 83.

[67] *Id.* at 80.

polluting source state.[68] Thus, plaintiffs seeking to regulate pollution could assert a state public nuisance claim against the offending source state; "[t]his [was] precisely the kind of cooperative federalism anticipated by the statute."[69] In addition, conflict preemption with the CAA did not apply to a private lawsuit seeking damages arising from property ownership.[70]

Finally, the Iowa Supreme Court ruled that the plaintiffs' action was not preempted by the Iowa state nuisance provisions. Like the CAA, the Iowa statute contained a savings clause preserving the rights of individuals to seek relief at statutory or common law. Like its reasoning concerning preemption under the CAA, the court further concluded that the Iowa statutory nuisance scheme did expressly or impliedly preempt the plaintiffs' public nuisance claim, nor did the Iowa nuisance provisions conflict with a common law claim.[71]

Federal courts have likewise determined that plaintiffs may assert public nuisance claims against out-of-state polluters by applying the state law in which the pollution source is located. Thus, a federal district court upheld the right of North Carolina to assert a public nuisance claim against the Tennessee Valley Authority concerning air pollution emissions from TVA's coal-fired electric generating units installed in power plants in Tennessee, Alabama, and Kentucky. North Carolina alleged violations of public nuisance law under Alabama's statutory and common, Kentucky's common law, and Tennessee's common law. The complaint sought injunctive relief to abate the harm.[72]

The defendant moved for partial summary judgment. In rejecting the motion, the court observed that state and local authorities had two means to address environmental pollution harms. One was to seek relief under a federal pollution control scheme, such as set forth in the CAA. A second method was to proceed under state law. The CAA anticipated this method through its savings clause permitting state law actions notwithstanding the existence of federal laws, and federal law did not preempt relief under state common law.[73]

Moreover, it was well-established that when considering state law public nuisance claims, the court must apply the state law where the source of the pollution was located. Surveying the laws of the source states, the court concluded that the nuisance laws of Alabama, Kentucky, and Tennessee all agreed that air pollution created an actionable public nuisance claim. In

---

[68] *Id.* at 82–85.
[69] *Id.* at 84.
[70] *Id.* at 85.
[71] *Id.* at 85–89.
[72] North Carolina *ex rel.* Cooper v. T.V.A., 549 F.Supp.725, 727, 729 (W.D.N.C. 2008).
[73] *Id.* at 729.

addition, the source states' laws specifically recognized injunctive relief as an equitable remedy to abate a public nuisance.[74]

Poultry grower defendants attempted to invoke federal preemption to prevent public nuisance litigation by Tulsa and its municipal utility district alleging phosphorus wastewater pollution that contaminated the Tulsa water supply.[75] The defendants claimed that the federal Packers and Stockyards Act and the Agricultural Fair Practices Act implicitly preempted Oklahoma statutory and common law nuisance claims. The Oklahoma federal district court held that there was no implied preemption under these acts; it neither evinced a Congressional intent to occupy the field of agricultural production and marketing nor to foreclose application of state law.[76]

7.4 GOVERNMENTAL ENTITIES AS ENVIRONMENTAL PUBLIC NUISANCE CLAIMANTS

At times defendants sued in public nuisance claims challenge the plaintiffs' standing to assert the claim. Governmental entities or private citizens may bring public nuisance claims against polluters and standing requirements may differ depending on the nature of the litigation and the plaintiff seeking relief.

State statutes may define the standing of plaintiffs to pursue public nuisance litigation. For example, the California civil code permits two types of nuisance claims: (1) actions for damages or abatement by one whose property was injuriously affected, and (2) a civil action brought in the name of the people of California to abate a nuisance.[77] In a lawsuit by Los Angeles County and the Los Angeles County Flood Control District against Monsanto for polychlorinated biphenyl (PCB) contamination of the plaintiffs' wastewater system, the defendants contended that the plaintiffs lacked standing because they had failed to identify any property rights belonging to them.

The court disagreed, first noting that the plaintiffs' lawsuit was not brought on behalf of the people of California, so the plaintiffs needed to show that their property was injuriously affected by the alleged nuisance. The court held that the plaintiffs had sufficiently identified property ownership and had adequately alleged injury to their property. Furthermore, the plaintiffs sufficiently pleaded their nuisance claim because they had shown that they had a property interest in the area stormwater.[78]

---

[74] *Id.* at 735.
[75] Tulsa v. Tyson Foods, Inc, 258 F. Supp. 1263, 1292–93(N.D. Okla. 2003).
[76] *Id.*
[77] Los Angeles v. Monsanto Co., 2019 WL 13064885, at *10 (C.D. Cal. Nov. 21, 2019), citing Cal. Code of Civil Procedure § 731.
[78] *Id.* at ** 10-11.

Similarly, the TVA defendants in the North Carolina litigation challenged North Carolina's standing, contending that North Carolina was
not authorized to bring a suit to abate a public nuisance under the laws of
Alabama, Kentucky, or Tennessee.[79] The TVA alleged that the source states'
law (Alabama, Kentucky, and Tennessee) did not permit foreign sovereigns
such as North Carolina to bring causes of action alleging public nuisance.
The TVA contended that the source states' law required that public nuisance suits could either only be brought by the attorney general or other arm
of the state in which the alleged nuisance was located, or by an individual
who had sustained a special harm that was different in kind than that suffered by the public.[80] The TVA defendant further argued that since North
Carolina was not the state in which the alleged nuisance was located, it
belonged in the category of private individuals, and therefore, had to show
a special injury.[81]

In rejecting this challenge, the federal court noted that the Supreme Court
had long authorized lawsuits by sovereign states seeking to address interstate
pollution problems.[82] The court was unconvinced that North Carolina's status
as a quasi-sovereign relegated it to the same category as individuals who wish
to recover pursuant to a public nuisance claim. Nor could the court conclude that the source states' laws should be interpreted to require that North
Carolina show a special injury as if it were any individual wishing to proceed
with a public nuisance suit under the color of state law.[83]

Furthermore, the analytical framework addressing the special injury requirement did not contemplate the situation in which a sovereign or quasi-sovereign
sought to recover, in a *parens patriae* capacity, for a public nuisance. North
Carolina, as *parens patriae*, effectively sued on behalf of North Carolina at
large. As such, it made no sense to interpret the source states' laws as requiring North Carolina to prove that its damages were different from the public.
Allowing North Carolina to proceed as *parens patriae* served the policy goal of
avoiding a multiplicity of lawsuits by North Carolinians asserting that they were
affected by the TVA's actions.[84]

An Oklahoma federal district court similarly upheld the rights of Tulsa
and its metropolitan utility authority to assert a public nuisance claim against
poultry businesses and the Arkansas wastewater treatment plant the businesses

---

[79] North Carolina *ex rel.* Cooper, *supra* note 73, at 728.
[80] *Id.* at 729.
[81] *Id.* at 730.
[82] *Id.* at 728.
[83] *Id.* at 729.
[84] *Id.* at 731.

used in their operations.[85] The plaintiffs sued under the Comprehensive Environmental Response, Compensation, and Liability Act (CERCLA), alleging that the defendants' acts and omissions polluted lakes from which Tulsa drew its water supply. The plaintiffs sought cleanup costs recovery.[86]

The plaintiffs alleged that the poultry growers' practises and the Arkansas wastewater effluent discharged excessive phosphorous into the watershed, resulting in physical invasion, interference, and impairment of the lakes. This was especially true regarding the effects on the Tulsa water supply. Moreover, the defendants knew or should have known their phosphorus invaded and interfered with the plaintiffs' and publics' use of the lakes, yet they knowingly and intentionally continued their disposal practices.[87]

The defendants challenged the standing of the Tulsa Municipal Utility Authority, contending that the utility authority bore all the costs of investigation, formulation, and treatment of the contaminated water supply to make it potable. Therefore, the utility authority could not show that it had sustained or would sustain an injury in fact. The court rejected this argument finding that the utility had independent sources of revenue and had incurred operation and maintenance expenses.[88]

The defendants further contested Tulsa's ability to bring a nuisance action, arguing that the city lacked the requisite property interest to bring a nuisance claim. The court rejected this argument holding that a water right was considered real property, and that "any wrongful and direct interference with the rights of another in possession of water rights constitutes a trespass or tort. A wrongful interference with rights in respect of waters may also constitute a nuisance."[89] Citing the *Restatement (Second)*,[90] the court held that Tulsa, as a municipality, had the right to bring a public nuisance claim on behalf of municipal users of the water supply under both the common law and Oklahoma statutes.[91] The state could maintain common law and statutory public nuisance claims to remedy the alleged injury to the public's groundwater and to vindicate the state's interest in making that groundwater available for public use.

A federal district court likewise upheld the ability of New Mexico to sue various petroleum handlers and distributors located near an industrial site for groundwater contamination based on a public nuisance

---

[85] Tulsa v. Tyson Foods, Inc., *supra* note 75, at 1275.
[86] *Id.* at 1270–74.
[87] *Id.* at 1289.
[88] *Id.*at 1275–76.
[89] *Id.*
[90] *Id.* at 1290, citing § 821(2)(b).
[91] *Id.* citing Okla. Stat. tit. 50, §§ 1-3, Okla. Stat. tit. 27A, §§ 2-6-105; Okla. Stat. 11, §§ 37-115.

theory.[92] Invoking the special injury rule, the court indicated that absent a showing of some discrete special injury to the state apart from the public's interest in uncontaminated groundwater, the plaintiff would be limited to equitable relief seeking abatement of the claimed nuisance.[93]

In addition, New Mexico nuisance statutes did not provide for the recovery of damages by private plaintiffs in the name of the state and acting for the citizenry. The New Mexico public nuisance statute made no distinction between actions brought by public officers or private citizens, including the state attorney general. In each instance, the available relief would be the same: abatement of the nuisance rather than an award of pecuniary damages.[94]

On the contrary, a Texas federal district court rejected a public nuisance claim brought by Louisiana *parens patriae* on behalf of Louisiana citizens against an offshore oil driller for violations of federal environmental laws.[95] The court held that although pollution from the oil drilling operation was a significant interference with public health and safety, Louisiana failed to establish that it suffered significant harm different in kind than the public. Moreover, Louisiana's assertion that pollution was inherently harmful did not reach the special damages threshold that common law public nuisance required. Therefore, because Louisiana could not establish it suffered actual harm and that its territory or citizens suffered damages substantially greater than the public.[96]

7.5 PRIVATE CITIZENS AS ENVIRONMENTAL PUBLIC NUISANCE CLAIMANTS

Private individuals also may pursue public nuisance claims. Generally, in environmental litigation, an individual plaintiff has standing to sue as a representative of the public, as a citizen in a citizen's action, or as a class member in a class action. To be awarded monetary damages on a public nuisance claim, a plaintiff must show a special injury, but this special injury requirement does not apply if the plaintiff requests relief to enjoin or abate the nuisance.[97]

Often it is difficult for individuals to satisfy the special injury requirement when asserting a public nuisance claim. Nonetheless, several plaintiffs have successfully satisfied this standard.

---

[92] New Mexico v. Gen. Elec. Co., 335 F.Supp.2d 1185, 1235 (D.N.M. 2004).
[93] *Id.* at 1241.
[94] *Id.* at 1242–43.
[95] Louisiana v. Rowan Companies, 728 F.Supp.2d 896, 900 (S.D. Tex. 2010).
[96] *Id.* at 905.
[97] Severa v. Solvay Specialty Polymers USA, LLC, 524 F.Supp.3d 381, 393–94 (D.N.J. 2021).

A federal appellate court reversed a Pennsylvania lower court's decision to dismiss a public nuisance case, finding the plaintiffs sufficiently alleged a particular damage necessary to state a private claim for public nuisance.[98] The homeowner plaintiffs brought a class action against Bethlehem Landfill Company alleging that the defendant's operation of a local landfill permitted waste to decompose and release odorous landfill gas, leachate, and other byproducts. The class action asserted public and private nuisance claims on behalf of homeowner occupants and renters within a 2.5-mile radius of the landfill and claimed damages more than five million dollars.[99]

The appellate court concluded that there was no dispute that the plaintiffs had alleged the existence of a public nuisance based on the defendant's failure to operate the landfill in accordance with Pennsylvania's Solid Waste Management Act. The court additionally concluded that the plaintiffs had properly pleaded a private claim for public nuisance. Thus, when a public nuisance interfered with an individual's personal rights, such as the right to use and enjoy private property, the aggrieved person had a private cause of action to remedy the infringement of his personal rights. To be actionable, the infringement of personal rights had to result in significant harm.[100]

The plaintiffs identified cumulative harms that were unique to themselves and their fellow residents as homeowners or renters, such as the inability to use and enjoy their pools, porches, and yards. The presence of odors was especially injurious to class members compared with the public at large, given the impact on their homes. In short, the plaintiffs had alleged a particular damage to sustain a private claim for public nuisance.[101]

Plaintiffs have been successful in pleading private nuisance claims where the plaintiffs are pleading and requesting a damage remedy for diminution of property values. Thus, neighbors brought a class action against an adjacent petroleum storage facility, alleging that unreasonable odors emanating from the storage facility constituted both a private and public nuisance.[102] The court noted that to plead a public nuisance claim, the plaintiff had to allege plausible facts that the odors emanating from the defendant's facility interfered with a right common to the public.

The plaintiff alleged the interference with the use and enjoyment of their property, but also that each class member suffered special injury in the form

---

[98] Baptiste v. Bethlehem Landfill Co., 965 F.3d 965 (3d Cir. 2020).

[99] *Id.* at 218.

[100] *Id.* at 220.

[101] *Id.* at 221.

[102] Agudelo v. Sprague Operating Resources, LLC, 528 F.Supp.3d 10, 12 (D.R.I. 2021).

of diminished property values and/or loss of use and enjoyment of their private properties. The court sustained these allegations, concluding that the plaintiff individually and on behalf of the class asserted a legally valid claim for public nuisance because she asserted plausible facts showing specific special injury to her, the neighbors, and their properties, as well as injury of a right common to the public.[103]

In another noxious odor litigation, an environmental advocacy group, the Fresh Air for the Eastside, sued a landfill operator alleging violations of the Resource Conservation and Recovery Act, the Clean Air Act, and common law public nuisance arising from the defendant's operation of the landfill.[104] The plaintiffs claimed that the landfill operations prevented the quiet use and enjoyment of their property because of the noxious odors emanating from the landfill, which created an environment conducive to the spread of vector species. Plaintiffs experienced headaches, eye, nose, and throat irritations. In addition, the stigma of owning property near the landfill resulted in diminished property values.[105]

The federal court held that diminished property values could constitute a special injury under New York law. A special injury need not be unique; simply because many individuals suffered a peculiar injury did not mean that the injury was not different in kind from that sustained by the public. The plaintiffs alleged that they were additionally impacted by a decrease in their homes' property values, the inability to use and enjoy their homes and physical ailments resulting from continuous exposure to the noxious emissions. Thus, compared to individuals who did not own property or live nearby and were merely affected by the landfill's impact on public spaces, the plaintiffs' alleged that these injuries constituted a special injury.[106]

Like noxious odor cases, some plaintiffs have successfully alleged a special injury in environmental litigation related to water contamination.[107] Property owners who lived adjacent to a landfill sued the landfill operators alleging the landfill caused groundwater contamination of their properties. The New Jersey district court held that private citizens had standing to bring the public nuisance claim and they had experienced special injuries because the defendants' pollution contaminated their drinking water and migrated onto their properties. In addition, the court held that if a private plaintiff had a right to sue for

---

[103] *Id.* at 14–15.
[104] Fresh Air for the Eastside, Inc., v. Waste Management of N.Y., L.L.C., 405 F.Supp.3d 408, 420 (W.D.N.Y. 2019).
[105] *Id.* at 441–42.
[106] *Id.* at 444.
[107] Corradetti v. Sanitary Landfill, Inc., 912 F. Supp.2d 156, 163 (D.N.J. 2012).

damages because of a harm that was different in kind, then the party also could pursue an action to abate the nuisance as it affected all members of the public. Therefore, the plaintiff had the right to seek damages and injunctive relief.[108]

Similarly, a New York federal district court upheld the right of Maryland homeowners to pursue a class action against an Exxon Mobil Corporation and a gas station owner in the multidistrict litigation over contamination of groundwater from methyl tertiary butyl ether (MTBE).[109] The plaintiffs sought relief from the defendants' alleged groundwater contamination from the gasoline additive chemical MBTE. Maryland law recognized three categories of public nuisance: (1) statutory per se nuisance, (2) nuisance that prejudiced the public health or comfort, and (3) nuisances which by reason of their locality, surroundings or manner in which they were maintained.[110] The court held that the plaintiffs' allegations were sufficient to allege public nuisance under any of the three prongs of the *Restatement (Second)*.[111]

The public interest central to the plaintiff's case was the use of the state's groundwater. The court rejected Exxon's argument that the use of the state aquifer was a shared individual right rather than a public right. "Though a plaintiff may have usufructuary rights to groundwater, this does not eliminate the public quality of the state's water resources."[112] Thus, the release of contaminants harmful to human health into the environment unreasonably infringed upon a public right regardless of whether the release occurred in the groundwater or surface water.

On the contrary, courts may dismiss individual public nuisance claims where the plaintiffs cannot demonstrate the requisite special injury, even where the allegations are sufficient to satisfy the definition of a public nuisance. The special injury requirement has proven problematic in water contamination litigation where some courts have been willing to find a plaintiff's special injury from the water contamination,[113] while many other courts have not.

For example, an appellate court held that West Virginia residential customers of a water district had not satisfied the special injury requirement to pursue a public nuisance claim against a Dupont chemical company for alleged contamination of their drinking water.[114] The court noted that when a private

---

[108] *Id.*

[109] *In re* Methyl Tertiary Butyl Ether ("MTBE") Prods. Liab. Litig., MDL 1358, 457 F.Supp.2d 298, 309–10 (S.D.N.Y. 2007).

[110] *Id.* at 308–09.

[111] *Id.* at 309, citing *Restatement (Second) of Torts* § 821B.

[112] *Id.* at 310.

[113] *See supra* notes 107–112.

[114] Rhodes v. E.I. Du Pont de Nemours and Co., 636 Fed.Rptr.3d 88, 97–98 (4th Cir. 2011).

citizen's claim of public nuisance was not based on a special injury, such a claim was insufficient as a matter of law. The plaintiffs filed a class action to enjoin a public nuisance on behalf of the class. They contended that where individual plaintiffs sought to enjoin a public nuisance on behalf of a class, the *Restatement (Second)* created an exception to the special injury.[115]

Relying on West Virginia precedent, the appellate court refused to recognize a class action exception to the special injury requirement. In the alternative, the court held that the plaintiffs failed to allege facts supporting a special injury because they suffered a personal injury or property damage that was not normally different in kind from that suffered by other public members. Moreover, the plaintiffs' class pleadings refuted the contention of special injury because the plaintiffs pleaded that the class members had suffered the same injury.[116]

It is possible for an individual to successfully plead a public nuisance claim on behalf of the public but fail to plead a claim for individual damages. For example, a New Jersey federal court concluded that town residents who brought a class action against a polymer plant operator for claims arising from the defendants' alleged contamination of the town water supply had properly pleaded a nuisance claim. The plaintiffs had not alleged that the municipal water supply was the public nuisance, but rather the defendants' chemicals they discharged that wound up in the plaintiffs' water supply.[117] Pursuant to New Jersey precedent and the *Restatement (Second)*, the plaintiffs satisfied the description of a public nuisance: "A public nuisance, by definition, is related to conduct, performed in a location within the actor's control, which has an adverse effect on a common right."[118]

Nonetheless, a private party could seek to recover damages only if the individual had a special injury.[119] The New Jersey federal court concluded that the plaintiffs had not pleaded an injury that was different from the injury that constituted the public nuisance itself. The public right was the residents' access to an uncontaminated water supply and the public nuisance was the defendants' interference with that right by their discharge of chemical pollutants into the environment.[120]

---

[115] *Id.* at 97, citing *Restatement (Second) of Torts* § 821C(2)(c).

[116] *Id.* at 98.

[117] Severa, *supra* note 97, at 394. *See also* Rowe v. E.I. De Nemours and Co., 262 F.R.D. 451 (D.N.J. 2009).

[118] Severa, *Id.* at 393–94, citing In re Lead Paint Litig., 191 N.J. 405, 924 A.2d 484, 496 (2007), quoting *Restatement (Second) of Torts* § 821B (1979).

[119] *Id.* at 394; *In re* Lead Paint, 924 A.2d at 496.

[120] *See also* Duquesne Light Co. v. Penn. Am. Water Co., 850 A.2d 701, 704–05 (Pa. Super 2004).

The court, however, determined not to dismiss the public nuisance claim. The court noted that the special injury requirement was not necessary when an individual sought relief to enjoin or abate the nuisance. A plaintiff had standing to sue as a representative of the public, as a citizen in a citizen's action, or as a member of a class. Because the plaintiffs' class action nuisance claim was not for money damages but for an order directing the defendants to abate the public nuisance, the claim could proceed.[121]

In another public nuisance action property owners sued an aircraft parts manufacturer, alleging toxic waste from its operation caused groundwater and soil contamination.[122] The court indicated that the general rule was that public nuisance actions must be brought by government officials, but that a private party could bring a public nuisance claim where the nuisance was "specially injurious" to the private party, beyond the harm caused by the nuisance to the public. The court held that the plaintiffs had not alleged a plausible claim for public nuisance; their claim that they had been specially injured by contamination of their groundwater and soil by the defendant's waste plume was a harm too like that suffered by the public.[123]

Similarly, in the public nuisance litigation brought by an individual against an alleged polluting nuclear power facility, the Connecticut Supreme Court upheld the trial court's dismissal of her public nuisance claim for a lack of standing. The court indicated that to assert and prevail in a public nuisance claim, a plaintiff had to satisfy four elements: (1) the condition complained of had a natural tendency to create danger and inflict injury on a person or property, (2) the danger created was a continuing one, (3) the use of the land was unreasonable or unlawful, and (4) the existence of the nuisance was the proximate cause of the plaintiff's injuries and damages.[124]

The Connecticut Supreme Court indicated that courts uniformly held that a private individual had no right to pursue an action for the invasion of a purely public right, unless their damage was in some way distinguished from the injuries the public sustained. The community's appointed representatives were the proper people to seek redress for wrongs to the community. "There is general agreement on the requirement that the plaintiff's damage be different in kind, rather than degree, from that shared by the public."[125]

Applying this special injury standard, the Connecticut Supreme Court determined that the plaintiff lacked standing to pursue her public nuisance claim

---

[121] *Id.* at 395.
[122] Greenfield MHP Associates, L.P. v. Ametek, Inc., 145 F. Supp. 3d 1000, 1004 (S.D. Cal. 2015).
[123] *Id.* at 1015–16.
[124] Burton, *supra* note 36, at 561–62.
[125] *Id.* at 562, citing cases and the *Restatement (Second) of Torts* § 821C(1).

relating to the harm caused by the elevated temperature of the thermal plume emitting from the defendant's nuclear power plant. The plaintiff's allegations of harm chiefly related to the effects of increased water temperature on wildlife, as opposed to members of the public who might use the Long Island estuary for recreational purposes. In addition, the plaintiff's allegations consisted almost entirely of statements about the possible effects of global warming on marine life generally, instead of marine life inhabiting the Long Island Sound. The plaintiff failed to explain how the nature and harm she suffered was special, distinct, or different in kind from the harm suffered by other members of the public.[126]

7.6 DEFENSES TO ENVIRONMENTAL PUBLIC NUISANCE CLAIMS

Defendants commonly raise the compliance defense and, therefore, their activities cannot constitute a public nuisance. Courts substantially have rejected this defense. This issue often is complicated by the intersection of federal regimes and separate state statutory or common law requirements. Federal jurisprudence has long recognized states' ability to supplement federal regulatory law with their own state standards. The Supreme Court has balanced the competing federal and state interests, ultimately concluding that in restricting public nuisance suits to those brought under source state law, this prevented a defendant from being subjected to an indeterminate number of possible regulations.[127]

Thus, in the North Carolina public nuisance litigation brought against the TVA defendants, the federal court held that the TVA was open to suit despite its alleged compliance with federal permits, based on the authority of source states' nuisance laws.[128] The court noted that the source states' laws were unanimous in concluding that a defendant's otherwise lawful activities might be the subject of a public nuisance action.[129]

Defendants also have invoked source states' law concerning comparative fault to require that courts consider the plaintiffs' state contribution to the public nuisance. However, if the plaintiffs' lawsuit is for injunctive relief, then comparative fault is not a proper consideration.[130] The Supreme Court had determined that the damage a sovereign state had done to its own environment did not preclude a state from suing others who polluted it.[131] Thus, a

---

[126] *Id.* at 563.
[127] North Carolina ex rel. Cooper, *supra* note 73, at 732, citing Ouellette, *supra* note 62, at 499.
[128] North Carolina *ex rel.* Cooper, at 732.
[129] *Id.*
[130] *Id.* at 733.
[131] *Id.* at 733, citing Georgia v. Tennessee Copper Co., 206 U.S. 230, 238, 27 S.Ct. 618 (1907).

federal court rejected a comparative fault defense in the North Carolina public nuisance litigation against the TVA and polluting power plants. The TVA argued that two source states – Kentucky and Tennessee – were comparative fault jurisdictions and any relief granted under these states' law must consider North Carolina's own contributions to pollution in its state.[132]

Other defendants have sought to interpose a contributory negligence defense to a public nuisance claim. Thus, in Tulsa's litigation against poultry growers and an Arkansas wastewater facility, the defendants argued that they were entitled to a contributory negligence defense because the plaintiffs' nuisance claims were inherently based on negligence.[133] The federal district court rejected this argument, holding that the plaintiffs had made out a claim of nuisance that was intentional. As such, the court concluded that where a plaintiff alleged a harm that was intentional, or the result of recklessness, contributory negligence was not a defense.[134]

More recently, in litigation against Monsanto company concerning polychlorinated biphenyl (PCB) contamination of the Los Angeles County stormwater system, defendants alleged that the plaintiff's claim failed to state a plausible nuisance claim because the plaintiffs were using the nuisance claim as a surrogate for a products liability action.[135] The California federal court rejected this argument, noting that in order to plead a viable nuisance claim in California, a plaintiff had to plead affirmative conduct by a manufacturer that directly contributed to the creation of a nuisance. This required actual knowledge of the hazard that the defendant's affirmative conduct would create.[136]

The court held that the defendants knew as early as the 1930s that PCBs were toxic, and certainly by the 1950s. Despite this knowledge, Monsanto continued to promote the use of PCBs and instructed its customers to dispose of PCB containing wastes in local landfills, knowing that landfills were not suitable for PCB contaminated waste. Thus, the defendants had affirmatively instructed users to dispose of PCBs in harmful ways.[137]

---

[132] *Id.* at 732.
[133] Tulsa v. Tyson Foods, Inc., *supra* note 75, at 1301, citing *Restatement (Second) of Torts* § 840(B)(1).
[134] *Id.* at 1302, citing *Restatement (Second) of Torts* § 840B(2).
[135] Los Angeles., *supra* note 77, at *9 (C.D. Cal. Nov. 21, 2019).
[136] *Id.*
[137] *Id.* at *10.

8

Opioids as Public Nuisance Health
and Welfare Harm

Environmental pollution represents the most prevalent type of public nuisance litigation. This is hardly surprising because plaintiffs typically allege that the polluting defendants' activities interfere with the plaintiffs' use and enjoyment of property. With rare exception, environmental public nuisance litigation defaults to jurisprudence relating to an offender's invasion of property, rather than harm arising from, or related to product defects.

Most environmental public nuisance litigation proceeds on conventional *Restatement (Second)* principles, including the assertion of conventional defenses to public nuisance claims. Although there continues to be an abundance of environmental public nuisance litigation, these cases rarely raise claims intersecting with product liability law. The modern twenty-first century era of innovative public nuisance litigation, then, has sought to recast public nuisance as a vehicle for adjudicating harms relating to products. The pursuit of public nuisance claims in products cases is evidence of the plaintiff bar's creative lawyering in the mass tort arena.

This novel approach gave rise to the current controversy concerning the deployment of public nuisance as a surrogate for products liability litigation. Massive litigation relating to lead paint, opioids, firearms, and e-cigarettes has inspired the debate over the extension of public nuisance law to capture what otherwise would be conventional mass tort litigation. Courts have split concerning the legitimacy of using public nuisance claims in the products setting, and few cases have progressed to jury trial resolution. However, national and state litigation suggests the contemporary power of public nuisance claims to achieve lucrative settlements from defendants.

The national and state opioid litigation illustrates the contemporary adjudication and settlement power of public nuisance claims, with competing views from federal and state courts. The narrative history of opioid litigation charts the development of emerging theories of public nuisance and judicial reception of such public nuisance claims. Thus, plaintiffs' initial opioid litigation focused on public nuisance as a vehicle for claims arising out of the marketing and sale of federally approved pharmaceuticals. Although some defendants initially were successful in persuading courts to decline to expand public nuisance claims, several courts refused to dismiss opioid public nuisance lawsuits.

Beginning in 2014, local government plaintiffs implemented a strategy to pursue multiple opioid defendants, including manufacturers, distributors, retail pharmacies, and pill mill doctors. Plaintiffs filed hundreds of opioid lawsuits in federal and state courts. In 2017, the Judicial Panel on Multidistrict Litigation consolidated all federal opioid litigation in the national opiate MDL, transferred to the federal district court for the Northern District of Ohio under the supervision and management of Judge Dan Polster.[1] In separate actions dealing with discrete defendant cohorts, Judge Polster allowed plaintiffs to proceed with public nuisance claims.

Governmental entities successfully prosecuted a public nuisance claim against retail drug sellers in 2021. After a six-week trial presided over by Judge Polster, a jury found that retail pharmacies CVS Health, Walmart, and Walgreens created a public nuisance that contributed to the opioid crises in two northeastern Ohio counties when the pharmacies overlooked the so-called red flags when filling opioid subscriptions. Because of ongoing federal litigation several pharmaceutical company defendants then reached multibillion-dollar settlements with states and municipalities.[2]

In contrast to the successful prosecution and settlement of opioid public nuisance claims in the federal multidistrict litigation (MDL), several state courts have been less receptive to opioid litigation pursued based on public nuisance theories. For example, in 2019, a Connecticut judge dismissed a public nuisance lawsuit brought by 37 municipalities against 25 drug companies.[3] The judge indicated that the consequence of imposing a duty on commercial enterprises to guard against the criminal misuse of their products would represent an unprecedented expansion of public nuisance law. In rejecting the plaintiffs' public nuisance theory, the judge concluded that allowing the case to proceed "would risk letting everyone sue almost everyone else about pretty much everything that harms us."[4]

[1] In re Nat'l Prescription Opiate Litig., 290 F. Supp.3d 1375 (J.P.M.D.L 2017).
[2] Jan Hoffman, CVS, Walgreens and Walmart Fueled Opioid Crisis, Jury Finds, N.Y. Times, Nov. 23, 2021, available at https://nytimes.com/2021/11/23/health/walmart-cvs-opioid-lawsuit-verdict.html.
[3] New Haven v. Purdue Pharma, L.O., 2-19 WL 423990 (Conn. Super. Ct. Jan. 8, 2019).
[4] Id.

The Connecticut judge also pushed back against allowing plaintiffs to deploy a public nuisance claim to leverage a lucrative settlement from defendants. Thus, "it might be tempting to wink at the whole thing and add pressure on parties who are presumed to have lots of money and moral responsibility. Maybe it would make them pay up and ease straining municipal fiscs across the state. But it's bad law."[5]

Likewise, in 2021, a California superior court ruled against several local governments and in favor of four large pharmaceutical companies in an opioid litigation that pleaded a public nuisance claim. The court concluded that the plaintiffs had failed to prove how physicians had written medically unnecessary opioid prescriptions because of the manufacturers' alleged misleading marketing efforts. In addition, the plaintiffs failed to show whether and how such prescriptions contributed to a public nuisance.[6]

A few weeks later, the Oklahoma Supreme Court reversed a district court's judgment against opioid manufacturers.[7] The court concluded that the Oklahoma courts had not extended the state's public nuisance statute to the manufacturing, marketing, and selling of products. In addition, the Oklahoma Supreme Court declined the invitation to expand Oklahoma's public nuisance law. The Oklahoma decision embodied the emerging critique of opioid public nuisance litigation, contending that the solution to the opioid crisis should lie with the political branches of government and not through the unwarranted judicial expansion of the law of public nuisance.

8.1 THE OPIOID CRISIS AND INITIAL OPIOID LITIGATION

Opioids embrace an array of pharmaceuticals prescribed by physicians to provide relief to millions of American patients suffering from chronic pain. Perhaps the most recognizable opioid drug was Purdue Pharma's OxyContin, which the company began marketing in 1996. The Federal Food and Drug Administration endorsed the properly managed medical use of opioids and, when taken properly as prescribed, considered opioids a safe and effective pain management pharmaceutical.

Beginning in the early twenty-first century, extending over two decades, the U.S. experienced a flood of abuse and misuse of opioid medications that resulted in increased addiction to opioids. The high demand and lucrative market for opioids incentivized some physicians to overprescribe opioids or

---

[5] *Id.*

[6] California v. Perdue Pharma, L.P., Case No.: 30-2014-007-CU-BT-CXC (2021).

[7] Oklahoma *ex rel.* Hunter v. Johnson & Johnson, 499 P.3d 719 (2021).

otherwise engage in enterprising pill mills. The popularity of opioids also contributed to the criminalization of black-market opioid sales.

As opioid prescriptions became prevalent and easily available, opioid deaths from overdosing increased during the early 2000s, giving rise to a complex social problem. Governmental entities experienced increased health and emergency service costs in addressing opioid addiction and deaths; municipalities incurred additional costs in administering the criminal justice system relating to the illicit sale of opioid pills.

The Centers for Disease Control and Prevention calculated that the opioid prescription rates peaked in 2012 at more than 255 million prescriptions, roughly equivalent to 81.3 prescriptions per one hundred persons.[8] As of 2021, approximately more than 100,000 Americans had died of drug overdoses, a more than 70 percent increase from the previous year. Although some deaths were attributable to fentanyl-laced drugs, a sizeable percentage of the overdose deaths were related to prescription pain medication: both natural and semi-synthetic opioids. The drug overdose deaths for the first time exceeded combined deaths from car crashes and gun violence.[9]

The Council of Economic Advisers estimated that in 2015 the economic costs associated with opioid abuse were estimated at $504 billion, consisting of health care costs, foregone earnings, and criminal justice costs.[10] Another source estimated that between 2001 and 2018, the estimated toll of the opioid crisis in the U.S. exceeded $1 trillion, and projected that the opioid crisis would cost an additional $500 billion over the next three years.[11]

To seek redress for the societal expenses incurred with dealing with the societal opioid crisis, several individuals filed lawsuits targeting opioid manufacturers, some individual physicians, and physician-run pill mills. These manufacturing defendants included Janssen Pharmaceuticals, a wholly owned subsidiary of Johnson & Johnson; Purdue Pharma L.P. and related entities; and Teva Pharmaceuticals, USA, Inc.

In the initial opioid litigation plaintiffs claimed that the defendant manufacturers, in marketing and selling their opioid products, contributed to

---

[8] Department of Justice, Drug Enforcement Administration, Diversion Control Division, *Cases Against Doctors*, Nov. 29, 2021, available at https://apps2.deadiversion.usdoj.gov/CasesAgainstDoctors/spring/main.

[9] John Malcom, Using Public Nuisance Law to "Solve" the Opioid Crisis Sets a Dangerous Precedent (Dec. 20, 2021), available at www.heritage.org/crime-and-justice/report/using-public-nuisance-law-solve-the-opioid-crisis-sets-dangerous -precedent.

[10] Council of Econ. Advisors, The Underestimated Cost of the Opioid Crisis, 2–3 (Nov. 2017), available at https://perma.cc/4YEGFNZR.

[11] Altarum, Economic Toll of Opioid Crisis in U.S. Exceeded $1 Trillion Since 2001, Feb. 13, 2018, available at https://altarum.org/news/economic-toll-opioid-crisis-us-exceeded-1-trillion-2001.

physicians' overprescribing opioids. The plaintiffs alleged that the defendants used branded and unbranded marketing to actively promote the concept that physicians were undertreating pain. In addition, the plaintiffs contended that the defendants overstated the benefits of opioid use, downplayed dangers, and failed to disclose the lack of evidence supporting the long-term use of opioids.

In lawsuits against the manufacturer defendants, the allegations of false and misleading information fell into three categories: (1) information contrary to or inconsistent with the manufacturer's product information or package insert of warnings for a specific opioid, (2) information which was not directly contradicted in a manufacturer's product information/insert due to an absence of contrary fact in the package insert, and (3) scientific insufficiency of the manufacturer's insert, including warnings.[12]

These initial opioid lawsuits invoked conventional product liability tort theories, sounding in strict liability, fraud, and negligence. The manufacturers defended against these lawsuits by either blaming users for their addiction or misusing their products, or by blaming physicians for prescribing the drugs improperly or despite knowing the risks. Most of these initial individual lawsuits failed.[13]

However, some state attorney generals and the Department of Justice successfully pursued opioid manufacturers and distributors in this first wave of opioid litigation. In 2007, the federal government secured a settlement and plea agreement with Purdue Pharma for misbranding; the company was fined $600 million, and its top corporate executives were fined $34.5 million. In 2016 and 2017, the Department of Justice and West Virginia settled a lawsuit with Cardinal Health, a major distributor of OxyContin, for about $64 million. And in 2017, the Department of Justice obtained a $150 million penalty against McKesson for civil violations of the Controlled Substances Act.[14]

A second wave of opioid litigation began in 2014 when local government plaintiffs targeted an expanded universe of defendants, including the manufacturers, distributors such as McKeeson, Cardinal Health, and AmerisourceBergen, pill mill physicians, and local pharmacies like CVS and Walgreens. By 2017, local government plaintiffs, individuals, and entities had filed more than 150 lawsuits in twenty-five federal district courts. Private attorneys for forty-six local governments petitioned the Judicial Panel on Multidistrict Litigation to create an opioid multidistrict litigation and to transfer all the federal opioid litigation to one judicial district for coordinated pretrial proceedings and disposition.[15]

[12] *See* Hunter, *supra* note 7, at 747 (Edmonson, J., dissenting).
[13] Abbe R. Gluck & Elizabeth Chamblee Burch, MDL Revolution, 96 N.Y.U. L. Rev. 1, 21–22 (2021).
[14] *Id.* at 22.
[15] *Id.* at 22–23.

8.2 THE NATIONAL OPIOID MDL LITIGATION

With burgeoning opioid litigation throughout the federal court system, the Judicial Panel on Multidistrict Litigation approved the creation of an opioid MDL in 2017 assigned to Judge Dan Polster's management.[16] The opioid MDL represented one of the largest, sprawling, and complex MDL litigations in MDL history. The MDL captured approximately 3,000 lawsuits involving arrays of different plaintiffs and defendants. Plaintiffs included cities, municipalities, and counties; school districts; third-party payors such as health and welfare funds; insurance benefits trusts; hospitals; and Native American tribes. Defendants included two dozen opioid manufacturers; distributors; pharmacy retailers; pill mill physicians; and individual defendants such as the owners of Purdue Pharma, the Sackler family.[17]

The second wave of opioid litigation culminating in the MDL not only expanded the universe of plaintiffs and defendants but also the legal theories for holding the defendants accountable for the consequences of the opioid crisis. The claims in the MDL proceedings included violation of the RICO statutes, the federal Controlled Substances Act and state analogues, state consumer protection laws, common law negligence, negligent misrepresentation, fraud, unjust enrichment, statutory negligence, statutory nuisance, and common law public nuisance.[18]

Given the complicated array of plaintiffs, defendants, applicable law, and claims, Judge Polster organized the MDL into litigation tracks, with the intention to promote settlements through these discrete aggregations. Track One consisted of three Ohio bellwether cases brought by two Ohio counties against several manufacturers and distributors that included a public nuisance claim. On October 1, 2019, almost all the Track One defendants settled with the Ohio counties and the bellwether cases never went to trial against these defendants.[19] Judge Polster created a new Track One-B which included non-settling pharmacy defendants Walgreen, CVS, Rite Aid, HBC, and Discount Drug Market. Track Two cases consisted of two West Virginia bellwether cases. Track Three was comprised of two Ohio cases involving public nuisance claims against pharmacies in their roles as distributors and dispensers of opioids.[20]

Other cohorts of specialized plaintiffs requested creation of their own tracks and Judge Polster granted tracks for Native American tribes, third-party payors,

---

[16] *See supra* note 1.

[17] Gluck & Burch, *supra* note 12, at 24.

[18] *Id.* at 24–25.

[19] *See* Johnson & Johnson Settles Ohio Lawsuits to Avoid Federal Trial in National Prescription Opiate Litigation, 35 No. 09 Westlaw J. Pharmaceutical 01 (Oct. 8, 2019).

[20] *Id.* at 28.

and hospitals. He declined to create a separate track for babies who developed neonatal abstinence syndrome (NAS babies).[21]

Judge Polster initially devoted his energies to organizing the MDL and encouraging settlement. His concerted settlement efforts encouraged plaintiffs' counsel to propose to resolve the massive opioid litigation through approval and implementation of a novel Rule 23 negotiation class action. In the proposed class action, cities and counties sued multiple manufacturers, distributors, and retailers of prescription opioid drugs, asserting claims under RICO, the Controlled Substance Act, and statutory and common law claims, seeking reimbursement for costs of addressing the opioid crisis. The purpose of the negotiation class was to allow the plaintiffs to negotiate a lump sum settlement. Class members would then be afforded the opportunity to assess the plan for allocating the settlement, after being given notice and the opportunity to opt out of the settlement. After extensive briefing and argument, Judge Polster certified a negotiation class.[22]

Judge Polster's approval of the negotiation class was short-lived. In 2020 the appellate court reversed and remanded the litigation to Judge Polster for further proceedings.[23] The appellate court rejected the trial court's approval indicating that judges were bound by Rule 23's text and that the rule imposed demanding standards for class certification, which the negotiation class failed to satisfy. Because of the appellate repudiation of the negotiation class, the MDL opioid cases proceeded to bellwether trials pursuant to Judge Polster's track structure. Despite pleading numerous statutory and common law liability theories, the focal point of the remaining opioid litigation centered on the viability of the plaintiffs' public nuisance claims.

Although the MDL's first two years was consumed with Judge Polster's organization of the MDL and consideration of a negotiation class, the plaintiffs' novel assertion of a public nuisance theory played a central role in Judge Polster's thinking. Early in the proceedings Judge Polster signaled his sympathy for and appreciation of the public nuisance claims, indicating that "[I]t is hard to find anyone in Ohio who does not have a family member, a friend, a parent ... or a child of a friend who has ... been affected ... While these allegations do not fit neatly into the legal theories chosen by the Plaintiffs, they fit nonetheless."[24] Throughout the progress of the opioid tracks, Judge Polster consistently recognized and upheld the plaintiffs' right to assert

---

[21] *Id.*

[22] In re Nat'l Prescription Opiate Litig., 332 F.R.D. 532 (N.D. Ohio 2019); *see also* Gluck & Burch, *supra* note 12, at 29–32.

[23] In re Nat'l Prescription Opiate Litig., 976 Fed.R.3d 664 (6th Cir. 2020). *See* Linda S. Mullenix, The Short Unhappy Life of the Negotiation Class, 56 Mich. J.L. Ref. 613 (2023).

[24] In re Nat'l Prescription Opiate Litig, 2018 WL 6628898, at *21 (N.D. Ohio Dec. 19, 2018).

public nuisance claims, eventually permitting a jury trial of the public nuisance claim in Track Three cases.

8.3 PUBLIC NUISANCE CLAIMS IN THE NATIONAL OPIOID LITIGATION: THE TRACK ONE LAWSUITS

In July 2019, during pretrial motions practice relating to the Track One cases, the defendants and plaintiffs moved for summary judgment on the plaintiffs' relatively novel public nuisance claims. The county plaintiffs pleaded a claim for absolute public nuisance under Ohio common law and a statutory public nuisance claim under the Ohio Revised Code.[25] The plaintiffs' alleged that the defendants' actions caused and/or contributed to the public nuisance and health crisis related to opioid abuse and addiction. They contended that the defendants' actions interfered with the public's health, welfare, and safety, and asserted an abatement claim seeking over seven billion dollars to address various societal impacts, such as costs related to law enforcement, health care, foster care, and lost worker productivity.

The litigants' Track One summary judgment arguments and Judge Polster's rulings are instructive concerning articulation of the public nuisance claims in the opioid litigation. In Track One cases, Judge Polster denied defendants' summary judgment to dismiss the public nuisance claim,[26] and the plaintiffs' summary judgment motion to prevail on the public nuisance claim as a matter of law.[27]

On July 19, 2019, in Track One litigation, Purdue Pharma, joined with other manufacturers, distributors, and pharmacy defendants, moved for summary judgment.[28] The defendants contended that the plaintiffs' common law public nuisance claim failed because merely placing the label "nuisance" on an unspecified set of conditions was insufficient to state a claim. The defendants argued that the plaintiffs failed to define the public nuisance. While the plaintiffs pleaded general allegations of public nuisance that might have sufficed at the pleading stage, simply labeling a broad set of conditions as nuisance – such as increased addiction and employers' loss of productivity – did

---

[25] Ohio Revised Code §§ 715.44(A), 3767.01, 3767.3 & 4729.35.

[26] Opinion and Order Denying Manufacturer Defendants' Motion for Summary Judgment on Plaintiffs' Public Nuisance Claims, In re Nat'l Prescription Opiate Litig., No. 17-md-02804 (N.D. Ohio Sept. 9, 2019).

[27] Opinion and Order at 1–4, In re Nat'l Prescription Opiate Litig., No. 17-md-02804 (N.D. Ohio Sept. 4, 2019).

[28] Manufacturer Defendants' Memorandum in Support of Motion for Summary Judgment on Plaintiffs' Public Nuisance Claims, In re Nat'l Prescription Opiate Litig., 2019 WL 9468029 (N.D. Ohio July 19, 2019).

not satisfy the plaintiffs' burden to define the scope of the nuisance tort at the conclusion of discovery.[29]

In addition, even if the court accepted a nuisance concept without a defined scope, the claim failed because the plaintiffs could not prove the necessary elements of a common law public nuisance claim: that is, violation of a public right, proximate causation of the nuisance, and defendants' intent or inherently injurious conduct. The defendants contended that the plaintiff carried the burdens of showing that the defendants had control of the instrumentalities of the nuisance and establishing a proximate cause between the defendants' unreasonable conduct, the nuisance, and the alleged injuries.[30]

The defendants argued that none of the rights the plaintiffs claimed constituted a public right under Ohio common law. Citing the *Restatement (Second)*, the defendants noted that the *Restatement* defined public nuisance as consisting of a collective right that everyone had been injured and not individual rights.[31] The defendants disputed that simply invoking terms "public health, public safety, or public peace" did not transform a series of vague allegations into a public nuisance. Only claims that sought redress for an invasion of a collectively shared public right – such as shooting fireworks in the public street, or loud and disturbing noises – could properly be the basis for a public nuisance claim.[32]

The defendants further argued that the plaintiffs could not establish the requisite proximate cause between the defendants' actions and the alleged nuisance. To satisfy proximate causation, a plaintiff needed to demonstrate that the defendant exercised sufficient control over the product that caused the injury. The manufacturers argued that they did not exercise any control over illegal drugs, and the plaintiffs' inability to establish harms caused by prescription opioids as opposed to harms caused by illegal drugs doomed their claim. In addition, plaintiffs needed to show that the defendant's conduct was not too remote from the plaintiffs' injuries, but the plaintiffs could point to no evidence that linked the manufacturers to the illegal drug harms for which the plaintiffs sought recovery.[33]

To prevail on a claim for absolute public nuisance at common law, a plaintiff also carried the burden of showing that the defendants' conduct was intentional or based on an abnormally dangerous condition; the plaintiff needed to demonstrate that the defendant intended to bring about the conditions that constituted the nuisance. The defendants pointed out that the record was

---

[29] *Id.*
[30] *Id.* citing, the *Restatement (Second) Torts* § 821B.
[31] *Id.*
[32] *Id.*
[33] *Id.*

devoid of any evidence that the manufacturers intended the abuse, misuse, or addiction that constituted the opioid crisis.[34]

The defendants also contended they were entitled to summary judgment on the plaintiffs' statutory public nuisance claim.[35] Various Ohio code provisions defined a public nuisance to consist of the violation by a pharmacist or other person of any laws or rules of the board of pharmacy controlling distribution of pharmaceuticals. To assert a statutory claim, the plaintiff needed evidence showing that the manufacturers violated a federal or state enactment controlling the distribution of opioids or committed an act in the Ohio code. The manufacturing defendants contended that the plaintiffs' vague aid-and-abetting allegations of liability were insufficient because the plaintiffs offered no proof of an actual predicate statutory violation.

The plaintiffs Cuyahoga and Summit Counties filed their own motion for partial summary judgment of their absolute public nuisance claim. They maintained that there were no genuine issues of fact, entitling them to a judgment as a matter of law, relating to three aspects of their claim: (1) the opioid epidemic constituted a public nuisance in the two counties because it significantly interfered with public health in those communities, (2) under Ohio common law any defendant found to have been a substantial factor in the creation or maintenance of a public nuisance was jointly and severally liable, and (3) the defendants' statutory apportionment defense was inapplicable to the plaintiffs' abatement claim.[36]

The plaintiffs contended that there could be little doubt that the epidemic of opioid availability and use significantly interfered with the public health and constituted a public nuisance in the two counties. The defendants simply could not deny that a nuisance existed. The opioid crisis represented the deadliest drug epidemic in the nation's history that devastated families and communities. The epidemic affected addicted patients seeking help and community members caring for them. It affected children born to opioid addicts. It affected finite community resources and the ability to provide services. It affected first responders who daily confronted the real-world consequences of the epidemic. The defendants had admitted that addiction was a disease and not a matter of private choice, and that the opioid epidemic cost the public tens of billions of dollars annually.

Relying on the *Restatement (Second)* and noting the *Restatement's* numerous examples of public nuisance dealing with interferences with public

---

[34] *Id.*

[35] *See supra* note 25.

[36] Motion of Plaintiffs Cuyahoga and Summit Counties for Partial Summary Adjudication of Their Equitable Claims for Abatement of an Absolute Public Nuisance, In re Nat'l Prescription Opiate Litig., 2019 WL9468030 (N.D. Ohio July 19, 2019).

health, the plaintiffs argued that "the point of such examples is not to define public nuisances by drawing vague lines between public health issues that may impede the public's right safely to move about and be in the public from those that may not. It is to illustrate how the common law is not a fossil but remains responsive to contemporary societal needs by defining public nuisance in terms of harms that 'affect the health of so many persons as to involve the interests of the public at large.'"[37]

Supporting their summary judgment motion with discovery materials, Summit County documented that the opioid epidemic disproportionately impacted Summit treatment providers, first responders, hospitals, child services, the criminal justice system, the medical examiner, and the county families. The county public health department concluded that the grim opioid statistics made it clear that the opioid epidemic was a community-wide crisis striking all parts of the community: city and suburban, white and black, male and female, young and old. The facts made clear that the opioid epidemic constituted a significant interference with the public health in Summit County and, thus, was a public nuisance, citing the *Restatement (Second)* definition of a public nuisance.[38]

Cuyahoga County presented similar facts relating to the impact of the opioid epidemic on its community, concluding that the opioid crisis was consonant with the *Restatement's* definition of a public health nuisance. Cuyahoga County noted the effects of opioid addiction: increased rates of opioid-addicted children at birth; child abuse and neglect resulting in increased placement of children in child services; increased criminal activity and county jail placements; increased medical costs for addicted inmates; greater numbers of persons processed through the justice system placing strains on the juvenile court, the prosecutors' office, the public defender, and probation officers. The county further noted that because of increased spending on opioid-related services, the county had even less money to spend on non-opioid-related services.

The plaintiffs argued that, considering this evidence, the manufacturer, distributor, and pharmacy defendants could not legitimately dispute that the opioid epidemic was a public nuisance and when the defendants reviewed statistics relating to opioid abuse and addiction, they consistently concluded that the epidemic was a significant and deadly public health crisis. Moreover, the plaintiffs contended that the defendants' conduct was a substantial factor in producing the public nuisance. The only question remaining concerned the defendants' liability for creating the nuisance.

---

[37] *Id.* citing *Restatement (Second) of Torts* § 821B(1), § 821B, cmt. g.
[38] *Id.* citing *Restatement (Second) of Torts* § 821B(1), (2).

The counties requested partial summary judgment of the defendants' joint and several liability for the opioid public nuisance they created. The plaintiffs argued that under Ohio common law any defendant whose conduct was a substantial contributing factor in causing a public nuisance could be held jointly and severally liable for abating the nuisance. Although an Ohio statute limited joint and several liability for compensatory damages in tort that represented economic damages,[39] that statutory limitation did not apply to the plaintiffs' equitable action for abatement. An action for abatement of a public nuisance was not a tort action for compensatory damages and, therefore, was not subject to Ohio's apportionment statute.[40]

8.4 JUDGE POLSTER'S RULINGS ON THE PLAINTIFFS' OPIOID PUBLIC NUISANCE CLAIMS

On September 4, 2019, Judge Polster denied the plaintiffs' motion for partial summary judgment on the existence of a public nuisance.[41] The court rejected the plaintiffs' contention that separate adjudication of the harm and elements of a nuisance claim was useful. Instead, the *Restatement (Second)* used the phrase "unreasonable interference" to define both cognizable harm and actionable conduct. The two elements were intertwined and could not be independently determined as a matter of law; whether the opioid crisis was a public nuisance was a question "that must await full airing of the facts at trial."[42]

Concerning the possibility for the defendants' joint and several liability under Ohio law, the court noted that the fact that a nuisance was sometimes characterized as a variety of tort did not change the fact that it was an equitable claim to abate a nuisance, and not an action for compensatory damages. Abatement was equitable in nature and provided a prospective remedy that compensated a plaintiff for the costs of rectifying the nuisance.[43]

The court held that Ohio statutes did not bar joint and several liability for abatement of a nuisance; there was nothing in the Ohio statutes that precluded application of that doctrine. However, the statute would not bar the

---

[39] R.C. § 2307.22-2307.31.

[40] *See e.g.*, Pharmacy Defendants' Response to Plaintiffs' Partial Motion for Summary Judgment on Abatement of an Absolute Public Nuisance, 2019 WL 8759008 (N.D. Ohio Aug. 14, 2019); Reply in Support of Motion of Plaintiffs Cuyahoga and Summit Counties for Partial Summary Adjudication of Their Equitable Claims for Abatement of an Absolute Public Nuisance (N.D. Ohio Aug. 26, 2019).

[41] Order and Opinion, In re Nat'l Prescription Opiate Litig., 2019 WL 4194272 (N.D. Ohio Sept. 4, 2019).

[42] *Id.* at **1–2.

[43] *Id.* at *3.

ability of any defendant at trial from arguing that the liability for creating the nuisance should be determined on a proportional basis.[44] Because there were material questions of fact that had to be resolved at trial prior to any apportionment ruling, the court denied that plaintiffs' request to strike the defendants' affirmative defenses to such proportional liability.[45]

On September 9, 2019, Judge Polster denied the manufacturers' summary judgment motion, disagreeing on the three broad grounds asserted in their motion.[46] First, the court rejected the defendants' contention that the plaintiffs had failed sufficiently to allege a public nuisance. This argument was "amply contradicted" by the extensive factual details and evidence the counties produced through discovery in support of their public nuisance claim.

The Ohio Supreme Court had recognized the breath of an absolute public nuisance claim under the *Restatement (Second)'s* broad definition that a public nuisance could be maintained where facts established that "the design, manufacturing, marketing or sale of [a] product unreasonably interfere[d] with a right common to the public."[47] Reviewing the plaintiffs' evidence, the court concluded that a factfinder could reasonably conclude that this evidence demonstrated an interference with public health and public safety rights.[48]

The court further concluded that the plaintiffs had made a sufficient showing to withstand the defendants' summary judgment on causation issues.[49] Adopting the conclusions reached in an earlier order relating to causation issues, the court rejected the defendants' argument that the plaintiffs could not establish, as a matter of law, that the manufacturers had proximately caused the public nuisance. The court indicated that the defendants misconstrued the plaintiffs' theory of nuisance liability. The plaintiffs were not contending that the nuisance was a consequence of the use or misuse of opioids, but rather the result of the defendant's business conduct: the defendants' control over the instrumentality of the nuisance by virtue of their marketing, distribution, or dispensing practices.[50] In addition, the court noted that the plaintiffs presented fact and expert evidence showing that the injuries they alleged would be an expected consequence of the manufacturers' alleged misleading marketing activities and their failure to maintain anti-diversion controls.[51]

---

[44] *Id.* at *4.

[45] *Id.* at **4–5.

[46] In re Nat'l Prescription Opiate Litig., 406 F.Supp.3d 672, 677 (N.D. Ohio 2019).

[47] *Id.* at 673, citing Cincinnati v. Beretta, U.S.A., Corp., 95 Ohio St.3d 416, 768 N.E.2d 1136, 1142 (2002).

[48] In re Nat'l Prescription Opiate, *supra* note 42, at 674.

[49] *See* Opinion and Order Regarding Defendants' Summary Judgment Motions on Causation, 2019 WL 4178617 (N.D. Ohio Sept. 9, 2019).

[50] *Id.* at 674–75.

[51] *Id.* at 675.

Additionally, the court recognized that the intentional conduct to support a public nuisance claim meant a showing that the creator of the nuisance intended to bring about the conditions which were in fact a nuisance. As to the manufacturers' intent to bring about the conditions creating the alleged nuisance, the court determined that the factfinders could reasonably infer that the defendants' marketing and failure to maintain anti-diversion controls were substantial factors in producing the harm the plaintiffs alleged.[52]

Turning to statutory allegations, the court indicated that the plaintiffs had presented sufficient evidence to preclude the defendants' summary judgment under the Controlled Substances Act. The court found that the record was replete with disputed material facts concerning whether each defendant complied with its obligations under the CSA.[53] The court held that the manufacturers' contention that there was no violation supporting the statutory nuisance claim was without merit.[54]

Judge Polster's summary judgment orders relating to the public nuisance claims cleared the way for trial, which would address solely the plaintiffs' common and statutory public nuisance claims. The defendants moved for an order that all aspects of the plaintiff's public nuisance claims – whether there existed a public nuisance caused by any defendant, and what abatement remedies should be imposed – should be tried by a jury. On September 24, 2019, Judge Polster issued a lengthy opinion surveying the right to trial by jury in litigation involving legal and equitable claims. He determined that liability for the public nuisance claims would be determined by a jury and, if found, the court would separately fashion remedies.[55] By the time Judge Polster issued his summary judgment and jury trial orders, he had narrowed Track One cases solely to the common and statutory public nuisance claims, thus making the litigation a test case for the viability of opioids-as-public nuisance.

As the national opioid litigation progressed to trial, an Oklahoma state judge conducted a 33-day bench trial against three opioid manufacturers, including Johnson & Johnson, on the single claim of public nuisance. The court held J&J liable under Oklahoma's public nuisance statute for conducting "false, misleading, and dangerous marketing campaigns" about prescription opioids. The court ordered J&J to pay $465 million to fund one year of the state's

---

[52] *Id.* at 675–76.
[53] *Id.* at 676.
[54] *Id.* at 676–77.
[55] Opinion and Order Regarding Adjudication of Plaintiffs' Public Nuisance Claims, In re Nat'l Prescription Opiate Litig., 2019 WL 4621690 (N.D. Ohio Sept. 24, 2019).

abatement plan, with the court appropriating money to 21 government programs for services to combat opioid abuse.[56]

Against this background of Judge Polster's denial of summary judgment and the substantial Oklahoma verdict against Johnson & Johnson, on October 21, 2019 – the eve of the first trial in the federal opioid MDL – three major pharmaceutical drug distributors settled.[57] McKeeson, Cardinal Health, and AmerisourceBergen – which distributed about 90 percent of all medicines to pharmacies, hospitals, and clinics – agreed to pay $215 million to the two plaintiff counties. In addition, Teva agreed to pay $20 million in cash over three years and donate $25 million worth of addiction treatment drugs.[58] The combined total of the settlements to the two counties amounted to $260 million.[59]

Coming on the eve of the first national trial, it was generally perceived that the distributors' last-minute settlements were intended to avoid the landmark federal trial, which would have served as a test case for legal arguments and evidence on the novel public nuisance claim. Because these opioid claims were not litigated in a jury trial, the settlement failed to establish any precedent concerning the legitimacy or viability of the plaintiffs' public nuisance claims at trial.

8.5 TRACK THREE NATIONAL OPIOID CLAIMS AGAINST RETAIL PHARMACIES

Walgreens, a defendant in Track One litigation was the only defendant that did not settle in October 2019. Walgreen's refusal to settle along with the opioid distributors set the stage for a trial of public nuisance claims against retail pharmacies. In this litigation, two new Ohio counties sued pharmacies' owners based on a claim of absolute public nuisance under Ohio common law, which arose out of the pharmacies' alleged violations of the federal Controlled Substances Act (CSA) and the Ohio controlled substances laws. The plaintiffs claimed that the defendants created a public nuisance by failing to comply with the controlled substances laws in dispensing of opioids to customers.[60] The gravamen of the complaint asserted that under the CSA and analogous Ohio statutes,

---

[56] Hunter, *supra* note 7. In the Oklahoma opioid litigation, the state additionally sued Purdue Pharma and related entities and Teva Pharmaceutical and related entities. The state settled with Purdue for $270 million and settled with Teva for $85 million.

[57] Jan Hoffman, $260 Million Opioid Settlement Reached at Last Minute with Big Drug Companies, N.Y. Times (Oct. 21, 2019).

[58] *Id.*

[59] *Id.* The counties announced programs to abate the local opioid crisis in their jurisdictions.

[60] In re Nat'l Prescription Opiate Litig., 477 F.Supp.3d 613, 616–17 (N.D. Ohio Aug. 6, 2020).

the defendants violated these laws because the pharmacies dispensed and sold opioids without effective controls against the diversion of opioids.[61]

In pretrial proceedings the pharmacy defendants objected to the plaintiffs' claims of absolute public nuisance based on the pharmacies' activities in distributing and dispensing opioids to customers. Just like Judge Polster ruled in the Track One litigation against the manufacturers and distributors, Judge Polster denied the pharmacy defendants' motions to dismiss for failure to state a claim,[62] and summary judgment.[63]

The court rejected defense arguments raised in opposition to the plaintiffs' public nuisance claims. The defendants argued that the Ohio occupational statutes governing pharmacies displaced the common law and precluded the absolute nuisance claim. The pharmacies further raised defenses sounding in state and federal field and conflict preemption. The court rejected these arguments construing the Ohio statutory scheme and its legislative intent.[64]

The court concluded that the plaintiffs were not asserting a claim under Ohio's occupational statutes, but rather were asserting a common law absolute public nuisance claim alleging the defendants' violation of the anti-diversion laws.[65] The court concluded that the Ohio legislature had not intended to abrogate public nuisance claims or remedies when it enacted its occupational laws. Moreover, Ohio courts repeatedly held that the general nuisance statute did not supersede or preempt common law public nuisance claims,[66] and although the distribution of controlled substances was regulated under a comprehensive federal scheme, this did not foreclose an absolute public nuisance claim under Ohio common law.[67]

Surveying public nuisance jurisprudence and facts surrounding the defendants' distributing and dispensing activities, Judge Polster concluded that the plaintiffs had sufficiently stated common law claims for absolute public nuisance.[68] He further rejected the pharmacies' objections based on a lack of proximate causation and the learned intermediary defense.[69] The court held that under various states' laws a physician's prescribing decision did not break the causal chain between the pharmacies' dispensing conduct and the plaintiffs' injuries. Moreover, the learned intermediary defense was inapplicable because

---

[61] *Id.* at 617.

[62] *Id.*

[63] Order and Opinion Denying HBC Service Company and Giant Eagle's Motion for Summary Judgment, In re Nat'l Prescription Opiate Litig., 2021 WL 3917174 (N.D. Ohio Sept. 1, 2021).

[64] In re Nat'l Prescription Opiate Litig., *supra* note 60, at 618–23.

[65] *Id.* at 618–19.

[66] *Id.* at 620.

[67] *Id.* at 621.

[68] *Id.* at 631–35.

[69] *Id.* at 635–36.

the plaintiffs were not seeking to hold the defendants liable for personal injuries for harm caused by products or related wrongs. Instead, the plaintiffs' public nuisance claim related to broad harms to the public caused by the defendants' dispensing conduct that implicated legal obligations independent of manufacturers, physicians, or any other participant in the opioid supply chain.[70]

Judge Polster further rejected some defendants' attempts to dismiss on summary judgment the public nuisance claims against them, arguing that they were entitled to a safe harbor immunity for having fully complied with all regulatory requirements involving anti-diversion laws. The defendants contended that they had been in full compliance with the Drug Enforcement Agency and Ohio Board of Pharmacy regulations and had passed numerous audits and inspections. The court concluded that the plaintiffs had submitted evidence that showed the defendants were not in compliance with the CSA as well as evidence that tended to show that the defendants knew that they were not in full compliance. The defendants were not entitled to summary judgment because there were material facts in dispute concerning their compliance, and therefore, they did not qualify for safe harbor immunity.[71]

Judge Polster's pretrial rulings relating to the pharmacy defendants' litigation cleared the way for trial solely on the plaintiffs' public nuisance claims. Unlike the Track One opioid litigation, the pharmacy defendants did not settle before trial.

8.6 THE NATIONAL OPIOID TRIAL OF THE PUBLIC NUISANCE CLAIM

In November 2021, the Track Three pharmacy litigation by two Ohio counties proceeded to trial against three pharmacy defendants, CVS, Walgreens, and Walmart. The case was tried based on the plaintiffs' absolute public nuisance claim arising from the allegations that the pharmacies' unlawful or intentional dispensing conduct substantially contributed to an oversupply of legal prescription opioid drugs, and to a diversion of opioids into the illicit market. The defendants' conduct consequently had endangered the public health or safety, creating a public nuisance.[72]

---

[70] *Id.*

[71] Order and Opinion Denying HBC Service Company and Giant Eagle's Motion for Summary Judgment, *supra* note 63, at **1–3. The court further denied the defendants' summary judgment motion on proximate causation grounds. *Id.* at *4. *See* In re Nat'l Prescription Opiate Litig., 2019 WL 4179617, at *4 (N.D. Ohio Sept. 3, 2019); In re Nat'l Prescription Opiate Litig., 202 WL 425830, at *2 (N.D. Ohio Jan. 27, 2020).

[72] In re Nat'l Prescription Opiate Litig., 589 F.Supp.3d 790, 795 (N.D. Ohio 2022).

After an eight-week trial, a jury found grounds in favor of the two counties in the liability phase of the litigation. The jury determined that the defendants created a continuing public nuisance because even though the supply of opioids had decreased by the time of trial, opioid patients who were addicted to pain killers had turned to illegal heroin and fentanyl. This was a foreseeable, direct consequence of the flood of opioid pills the defendants dispensed in the marketplace. In addition, the jury found that the defendants had engaged in intentional or illegal conduct.[73] The jury left to the court, in a bench trial, to determine the abatement remedy.[74]

The defendants moved for a judgment as a matter of law. In March 2022, Judge Polster issued a lengthy opinion denying the defendants' posttrial motion.[75] With an eye toward the certainty that the defendants would appeal, Judge Polster carefully canvassed the reasons the jury reasonably concluded that the defendants had created and sustained a public nuisance. Judge Polster's opinion discussed two broad challenges: (1) the jury's finding of an actionable public nuisance claim, and (2) an array of technical defense arguments disputing the legality of the public nuisance claim. Many of Judge Polster's holdings rejecting the defendants' contentions reiterated his numerous pretrial orders governing the Track Three cases.[76]

Reviewing the plaintiffs' extensive trial evidence concerning the activities of each pharmacy defendant, Judge Polster rejected arguments that the plaintiffs had failed to establish that the defendants had engaged in unlawful or intentional conduct, or their conduct proximately caused a public nuisance. He instructed the jury that to find a person had engaged in intentional conduct, "it [was] enough that the person intended to act and knew, or was substantially certain, that the circumstances resulting from that act would interfere with the public health or public safety."[77] He concluded that the plaintiffs' trial evidence was sufficient for a jury to reasonably conclude that each defendant knowingly engaged in unlawful dispensing conduct.[78]

Judge Polster further upheld the jury's finding that the defendants proximately caused public nuisance. Referencing the defendants' prior summary judgment causation motion, Judge Polster indicated he previously found that the aggregate

---

[73] *See* Jan Hoffman, CVS, Walgreens and Walmart Fueled Opioid Crisis, Jury Finds, N.Y. Times (Nov. 23, 2021).

[74] In re Nat'l Prescription Opiate Litig., *supra* note 72, at 795.

[75] *Id.*

[76] *Id.* at 800. Judge Polster also rejected defendants' challenges to the admission of five expert witnesses at trial. *Id.* at 826–31.

[77] *Id.* at 805.

[78] *Id.* at 796–97.

evidence of the massive increase in the opioid supply, combined with evidence that the defendants failed to maintain effective controls against opioid diversion, supported a reasonable jury inference that the defendants' conduct was a substantial factor in creating the nuisance.[79] Moreover, the existence of other possible causation factors did not preclude the jury from determining that each defendants' conduct played a substantial role in creating the nuisance.[80]

Turning to other legal challenges, Judge Polster rejected defense arguments that various doctrines barred the public nuisance claim: (1) preclusion by Ohio statutory or common law, (2) primary jurisdiction, (3) standing, (4) economic loss rule, (5) statewide concern, and (6) the municipal cost recovery rule. Judge Polster rejected defense challenges to plaintiffs' alleged failures to demonstrate violation of a public right, or an ongoing public nuisance. He rejected defendants' contentions that the action penalized them for lawful conduct because federal and state laws authorized and regulated their controlled substance dispensary business; the court rejected the corollary safe harbor immunity. Judge Polster rejected the defense argument that the pharmacies lacked control over the instrumentality allegedly causing the nuisance. Globally, Judge Polster rejected the defendants' policy argument that the plaintiffs' action illegitimately extended the law and would permit consumers to convert almost every products liability claim into a public nuisance claim.[81]

Judge Polster subsequently held a bench trial to determine the remedies following the Track Three jury verdicts. On August 17, 2022, he issued his abatement order.[82] The court held that the pharmacy defendants would be jointly and severally liable for $306.2 million compensation over fifteen years to Lake County and for $344.4 million compensation to Trumbull County, for a total of $650.6 million.[83] Judge Polster ordered an administrator to oversee the abatement fund and the court retained continuing jurisdiction over its administration. The court further entered an injunction directing the pharmacy defendants to undertake certain actions to ensure compliance with the Controlled Substances Act, to avoid further improper dispensing conduct.[84]

Judge Polster's abatement order extensively set forth the principles of public nuisance jurisprudence undergirding the jury verdict and his abatement

---

[79] *Id.* at 808–11.

[80] *Id.* at 811.

[81] *Id.* at 811–26.

[82] In re Nat'l Prescription Opiate Litig., 2022 WL 3443614 (Aug. 17, 2022).

[83] Jan Hoffman, CVS, Walgreens and Walmart Must Pay $650.5 Million in Ohio Opioids Case, N.Y. Times (Aug. 17, 2022); Amanda Robert, Federal Judge Orders 3 Pharmacy Chains to Pay Over $650M for Role in Opioid Epidemic, A.B.A.J (Aug. 18, 2022).

[84] In re Nat'l Prescription Opiate Litig., *supra* note 82, at *3.

remedy order. Like his opinion denying the defendants' post-trial motion for a judgment as a matter of law, Judge Polster's abatement order was written in contemplation of an appeal. In this opinion he reiterated the same principles and conclusions he had articulated throughout the MDL public nuisance litigation.

After narrating the extensive MDL opioid litigation history and the equitable principles underlying the litigation, Judge Polster comprehensively reviewed Ohio law on public nuisance, the nuisance the jury found, abatement of nuisance versus damages, the scope of the abatement remedy, allocation of costs attributable to the defendants' conduct, standards regarding apportionment, contribution by other actors, other defense arguments, and administration of the abatement fund.[85]

In December 2022 the pharmacy defendants appealed the underlying judgments,[86] followed by responsive briefing by the plaintiff–appellees during February 2023.[87] Numerous amici filed briefs in support of the appellants and appellees.[88] On February 10, 2023, Judge Polster denied the pharmacy defendants' motion to stay his August 2022 injunction order pending the appeal.[89] When the appellate court decides this appeal, its determination of the viability of a public nuisance claim will lay the groundwork for a Supreme Court appeal.

8.7 OTHER PUBLIC NUISANCE CLAIMS IN THE NATIONAL OPIATE LITIGATION

Judge Polster managed the public nuisance claims in Track One and Track Three cases aggregated in the MDL. The Track One public nuisance claims settled and never went to trial, generating no appealable issue. The Track Three public nuisance claims were tried by a jury and resulted in Judge Polster's abatement order. Judge Polster's numerous opinions in the Track Three opioid cases are now subject to appellate review.

While Judge Polster retained the management of Track One and Three cases, other MDL opioid cases proceeded in West Virginia state court and

---

[85] *Id.* at **3–32.

[86] Consolidated Brief for Appellants, In re Nat'l Prescription Opiate Litig., 2022 WL 17551447 (6th Cir. Dec. 1, 2022).

[87] Consolidated Brief for Plaintiffs-Appellees Trumbull County and Lake County, Ohio, In re Nat'l Prescription Opiate Litig., 2023 WL 2161658 (6th Cir. Feb. 14, 2023).

[88] *See e.g.*, Brief of the Ohio Chamber of Commerce as Amicus Curiae in Support of Defendant-Appellants, In re Nat'l Prescription Opiate Litig., 2022 WL 17688026 (6th Cir. Dec. 8, 2022); Brief of American Public Health Association and National Association of County and City Health Officials as Amici Curiae in Support of Appellees, In re Nat'l Prescription Opiate Litig., 2023 WL 2261164 (6th Cir. Feb. 21, 2023).

[89] Opinion and Order Denying Motion to Stay Injunction Order Pending Appeal, In re Nat'l Prescription Opiate Litig., 2023 WL 1878580 (N.D. Ohio Feb. 10, 2023).

California federal court. The adjudication of these cases resulted in conflicting holdings concerning the viability of opioid public nuisance claims, even within the context of the national MDL. Judge Polster's lengthy justification of the public nuisance claims, and the conflicting analysis in the West Virginia and other state public nuisance cases, suggested that the controversy over public nuisance litigation was ripening for Supreme Court resolution.

Two West Virginia political subdivisions brought lawsuits against three opioid distributors: McKesson, Cardinal, and AmerisourceBergen. Before trial, the distributors settled with all political subdivisions in 49 states for about $21 billion, but the West Virginia subdivisions did not participate. The West Virginia trial judge issued an opinion that the Supreme Court of West Virginia would not extend the law of public nuisance to the sale, distribution, and manufacture of opioids, and that even if it did, the plaintiffs failed to show that the defendants' conduct interfered with a public right.[90]

San Francisco pursued opioid litigation solely against Walgreens that was conducted in a bench trial. The judge bifurcated the trial in a fashion similar to Judge Polster's adjudication of the Track Three cases. The first phase was to determine Walgreen's liability for a public nuisance. The judge held that Walgreens substantially contributed to an opioid epidemic with far-reaching and devastating effects across San Francisco. He indicated that a second trial phase would determine the extent to which Walgreens had to abate the public nuisance it helped to create.[91]

8.8 PUBLIC NUISANCE CLAIMS REJECTED IN STATE OPIOID LITIGATION

The state courts' resolution of opioid litigation did not follow in lockstep agreement with Judge Polster's extensive analysis of the opioid crisis as presenting an actionable public nuisance claim. At the same time in November 2021 that the national opioid cases were proceeding to a jury trial in Ohio before Judge Polster, the Oklahoma Supreme Court – in a five to one decision – reversed a trial court judgment holding an opioid manufacturer liable for a public nuisance in manufacturing, marketing, and selling of prescription opioids.[92]

---

[90] In re Nat'l Prescription Opiate Litig., *supra* note 82, at 1, citing Huntington v. AmerisourceBergen Drug. Corp., 2022 WL 2399876, at *59 (S.D.W.Va. July 4, 2022).

[91] In re Nat'l Prescription Opiate Litig., *supra* note 82, at 1, citing San Francisco v. Purdue Pharma, 2022 WL 3224463, at *60 (N.D. Cal. Aug. 10, 2022).

[92] Hunter, *supra* note 7. *See* Jan Hoffman, Oklahoma Supreme Court Throws Out $465 Million Opioid Ruling Against J & J, N.Y. Times (Nov. 9, 2021); Jennifer Calfas, Johnson & Johnson Opioid Verdict Overturned by Oklahoma Supreme Court, Wall. St. J. (Nov. 9, 2021).

In 2017 the Oklahoma attorney general sued three opioid manufacturers, Johnson & Johnson, Purdue Pharma, and Teva alleging that the defendants deceptively marketed opioids in Oklahoma. The state settled with the other opioid manufacturers and dismissed all claims against J & J except for public nuisance under the Oklahoma nuisance statute.[93]

The district court conducted a 33-day bench trial limited to the single issue whether J & J was responsible for creating a public nuisance in marketing and selling its opioids products. The court held J & J liable under Oklahoma's public nuisance statute for conducting false, misleading, and dangerous marketing campaigns about prescription opioids and ordered J & J to pay $465 million to fund one year of the state's abatement plan. The district court was to appropriate the money to fund twenty-one governmental programs for services to combat opioid abuse.[94] J & J appealed and the state cross-appealed, arguing that the monetary judgment was insufficient. The state argued that J & J should be responsible for paying twenty years of the state's abatement plan or approximately $9.3 billion to fund the state's governmental programs.[95]

The Oklahoma Supreme Court limited its review to the question whether J & J's marketing and selling of opioids constituted a public nuisance under Oklahoma statutes. The court held that the district court's expansion of public nuisance law to embrace the defendant's conduct went too far, and does not extend to the manufacturing, marketing, and selling of prescription opioids.[96] The court noted that the litigation primarily concerned a question of statutory construction.

The court signaled that it would take a narrow approach by limiting public nuisance claims to traditional interferences with property. Reviewing the history of public nuisance jurisprudence, the court noted that public nuisance evolved into a common law tort that historically was linked to the use of land by a person creating the nuisance. The Oklahoma Supreme Court concluded that courts had cabined public nuisance claims to these traditional bounds, citing the New Jersey Supreme Court's decision in its lead paint public nuisance litigation.[97] Moreover, abatement was the sole remedy for available for public entities seeking relief from public nuisance violations.[98]

---

[93] 51 O.S.2011, §§ 1 & 2.
[94] *Id.* at 721–23.
[95] *Id.* at 723.
[96] *Id.* at 721.
[97] *Id.* at 724, citing In re Lead Paint Litig., 191 N.J. 405, 924 A.2d 484, 499 (2007).
[98] Hunter, *supra* note 7, at 724.

The Oklahoma Supreme Court determined that the state nuisance statute enacted in 1910, codified the common law.[99] Surveying 100 years of Oklahoma public nuisance litigation, the Supreme Court noted that courts had limited defendants' liability to two situations where defendants: (1) committed crimes constituting a nuisance, or (2) caused physical injury to property or participating in offensive activity that rendered property uninhabitable. The court concluded that the plaintiff's allegation did not fit within the Oklahoma statutory provisions as construed by the Oklahoma Supreme Court.[100]

Citing the *Restatement (Third)*,[101] the court indicated that it had never applied public nuisance law to the manufacturing, marketing, and selling of lawful products. "Applying nuisance statutes to lawful products as the State requests would create unlimited and unprincipled liability for product manufacturers."[102] The plaintiff's view of J & J's responsibilities presented a classic articulation of tort law duties – to warn or make safe – that sounded in product-related liability. But public nuisance law and product liability were two distinct causes of action "each with boundaries that are not intended to overlap."[103]

Elaborating on this policy consideration, the Oklahoma Supreme Court indicated that public nuisance claims were ill-suited to resolve claims against product manufacturers. The court identified three reasons not to extend public nuisance jurisprudence to J & J's activities: (1) the manufacture and distribution of products rarely caused a violation of a public right, (2) manufacturers do not generally have control of their products once they are sold, and (3) manufacturers could be held perpetually liable for its products under a nuisance theory.

The court indicated that J & J had failed to show a violation of a public right. Taking the narrowest view, the court held that a "public right was a right to a public good, such as an indivisible resource shared by the public at large,

---

[99] The Oklahoma statute provides:

> A nuisance consists in unlawfully doing an act, or omitting to perform a duty, which act or omission either:

> First. Annoys, injures or endangers the comfort, response, health, or safety of others; or
> Second. Offends decency; or
> Third. Unlawfully interferes with, obstructs or tends to obstruct, or renders dangerous for passage, any lake or navigable river, stream, or canal or basin, or any public park, square, street or highway; or
> Fourth. In any way renders other person insecure in life, or in the use of property, provided, this section shall not apply to preexisting agricultural activities.

50 O.S. 2011 § 1.
[100] Hunter, *supra* note 7, at 723–24.
[101] *Id.* at 725; *Restatement (Third) of Torts: Liab. For Econ. Harm* § 8 cmt. g (Am Law. Inst. 2020).
[102] Hunter, *supra* note 7, at 725.
[103] *Id.*

like air, water, or public rights-of-way."[104] The court rejected that state's characterizing the interference with the public right of health. According to the court, the case did not involve activities that anticipated injury to the public health, such as diseased animals, pollution in drinking water, or the discharge of a sewer on property.[105]

Furthermore, a product manufacturer's responsibility was to place a lawful non-defective product in the marketplace, but there is no common law tort duty to monitor how a consumer subsequently uses or misuses the product after it is sold. J & J had no control over its products once they were sold through multiple levels of distribution to wholesalers, retail pharmacies, and physicians' offices.[106]

In addition, without continuing control over the product J & J could not remove or abate the alleged nuisance. Even if J & J paid for the state's abatement plan, opioid use and addiction would not cease to exist; the plan would not stop the act or omission that constituted the nuisance.[107] For more than 100 years in deciding public nuisance cases the Oklahoma Supreme Court had never allowed the state to collect cash payments from a defendant with the district court apportioning the money to address social, health, and criminal consequences allegedly arising from the nuisance. Moreover, Oklahoma law rejected manufacturers' perpetual liability for their products in relation to all other traditional tort theories.[108]

In conclusion the Oklahoma Supreme Court offered the most robust statement opposing the use of public nuisance claims in products cases. The court noted that the state presented a novel public nuisance theory that challenged the court to rethink traditional notions of liability and causation, and that tort law was ever-changing, reflecting "the complexity and vitality of daily life."[109] The court had recognized and allowed public nuisance claims to address discrete, localized problems, but not policy questions. The trial court's decision expanded public nuisance law and permitted the court to manage public policy matters that were better handled by the legislative and executive branches. The legislative and executive branches were better suited to balance the competing interests involved in societal problems.[110]

---

[104] *Id.* at 726.

[105] *Id.*

[106] *Id.* at 727.

[107] *Id.* at 729. The court pointed out that an injunction against J & J to cease promoting and marketing opioids would be ineffective because J & J had halted promotional activities for several years.

[108] *Id.*

[109] *Id.* at 731.

[110] *Id.* "The court defers the policy-making to the legislative and executive branches and rejects the unprecedented expansion of public nuisance law."

The court held that extending public nuisance jurisprudence to the manufacturing, marketing, and selling of products would allow consumers to convert almost every products liability action into a public nuisance claim:

> The common law criminal and property-based limitations have shaped Oklahoma's public nuisance statute. Without those limitations, businesses have no way to know whether they might face nuisance liability for manufacturing, marketing, or selling products, i.e., will a sugar manufacturer or the fast-food industry be liable for obesity, will an alcohol manufacturer be liable for psychological harms, or will a car manufacturer for health hazards from lung disease to dementia or for air pollution. We follow the limitations set by this Court for the past one hundred years: Oklahoma public nuisance law does not apply to J & J's conduct in manufacturing, marketing, and selling prescription opioids.[111]

In addition to the Oklahoma Supreme's Court's repudiation of expanding public nuisance law to reach J & J's manufacturing activities, North and South Dakota courts reached the same conclusions to reject public nuisance claims against opioid manufacturers, based on nuisance statutes identical to Oklahoma's statute. In North Dakota, a district court dismissed litigation brought by the state against opioid defendants holding that its public nuisance law did not apply to the sale of goods.[112] A South Dakota court dismissed a public nuisance claim by the state against opioid manufacturers for the same reason as the North Dakota court, but for the additional reason that the defendants did not have control of the instrumentality of the nuisance – the opioids – when the alleged injuries occurred.[113]

8.9 PUBLIC NUISANCE CLAIMS UPHELD IN STATE OPIOID LITIGATION

Several states, including the Commonwealth of Massachusetts, fared better in their public nuisance litigation against Purdue Pharma and declined to dismiss public nuisance opioid claims against this manufacturing defendant.[114] In 2007 Purdue reached a consent decree with Massachusetts and several other states that prohibited Purdue from making any written or oral representation that was false, misleading, or deceptive in the marketing of OxyContin's addictive properties. It also required that Purdue establish and follow an abuse

[111] *Id.*

[112] State *ex rel.* Stenehjem v. Purdue Pharma, L.P., 2019 WL2245734, at *13 (N.D. Dist. Ct. May 10, 2019).

[113] State *ex rel.* Ravnsborg v. Purdue Pharma L.P., No. 32CIV18-000065 (S.D. Cir. Ct. Jan. 13, 2021).

[114] Massachusetts v. Purdue Pharma, L.P., 36 Mass. L. Rptr. 56 (2019).

diversion program to detect and identify high-prescribing doctors who showed signs of inappropriate prescribing, to stop prescribing drugs to them, and to report them to the authorities.

In the years following the consent decree, Massachusetts alleged that Purdue failed to comply with the consent decree. It continued its prior marketing practice, minimizing the dangers associated with the use of OxyContin, knowing that its marketing tactics led to more addiction among patients and increased the likelihood that patients would overdose and die. Massachusetts sued Purdue Pharma alleging that because of its unfair and deceptive marketing activities the state sustained substantial damages. The state sought damages from Purdue to offset the costs of the opioid epidemic which Massachusetts had declared a public health emergency. The state asserted a claim for violation of statutory law as well as public nuisance.[115]

In 2019, the Superior Court of Massachusetts denied Purdue Pharma's motion to dismiss the case for failure to state a claim upon which relief could be granted. The court rejected the defendant's claim that it was not subject to a statutory violation because its activities were a "permitted practice" under the statute, and therefore, exempted from liability. Purdue further claimed that it was not liable because the plaintiff could not show that the defendant had infringed any public right and the learned intermediary broke the chain of causation between its conduct and the harms the state alleged.[116]

In declining to dismiss the state's public nuisance claim, the court surveyed other state's opioid litigation against manufacturers. The Massachusetts court held that manufacturing defendants had raised similar arguments and courts in many other jurisdictions – Alaska, Arkansas, Minnesota, New Hampshire, Ohio, Oklahoma, Tennessee, and Vermont – had rejected these arguments.[117] In line with these other states, Massachusetts concluded that Purdue's arguments did not justify dismissal of the state's complaint.

In upholding the state's complaint, the court rejected Purdue's argument that its conduct conformed with Food and Drug Administration decisions approving the sale of opioids, and therefore, its marketing statements were not actionable as a matter of law. The court indicated that Purdue's theory

---

[115] *Id.* at **1–2.
[116] *Id.*
[117] *Id.* at *2, citing Alaska v. Purdue Pharma, L.P., 2018 WL 4468439 (Alaska Super. Ct. 2018); State of Arkansas v. Purdue Pharma, L.P., No. 60CV-18-2018 (Ark. Cir. Ct. Apr. 5, 2019); Minnesota v. Purdue Pharma, L.P., No. 27-CV-18-10788 (Minn. Dist. Ct. Jan. 4, 2019); New Hampshire v. Purdue Pharma, L.P., 2018 WL 4566129 (N.H. Super. Ct. 2018); Ohio v. Purdue Pharma, L.P., 2018 WL 4080052 (Ohio C.P. 2018); Oklahoma v. Purdue Pharma, L.P., 2017 WL 10152334 (Okla. Dist. Ct. 2017); Tennessee v. Purdue Pharma, L.P., No. 1-173-18 (Tenn. Cir. Ct. Feb. 22, 2019); Vermont v. Purdue Pharma, L.P., No. 757-9-18 (Vt. Super. Ct. March 19, 2019).

fell short of implied preemption under the FDA, a preemption argument that Delaware and New Jersey had rejected.[118] The court indicated that North Dakota's contrary finding seemed to be an outlier among state courts that had considered the issue.

Citing the *Restatement (Second)* and Massachusetts precedents, the court concluded that the state's allegations were sufficient to support a claim that Purdue's conduct had interfered with public health and safety. The court disagreed that the public nuisance claim was simply a repackaged product liability claim, citing cases where Massachusetts courts had refused to dismiss public nuisance claims involving dangerous products such as tobacco and firearms.[119]

The court further determined that the state's complaint contained sufficient allegations to show causation and the harm alleged. Cause in fact meant an injury or harm would not have occurred but for the defendant's conduct. Proximate cause was an injury to a plaintiff that was a foreseeable result of the defendant's conduct. The court further denied Purdue's invocation of the learned intermediary defense, noting that by actively undermining the warnings on its products, Purdue was alleged to have caused physicians to write opioid prescriptions they otherwise would not have written.[120]

In a companion lawsuit brought by Boston against Purdue Pharma, in 2020 the Superior Court of Massachusetts declined to dismiss the city's public nuisance lawsuit for failure to state a claim based on the same reasoning in the court's 2019 decision in favor of the Commonwealth.[121]

---

[118] Massachusetts, *supra* note 114, at *3, citing Delaware v. Purdue Pharma, L.P., 2019 WL 446382 (Del. Super. 2019); Grewal v. Purdue Pharma, L.P., 2018 WL 4829660 (N.J. Super. Ct. 2018).

[119] Massachusetts, *Id.* at *4, citing *Restatement (Second) of Torts* § 821B, Evans v. Lorillard Tobacco Co., 2007 WL 796175 at **18–19 (Mass. Super. Ct. 2007); and Boston v. Smith & Wesson Corp., 2000 WL 1473568 at *14 (Mass. Super. 2000).

[120] Massachusetts, *Id.* at *5.

[121] Boston v. Purdue Pharma, L.P., 2020 WL 416406 (Super. Ct. Mass. Jan. 3, 2020).

9

Firearms Violence as a Public Nuisance

The prevalence of gun violence in the U.S. has caused commentators to declare that the increasing number of deaths and injuries from firearms constituted a public health crisis. In the aftermath of the 1998 national tobacco settlement with states' attorneys generals, many observers predicted that litigation against the firearms industry would be the next great mass tort litigation to be resolved in similar ways.[1] Despite the efforts of many plaintiffs' attorneys, a mass tort against the firearms industry has not yet materialized.

Like the defendants sued in the opioid litigation, lawsuits against the firearms industry have sought to hold participants in the chain of manufacturing and distribution accountable for the consequences of gun violence. The firearms industry has long been represented by a powerful cadre of well-financed lobbyists who successfully have, through their efforts, persuaded the federal and state legislatures to provide blanket immunity to the firearms industry. This robust statutory immunity afforded to the industry has frustrated plaintiffs' ability to sue any firearms defendant either individually or in combination. For two decades in the twenty-first century virtually almost all firearms litigation has failed.

Notwithstanding the substantial barriers to litigation, plaintiffs' attorneys have nonetheless continued to attempt to sue the firearms industry. Plaintiffs' attorneys have sought to hold firearms defendants accountable by asserting claims pursuant to the few, limited exceptions in the immunity statutes. Almost all these efforts have failed. Among the plaintiffs' continuing efforts, however, the plaintiffs' litigation strategy has included assertion of novel public nuisance theories. While federal and state courts chiefly have rejected the

[1] *See generally* Andrew M. Dansicker, The Next Big Thing for Litigators, 37 MD. B.J., no.4, July–Aug. 2004, at 12–17; Molly McDonough, Lawyers, Guns and Lead, 89 A.B.A.J., No. 2, Feb. 2003, at 22–23; and Allan Rostron, Shooting Stories: The Creation of Narrative and Melodrama in Real and Fictional Litigation Against the Gun Industry, 73 U.M.K.C. L. Rev. 1047 (2005).

use of a public nuisance model against firearms defendants, at least some courts have been willing to approve litigation based on this theory.

The firearms industry has long been immunized from any litigation relating to the manufacture, selling, marketing, or distribution of firearms. After the 1998 national attorney general settlement of tobacco claims, the gun lobby reacted by seeking Congressional relief in the enactment of the Protection of Lawful Commerce in Arms Act (2005) (PLCCA),[2] which provided blanket immunity from suit to the firearms industry. Thirty-four states followed with similar statutes. Since 2005, plaintiffs have universally failed in attempts to sue firearm defendants.

The first wave of unsuccessful gun litigation between the 1990s and 2005 was based on claims for negligent distribution and/or marketing of firearms, deceptive advertising, the manufacture and/or selling of defective firearms, and public nuisance. Most of the gun lawsuits were dismissed before trial and resulted in few favorable jury verdicts. However, in 2019, Connecticut plaintiffs in the Sandy Hook mass shooting succeeded in state court litigation against firearms defendants by invoking the predicate statute exception to PLCAA. A $74 million settlement followed. This represented a rare victory for firearms plaintiffs.

In the twenty-first century plaintiffs' attorneys shifted strategies and began invoking public nuisance law more frequently to hold firearms defendants accountable. This strategy required plaintiffs' attorneys to recast the growing incidence of harm from gun violence as a public nuisance and an interference with the public health and safety. Like plaintiffs in the opioid litigation, governmental entity lawsuits also claimed increasing costs to state and local jurisdictions of the expenses related to firearms violence seeking abatement remedies. And, in an innovative legal action, Mexico filed litigation in federal district court alleging public nuisance claims resulting from gun trafficking into Mexico. The judicial reception of such lawsuits, however, predominately has been negative with a few courts approving public nuisance-based litigation.

Perhaps the most recent endeavor by gun violence advocates has been the innovative attempt to hold firearms defendants accountable directly by a specific public nuisance statute. In July 2021 the New York state legislature amended its public nuisance statute to create a cause of action for harms resulting from use of firearms.[3] This was the first statute in the U.S. to limit the gun liability shield afforded by PLCAA.

---

[2] *See* The Protection of Lawful Commerce in Arms Act (PLCAA), 15 U.S.C. § 7903 (5)(A) (iii) (2018) (exception that allows gun manufacturers to be sued); Connecticut Unfair Trade Practices Act, (CUTPA), CONN. GEN. STAT. ANN. § 42-110b(a) (West 2012).

[3] N.Y. Senate Bill S7179, effective Sept. 1, 2021.

The legislators carefully crafted the statute to comply with exemptions from federal PLCAA liability. It allows for civil lawsuits when a gun manufacturer knowingly took steps to violate underlying law (i.e., the state's public nuisance statute). State, local, and crime victims can file suit against gun manufacturers and distributors if they contribute to a public nuisance by failing to take adequate action to ensure their products are not used in any unlawful activity. In 2022, similar public nuisance statutes were enacted in New Jersey, California, and Delaware.

9.1 GUN VIOLENCE IN THE U.S.: SOME STATISTICS

In order to pursue a public nuisance theory for remediation of harm caused by the firearms defendants, plaintiffs need to establish the existence of a public nuisance; that is, an interference with the enjoyment of a public right. Like the theory underlying the opioid public nuisance claims, firearms plaintiffs recite data relating to the increased numbers of gun-related deaths and injuries to support the claim of group harm to public health and safety. Sources documenting gun-related injuries reflect constantly changing data; different sources report various statistics. Nonetheless, all sources reflect a constant, growing incidence of gun-related injuries from the 1990s into the twenty-first century.

The Pew Research Center, collecting data from the Center for Disease Control and Prevention, the Federal Bureau of Investigation, and other sources, reported that in 2020 – the most recent year for which there was collected information – more Americans died of gun-related injuries than in any other year on record. This included deaths resulting from murder or suicide.[4] In 2020, 45,222 people died from gun-related injuries in the U.S.[5] This total was by far the most on record, representing a 14 percent increase from the prior year and a 25 percent increase from five years earlier. The 45,222 total represented a 43 percent increase from the prior decade.[6]

The majority of gun deaths were suicides; in 2020, 54 percent of all gun-related deaths were suicides, while 43 percent were murders. Suicides by guns increased

---

[4] John Gramlich, What the Data Says About Gun Deaths in the U.S., The Pew Research Center (Feb. 3, 2022), available at www.pewresearch.org/fact-tank/2022/02/03/what-the-data-says-about-gun-deaths-in-the-us/.

[5] *Id.* This figure from the CDC included murders, gun suicides, unintentional shootings, gun-related events involving law enforcement, and gun-related deaths where the circumstances could not be determined. The total excluded deaths in which gunshot injuries played a contributing but no principal cause of death or injury. The CDC fatality statistics were based on death certification information which lists a single cause of death.

[6] *Id.*

by 10 percent over the five previous years and by 25 percent over the ten previous years. The 24,292 suicide deaths in 2020 was the highest in any year except 2018, when there were 24,432 reported suicide deaths by guns.[7]

Nearly 79 percent, or eight in ten murders in the U.S. involved a firearm. The Pew Research Center reported that gun murders had climbed sharply in recent years and the 19,384 gun murders in 2020 were the most since 1968.[8] The 2020 statistic on gun murders represented a 34 percent increase from 2019; a 49 percent increase over five years, and a 75 percent increase over ten years.

Mass shootings in the U.S. garner a great deal of public attention. It is difficult to compile statistics relating to mass shootings because different reporting agencies use different definitions of what constitutes a mass shooting event. The Gun Violence Archive, a frequently quoted online data base, defines a mass shooting as any incident in which four or more people are shot, even if no one is killed (excluding the shooter). In 2020, the Gun Violence Archive reported that 513 people died in mass shooting events.[9] Mass shooting fatalities comprise a small fraction of gun murders every year. Nonetheless, the FBI found that there has been a steady increase in active shooter incidents between 2000 and 2020.[10]

In 2020, handguns were involved in 59 percent of the 13,620 murders and non-negligent manslaughters. According to the FBI rifles – including weapons described as assault weapons – were used in 3 percent of firearm murders. Shotguns were involved in 1 percent of murders and the remainder of gun homicides and non-negligent manslaughters (36 percent) involved other types of firearms.[11]

For 2022, the Gun Violence Archive reported a total of 44,346 gun deaths, including 20,256 murders and 24,090 suicides.[12] The Archive reported 38,595 injuries, 646 mass shootings, and 36 deaths from mass shootings. The Archive reported separate data for children killed or injured in firearm incidents: 315 children between the ages 1–11 years had been killed in gun-related incidents and 682 had been injured. About 1,367 teenagers had been killed and 3,806 had been injured.[13]

According to the Giffords Law Center to Prevent Gun Violence, the U.S. has approximately 393 million guns, the most guns of any comparable country. The U.S. accounts for just 4 percent of the world's population but 35 percent

[7] *Id.*
[8] *Id.* The previous gun murder peak was in 1968, when there were 18,253 recorded gun murders.
[9] *Id.*
[10] *Id.*
[11] *Id.*
[12] Gun Violence Archive 2022, available at https://gunviolencearchive.org/past-tolls.
[13] *Id.*

of global firearms suicides. An American is twenty-five times more likely to be killed in a gun homicide than people in any other high-income country.[14] Approximately 43,000 Americans died every year from gun violence, an average of 116 persons a day. The majority of gun deaths are suicides and access to guns triples the suicide risk. The majority of suicides – 59 percent – involve a gun.[15]

The Gifford Law Center also documents demographic information relating to the victims of gun violence. Gun homicides disproportionately affect Black Americans, and domestic violence victims are five times more likely to be killed when their abuser has access to a gun. American women are twenty-one times more likely to be killed with a gun than women in other high-income countries. Twenty-five million American adults have been threatened or non-fatally injured by a partner with a firearm.[16] Three million children annually are directly exposed to gun violence that results in injury, death, or trauma; guns are the leading cause of death for children under 18.[17]

The emergence of widespread firearms casualties in the 1990s developed along with the advent of other massive personal injury victims, arising from the marketing, distribution, and retail sale of defective products. The increasing nationwide deaths and injuries from firearms-related incidents presented the plaintiffs' bar with the opportunity to hold accountable participants in the manufacture, distribution, and sale of firearms. Beginning in the 1990s through the early twenty-first century plaintiffs' attorneys made repeated attempts to sue actors engaged in the firearms industry. The firearms defendants aggressively resisted this litigation and largely remained impervious to lawsuits.

9.2 SUING THE FIREARMS INDUSTRY: THE 1990S THROUGH 2005

In the late 1990s and early twenty-first century, various victims of crime and gun violence attempted to sue gun industry defendants for harms that allegedly were caused by the misuse of firearms by third parties (including criminals).[18] One cluster of lawsuits were pursued by individuals.[19] Other gun

---

[14] Giffords Law Center, Statistics, available at https://giffords.org/lawcenter/gun-violence-statistics.
[15] *Id.*
[16] *Id.*
[17] *Id.*
[18] *See generally* Timothy D. Lytton, Tort Claims Against Gun Manufacturers for Crime-Related Injuries: Defining a Suitable Role for the Tort System in Regulating the Firearms Industry, 65 Mo. L. Rev. 1 (2000).
[19] *See e.g.*, Ileto v. Glock, Inc., 565 F.3d 1126, 1131 (9th Cir. 2009); Hamilton v. Beretta U.S.A. Corp., 264 F.3d 21, 25 (2d Cir. 2001); McCarthy v. Olin Corp., 119 F.3d 148, 151 (2d Cir. 1997); Merrill v. Navegar, Inc., 28 P.3d 116, 119 (Cal. 2001).

violence litigation was pursued by municipalities, government officials, or other entities.[20] Plaintiffs' attorneys pursued these lawsuits based on a variety of legal theories: chiefly "negligent distribution or marketing, making and selling defective firearms, deceptive advertising, and contributing to a public nuisance."[21]

These lawsuits largely either were dismissed before trial or were unsuccessful on the merits.[22] Commenting on the firearms lawsuits during this first wave of gun litigation, one commentator noted that "[t]he great majority [of such lawsuits] have been dismissed or abandoned prior to trial, and of the few favorable jury verdicts obtained by plaintiffs, all but one have been overturned on appeal."[23] Moreover, gun litigation that was based on theories of negligent marketing claims under state consumer statutes were particularly vulnerable to dismissal.[24]

Although the firearms defendants could take some comfort in their continued defeat of gun litigation, these defendants nonetheless had legitimate concerns about their continued vulnerability to litigation. The gun industry had growing concerns about its own exposure to mass liability against a backdrop of other evolving, successful mass tort litigation, as well as the increasing state and federal receptivity to entertain aggregate litigation pursuant to a variety of legal theories. Moreover, the states' attorney generals' massive 1998 settlement with the tobacco defendants signaled that even powerful industries that had long pursued "no settlement" strategies, coupled with a record of litigation victories, could be vulnerable to continued, extensive litigation.

9.3 BARRIERS TO SUING THE FIREARMS INDUSTRY: PLCAA

In response to the gun industry's growing concerns of exposure to liability for harms resulting from gun use, the firearms industry lobbied Congress to enact legislation to immunize manufacturers, distributors, and retailers from

---

[20] *See generally* New York v. Beretta U.S.A. Corp., 524 F.3d 384 (2d Cir. 2008); NAACP v. AcuSport, Inc., 271 F. Supp. 2d 435 (2d Cir. 2003); Cincinnati v. Beretta U.S.A. Corp., 768 N.E.2d 1136 (Ohio 2002); Chicago v. Beretta U.S.A. Corp., 785 N.E.2d 16 (Ill. App. Ct. 2002), rev'd, 821 N.E.2d 1099 (Ill. 2004); Hamilton v. Beretta U.S.A. Corp., 750 N.E.2d 1055 (N.Y. 2001); Ganim v. Smith & Wesson Corp., 780 A.2d 98 (Conn. 2001).

[21] *See* Gary Kleck, Gun Control After Heller and McDonald: What Cannot Be Done and What Ought to Be Done, 39 Fordham URB. L.J. 1383, 1391 (2012).

[22] *See* Bryce A. Jensen, From Tobacco to Health Care and Beyond – A Critique of Lawsuits Targeting Unpopular Industries, 86 Cornell L. Rev. 1334, 1371–77 (2001).

[23] Timothy D. Lytton, Suing the Gun Industry: A Battle at the Crossroads of Gun Control and Mass Torts 5 (Timothy D. Lytton ed., 2005).

[24] *See* Timothy D. Lytton, Halberstam v. Daniel and the Uncertain Future of Negligent Marketing Claims Against Firearms Manufacturers, 64 BROOK. L. REV. 681, 681 (1997).

liability to suit.[25] Congress enacted the Protection of Lawful Commerce in Arms Act in 2005.[26] The statute broadly protects firearms manufacturers and dealers from liability to suit when crimes have been committed with their products.[27] Gun industry advocates further lobbied state and local legislators for immunity statutes, and in the aftermath of PLCCA's enactment, thirty-four states enacted statutes providing "blanket immunity to the gun industry," in ways similar to PLCCA.[28]

Notwithstanding this broad immunity from suit, under certain circumstances, gun manufacturers, distributors, and retailers can still be held liable for damages resulting from defective products, breach of contract, and criminal misconduct. Firearm defendants may be held responsible for actions for which they are directly responsible, like any U.S.-based manufacturer of consumer products. Finally, if a firearms defendant has reason to know that a gun is intended for use in a crime, they may also be held liable for negligent entrustment – a theory unsuccessfully asserted by the Sandy Hook plaintiffs as well as plaintiffs in other cases.[29]

In PLCCA, Congress set forth six exceptions to firearm defendants' broad immunity from civil liability arising from the criminal or unlawful use of their

---

[25]   The statute states:

> The possibility of imposing liability on an entire industry for harm is solely caused by others is an abuse of the legal system, ... threatens the diminution of a basic constitutional right and civil liberty, invites the disassembly and destabilization of other industries and economic sectors lawfully competing in the free enterprise system ..., and constitutes an unreasonable burden on interstate and foreign commerce.

> 515 U.S.C. § 7901 (a)(6) (2018).

[26]   The Senate passed the Act on July 29, 2005, by a vote of 65–31. The House of Representatives passed the legislation on October 20, 2005, with 283 in favor and 144 opposed. *See* Ryan VanGrack, Recent Development, The Protection of Lawful Commerce in Arms Act, 41 HARV. J. ON LEGIS. 541, 541, 545–46 (2004).

[27]   *See generally* Recent Legislation, Tort Law – Civil Immunity – Congress Passes Prohibition of Qualified Civil Claims Against Gun Manufacturers and Distributors, 119 HARV. L. REV. 1939 (2006). The statute provides:

> [A] civil action or proceeding or an administrative proceeding brought by any person against a manufacturer or seller of a [firearm or ammunition] product ... for damages ... or other relief, resulting from the criminal or unlawful misuse of [the] qualified product by the person or a third party' ['may not be brought in any Federal or State court'].

> 15 U.S.C. §§ 7902(a), 7903(5)(A) (2018). Any action pending on the date of PLCCA's enactment was subject to immediate dismissal.

[28]   Gun Industry Immunity, *Giffords Law Center*, https://lawcenter.giffords.org/gun-laws/policy-areas/other-laws-policies/gun-industry-immunity/#state (last visited on Jan. 25, 2020).

> California repealed its gun immunity statute in 2002, following the California Supreme Court's decision in *Merrill v. Navegar*, 28 P.3d 116, 133 (Cal. 2001), which upheld the immunization of an assault weapons manufacturer from a negligence action brought by a California gun massacre.

[29]   *See* Soto v. Bushmaster Firearms Int'l, LLC, 202 A.3d 262, 275, 279–83 (Conn. 2019).

products by third parties.[30] PLCCA's third exception, known as the "predicate statute exception" provided the Sandy Hook plaintiffs' ground for relief from PLCCA's broad immunity.

PLCCA's third exception from broad immunity to suit permits "action[s] in which a manufacturer or seller of a [firearm or ammunition] knowingly violated a State or Federal statute applicable to the sale or marketing of the product, and the violation was a proximate cause of the harm for which relief is sought."[31] In order to invoke this exception, a plaintiff must present a cognizable claim along with a knowing violation of a predicate statute – that is, a statute that is applicable to the sale or marketing of firearms.[32]

Two types of claims come within PLCCA's predicate exception. First, a manufacturer or seller may be subject to suit if the manufacturer or seller knowingly falsifies or fails to keep records that are required to be kept under federal or state law with respect to the firearm or ammunition.[33] A manufacturer or seller may be subject to suit if they were involved in making a false statement with regard to the lawfulness of a firearms transfer.[34]

Second, a manufacturer may be subject to suit where the manufacturer aided, abetted, or conspired to sell a firearm or ammunition that it knew or had reasonable cause to know that the actual buyer as prohibited from possessing a firearm under federal law.[35]

---

[30] 15 U.S.C. § 7903(5)(A)(i)-(vi) (2018). These exceptions provide blanket civil immunity for the following:

    (1) [A]n action brought against a transferor convicted under section 924(h) of Title 18 [of "knowingly transfer[ing] a firearm, knowing that such firearm will be used to commit a crime of violence"] or a comparable or identical State felony law, by a party directly harmed by the conduct of which the transferee is so convicted;

    (2) an action brought against a seller for negligent entrustment or negligence per se;

    (3) An action in which a manufacturer or seller of a qualified product knowingly violated a State or Federal statute applicable to the sale or marketing of the product, and the violation was the proximate cause of the harm for which relief is sought;

    (4) an action for breach of contract or warranty in connection with the purchase of the product;

    (5) an action for death, physical injuries or property damage resulting directly from a defect in design or manufacture of the product, when used as intended or in a reasonably foreseeable manner, except where the discharge of the product was caused by a volitional act that constituted a criminal offense, then such act shall be considered the sole proximate cause of any resulting death, personal injuries or property damage; or

    (6) an action or proceeding commenced by the Attorney General to enforce the [Gun Control Act or the National Firearms Act.].

[31] 15 U.S.C. § 7903(5)(A)(iii).

[32] *See* Ileto v. Glock, Inc., 565 F.3d 1126, 1132 (9th Cir. 2009).

[33] 15 U.S.C. § 7903(5)(A)(iii)(I); 18 U.S.C. § 922(m) (2018).

[34] *See* 15 U.S.C. § 7903(5)(A)(iii)(I).

[35] 15 U.S.C. § 7903(5)(iii)(II); 18 U.S.C. § 922(g), (n) (2018).

9.4 SUING THE GUN INDUSTRY POST-PLCCA: THE CONTROVERSY OVER APPLICABILITY OF THE PREDICATE STATUTE EXCEPTION TO PUBLIC NUISANCE CLAIMS

Although Congress intended to broadly immunize the gun industry from liability from harm arising from the manufacture, distribution, or sale of firearms or ammunition, plaintiffs have nonetheless continued to pursue litigation, primarily seeking to utilize PLCCA's predicate statute exception as the basis for pursuing relief. Plaintiffs have taken broad and narrow approaches to suing firearm defendants post-PLCCA. Thus, a handful of gun violence suits have broadly challenged the constitutionality of PLCCA, but none of these constitutional challenges have been successful.[36] State and federal courts have upheld the constitutionality of PLCCA as a legitimate exercise of congressional legislative power.[37]

Channeling a narrower approach, plaintiffs have attempted to invoke PLCCA's statutory exceptions to federal pre-emption by relying on predicate nuisance statutes as a basis for relief. Relatively few courts have considered litigation against gun defendants pursuant to PLCCA's other exceptions for negligent entrustment,[38] negligence or negligence per se,[39] design defects,[40] failure to warn,[41] or breach of implied warranty of merchantability.[42] Plaintiffs have been unsuccessful in nearly all the cases advancing claims based on these PLCCA exceptions.[43]

Only the Second and Ninth Circuits have considered the viability of gun litigation under PLCCA's third exception, the predicate statute exception as it relates to public underlying public nuisance statutes.[44] These two divergent

---

[36] *See e.g.*, Ileto, 565 F.3d at 1138–44; New York v. Beretta U.S.A. Corp., 524 F.3d 384, 392–98 (2d Cir. 2008); Adames v. Sheehan, 909 N.E.2d 742, 764–65 (Ill. 2009).

[37] *See, e.g.*, Ileto, 565 F.3d at 1138–44; Beretta U.S.A. Corp., 524 F.3d at 392–98; Adames, 909 N.E.2d at 764–65.

[38] *See, e.g.*, Soto v. Bushmaster Firearms Int'l, LLC, 202 A.3d 262, 275 (Conn. 2019); Phillips v. Luck Gunner, LLC, 84 F. Supp. 3d 1216, 1225, 1227 (D. Colo. 2015); Noble v. Shawnee Gun Shop, Inc., 409 S.W. 3d 476, 485 (Mo. Ct. App. 2013); Estate of Kim v. Coxe, 295 P.3d 380, 395 (Alaska 2013). *But cf.* Williams v. Beemiller, Inc., 952 N.Y.S.2d 333, 338–39 (App. Div. 2012), *amended by* 103 A.D. 3d 1191 (App. Div. 2013).

[39] *See, e.g.*, *Phillips*, 84 F. Supp. 3d at 1225, 1227; Estate of Charlot v. Bushmaster Firearms, Inc., 628 F. Supp. 2d 174, 180–81 (D.D.C. 2009); *Estate of Kim*, 295 P.3d at 394.

[40] *See, e.g.*, *Adames*, 909 N.E.2d at 765.

[41] *See, e.g.*, *id.*

[42] *Id.*

[43] *See supra* notes 63–67.

[44] *See* Ileto v. Glock, Inc. 565 F.3d 1126, 1133–35 (9th Cir. 2009); New York v. Beretta U.S.A. Corp., 524 F.3d 384, 389–90 (2d Cir. 2008).

opinions have engendered a circuit court split concerning the interpretation and applicability of PLCCA's third exception when the predicate statute relies on a nuisance theory.[45] In both decisions, the appellate courts agreed that PLCCA barred claims that plaintiffs pursued under generally applicable public nuisance statutes.[46] Several state courts and one federal district court similarly have concluded that PLCCA does not permit litigation based on applicable public nuisance statutes.[47] However, two state courts permitted such lawsuits to proceed under this theory.[48]

9.5 A BROAD INTERPRETATION OF PUBLIC NUISANCE AS A PREDICATE STATUTE EXCEPTION

In *New York v. Beretta U.S.A. Corp.*,[49] the Second Circuit handed victories to the firearms industry as well as gun violence victims. In a rambling and discursive opinion, the Second Circuit simultaneously upheld the constitutionality of PLCCA and reinforced the Congressional intention to immunize the gun industry from lawsuits – ultimately dismissing litigation against the firearm defendants.[50] However, in the same opinion, the court offered a statutory interpretation of PLCCA's predicate statute exception,[51] which opened the door for the Connecticut Supreme Court to hold that its unfair trade practices statute fell within PLCCA's predicate exception, thereby allowing the Sandy Hook plaintiffs' litigation to proceed.

In the *Beretta U.S.A. Corp.* litigation, New York filed a complaint against the firearms suppliers seeking injunctive relief and abatement of the alleged public nuisance caused by their distribution practices.[52] The city claimed that the firearm suppliers marketed guns to legitimate buyers with the knowledge that those guns would be diverted through various mechanisms into illegal markets. The city also claimed that the firearm suppliers failed to take

---

[45] *See infra* notes 74–107.

[46] This circuit split represents a conflict of statutory construction that the U.S. Supreme Court declined to consider when denying certiorari in the Sandy Hook appeal. *See* Soto v. Bushmaster Firearms Int'l, LLC, 202 A.3d 262 (Conn. 2019), *cert denied*, 140 S. Ct. 513 (2019).

[47] *See* Estate of Kim v. Coxe, 295 P.3d 380, 388 (Alaska 2013); *Adames*, 909 N.E.2d at 765; Estate of Charlot v. Bushmaster Firearms, Inc., 628 F. Supp. 2d 174, 177, 180, 186 (D.D.C. 2009).

[48] *See* Williams v. Beemiller, Inc., 952 N.Y.S.2d 333, 338, 339 (App. Div. 2010), *amended by* 103 A.D.3d 1191 (App. Div.2013); Smith & Wesson Corp. v. Gary, 875 N.E.2d 422, 434–35 (Ind. Ct. App. 2007).

[49] 524 F.3d 384 (2d Cir. 2008).

[50] *Id.* at 389.

[51] *See id.* at 400–03.

[52] *Id.* at 390–91.

reasonable steps to inhibit the flow of firearms into illegal markets, thus creating a public nuisance.[53]

The firearms defendants moved to dismiss based on immunity under PLCCA. In response, the city argued that PLCCA "did not bar its causes of action because this case fell within an exception to the forbidden qualified civil liability actions" – the predicate statute exception.[54] The plaintiff invoked as the predicate statute the New York Penal Law § 240.45.[55]

The defendants claimed that New York Penal Law § 240.45 could not serve as a predicate statute to remove its PLCCA immunity "because the predicate exception was meant to apply to statutes that were 'expressly and specifically applicable to the sale and marketing of firearms, and not to statutes of general applicability,' such as § 240.45."[56]

On December 2, 2005, the U.S. District Court for the Eastern District of New York denied the defendants' motion to dismiss, finding that PLCAA did not require dismissal of the case.[57] The district court held that "[b]y its plain meaning, New York Penal Law § 240.45 satisfies the language of the predicate exception requiring a 'statute applicable to the sale or marketing of [a firearm].'"[58] The district court certified its December 2, 2005, order for immediate appeal pursuant to 28 U.S.C. § 1292(b).[59]

The Second Circuit concluded that the city's claim – predicated on New York Penal Law § 240.45, a penal nuisance statute – did not fall within a PLCCA exception because that New York statute did not "fall within the contours of the Act's predicate exception."[60] The Second Circuit held that a statute upon which a case was brought was meant to apply to statutes that expressly and specifically were applicable to the sale and marketing of firearms, and not to statutes of general applicability, such as § 240.45.[61]

The Second Circuit noted that the core issue was "what Congress meant by the phrase 'applicable to the sale or marketing of [firearms],'" and "what Congress meant by the term 'applicable.'"[62] The Court concluded that "the meaning of the term 'applicable' must be determined in the context of the

---

[53] *Id.* at 391.
[54] *Id.* at 389–90.
[55] *Id.* at 390.
[56] *Id.*
[57] New York v. Beretta U.S.A. Corp., 401 F. Supp. 2d 244, 298 (E.D.N.Y. 2005) *aff'd in part, rev'd in part,* 524 F.3d 384 (2d Cir. 2008).
[58] *Id.* at 261.
[59] *Id.* at 298.
[60] *Beretta U.S.A. Corp.,* 524 F.3d at 390.
[61] *Id.* at 404.
[62] *Id.* at 399.

statute."[63] However, the court found that "nothing in [PLCCA] require[d] any express language regarding firearms to be included in a statute in order for that statute to fall within the predicate exception."[64] Thus, the court decided:

> [T]o foreclose the possibility that, under certain circumstances, state courts may apply a statute of general applicability to the type of conduct that the City complain[ed] of, in which case such a statute might qualify as a predicate statute.... Accordingly, while the mere absence in New York Penal Law § 240.45 of any express reference to firearms did not, in and of itself, preclude that statute's eligibility to serve as a predicate statute under the PLCAA, New York Penal Law § 240.45 [was] a statute of general applicability that [did] not encompass the conduct of firearms manufacturers.... It therefore [did] not fall within the predicate exception to the claim restricting provisions of the PLCAA.[65]

The Second Circuit opined that: "[T]he term 'applicable' must be examined in context." The PLCAA provides that predicate statutes are those that are "applicable to the sale or marketing of [firearms]." The universe of predicate statutes is further defined as "including" the examples set forth in subsections (I) and (II).... These examples refer to statutes that specifically regulate the firearms industry.[66]

Yet, the court did not agree "that the PLCAA requires that a predicate statute expressly refer to the firearms industry. Thus, the contours of the universe of predicate statutes – i.e., those statutes that are 'applicable' to sale or marketing of firearms' – are undefined."[67]

9.6 THE NARROW INTERPRETATION OF PUBLIC NUISANCE AS A PREDICATE STATUTE EXCEPTION

A year after the Second Circuit's decision in the *New York v. Beretta* litigation, the Ninth Circuit upheld PLCCA against an array of constitutional challenges, including arguments that PLCCA violated the constitutional requirement for separation of powers,[68] equal protection principles, and substantive and procedural due process rights.[69] In addition, the Ninth Circuit

---

[63] *Id.*

[64] *Id.* at 399–400.

[65] *Id.* at 400 ("We decline to foreclose the possibility that, under certain circumstances, state courts may apply a statute of general applicability to the type of conduct that the City complains of, in which case such a statute might qualify as a predicate statute.").

[66] *Id.*

[67] *Id.*

[68] Ileto v. Glock, Inc., 565 F.3d 1126, 1138 (9th Cir. 2009).

[69] *Id.* at 1140–41.

held that the victims of gun violence in California did not have a vested property right in their accrued state causes of action.[70]

Perhaps most important for the firearms liability debate, the Ninth Circuit affirmatively ruled that PLCCA preempted California tort claims brought by shooting victims against federally-licensed manufacturers, distributors, and firearms dealers for firearms that an assailant possessed and used during an assault.[71] Construing PLCCA's third predicate statute exception, the court ruled that the exception did not apply to claims brought by shooting victims under California civil codes pertaining to nuisance, public nuisance, and negligence.[72]

The California litigation arose out of events on August 10, 1999, in which a gunman shot and injured three children, a teenager, and an adult at a Jewish Community Center summer camp in Granada Hills, California. Later that day the gunman killed Joseph Ileto, a postal worker. The gunman carried at least seven firearms, which he possessed illegally. In 2001, the shooting victims and Ileto's surviving wife filed a lawsuit against the manufacturers, marketers, importers, distributors, and sellers of firearms.[73]

The "[p]laintiffs brought their claims ... solely under California common law tort statutes for foreseeably and proximately causing injury, emotional distress, and death through knowing, intentional, reckless, and negligent conduct."[74] They did not allege that the defendants "violated any statute prohibiting manufacturers or sellers from aiding, abetting, or conspiring with another person to sell or otherwise dispose of firearms to illegal buyers."[75]

The court opined that the plaintiffs' negligence and public nuisance allegations stated cognizable claims under California law. However, the plaintiffs failed to "point to an allegation of a knowing violation of any *separate* statute."[76] Instead, the plaintiffs had pointed out that "unlike many other jurisdictions, California's general tort law [was] codified in its civil code."[77] Citing these civil code provisions, the plaintiffs contended that the California Code sections satisfied PLCCA's predicate statute exception. The defendants argued that only a separate statute regulating firearms explicitly or exclusively could be a predicate statute to satisfy PLCCA.[78]

[70] *Id.*
[71] *Id.* at 1145.
[72] *Id.* at 1137–38.
[73] *Id.*
[74] *Id.*
[75] *Id.*
[76] *Id.* at 1132.
[77] *Id.* at 1132–33 (citing Cal. Civ. Code § 1714(a) (negligence); § 3479 (nuisance); § 3480 (public nuisance).
[78] *Id.* at 1133.

Examining the text and legislative history of PLCCA, the Court construed PLCAA's "applicable" statute should be given a narrow construction, rather than the plaintiffs' proposed all-encompassing meaning.[79] Consequently, the court concluded that "Congress intended to preempt general tort theories of liability even in jurisdictions, like California, that [had] codified such causes of action."[80]

9.7 PUBLIC NUISANCE FIREARMS LITIGATION IN STATE COURTS

In the pre-PLCCA era state courts in Connecticut, New York, Illinois, and California rejected firearms litigation. These decisions rehearsed many of the standard objections to public nuisance claims: narrow definitions of public nuisance; remoteness doctrine; lack of causation; lack of control over the instrumentality; lawful manufacture and sale of a defect-free product; economic loss doctrine; municipal recovery rule; and social policy considerations best left to the legislative branches.

In 2001 a Connecticut municipality sued firearms manufacturers, trade associations, and retail sellers based on nine claims, including a public nuisance claim.[81] The plaintiffs alleged that the manufacturers had failed to provide self-locking mechanisms to make guns childproof, and failed to take adequate, reasonable measures to make guns safer to prevent foreseeable deaths. In addition, the manufacturers engaged in a conspiracy for years that deceived residents, through their advertising, of the safety of handguns. The defendants had knowingly sold guns in a manner that foreseeably led to guns flowing into an illegal market that supplied guns to criminals or other unauthorized users. The plaintiffs alleged that the retailers regularly sold or advertised guns that had been or could be used by unauthorized users. The plaintiffs sought monetary and injunctive relief.[82]

The Connecticut Supreme Court upheld the trial court's dismissal of the case for a lack of plaintiffs' standing.[83] The court defined public nuisance as the violation or obstruction of public rights that produced a common injury.

---

[79] *Id.* at 1134. However, in construing the textual meaning of the term "applicable," the court concluded that neither the plaintiffs' nor the defendants' asserted meaning was correct. Instead, the court agreed with the Second Circuit's decision in *Beretta* that the text of a statute alone was inconclusive as to Congressional intent.

[80] *Id.* at 1136.

[81] Ganim v. Smith and Wesson Corp., 258 Conn. 313, 780 Atl. Rptr.2d 98, 108 (2001).

[82] *Id.* at 108–110.

[83] *Id.* at 131.

The test was not the number of persons annoyed, but the possibility of annoyance to the public by the invasion of its rights. The Connecticut Supreme Court noted the litany of traditional circumstances constituting public nuisance: pollution and obstruction of waterways, maintenance of a fire or explosion hazard, or other unsafe premises, obstruction or unsafe highway travel, maintenance of a house of prostitution, or maintenance of a junkyard or dump.[84]

Although the court noted that the definition of public nuisance was "capacious" enough to include the plaintiffs' allegations against the firearms defendants, the court indicated this was not enough to answer the antecedent question whether the harms were too remote from the defendants' conduct to confer standing on the plaintiffs. The causal chain from the defendants' actions to the alleged harms was too remote to support a public nuisance claim. The court could find no case in which a plaintiff situated as remotely from the defendants' conduct, who presented as lengthy a causal chain, had been held to have standing to assert a public nuisance claim.[85]

In the early twenty-first century several New York state decisions likewise dismissed public nuisance firearms litigation. New York State's attorney general sued handgun manufacturers, wholesalers, and retailers for contributing to and maintaining a public nuisance by their marketing practices that placed a disproportionate number of handguns into persons who used them unlawfully. The plaintiff alleged that illegally possessed handguns were a public nuisance because the guns endangered the health and safety of a significant portion of the population, and interfered with, offended, and caused damage to the public in their exercise of common rights. The plaintiff sought an order to abate the nuisance, directing each defendant to cease contributing to and maintaining the public nuisance.[86]

The appellate court upheld dismissal of the lawsuit because the plaintiffs failed to state a cause of action for public nuisance. The court held that the defendants were engaging in the lawful manufacture and marketing of defect-free products in a highly regulated commercial industry. Citing numerous New York and other federal and state precedents involving the firearms industry, the court noted that the New York Court of Appeals had never recognized a common law public nuisance claim based on allegations in the plaintiff's complaint.[87] The defendants' conduct was far removed from the downstream

---

[84] *Id.* at 132.
[85] *Id.* at 132–33.
[86] New York v. Sturm, Ruger & Co., 761 N.Y.S.2d 192, 309 A.D.2d 91, 92–93 (2003).
[87] *Id.* at 94, citing cases.

unlawful use of handguns, which was out of their control, and which constituted the alleged nuisance. The causal connection between the alleged business conduct and harm was just too tenuous and remote.[88]

In prior litigation, a New York Appellate Court rejected a negligent marketing claim against firearms defendants.[89] That court's reasoning applied
with equal force to the plaintiff's public nuisance claim. Thus, defendant gun
manufacturers did not owe a duty to control the conduct of third persons
to prevent them from harming others, even where as a practical matter the
defendant could exercise such control. The court rejected that gun manufacturers had a duty of care to lessen the risks of illegal gun trafficking because
they had the power to restrict marketing and distribution.[90]

Finally, the court offered numerous policy rationales for rejecting the
plaintiff's public nuisance claim, contending that the legislative and executive branches of government were better suited to address the societal concerns the plaintiffs raised. Pointing to New Jersey precedents, the court
noted that no New Jersey court had ever permitted a public nuisance claim
to proceed against manufacturers who had lawfully placed lawful products
in the stream of commerce. Courts consistently enforced the boundaries
between well-developed product liability tort law and public nuisance law.
"Otherwise, if public nuisance law were permitted to encompass product
liability, nuisance law 'would become a monster that would devour in one
gulp the entire of tort law.'"[91]

The judicial resistance to imposing a duty on the gun manufacturers
arose out of practical concerns about the "potentially limitless liability and
about the unfairness of imposing liability for the acts of another."[92] The court
sounded a generalized alarm at the consequences of sustaining the plaintiff's
public nuisance lawsuit: "However, giving the green light to a common-law
public nuisance cause of action today, will, in our judgment, likely open the
courthouse doors to a flood of limitless, similar theories of public nuisance,
not only against these defendants, but also against a wide and varied array of
other commercial and manufacturing enterprises and activities."[93] The court
suggested the ultimate negative consequence of expanding public nuisance
doctrine:

---

[88] *Id.* at 93–94, 102–04.
[89] Hamilton v. Beretta U.S.A. Corp., 96 N.Y.2d 222 (2001).
[90] New York, *supra* note 86, at 95, 101–02, citing Hamilton, *id.* at 233.
[91] New York at 96–97.
[92] *Id.* at 95–96.
[93] *Id.* at 96.

All a creative mind would need to do is construct a scenario describing a known or perceived harm of a sort that can somehow relate back to the way a company or an industry makes, markets/sells its nondefective, lawful product or service, and a public nuisance claim would be conceived and a lawsuit born.[94]

In a firearms action by Chicago for public nuisance against firearms manufacturers, distributors, and dealers, the state sought to recover $433 million in operating expenses for the costs of law enforcement and medical services resulting from gun violence. The Supreme Court of Illinois rejected the public nuisance claim.[95] The court questioned whether the plaintiffs stated an infringement of a public right as opposed to an individual right to be free from the threat of illegal conduct by others. The court could find no Illinois case that recognized such a public right to be free from the threat that members of the public might commit crimes against individuals.[96] The court was reluctant to recognize a public right so broad and undefined, consisting of any dangerous instrumentality that might otherwise be a lawful product (a gun, liquor, a car, cell phone), be deemed a threat to the community, and therefore, a public nuisance.[97]

The court also expressed doubt that the plaintiffs could recover compensation for their alleged injuries. Citing the *Restatement (Second)* concerning damage remedies for public nuisance, the court noted that the *Restatement* made no mention of the ability of a public official or entity to recover for damages in an action for public nuisance brought on behalf of the public.[98] Furthermore, the plaintiffs' action for damages was barred by the economic loss doctrine and the municipal cost recovery rule.[99]

The court indicated that to sustain the public nuisance claim would be to create "an entirely new species of public nuisance liability."[100] Even if the court were to grant that the defendants had infringed some public right, the plaintiffs' assertions of negligent conduct were not supported by a recognized duty on the part of the manufacturers or distributors. Moreover, the plaintiffs' allegations of intentional conduct were deficient as a matter of law. The plaintiffs could not establish proximate cause in relation to the dealers because the harm to the plaintiffs was the result of numerous, unforeseeable intervening criminal acts by third parties who were not under the defendants' control.

[94] *Id.*
[95] Chicago v. Beretta U.S.A. Corp., 231 Ill.2d 351, 821 N.E.2d 1099, 1138, 1148 (Ill. 2004).
[96] *Id.* at 1113–15.
[97] *Id.* at 1116.
[98] *Id.* at 1138, citing *Restatement (Second) of Torts* § 821C(1)(1979).
[99] Chicago, *supra* note 95, at 1139–47.
[100] *Id.* at 1148.

By implication, proximate cause was lacking in relation to the manufacturers and distributors who were even further removed from the intervening criminal acts of third parties.[101]

Finally, the Illinois Supreme Court concluded that "Any change of this magnitude in the law affecting a highly regulated industry must be the work of the legislature, brought about by the political process, not the work of the courts. I response to the suggestion of *amici* that we are abdicating our responsibility to declare the common law, we point to the virtue of judicial restraint."[102]

A California appellate court similarly rejected the public nuisance allegations of cities that the manner in which the defendants distributed firearms enabled criminals to acquire the firearms and thereby created a public nuisance. The plaintiffs alleged that the defendants' conduct resulted in supplying handguns to the criminal market that remained in criminal hands for years and caused deaths and injuries to the public.[103] The appellate court held that the trial court properly rejected the plaintiffs' nuisance theory.

The appellate court upheld the trial court's finding that the public nuisance claim failed because the plaintiffs could not show causation, a necessary element of a public nuisance claim. The court indicated that the *Restatement (Second)* presumed that the necessary elements for proof of a public nuisance claim included existence of a duty and causation. Although it was not necessary to show that harm occurred, plaintiffs must show that a defendant's acts were likely to cause an invasion of a public right. A public nuisance did not consist of defendants merely engaging in what the plaintiffs deemed to be a risky practice, without connecting a causative link to the threatened harm. Because there was no causal connection between the defendants' conduct and any illegal acquisition of handguns, criminal acts, or accidental injuries by a firearm, there was no actionable public nuisance claim.[104]

Finally, the appellate court invoked federal Circuit Judge Alex Kozinski's cautionary warning against extending tort nuisance liability to lawful economic activity, suggesting that this expansion of public nuisance law was a blunt and capricious form of regulation administered by courts rather than state regulatory agencies. This expansion of public nuisance doctrine would depend on the vicissitudes of the legal system, making results unpredictable in probability and magnitude: "Courts should therefore be chary of adopting

---

[101] *Id.*
[102] *Id.*
[103] In re Firearms Cases, 126 Cal. App.4th 959, 967–70, 986, 24 Cal. Rptr.3d 659, 678 (2005).
[104] *Id.* at 986–89.

broad new theories of liability, lest they undermine the democratic process through which the people normally decide whether, and to what degree, activities should be fostered or discouraged within the state."[105]

9.8 PLCAA WORKAROUNDS: STATE LEGISLATIVE PUBLIC NUISANCE ENACTMENTS

In response to the PLCAA limitations on federal and state firearms litigation, in 2021–22, four states – New York, New Jersey, Delaware, and California – reacted by enacting firearms statutes that, for the first time, made gun-related litigation an actionable public nuisance claim under state law. The legislatures deliberately crafted these statutes to conform with PLCAA's exemption for state claims based on a predicate statute.[106] The theory underlying these specific public nuisance statutes was that, in comparison to other efforts to invoke a predicate statute based on state consumer protection laws, state public officials now had the ability to rely directly on a predicate state statute that created liability for marketing, sale, and distribution of firearms as constituting a public nuisance.[107] The constitutionality of these new state statutes, in relation to PLCAA and Congress's virtual blanket immunity to the firearms industry, is destined to be resolved by the Supreme Court.[108]

9.9 NEW YORK STATE'S GUN PUBLIC NUISANCE STATUTE JULY 2021

The New York State legislature led the country in enacting the first targeted firearms public nuisance statute that subsequently became the model for similar public nuisance statutes enacted in New Jersey, Delaware, and California.[109] The New York statute, Senate bill 7196 and Assembly bill 6762B, was intended to permit civil lawsuits to be brought against firearms manufacturers, distributors, and dealers and to circumvent the broad immunity that

---

[105] *Id.* at 991, citing Ileto v. Glock, Inc., 349 F.3d 860, 868 (9th Cir. 2004).

[106] Timothy D. Lytton, An End Run Around the Gun Industry Liability Shield, The Regulatory Review (July 6, 2021); Keshia Clukey, New York Enacts First-in-U.S. Law to Limit Gun Liability Shield, Bloomberg News (July 6, 2021).

[107] Gregory N. Heinen, How New Public Nuisance Claims Are Targeting Gun Cos., Law360 (Sept. 16, 2022).

[108] Tobi Raji, The Brewing Gun-Control Fight That Could be Headed to the Supreme Court, Wash. Post (Feb. 21, 2023).

[109] *See infra* at notes 114–61.

these defendants enjoyed under PLCAA.[110] The bill specifically was intended to rely on the PLCAA's predicate statute exception to industry immunity: the exception allowing manufacturers to be sued under a federal or state law that specifically regulated the sale or marketing of products.[111]

The New York law indicated that a violation of the statute that resulted in harm to the public "shall hereby be declared a public nuisance." The existence of this public nuisance would not depend on whether the gun industry member acted for the purpose of causing harm.[112] The statute stated that no gun industry member by either unlawful or unreasonable conduct shall knowingly or recklessly maintain or contribute to a condition that endangered the health or safety of the public through the sale, manufacturing, importing, or marketing of a firearms product.[113] The statute required all industry members who manufactured, marketed, imported, or offered firearms for sale to establish reasonable controls to prevent their guns from being used, marketed, or sold illegally in New York. A manufacturer's conduct would be deemed a public nuisance if it failed to institute such reasonable controls and endangered the public.[114]

The law permitted the state attorney general on behalf of the people of the state, or city corporation counsel on behalf municipal governments, to bring lawsuits against gun industry members for failing to institute or to exercise reasonable controls. These officials could institute actions in New York state or federal district court to enjoin or restrain violations, and to obtain restitution and damages.[115] The law also provided a private right of action to authorized persons, firms, corporations, or associations that were damaged as a result of a gun industry member's acts or omissions in violation of the statute to bring an action for damages to enforce the statute in state or federal district court.[116]

The legislative findings accompanying the statute's enactment stated that the legislature found illegal use of firearms not only constituted a public nuisance in the penal law but contributed to the public health crisis of gun

---

[110] Luis Ferré-Sadurni, It's Hard to Sue Gun Makers. New York is Set to Change That, N.Y. Times (Nov. 2, 2021); Clukey, *supra* note 106; Gabriel Sandoval, Bill Evading Federal Blockade on Lawsuits against Gunmakers Passes Legislature, The City (June 9, 2021).

[111] Everytown for Gun Safety, Support S.7196 and A.6762B: Creating a Path to Gun Industry Accountability (June 24, 2021).

[112] § 898-c1,2. Prohibited Activities. McKinney's Gen. Bus. L. Chap. 20, Art. 39-DDD. Sale Manufacturing, Importing, and Marketing of Firearms (July 6, 2021).

[113] *Id.* § 898-b1.

[114] *Id.* § 898-b2.

[115] *Id.* § 898-d.

[116] *Id.* § 898-e.

violence in the state.[117] This nuisance posed specific harms to state citizens based largely on their zip codes and certain "immutable characteristics such as race and ethnicity." Illegal firearms violence disproportionately affected minority communities despite stringent state and local laws against the illegal possession of firearms. Given the ease of firearms flow into the illegal market and the specific harm illegal firearms violence caused to New Yorkers, those responsible for the firearms' manufacture, distribution, importing, or marketing might be held liable for the public nuisance created by such activities. The failure of the firearms industry to implement reasonable safety measures warranted liability for the many New Yorkers, including children, who were killed unintentionally from these failures.[118]

The National Shooting Sports Foundation immediately challenged the constitutionality of the new statute in federal court. In May 2022, the district court for the Northern District of New York upheld the statute's constitutionality,[119] setting up an appeal to the Second Circuit.[120]

The NSSF plaintiffs consisted of fourteen gun-industry members and a trade association. They sued the New York state Attorney General Letitia James alleging that N.Y. Gen. Bus. Law §§ 898-a-e was unconstitutional, seeking a preliminary and permanent injunction prohibiting enforcement of the statute. The NSSF advanced three chief arguments: (1) the statute was preempted by PLCAA, (2) violated the dormant Commerce Clause, and (3) was void for vagueness.[121] The district court rejected all three arguments.

Reviewing the industry immunity afforded by PLCAA, the court noted that because the New York statute established liability against gun industry members resulting from the criminal or unlawful misuse of a firearm, PLCAA would expressly preempt liability unless it fell within PLCAA's predicate statute exception. Distinguishing the Second Circuit's holding in *New York v. Beretta U.S.A. Corp.*[122] – that PLCAA preempted the gun litigation as not within the predicate statute exception – the district court held that the public nuisance provisions in § 898 expressly regulated firearms constituting a predicate statute; therefore, PLCAA federal preemption did not apply.[123]

---

[117] *Id.* § 898-a *et seq.*; Section 1. Legislative findings and intent (approved and effective July 6, 2021).

[118] *Id.*

[119] Nat'l Shooting Sports Foundation v. James, 604 F. Supp.3d 48 (2022).

[120] Nat'l Shooting Sports Foundation v. James, Case No. 0:22-cv-01374 (2d Cir.), filed June 24 2022.

[121] Nat'l Shooting, *supra* note 119, at 56.

[122] 524 F.3d 384 (2d. Cir. 2008).

[123] Nat'l Shooting, *supra* note 119, at 59–60.

The only question before the court was whether the New York statute expressly regulated firearms. Because the law established liability of gun industry members for failures to institute screening, security, inventory, and business practices to prevent thefts of firearms, as well as sales to straw purchasers, traffickers, and persons prohibited from possessing firearms under federal and state laws, the court held that the New York statute expressly regulated firearms.[124]

The court likewise dismissed the NSSF's argument that the state's public nuisance statute was prohibited by conflict preemption with PLCAA. The court concluded that the statute as a whole and its legislative history establishing liability for the improper sale or marketing of firearms was not an obstacle to any objective of PLCCA. There was no statutory indication in PLCAA that Congress intended to preempt state statutes that expressly regulated firearms.[125]

The NSSF claimed that New York's public nuisance statute violated various theories of the dormant Commerce Clause. The court noted that a state statute violated the dormant Commerce Clause if it (1) clearly discriminated against interstate commerce in favor of intrastate commerce, (2) imposed a burden on interstate commerce incommensurate with the local benefits secured, or (3) had the practical effect of extraterritorial control of commerce occurring entirely outside the boundaries of the state.[126]

The court rejected NSSF's argument that the public nuisance statute was facially discriminatory, holding that because there was no in-state competitor, New York could not discriminate against out-of-state commerce in favor of in-state commerce. In the same vein, § 898 did not place an undue burden on interstate commerce because there were no in-state commercial interests that benefitted from the statute. Finally, the statute did not impermissibly regulate out-of-state commerce. Compliance with the statutory regulations regarding the safe manufacture, marketing, or selling of a product were wholly outside the concerns of the extra-territorial-dormant Commerce Clause doctrine. Section 898 did not differ in any way from the extraterritorial effect of numerous safety state laws and regulations that every industry must comply.[127]

Reviewing all sections of New York's public nuisance law, the court concluded that the statute did not fail for unconstitutional vagueness. The court pointed out that the statute closely tracked the language of New York's public nuisance law, which had been good law since 1965.[128] In over 50 years, the public

---

[124] *Id.*
[125] *Id.* at 60–61.
[126] *Id.* at 61–62.
[127] *Id.* at 62–65.
[128] *Id.* at 68, citing N.Y. Penal Law § 240.45.

nuisance law had never been held as void for vagueness. Section 898-b(1), providing the definition of the public nuisance, gave "the person of ordinary intelligence a reasonable opportunity to know what was prohibited."[129] Section 898-b(2), setting forth gun industry members' duties, was not so vague and indefinite as to be no rule at all. Moreover, this section constitutionally applied to a wide range of conduct, so it could not be said that "no set of circumstances exists under which [the] law would be valid." The court held that the section was not "permeated" with vagueness.[130]

In June 2022, the NSSF appealed the district court's decision upholding the constitutionality of the New York statute,[131] which appeal is pending. Numerous interested groups and parties have filed amici briefs, including a coalition of eighteen states' attorneys generals.[132] Shortly after the district court held that the New York public nuisance statute was not constitutionally infirm, the state's Attorney General and New York City each filed a lawsuit in state court against ten defendants involved in the manufacture or sale of unfinished firearm frames and receivers that could quickly and easily be converted into functioning firearms, commonly known as "ghost guns."[133]

According to the two lawsuits, ghost guns are not stamped with serial numbers or otherwise registered, and therefore, they are untraceable when law enforcement officials recover these firearms in connection with a crime. In its lawsuit, the state asserted that the defendants' products were illegal and contributed significantly to the public health crisis caused by gun violence. The complaint alleged two claims under New York's new public nuisance statute, and sought damages, injunctive relief, restitution and disgorgement of profits.[134]

The defendants removed the lawsuit to federal court on the grounds that one or more of the state claims represented a substantial federal question. The state moved to remand the case back to state court, countering that there was no substantial federal question and that adjudication in federal court would upset the balance between federal and state judicial responsibilities. The court denied the plaintiff's motion to remand the litigation, holding that the case fell

---

[129] Nat'l Shooting, *supra* note 119, at 68.

[130] *Id.*

[131] *See supra* note 120.

[132] Bruce Walker, Eighteen State AGs Voice Support for New York Gun-Industry Liability Law, The Center Square (Jan. 18, 2023).

[133] New York v. Arm Or Ally, LLC, 2022 WL 17496413, at *1-2 (S.D.N.Y. Dec. 8, 2022); *see* Sarah Lim, Litigation Highlight: New York Officials Alleged Ghost Gun Manufacturers Created a Public Nuisance – Now the Settlements Have Started, Duke Center for Firearms Law (Nov. 23, 2022), available at https://firearmslaw.duke.edu/lawsuits/.

[134] *Id.*

into the small, limited categories of cases embraced by the substantial federal question doctrine. Also, given the longstanding federal interest in regulating the manufacture and sale of firearms in interstate commerce, the exercise of federal jurisdiction would not upset the federal-state judicial balance.[135]

The court concluded that questions of statutory construction of N.Y. General Business Law §§ 898 et seq. necessarily raised federal questions that were substantial and actually disputed.[136] Moreover, in interpreting the public nuisance statute the court further concluded that the statute did not speak to whether actions under the law belonged in state or federal court. In drafting the statute the state chose to piggyback its definition of gun firearms products in applicable federal law and having done so, assumed the risk that an action to enforce the statute would be subject to removal.[137]

In the second New York City ghost gun litigation brought under the public nuisance statute, the city reached settlements with four of the five online firearms distributor defendants. These defendants agreed to stop selling and delivering gun components to New York residents used to assemble ghost guns. Two defendants also agreed to provide identifying information for the purchasers of their ghost gun parts. The city agreed not to publicize this information, but the agreement permitted the city to share this information with any city agency, including the police department. The state's claims against the other five defendants did not settle.[138]

In November 2022 one of the defendants filed its answer to the New York City complaint alleging that it did not sell unfinished frames directly to New York customers and that even if it did, the plaintiff's complaint failed to adequately allege that the defendant's sales proximately caused the harm alleged by the plaintiff.[139]

9.10 NEW JERSEY STATE'S GUN PUBLIC NUISANCE STATUTE JULY 2021

On June 5, 2022 – one year after New York's enactment of its gun public nuisance statute – New Jersey enacted a similar firearms public nuisance law.[140] The statute substantially replicated the New York statute's provisions.

[135] *Id.* at **3–9.
[136] *Id.* at **5–8.
[137] *Id.* at *9.
[138] Lim, Litigation Highlights, *supra* note 133.
[139] *Id.*
[140] N.J.S.A. 2C:58-35 (2022); *see* Official Site of the State of New Jersey, Governor Murphy Signs Sweeping Gun Safety Package 3.0 to Continue Fight Against Gun Violence (July 5, 2022).

It created a cause of action for public nuisance applying to gun industry members that were engaged in the sale, manufacturing, distribution, importing, or marketing of a gun-related product. The statute reached any officer, agent, employee or person authorized to act on behalf of the gun industry members, who acted in concert with one another. The law established liability for any gun industry member that failed to establish, implement, and enforce reasonable controls regarding the manufacture, sale, distribution, importing, and marketing of gun-related products.[141]

The statute provided for enforcement mechanisms, permitting the state attorney general to seek an injunction to prohibit gun industry members from engaging in or continuing harmful conduct. The statute provided for the creation of an enforcement committee within the attorney general's offices or the Department of Law and Public Safety.[142]

On November 16, 2022, the National Shooting Sports Foundation sued New Jersey's state attorney general in federal court, seeking a preliminary injunction, declaratory and permanent injunctive relief, and nominal damages to enjoin the defendant from implementing or enforcing the act.[143] Although the NSSF had failed to have New York's public nuisance statute declared constitutionally infirm, the NSSF succeeded in obtaining a preliminary injunction from the New Jersey federal court against the New Jersey public nuisance statute.[144] The state's attorney general appealed that order granting the NSSF its preliminary injunction.[145]

In its decision granting the NSSF's request for a preliminary injunction, the district court opined on several issues relating to the New Jersey statute. First, the court rejected the argument that the NSSF could not succeed on the merits of its injunction action because the lawsuit was premature, hypothetical, and unripe, and the plaintiffs lacked standing. The court concluded that the plaintiffs satisfied the three elements of constitutional standing: injury in fact, traceable to the defendant's conduct, for which the law supplied a remedy. The threat of liability under the statute for their conduct satisfied the first two requirements; the threat of future enforcement satisfied the third standing element.[146]

---

[141] N.J.S.A. 2C:58-35.

[142] N.J.S.A. 2C:-35(a)(3)(b).

[143] Nat'l Shooting Sports Foundation v. Platkin, 2023 WL 1380388, at * 1 (D.N.J. Jan. 31, 2023).

[144] *See* NRA-ILA, Institute for Legislative Action, Biden-Appointed Judge Issues PI Against New Jersey Anti-Gun "Public Nuisance Law," (Feb. 6, 2023).

[145] *See* Nat'l Shooting Sports Foundation v. Platkin, 2023 WL 2344635 (D.N.J. Mar. 3, 2023) (opinion denying state attorney general's motion to stay former order, pending appeal).

[146] Nat'l Shooting, *supra* note 143, at **2–3.

Second, as it argued in its New York lawsuit, the NSSF asserted that PLCAA conflicted with and preempted New Jersey's state efforts to subject firearms manufacturers or sellers to liability for harm resulting from the criminal or misuse of a qualified product by a third party. NSSF argued that the New Jersey statute did not fall within PLCAA's predicate statute exception. After lengthy statutory construction of PLCAA and the New Jersey public nuisance provisions, the district court concluded that the predicate exception did not apply. The court held that the New Jersey statute would subject firearms manufacturers, distributors, dealers, and importers of firearms or ammunition products and their trade associations to civil liability for harm by the criminal conduct or misuse of their products by others. The New Jersey statute was in direct conflict with PLCAA's purpose and to read the statute as coming within the predicate exception would run afoul of PLCAA's goal and gut the PLCAA.[147]

The court further found that the NSSF would suffer irreparable injury if the court did not grant its motion for an injunction. The statutory enforcement mechanisms placed NSSF members in a dilemma: either they complied with the statutory subjecting them to vague requirements to enforce reasonable controls regarding the manufacture, sale, distribution, importing, and marketing of gun-related products, or face prosecution and fees for noncompliance with the statute. If the court ultimately should find the statute preempted by PLCAA unconstitutional, recovering damages for fines assessed for noncompliance would be unrecoverable in state or federal court under the Eleventh Amendment.[148]

Balancing the harm of issuing a preliminary injunction against the state, the court found that the state had no legitimate interest in enforcing an unconstitutional statute, nor could the state present any argument of potential damages that would result if the court issued the injunction. The court further indicated that the public interest favored suspension of the state's policy pending the outcome of litigation on the merits. "The Court is mindful that firearms are inherently dangerous and even more so in the wrong hands, but it is also mindful that the PLCAA embodies Congress's earnest effort to balance those dangers against the national interest in protecting access to firearms."[149]

---

[147] *Id.* at 3–7.
[148] *Id.* at 7–9, citing Royster v. New Jersey State Police, 227 N.J. 482, 494–95 (2017); Edelman v. Jordon, 415 U.S. 651, 663 (1974) (suit by private parties seeking to impose liability which must be paid from the public funds in the state treasury is barred by the Eleventh Amendment).
[149] *Id.* at 9–10.

The New Jersey district court's construction of the state's public nuisance statute, particularly regarding PLCAA preemption and the applicability of PLCAA's predicate statute exception, places the court squarely in conflict with the New York federal district's court's conclusion concerning a virtually identical public nuisance statute. The decisions currently are on appeal with the Second and Third Circuits and, depending on the outcome in those appeals, the legitimacy of these new state gun-related public nuisance statute may be headed to the Supreme Court for resolution on the public nuisance laws.

9.11 CALIFORNIA AND DELAWARE GUN PUBLIC NUISANCE STATUTES JULY 2022

The Delaware and California state legislatures followed New York and New Jersey in enacting firearms public nuisance statutes in 2022–23. The California statute AB 1594 was signed into law in July 2022 and similarly provides for holding the firearm industry liable for their misconduct. The statute governs the sale and marketing of firearms by manufacturers and distributors who do business in California and requires them to take reasonable efforts to prevent their products from being used unlawfully. If industry members fail to take proper precautions in marketing and sale of firearms, the state attorney general and citizens are authorized to file civil litigation to recoup damages.[150]

On June 30, 2022, the Delaware governor signed Senate Bill 302, Delaware's redefined tort of public nuisance.[151] The Delaware statute is the most sweeping of the new state public nuisance laws. The statute covers not only firearm industry members, but also firearm traffickers and straw purchasers.[152] It defines a public nuisance as a condition which injures, endangers, or threatens to injure or endanger or contributes to the injury or endangerment of the health, safety, peace, comfort, or convenience of others or otherwise constitutes a public nuisance under common law.[153]

---

[150] Cal. Civ. Code tit. 20 §§ 3273.50-55 et seq. Firearm Industry Responsibility Act (effective July 1, 2023). *See* Office of the Attorney General, Attorney General Bonta Celebrates the Signing of AB 1594 to Prevent Gun Violence (July 12, 2022); Everytown for Gun Safety, Victory for Gun Safety: Following Tireless Advocacy from Moms Demand Action and Students Demand Action, Governor Newsome Signs Historic Bill to Hold Firearm Industry Accountable for Role in Gun Violence (July 12, 2022). *See also* Eva Symon, Judge Blocks Major Part of California Gun Control Bill, California Globe (Dec. 17, 2022).

[151] Del. Code tit. 10 § 3930.

[152] *Id.* § 3930(a)(1), (3), (7).

[153] *Id.* at § 3930(a)(5).

Like the other state public nuisance statutes, it imposes a duty on industry members to establish and implement reasonable controls regarding the
manufacture, sale, distribution, use, and marketing of firearms.[154] The statute
specifically indicates that a firearm members' conduct constitutes a proximate
cause of a public nuisance if the harm to the public is a consequence of
the firearm members' failure to carry out its statutory duties.[155] The statute
provides for remedies including injunctions, abatement orders, restitution,
compensatory and punitive damages, reasonable attorney fees and costs, and
any other appropriate relief.[156]

The statute provides individuals with a private right of action to seek injunctive relief, compensatory and punitive damages, and reasonable attorney fees,
and to notify the attorney general's office of the filing of an action.[157] To prevail in a firearms public nuisance action, a plaintiff is not required to show
that the firearm industry member acted with the intent to engage in a public
nuisance or otherwise cause harm to the public.[158] In addition, nothing in the
statute is intended to restrict or alter the availability of an action for relief to
remedy a public nuisance at common law.[159]

On November 16, 2022, the NSSF filed a lawsuit against the Delaware
state attorney general in the federal district court for Delaware, seeking an
injunction against enforcement of the Delaware public nuisance statute.[160]
The complaint alleged the same arguments advanced in the New York and
New Jersey litigation, challenging (1) the constitutionality of the statute,
(2) the statute's violation of the Commerce Clause, and (3) PLCAA preemption of the state nuisance statute as not within PLCAA's predicate statute
exemption.[161]

In suing to restrain enforcement of the Delaware public nuisance statute,
the NSSF is following a strategy of assembling federal district decisions inval-
idating state efforts to create state statutory exemptions to PLCAA firearms
industry immunity. It remains to be seen how successful this industry defense
strategy succeeds, perhaps all the way to the Supreme Court. At the same
time, state attorney generals have been tracking litigation over the new state

---

[154] *Id.* at § 3930(c).
[155] *Id.* at § 3930(e).
[156] *Id.* at § 3930(f).
[157] *Id.* at § 3930(g).
[158] *Id.* at § 3930(h)
[159] *Id.* at § 3930(k).
[160] Nat'l Shooting Sports Foundation v. Jennings, Case 1:22-cv-01499-UNA (D. Del. Nov. 11, 2022)
(NSSF complaint).
[161] *Id.*

public nuisance statutes in the hope that judicial validation of these statutes will provide an inroad into holding firearms industry members accountable for harms to citizens of their states. If the New York precedent prevails and federal appellate courts agree, then one may expect a cascade of imitation firearms statutes enacted in many states.

E-Cigarettes and Vaping as a Public Nuisance Harm

Beginning in 2018, dozens of school districts across the U.S., including districts in Missouri, Kansas, Arizona, West Virginia, New York, and California, instituted lawsuits against e-cigarette companies alleging public nuisance claims.[1] Plaintiffs' attorneys – many of whom were involved with the opioid litigation – modeled these lawsuits based on the opioid public nuisance litigation. Target defendants included JUUL and the Altria Group Inc., which had acquired an interest in JUUL. The lawsuits alleged that the deceptive marketing of e-cigarettes to minors created an epidemic of student nicotine use, requiring significant expenditures by school districts to address the vaping crisis.

The opioid litigation greatly influenced the development and reception of e-cigarette lawsuits, which followed a similar trajectory. The multidistrict litigation (MDL) panel consolidated hundreds of federal e-cigarette cases in the Northern District of California.[2] Like the RICO claims asserted in the opioid litigation, the e-cigarette lawsuits accused the defendants of racketeering related to marketing to minors and being a public nuisance by creating an epidemic of student vaping, burdening schools in managing e-cigarette use. The lawsuits claimed the defendants purposefully targeted student-aged youth and used language in its marketing that represented that their vaping products were totally safe. The school districts sought to recoup financial losses incurred by managing the exploding numbers of students using e-cigarettes.

The filing of numerous federal court cases spurred the Judicial Panel on Multidistrict Litigation to create an e-cigarette MDL, as the Panel had done for the opioid litigation. In 2020, the federal district judge overseeing the e-cigarette MDL ruled the plaintiffs could proceed on a public nuisance

---

[1] Kari Paul, More Than a Dozen US School Districts Sue JUUL and Other Vape Companies, The Guardian (Dec. 1, 2019).

[2] In re JUUL Labs, Inc., Marketing, Sales Practices, and Prods. Liab. Litig, 396 F.Supp.3d 1366 (J.P.M.D.L. 2019).

theory. He determined the plaintiffs had adequately pled their public nuisance claims because JUUL's conduct, such as targeted marketing and the sale of flavored products, created and maintained a youth market of school-aged students addicted to nicotine, causing extreme disruption in classrooms and unique harm to schools.[3]

The pattern of e-cigarette litigation followed closely on the opioid model of federal and state court developments. Like the other public nuisance litigation pursued in the twenty-first century, the e-cigarette public nuisance lawsuits reflected a similar judicial ambivalence towards societal recovery for amorphously alleged interference with and harm to a public right. The contrasting federal and state decisions in e-cigarette litigation suggest the nascent and evolving state of mass tort public nuisance jurisprudence.

10.1 THE E-CIGARETTE AND VAPING CRISIS AMONG AMERICAN YOUTH

The 1998 national tobacco Master Settlement Agreement with 48 states' attorney generals imposed an array of restrictive provisions on tobacco company defendants regarding the companies' advertising, sponsorship, and lobbying activities, especially targeted to youth.[4] The settlement specified bans on outdoor billboards, advertising on transit vehicles, sports marketing, event sponsorships, and promotional products. Tobacco companies were required to place dramatic and effective warnings about the health dangers of cigarette smoking on cigarette packaging, coupled with media campaigns to inform the public of the health consequences of cigarette smoking.

In 2023, the National Association of Attorneys General reported that the Master Settlement Agreement had a profound effect on cigarette smoking in the U.S., particularly among youth; between 1998 and 2019, U.S. cigarette consumption dropped by more than 50 percent.[5] In that same period, smoking by high school students dropped from its near peak of 36.4 percent in 1997 to 6 percent in 2019. In 2006 the New York attorney general reported that cigarette sales had dropped to the lowest level since 1951 with a 21% sales drop since implementation of the Master Settlement Agreement.[6] The U.S. Department

---

[3] In re JUUL Labs, Inc., Marketing, Sales Practices, and Prods. Liab. Litig, 497 F.Supp.3d 1366 (N.D. Cal. 2020).

[4] Nat'l Assoc. of Attorneys Gen., Master Settlement Agreement at § III(a)(1998).

[5] National Association of Attorneys General, The Master Settlement Agreement (2023), available at www.naag.org/our-work/naag-center-for-tobacco-and-public-health/the-master-settlement-agreement/#

[6] Office of the New York State Attorney General, Cigarette Sales Hit 55-Year Historic Low (Mar. 8, 2006), available at https://ag.ny.gov/press-release/2006/cigarette-sales-hit-historic-55-year-low.

of Health likewise documented the marked decline of traditional cigarette smoking over several decades among youth and young adults.[7]

The relative decline of cigarette sales prompted tobacco companies to recast delivery systems for their nicotine products and, in 2006, e-cigarettes were introduced to the marketplace. In 2016, the U.S. Surgeon General issued a major report documenting the advent of e-cigarettes in the market and the emerging effects on youth and young adults. The study reported that the decline in traditional cigarette smoking among the youth was accompanied by a dramatic rise in the use of emerging tobacco products, most notably e-cigarettes.[8]

E-cigarettes included an array of devices containing nicotine, flavorings, and other additives that permitted users to inhale an aerosol. The e-cigarette aerosol was not harmless, containing injurious and potentially damaging constituent chemical elements. The devices went by several names, including vapes, vaping pens, and tank systems, and represented a rapidly emerging and diversified product class.[9] In May 2016, the Food and Drug Administration exercised its authority over e-cigarettes as a tobacco product.

The tobacco companies marketed and advertised their e-cigarette devices through multiple media channels, which promoted the flavors and appeal of e-cigarettes. The marketing programs employed approaches the tobacco companies had used in the past to promote conventional cigarettes, including sexual content and projections of consumer satisfaction. E-cigarette products were marketed through television, magazines, promotional activities, radio, the internet, and at point-of-sale.

The Surgeon General's report concluded that use of nicotine products posed dangers to youth, pregnant women, and fetuses; the use of products containing nicotine in any form was unsafe. Exposure to nicotine products during adolescence could cause addiction and damage to developing brains. The Surgeon General's report further concluded that e-cigarette use among youth and young adults had become a public health concern. In 2019, doctors and patients reported a rash of lung diseases tied to e-cigarette use, with more than 2,000 cases of vaping-related lung injury.[10] The Centers for Disease Control and Prevention documented that since March 2019, 2,807 people had been hospitalized for vape-product-use associated lung injury, with 68 confirmed

---

[7] U.S. Dept. of Health and Human Services, Preventing Tobacco Use Among Youth and Young Adults: A Report of the Surgeon General (2012).

[8] Centers for Disease Control and Prevention, E-Cigarette Use Among Youth and Young Adults: A Report of the Surgeon General (2016), available at www.ncbi.nih.gov/books/NBK538634

[9] *Id.*

[10] *See* Paul, *supra* note 1.

deaths. The cases were reported in all 50 states, the District of Columbia, Puerto Rico, and the Virgin Islands.[11]

As of 2014, e-cigarette use among young adults between 18–24 years of age surpassed that of adults 25 years or older and were the most used tobacco products among youth, surpassing conventional cigarettes in 2014. Data collected by the Center for Disease Control indicated that e-cigarette use among middle and high school students more than tripled since 2011. The most cited reasons for e-cigarette use were curiosity, flavoring and taste, and a low perceived harm compared to other tobacco products. Using e-cigarettes to quit conventional smoking was not viewed as a primary reason for adopting e-cigarettes use.[12]

Since the introduction of e-cigarette products in 2006, the market for nicotine devices grew rapidly with "notable increases in total sales of e-cigarette products, types of products, consolidation of companies, marketing expenses, and sales channels."[13] As prices for e-cigarettes devices declined, sales greatly increased. JUUL, a primary defendant in subsequent e-cigarette litigation, saw its revenues grow by 700% to $200 million, and revenues hit $1 billion in 2018. The company forecasted revenue more than $3 billion for 2019.[14]

In December 2018, the U.S. Surgeon General declared that e-cigarette use "ha[d] become an epidemic among our nation's young people."[15] Subsequently, thirty-nine states' attorney generals announced an investigation into the marketing and sales practices by JUUL Labs. Attorney generals in New York, California, North Carolina, Massachusetts, and Illinois sued JUUL Labs, alleging that JUUL engaged in deceptive marketing practices targeting youth and misleading consumers about the nicotine content and safety of its products.[16]

For the first ten years after the introduction of e-cigarettes to the market, the vaping industry did not face any product liability lawsuits. However, school districts across the country were among the first to experience the effects of the rapid growth of the e-cigarette industry and the explosion of school-age youth using vaping products. Beginning in 2018 vape product manufacturers began to face hundreds of lawsuits filed in federal and state courts throughout the U.S.

---

[11] Richtel & Kaplan, First Death in a Spate of Vaping Sicknesses Reported by Health Officials, N.Y. Times (Aug. 24, 2019).

[12] Paul, *supra* note 1.

[13] Centers for Disease Control and Prevention, *supra* note 8.

[14] Paul, *supra* note 1.

[15] Center for Disease Control and Prevention, Surgeon General's Advisory on E-Cigarette Use Among Youth, at 2 (Dec. 18, 2018).

[16] Keelin Kavanagh & Christopher Gismondi, The Litigation Environment in the Vape Industry, N.Y.L.J. (Apr. 3, 2020).

Local municipalities and school districts followed with lawsuits against JUUL, seeking to recover costs associated with the time, money, and resources the districts expended to combat the nuisance created by vaping products. In 2019, a rural Missouri school district became one of the first to file a federal lawsuit against JUUL, complaining that the prevalence of student vaping required significant expenditures to address the epidemic in the community.[17] The lawsuit accused JUUL of racketeering relating to the marketing to minors and being a public nuisance by creating an epidemic of nicotine use among students. The complaint alleged that JUUL purposefully targeted youth with misleading marketing that told students that its vaping products were harmless. The school district accused the defendant of conducting viral marketing campaigns that user influencers that would appeal to young people.[18]

A Los Angeles school district filed a similar lawsuit against JUUL, complaining that the loss of instructional time due to discipling students using vaping products had a significant impact on district schools. In 2021, various West Virginia counties sued JUUL, with the plaintiff county boards of education declaring nicotine e-cigarettes a public nuisance.[19]

In the school district lawsuits, plaintiffs documented the costs of the expanding e-cigarette epidemic among student populations. The cost of installing vaping detection systems ran as high as $40,000, and some schools had to hire full-time staff members to monitor hallways and bathrooms for vaping students. Other schools took extreme measures to address the vaping problem, including removing bathroom stall doors, installing vape sensors in bathrooms, and banishing USB drives.

The development of litigation against the e-cigarette industry paralleled the way in which the opioid litigation against the opioid manufacturers, distributors, and sellers progressed. Thus, in addition to school district and municipal lawsuits, states attorney generals sued JUUL and the vaping industry as state plaintiffs, as did various individuals affected by e-cigarette addiction.

10.2 E-CIGARETTE AND VAPING MDL

On October 2, 2019, the Judicial Panel on Multidistrict Litigation authorized the creation of an MDL at JUUL's request to handle the burgeoning e-cigarette

---

[17] Paul, *supra* note 1.
[18] *Id.*
[19] Lyra Bordelon, BoE Declares Nicotine E-Cigarettes a 'Public Nuisance,' W.Va. Daily News (Apr. 15, 2022). *See also* Whatcom County v. JUUL Labs., Inc, Case No. 2:20-cv-499 (W.D. Wash. 2020) county lawsuit against JUUL).

litigation throughout the federal system.[20] At the time the MDL was requested, 10 actions had been filed: 5 in the Northern District of California, 2 in the Middle District of Alabama, and one case each in the Middle District of Florida, the Southern District of Florida, and the Southern District of New York. The panel was notified of more than 40 potentially related federal e-cigarette actions.

The lawsuits included both class actions and individual personal injury claims. The complaints alleged that JUUL had marketed its nicotine products in a fashion designed to attract youth and that its marketing practices failed to alert consumers to the potentially harmful and addictive nature of e-cigarettes. The complaints alleged that the JUUL products were defective and unreasonably dangerous due to their attractiveness to minors.[21]

The Panel held that the actions involved common questions of fact that justified the transfer and centralization of all the cases to one judicial forum. Tracking the language of the MDL statute,[22] the Panel noted that centralization of the cases would serve the convenience of the parties and witnesses and promote the just and efficient conduct of the litigation. Centralization of the litigation would eliminate duplicative discovery, inconsistent rulings on motions practice, and conserve judicial and party resources.[23]

The Panel selected the Northern District of California as the transferee district and assigned the MDL to Judge William H. Orrick III. Judge Orrick had been presiding over the California JUUL actions since they were filed in 2018, so he was familiar with allegations in the emerging e-cigarette litigation.[24] The Northern District of California was selected, in part, because it was the location of JUUL's headquarters.[25]

In October 2020, Judge Orrick ruled on the first wave of defendants' motions to dismiss the litigation.[26] The MDL structure had become complex, embracing three different amended complaints: (1) an amended consolidated class action complaint, (2) an amended personal injury master complaint, and (3) governmental entity complaints. The major defendants named in all the complaints were JUUL Labs., Inc., an Altria corporate group of defendants, and current and former JUUL founders and directors. The plaintiffs in the personal injury complaint named as defendants retail sellers and distributors of e-liquid products.[27]

---

[20] In re JUUL Labs, *supra* note 2, at 1367.
[21] *Id.*
[22] 28 U.S.C. § 1407.
[23] *Id.*
[24] Colgate v. JUUL Labs, Inc., 402 F.Supp.3d 728 (N.D. Cal. 2019); Colgate v. JUUL Labs, inc., 345 F.Supp.3d 1178 (N.D. Cal. 2018).
[25] In re JUUL Labs, Inc., *supra* note 2, at 1367.
[26] In re JUUL Labs, Inc., *supra* note 3, at 573.
[27] *Id.*

The plaintiffs' class action and the personal injury complaints alleged a laundry list of claims and causes of action that did not include a public nuisance claim.[28] Several school districts comprised the plaintiffs in third consolidated complaint. By party agreement, they consented to having the viability of their complaint tested on the omnibus motions to dismiss the e-cigarette litigation.[29]

The governmental entities pursuing a public nuisance claim alleged that JUUL Labs, Altria, and the management defendants worked together to implement a multifaceted strategy in which they would share the market of vaping products. The strategies included creating highly addictive products that users would not associate with cigarettes and would appeal to a lucrative youth market; deceiving the public and especially youth that their products were fun and safe alternatives to cigarettes that would help smokers to quit; actively attracting youth consumers through targeted marketing; and employing a variety of tools to delay regulation of e-cigarettes through false and captive statements to the public and regulators.[30]

The school districts' consolidated MDL complaint detailed facts relating to the crisis created because of the defendants' conduct and the resulting costs to the school districts. The school districts incurred significant expenditures of time and resources to address the pervasiveness of youth e-cigarette use. This included costs to educate youth to the dangers of e-smoking, staff training, new counselling service, costs associated with disciplining and suspending students, disciplinary hearings, home tutoring, monitoring bathrooms, installing e-cigarette detectors, additional cameras, and the costs associated with safe disposal of hazardous waste contained in JUUL products.[31]

The municipal plaintiffs similarly documented the public costs of dealing with the vaping crisis. These included public staff time and resources addressing youth e-cigarette use, educational campaigns, ad purchases to combat the defendants' deceptive and misleading information, time and resources from local police departments, increased need for disciplinary hearings, trained addiction specialists, counselors and social workers, and development of effective cessation methods targeted to youth.[32]

Based on their allegations, the governmental entity plaintiffs pleaded four causes of action: (1) violation of RICO, (2) conspiracy to violate RICO, (3) public nuisance under Arizona, California, Florida, New York, and Pennsylvania

[28] Id.
[29] Id. at 577.
[30] Id.
[31] Id. at 577–78.
[32] Id. at 578.

laws, and (4) negligence and gross negligence under the same state laws.[33] The governmental entity plaintiffs sought abatement, injunctive relief, equitable relief to fund education and addiction treatment, actual and compensatory damages, statutory damages, punitive damages, attorney fees and costs, and pre- and post-judgment interest.[34]

10.3 MOTION TO DISMISS THE GOVERNMENTAL ENTITIES' E-CIGARETTE PUBLIC NUISANCE CLAIM

JUUL, Altria, and the corporate officers moved to dismiss all the pleaded claims in the three complaints, invoking the primary jurisdiction doctrine, as well as express and implied preemption. As courts had concluded in prior environmental and opioid public nuisance litigation, the MDL judge determined that the plaintiffs' claims in the e-cigarette litigation were not barred by the primary jurisdiction or preemption doctrines.[35]

In addition, defendants moved to dismiss the governmental entities' public nuisance claim, raising various arguments raised in prior environmental, opioid, and firearms litigation. These defenses included the municipal cost recovery rule, the product liability limitation, lack of interference with a public right, lack of control over the instrumentality allegedly causing the nuisance, and lack of special injury.[36]

The court rejected JUUL's motion to stay all MDL proceedings pending a federal Food and Drug Administration ruling on JUUL's recently filed pre-market tobacco application for its electronic nicotine delivery system. JUUL invoked the primary jurisdiction doctrine in support of this motion.[37] The court determined that the prevailing circuit precedent concerning primary jurisdiction depended on whether application of the doctrine would needlessly delay the resolution of claims.

In making this determination, efficiency was the deciding factor, and efficiency weighed against a stay of proceedings.[38] The court further noted that the unclear scope and unlikely relevance of any FDA actions on JUUL's pending application, coupled with the uncertainty of when the FDA might act, did not weigh strongly in favor of staying the large and complex MDL proceedings "that can and should move forward efficiently."[39]

---

[33] *Id.* Three governmental entity plaintiffs further alleged violations of the New York and Florida consumer protection laws. *Id.*

[34] *Id.*

[35] In re JUUL Labs, Inc., *supra* note 3, at 578–593.

[36] *Id.* at 643–53.

[37] *Id.* at 578–92.

[38] *Id.* at 580.

[39] *Id.* at 582.

JUUL and the retail e-cigarette defendants also moved to dismiss the complaints arguing that the plaintiffs' state law claims were preempted by the Family Smoking Prevention and Tobacco Control Act of 2009.[40] In prior decisions before authorization of the MDL, Judge Orrick determined that the plaintiffs' state law false advertising and consumer protection claims were not expressly preempted. Judge Orrick extended these holdings to the MDL lawsuits.[41] The court further noted that the Tobacco Control Act's express savings clause expressly preserved state law products liability claims and that savings clause preserved the majority of claims in the plaintiffs' MDL complaints.[42] The majority of the plaintiffs' claims could proceed and were not preempted.[43]

Judge Orrick further rejected the defendant's contention that all the plaintiffs' claims, including the products liability claims that fell within the statute's savings' clause, were impliedly preempted under conflict preemption.[44] He suggested that the defendants' objection based on implied preemption placed the cart before a cart; the court could not rule on implied preemption until the FDA exercised its regulatory authority to create a conflict with state law. Judge Orrick noted that the FDA could take actions that would impact the strength of some plaintiffs' claims, but if a conflict arose, he could address it then. Moreover, field preemption was clearly not contemplated by the Tobacco Control Act.[45]

The MDL judge assessed the defendants' objections against the public nuisance claim. The defendants argued that the municipal cost recovery rule barred the governmental entities from obtaining the monetary damages to recover the cost of providing educational and other public community services. The defendants contended that the common law municipal recovery rule held that the cost of public services like protection from fire and safety hazards be borne by the public and not assessed against a tortfeasor, whose negligence created the need for services.[46]

The MDL judge rejected the defense, citing circuit precedent for the proposition that governmental entities were able to recover costs where a private party's acts created a public nuisance that plaintiffs were seeking to abate.[47] The municipalities plausibly alleged damages resulting from the defendants'

---

[40] *Id.* at 583, 585–86. *See* Family Smoking and Prevention and Tobacco Control Act of 2009, 21 U.S.C. § 387 *et seq.*
[41] *Id.* at 584, citing Colgate v. JUUL Labs., Inc. (Colgate I and II), *supra* note 24.
[42] *Id.* citing 21 U.S.C. § 387p(b).
[43] *Id.* at 592–94.
[44] *Id.*
[45] *Id.* at 593–94.
[46] In re JUUL Labs, Inc., *supra* note 35, at 643.
[47] *Id.* citing Flagstaff v. Atchinson, Topeka & Sant Fe, 719 F.2d 322, 323 (9th Cir. 1983).

ongoing and persistent deceptive marketing campaign and intentional targeting of youth that led the municipalities and school boards to incur expenses that they could not reasonably have anticipated.[48]

Turning to the national MDL opioid litigation, the court noted that Judge Polster ruled that the municipal cost recovery rule did not bar the counties' and tribal public nuisance claims in that litigation.[49] And a New York state court in its opioid litigation similarly held that the municipal cost recover rule did not bar the plaintiffs' public nuisance claim; to conclude otherwise would distort the doctrine beyond recognition. The court could not find case law supporting the defendants' contention that the rule barred municipalities' recovery for expenses they incurred to remedy the harm caused by defendants' intentional, persistent course of deceptive conduct.[50]

In addition, the Ohio Supreme Court recognized similar distinctions and declined to apply the municipal cost recovery rule in firearms public nuisance litigation.[51] Thus, where a defendant's conduct was ongoing and persistent, the continuing nature of the misconduct might justify the recoupment of governmental costs.[52]

JUUL moved to dismiss the plaintiffs' claims arguing that the municipalities should not be allowed to expand public nuisance law beyond its traditional boundaries into product liability law. The public nuisance claim essentially was a products liability claim for economic damages masquerading as a public nuisance claim.[53]

The MDL judge disagreed, again finding support in Judge Polster's ruling on a similar contention in the national opioid MDL. The court held that the entities' public nuisance claims did not stretch into products' liability law.[54] The governmental entities' claim was not an attempt to expand public nuisance law to embrace causes of action against manufacturers for dangerous products or failure to warn in their product marketing. Rather, the plaintiffs' allegations did not concern JUUL's products, but rather the consequences of JUUL's conduct. The plaintiffs' public nuisance claim was predicated on

---

[48] In re JUUL Labs, Inc., *supra* note 36, at 645.

[49] *Id.* at 644, citing In re Nat'l Opiate Litig., 2019 WL 3737023, at *1 (N.D. Ohio June 13, 2019).

[50] In re JUUL Labs, Inc., *supra* note 36, at 644–45, citing In re Nat'l Prescription Opioid Litig., 2018 WL 3115102, at *2 (N.Y. Sup. Ct. June 18, 2018).

[51] In re JUUL Labs, Inc., *supra* note 36, at 644, citing Cincinnati v. Beretta U.S.A., Corp., 95 Ohio St.3d 416, 428, 768 N.E.2d 1136 (2002).

[52] In re JUUL Labs, Inc., *supra* note 36.

[53] *Id.* at 645–47.

[54] *Id.* at 646, citing In re Nat'l Prescription Opiate Litig. – Muscogee (Creek) Nation, 2019 WL 2468267 at *29 (N.D. Ohio Apr. 1, 2019).

JUUL's aggressive marketing and promotion of its products to teens and its efforts to create and maintain an e-cigarette market based on youth sales. In addition, the municipalities' public nuisance claim was not as novel as the defendant argued; it had been raised and rejected in numerous opioid and gun manufacturer cases.[55]

JUUL further contended that the plaintiffs had not shown that the relevant states involved (Arizona, California, Florida, Pennsylvania, and New York) recognized this type of public nuisance claim. The MDL judge disagreed. The court noted that California plaintiffs were permitted to bring public nuisance claims against manufacturers if the litigation was not premised on product liability theories. And any contrary jurisprudence from Pennsylvania, Florida, and New York courts was distinguishable on their facts. Because Arizona had a not yet recognized a public nuisance claim against the manufacturer of a consumer product based on its marketing, sales, and distribution, this was no reason to conclude that Arizona would not recognize a public nuisance claim based on similar allegations in the governmental entities' e-cigarette case.[56]

JUUL additionally contended that the governmental entities' public nuisance claim failed because the plaintiffs did not sufficiently allege an unreasonable interference with a public right, a required element to establish a public nuisance under the *Restatement (Second)*.[57] The MDL judge disagreed, rejecting JUUL's motion to dismiss the public nuisance claim for failure to plead interference with a public right.[58] The court pointed out that the *Restatement (Second)* included, as an unreasonable interference with a common public right, conduct that involved a significant interference with public health. The governmental entities adequately described a public health crisis of youth e-cigarette use and wholesale addiction to nicotine products. Each of the plaintiffs' state jurisprudence prohibited conduct that interfered with the public health, and each sufficiently alleged that JUUL had substantially interfered with the public health, negatively impacting school districts and their communities.[59]

JUUL argued that the governmental entity complaints from Arizona, Florida, New York, and Pennsylvania had to be dismissed because JUUL did not control the instrumentality that caused the nuisance. Reviewing state law, the court noted that Pennsylvania and Florida required control as an

---

[55] In re JUUL Labs, Inc., *supra* note 36, at 646 (citing opioid and firearms public nuisance cases).

[56] *Id.* at 646–47.

[57] *Id.* at 647, citing *Restatement (Second) of Torts* § 821B (1979). The court noted that Arizona, New York, and Pennsylvania courts adopted the *Restatement (Second)* approach, and that Florida and New York courts adopted similar principles.

[58] In re JUUL Labs, Inc., *supra* note 36, at 648.

[59] *Id.*

element for a public nuisance claim, but JUUL had not submitted briefing on the Arizona and New York laws. Even assuming Arizona and New York also required defendant's control over the instrumentality of the nuisance, the court concluded that the plaintiffs sufficiently alleged this element.[60]

JUUL's argument, the court responded, rested on the false premise that the instrumentality of the nuisance was the product itself. Instead, what was relevant was whether the defendant had control over the conduct that created and maintained the public nuisance. The MDL judge denied JUUL's motion to dismiss the public nuisance claim for failing to sufficiently plead the defendant's control over the instrumentality of the public nuisance.[61]

Citing opioid and firearms public nuisance decisions to this effect, the MDL e-cigarette judge stated that JUUL had control over the conduct that created the vaping crisis among youth. This included JUUL's direct and intentional marketing to youth, distributing free samples, presenting misleading information, and preserving availability of mint flavored e-cigarette kits. "These allegations," the court concluded, "match the type of public nuisance allegations that have preceded past the pleading stage in cases addressing opioids and firearms."[62]

Finally, JUUL moved to dismiss the plaintiffs' public nuisance claim for failure to plead a special injury as the *Restatement (Second)* required.[63] The court noted that a plaintiff cannot recover for pecuniary losses resulting from a public nuisance unless the plaintiff suffered damages that were different in kind from those suffered by the public. If a plaintiff suffered an injury that differed only in degree from the entire community, it was not a different harm, and the individual plaintiff could not recover for invasion of the public right.

The MDL judge rejected JUUL's motion to dismiss for failure to plead a special injury. The court found that the school districts had provided sufficient detail in their complaints about the kinds of harm caused by JUUL's conduct that was unique and different in kind than the harm suffered by the public in their communities. The court noted the numerous actions that the school districts had been required to take to deal with the vaping crisis among its youth, diverting limited resources to combat the problem. Again, the court relied on related findings by Judge Polster in the national opioid litigation, where similar allegations of governmental entity plaintiffs had passed the pleading stage in the opioid cases.[64]

---

[60] *Id.* at 647–48.
[61] *Id.* at 649.
[62] *Id.* citing opioid and firearms cases.
[63] *Id.* at 649, citing *Restatement (Second) of Torts* § 821C.
[64] *Id.* at 650, citing In re Nat'l Prescription Opiate Litig. – West Boca Medical Ctr., 452 F.Supp.3d 745, 774 (N.D. Ohio Apr. 3, 2020).

Altria separately sought to dismiss the public nuisance claim against it, arguing that the government entities failed to allege sufficient facts regarding its role
in creating or maintaining the alleged public nuisance.[65] The court disagreed,
finding that the plaintiffs pleaded sufficient facts showing JUUL's coordination
with Altria by sharing information on marketing and logistical efforts to expand
the youth vaping market as early as spring 2017. Altria actively participated in a
"Make the Switch" campaign to assist convincing the public the JUUL products were never marketed to youth but were intended as smoking cessation
devices. In addition, Altria exercised lobbying efforts to maintain the youth
e-cigarette vaping market and invested in JUUL. Two key Altria executives
became JUUL's CEO and head of regulatory affairs and agreed to use Altria's
logistical capacities to help JUUL expand its reach and efficiency.[66]

The officer and director defendants moved to dismiss based on comparable
arguments, which the court rejected on similar grounds relating to the Altria
defendants.[67] According to the court, the government entities identified that
each relevant state applied liability theories that recognized individual liability for a public nuisance tort.[68] If liable, the individual officer and director
defendants would contribute to the abatement fund, which would be used for
various measures to address the youth vaping epidemic. An abatement remedy
was not a thinly disguised damages award, but an equitable remedy designed
to eliminate the nuisance.[69]

10.4 THE DENOUEMENT OF THE E-CIGARETTE MDL

In June 2022, the Food and Drug Administration which regulated e-cigarettes
denied JUUL's application to allow it's vapes to remain in the market. JUUL
appealed this decision and received a temporary stay; the FDA put its decision on hold pending further review.[70] Beginning in autumn 2022, JUUL
began a cascade of settlements throughout spring 2023 involving various lawsuits within and apart from the MDL. In September 2022 JUUL agreed to pay

---

[65] In re JUUL Labs, Inc., *supra* note 36, at 650–51.
[66] *Id.*
[67] *Id.* at 651–52.
[68] *Id.*
[69] *Id.* at 653, citing People v. ConAgra Grocery Prod. Co., 17 Cal. App.5th 51, 132, 227 Cal.
Rptr.3d 499 (2017). Judge Orrick rejected an attempt by the officer and director defendants to
dismiss the governmental entity public nuisance claims in a second round of summary judgment motions. *See In re* JUUL Labs., Inc., Marketing, Sales Practices, and Prods. Liab. Litig.,
583 F.Supp.3d 858, 876–77 (N.N. Cal. 2021).
[70] Christina Jewett, Vaping Settlement by JUUL is Said to Total $1.7 Billion, N.Y. Times (Dec.
10, 2022).

$438.5 million to settle a multistate investigation by nearly three dozen states trying to find whether the company had targeted youth in its advertising and marketing campaigns.[71] The company did not admit to any wrongdoing.

In December 2022, JUUL agreed to settle more than 5,000 MDL lawsuits with school districts, municipalities, adolescents, and Native American tribes for between $1.2 and $1.7 billion.[72] In January 2023, Judge Orrick gave preliminary approval to this settlement; he also approved a $255 million settlement that resolved the MDL class action claims that JUUL had deceptively marketed its products.

Altria, which had acquired a 35 percent stake in JUUL in 2018, was not part of the December 2022 MDL settlement. A lawsuit filed by the San Francisco Unified School District against Altria remained in the MDL, and on April 10, 2023, Judge Orrick denied the defendant's summary judgment motions to dismiss this case. Judge ordered a bellwether case to be tried by a jury in late April 2023. He noted that the plaintiff school district had shown evidence of the students' widespread use of vaping products and the company's use of social media and other marketing techniques that Altria knew had and would continue to reach school-aged students. Altria helped JUUL market its products to a youth audience while concealing the harmful health risks and contributing to addiction.[73]

Judge Orrick held that the San Francisco School District was authorized under the California Code of Civil Procedure to sue for public nuisance for damage to its property and that the school district had sufficient evidence of injury for the case to proceed to trial.[74] He found sufficient disputed issues of fact to allow the plaintiff's negligence and RICO claims also to proceed.[75]

Judge Orrick indicated that some matters might be resolved after the trial,[76] and that he would provide the jury with a special verdict form that, if the jury found Altria liable, separated categories of damages or forms of abatement the school district sought. He held that the school district was not precluded from seeking an abatement remedy, given the different scope and purposes of damages versus abatement. It remained plausible that damages would be inadequate, and the judge could address any overlap between the remedies after the trial.[77]

[71] *Id.*

[72] *Id.*

[73] *Id.* at **2–3.

[74] *Id.* at *1, citing Cal. Code. Civ. Pro. § 731.

[75] *Id.* at **1–2.

[76] *Id.* at *2.

[77] *Id.* at *3.

10.5 THE E-CIGARETTE AND VAPING STATE LITIGATION

Apart from the federal e-cigarette litigation consolidated in the MDL, several states and some cities instituted their own lawsuits against JUUL, Altria, and other e-cigarette defendants in state courts. In 2019, the state attorney generals filed lawsuits against JUUL in Minnesota[78] and California.[79] In 2020, the state attorney generals for Massachusetts and Pennsylvania likewise sued JUUL and other vaping defendants.[80]

The state e-cigarette complaints largely followed the factual and legal allegations contained in the federal lawsuits. Thus, the lawsuits detailed how JUUL and other defendants created a public nuisance through their conduct: that is, the history of the traditional tobacco industry, the emergence of e-cigarettes, the dangers of e-cigarettes to youth, the youth-oriented design and marketing of vaping products, in-person marketing at schools, and pervasive misstatements and deceptive practices, causing a public health epidemic.[81] The complaints contained lengthy descriptions of the prevalence of e-cigarettes among their youth populations, accompanied by detailed descriptions of the impact and costs of the vaping epidemic on schools districts, municipalities, and state resources.[82]

The state complaints typically pleaded similar arrays of claims under state statutory and common law including but not limited to: consumer fraud, deceptive trade practices, unlawful trade practices, false statements in advertising, negligence and negligence per se, and unjust enrichment.[83] The California state complaint alleged several statutory claims under its business and professions provisions.[84] Many state complaints involving e-cigarette litigation – although not all – pleaded a claim for public nuisance, relying on state public nuisance statutes.[85]

---

[78] Complaint, State of Minnesota v. JUUL Labs., Inc., No.27-cv-19-19888, 2019 WL 6532989 (Minn. Dist. Ct. Dec. 4, 2019).

[79] Complaint for Permanent Injunction, Abatement, Civil Penalties, and Other Equitable Relief, The People of the State of California v. JUUL Labs., Inc., No. RG19043543, 2019 WL 6245842 (Cal. Super. Nov. 18, 2019).

[80] Complaint, Commonwealth of Massachusetts v. JUUL Labs, Inc. and Pac Labs, Inc., No. 20-0402, 2020 WL 6787752 (Mass Super. Feb. 12, 2020); Commonwealth of Pennsylvania v. JUUL Labs, Inc., No. 200200962, 2020 WL 704890 (Pa. Co. Pl. Feb. 10, 2020).

[81] *See e.g.*, Minnesota Complaint, *supra* note 78, at pp. 8–61; California Comp., *supra* note 79, at ¶¶ 31–105.

[82] Minnesota Complaint, *id.*; California Complaint, *id.* at ¶¶107–15, 121–26.

[83] Minnesota Complaint, *Id.* at pp. 59–78.

[84] California Complaint, *supra* note 79 at ¶ 194–221, 238–42.

[85] Minnesota Complaint, *Id.* at pp. 73–75. *See* ¶ 269, Minnesota Statutes, section 609.74.; California Complaint, *supra* note 79, at ¶¶ 222–37 (public nuisance under Cal. Civ. Code ¶ 3479, et seq.).

The state public nuisance claims stated that state residents, including its youth, had a public right to be free from interference with the public safety, health, comfort, and repose. Equity and the law empowered the state to allege a claim and seek redress for a public nuisance, in its capacity as a public litigant and as *parens patriae*. The state, as payor for the costs incurred in public education, health care programs, and governmental services had an important and unique interest in protecting the public's health and safety.[86] In pleading the public nuisance claim, the state plaintiffs alleged that JUUL, through its deceptive and unlawful conduct had intentionally maintained a public nuisance that annoyed, injured, and endangered (and would continue to unreasonably annoy, injure, and endanger) the common right of public health, comfort, or repose of considerable members of the public.[87]

The states' attorney generals typically sought several different remedies, including injunctions, funding for corrective public education campaigns, funding for clinical vaping cessation clinics, ordering defendants to take reasonable, necessary, and adequate steps to prevent the distribution of e-cigarettes to children under eighteen years of age, awarding maximum civil penalties, awarding judgment for monetary relief, awarding judgment for reimbursement of all state costs to control nicotine use among youth, ordering abatement of the nuisance in an amount necessary to accomplish the abatement, disgorgement of payments received as a consequence of the defendant's unlawful conduct, restitution under the *parens patrie* doctrine, awarding the state costs of investigation, attorney fees, expert consultants and any other relief the court should deed appropriate and just.[88]

Beginning in spring 2021, JUUL began settling a series of state lawsuits. In June 2021, JUUL agreed to pay $40 million to North Carolina in the first state lawsuit settlement for contributing to the youth vaping epidemic.[89] In November 2021, JUUL settled a lawsuit by the Arizona state attorney general for $14.5 million for the company's unlawful marketing practices targeted to younger consumers and for having downplayed the risks associated with their vaping products.[90] In April 2022, JUUL settled for $22.5 million with

---

[86] Minnesota Complaint, *supra* note 78, at ¶ 270.

[87] California Complaint, *supra* note 79, at ¶¶ 225–37 (similar allegations).

[88] Minnesota Complaint, *supra* note 78, at pp. 78–79 (Relief); California Complaint, *supra* note 79, at Prayer for Relief.

[89] Sheila Kaplan, JUUL to Pay $40 Million to Settle N.C. Vaping Case, N.Y. Times (June 28, 2021); Office of the Attorney General Josh Stein, Attorney General Stein Reaches Agreement with JUUL for $50 Million and Drastic Business Changes (June 28, 2021).

[90] Brendan Pierson, JUUL to Pay $14.5 MLN to Settle AZ Lawsuit Over Youth Marketing, Reuters (Nov. 23. 2021); Office of Arizona Attorney General Kris Mayes, Attorney General Mark Brnovicj Reaches $14.5 Million Settlement with JUUL, (Nov. 23, 2021).

Washington state, settling claims that JUUL marketed its products to minors and lied about the addictive nature of vaping. JUUL agreed to implement a secret shopper program to police whether retailers were prohibiting minors from buying its products.[91] In September 2022 JUUL reached a tentative agreement to pay about $440 million to settle investigations by nearly three dozen states over how JUUL might have marketed to teenagers.[92] In March 2023 JUUL agreed to pay $23.8 million to Chicago to settle claims that the e-cigarette makers deceptively marketed its products and sold vaping products to underage users.[93] In the beginning of April 2023, JUUL settled West Virginia claims for $7.9 million.[94]

In March 2023, the Minnesota state attorney general began its trial against the defendants JUUL and Altria over claims the defendants created a public nuisance by marketing addictive e-cigarettes to minors. The state presented eleven witnesses in support of its claims for deceptive marketing and addicting youth to their vaping products. This was the first-in-the-nation state trial against e-cigarette defendants.[95] The state rested its case on April 11th. On April 17, 2023, the state's attorney general announced that the defendants settled the case. Minnesota was the first state to go to trial and hold JUUL and Altria accountable for deceptive marketing of e-cigarette devices and creating a public nuisance. The terms of the settlement were not disclosed.[96]

Several states collectively accomplished the largest settlement with JUUL in April 2023, for $462 million to six states and the District of Columbia.[97] The agreement was the largest multistate agreement with JUUL and placed strict requirements on JUUL's marketing, sales, and distributions practices to

[91] David Gutman, E-cigarette Giant JUUL to Pay $22.5 Million to Settle Lawsuit, Seattle Times (Apr. 13, 2022); Office of the Attorney General Washington State, AG Ferguson: JUUL Must Pay Washington $22.5 Million Over Its Unlawful Advertising Practices (Apr. 12, 2022).

[92] Associated Press, JUUL Will Pay Nearly $440 Million to Settle States' Investigation into Teen Vaping (Sept. 6, 2022).

[93] Hank Sanders, JUUL E-Cigarette Company Settles $23 Million Lawsuit with City of Chicago Over Marketing Vapes to Minors, Chicago Trib. (Mar. 10, 2023); Office of the Mayor, City of Chicago Reaches $23.8M Settlement Agreement with E-Cigarette Maker JUUL Labs for Marketing and Selling Products to Underage Youth (Mar. 10, 2023).

[94] John Raby, Vaping Company JUUL Settles West Virginia Lawsuit for $7.9M, AP News (Apr. 10, 2023).

[95] Brendan Pierson, JUUL, Altria Face First Trial Over Claims of Marketing E-Cigarettes to Teens, Reuters (Mar. 27, 2023).

[96] The Office of Minnesota Attorney General Keith Ellison, Press Release, Minnesota Settles Historic E-Cigarette Lawsuit with JUUL and Altria (Apr. 17, 2023).

[97] Christina Jewett and Julie Creswell, JUUL Reaches $462 Million Settlement with New York, California, and Other States, N.Y. Times (Apr. 12, 2023). See also, New York State Attorney General, Attorney General James Secures $462 Million from JUUL for Role in the Youth Vaping Epidemic (Apr. 12, 2023).

protect and prevent underage minors from vaping. This settlement resolved the state claims of California, Colorado, the District of Columbia, Illinois, Massachusetts, New York, and New Mexico. The settlement resolved the states' claims that the JUUL had aggressively marketed its e-cigarettes to youth and fueled the vaping crisis. The state attorneys general had conducted investigations that found that JUUL executives were aware that their marketing attracted teenagers into buying its vaping pens but then did little to address the consequent problem of youth addiction as vaping use exploded.

Under the settlement terms, California would receive the largest amount, estimated at $176 million.[98] New York would receive $112.7 million over an eight-year period to support vaping abatement programs across the state. The agreement required JUUL to secure its products behind retail sales counters and verify the age of youngsters who directly sold or promoted JUUL products online. JUUL was required to refrain from marketing and promotional activities that directly or indirectly targeted anyone under the age of 35, through funding, operating, or sponsoring school-related activities. JUUL was required to limit the amount of retail and online purchases that an individual consumer could make, and refrain from providing free or nominally priced JUUL sample pods. In addition, the settlement required JUUL to fund a document depository by up to $5 million, and to place relevant documents in this depository to inform the public on how JUUL had created a public health crisis. The agreement's restrictions were binding on JUUL's former directors and executives.[99]

It may well be unknowable – or at least speculative – concerning what motivated the JUUL and Altria defendants to agree to the cascading series of state e-cigarette settlements beginning in 2021 and extending through the Minnesota state jury trial in April 2023. The state lawsuits against the e-cigarette defendants asserted numerous claims under state statutory and common law, including public nuisance claims. Because the state cases settled before trial, except for the Minnesota lawsuit, it is problematic to assess the extent to which the threat of a jury finding of liability for creating and maintaining a public nuisance persuaded the defendants to settle, or whether the other collected claims presented a forbidding prospect for a jury trial.

The states' attorney generals and the e-cigarette defendants, however, had information concerning the trial fate of the concurrent national opioid litigation to inform their thinking and strategy. Almost all the county, municipalities, Native American tribes, individuals, and other entities settled before trial.

[98] Jewett & Creswell, *id.*
[99] Office of New York State Attorney General, *id.*

These established settlement values and terms, but created no precedential law concerning the viability of an actual trial of a public nuisance claim.

In the opioid MDL Judge Polster distilled the one opioid bellwether case to its sole public nuisance claim, eliminating all other statutory and common law claims from the lawsuit. The Ohio jury found the opioid defendants liable for creating and maintaining a public nuisance, establishing the proposition that a jury could and would return a liability verdict for public nuisance for the effects of a harmful product. In addition, the e-cigarette defendants knew that Judge Polster imposed a substantial, multimillion-dollar abatement fund as a remedy for the defendants' liability.

JUUL and Altria chose to go to trial in the Minnesota e-cigarette lawsuit, against this background of a successful prosecution of an opioid harmful product public nuisance claim. Days after the Minnesota state's evidentiary presentation, the defendants on April 23, 2023, settled the e-cigarette lawsuit before the case was submitted to the jury. As with the opioid settlements, the vaping settlement resulted in no jury precedent of a finding of liability for a public nuisance.

In an almost anticlimactic ending to the e-cigarette MDL drama, on May 10, 2023, Altria announced that it had settled its outstanding MDL-related e-cigarette liabilities the day after the plaintiffs rested in a San Francisco bell-wether trial.[100] Rather than put on a defense, Altria settled as it had in previous vaping litigation that proceeded to trial. The $235 million settlement resolved all pending MDL litigation against Altria, consisting of approximately 8,500 personal injury cases, 1,400 governmental entity cases, and a massive consumer class action.

[100] Ananya Mariam Rajesh and Brendan Person, Altria Agrees to $235M Settlement to Resolve JUUL-Related Cases, Reuters (May 10, 2023), available at reuters.com/legal/altria-agrees-to-235m-settlement-to-resolve-juul-related-cases; Press Release, Lieff Cabraser Announces Historic $235M Comprehensive Settlement With Altria in National JUUL Youth E-cigarette Predatory Advertising, Addiction, and Injury Cases (May 10, 2023), available at lieffcabraser .com/2023/05/Lieff-cabraser-announces-historic-$235m-comprehensive-settlement-in-national-juul-youth-e-cigartee-predatory-advertising-addiction-and-injury-cases.

11

Evaluating the Competing Arguments Regarding the Contemporary Use of Public Nuisance in Mass Tort Litigation

The numerous contemporary federal and state lawsuits alleging public nuisance theories have elicited the array of arguments supporting the expansion of public nuisance law as well as the counterarguments challenging the legitimacy of these new applications of public nuisance theory. These arguments have been advanced by the various actors invested in the mass tort litigation landscape: the bench and bar, allies of the bench and bar, institutional reform organizations, and the scholarly community. The debate is evenly drawn, contentious, unsettled, rapidly evolving, and likely to wind up in the Supreme Court for resolution.

The swift development of public nuisance claims in the mass tort arena is a very recent twenty-first century phenomenon. Mass tort litigation that dominated federal and state court dockets since the late 1970s chiefly proceeded on conventional tort, personal injury, and product liability theories: negligence, negligence *per se*, gross negligence, strict product liability, design defect, manufacturing defect, warning defect, breach of warranty, fraud, fraudulent misrepresentation, fraudulent concealment, negligent entrustment, negligent marketing, inherently dangerous products, restitution, and unjust enrichment.

For nearly fifty years, plaintiffs' attorneys pursued mass tort remediation under legal, equitable, statutory, and common law principles, including violations of federal regulations and state consumer protection laws as negligence per se. Plaintiffs' attorneys expanded the universe of liability theories to reach entire industries, advancing claims sounding in RICO and conspiracy causes of action. Except for environmental pollution lawsuits, what was noticeable about the plaintiffs' mass tort litigation pleading for decades was the absence of private and public nuisance claims.

Attorneys develop litigation strategies from the learned experience of repeated litigation, and the absence of public nuisance claims from the plaintiffs' mass tort toolbox might be explained by judicial rejection of this theory relatively early in the history of asbestos litigation. Throughout the 1980s, in the heyday of asbestos mass tort litigation, federal courts dispensed with plaintiffs' attempts to assert public nuisance claims in lawsuits against the manufacturers, sellers, and installers of asbestos products.[1] Because courts repeatedly denied asbestos public nuisance claims, the plaintiffs' bar likely took note and abandoned public nuisance claims for relief, not only in asbestos litigation, but in any product-based mass tort.

The reasoning underlying judicial rejection of public nuisance claims in asbestos litigation was significant because it anticipated the arguments that twenty-first century judges would embrace for denying plaintiffs' public nuisance claims in litigation involving lead paint, firearms, opioids, and e-cigarettes. Thus, a Michigan appellate court contemplating a public nuisance claim against asbestos manufacturers noted that the alleged defendants' liability was premised on their roles as "creators" of a nuisance.[2] This formulation, the court opined, begged the question whether an asbestos product was a nuisance. If an asbestos product was not a nuisance, then the defendants could not be held liable on nuisance theory irrespective of their roles in creating the products. The court held that the case clearly was a products liability action, and that manufacturers, sellers, or installers of defective products could not be held liable on a nuisance theory for injuries caused by the defect.[3]

The Michigan court also noted the issue of recognizing a public nuisance claim where, in commercial transactions, defendants gave up ownership and control of their products when sold to plaintiffs. In such circumstances, defendants lacked the legal right to abate whatever hazards their products might pose; ownership and possession lay exclusively with the plaintiffs. Plaintiffs' proper remedies, then, were with products liability actions for negligence or breach of warranty.[4]

Finally, the court noted the adverse policy implications of expanding nuisance theory in products cases: to hold otherwise, the court cautioned, "would significantly expand, with unpredictable consequences, the remedies already available to persons injured by products, and not merely asbestos products."[5] In dicta, the

---

[1] *See e.g.,* Bloomington, Inc. v. Westinghouse Electric Corp., 891 F.2d 611, 614 (7th Cir. 1989); Manchester v. Nat'l Gypsum Co., 637 F.Supp. 646, 656 (D.R.I. 1986); Hooksett School Dist. V. W.R. Grace & Co., 617 F.Supp. 126, 133 (D.N.H. 1984); Johnson Co., Tenn. v. U.S. Gypsum Co., 580 F.Supp. 284, 294 (E.D. Tenn. 1984).

[2] Detroit Bd. of Educ. v. Celotex Corp., 196 Mich. App. 694, 493 N.W.2d 513, 520 (Mich. App. 1992).

[3] *Id.* at 521.

[4] *Id.* at 522.

[5] *Id.* at 521.

court explained: "We need not repeat the bewilderment expressed by the courts and secondary authorities concerning the exact boundaries of the tort of 'nuisance.' Suffice it to say that, despite attempts by appellate courts to rein in the creature, it, like the Hydra, has shown remarkable resistance to such efforts."[6]

It is difficult to identify when plaintiffs' lawyers began to assert public nuisance claims in twenty-first century mass tort cases, but this most likely was inspired, in part, by the 1998 tobacco Mass Settlement Agreement. This experience proved that it was entirely possible for states' attorney generals to collaborate with experienced mass tort trial lawyers to accomplish nationwide settlements against entire industries that allegedly caused widespread community harm. On the heels of the Master Settlement Agreement, attorneys and commentators predicted that the next big mass tort litigations in the twenty-first century would involve lead paint, firearms, and the fast-food industry. In this they were chiefly correct, but what the commentators did not foresee was the advent of massive drug abuse and revitalization of nicotine delivered in different packages.

The historical narrative of mass tort litigation is one of the ever-evolving litigation landscape over five decades. The reconceptualization of mass torts harms as public nuisance fits well within the mass tort paradigm, sharing attributes of historical mass tort cases. As in the landmark mass tort cases of asbestos, Agent Orange, DES, Bendectin, breast implants, and other medical devices, the twenty-first century mass tort cases – lead paint, firearms, opioids, and e-cigarettes – affected large, dispersed populations of the citizenry. Some, but not all, involved latent injury harms. Many of them involved harm to youth with collateral adverse effects on entire communities.

The harm involved in the emerging twenty-first century mass torts involved personal injury and property damage claims to aggregations of individuals, communities, municipalities, and states. The cases typically involved multiple defendants in entire industries: manufacturers, distributors, wholesalers, and retail sellers. Highly experienced mass tort plaintiffs' attorneys – with litigation skills honed on asbestos litigation and other mass torts – undertook prosecution of these new mass torts. The litigation proceeded on a predictable mass tort arc: filing of hundreds of cases in federal court, including individual and class actions, consolidation in federal multidistrict litigation, with concurrent jurisdiction of state court cases.

The twenty-first century mass tort cases largely resembled the historical mass tort cases in pleading, development, and prosecution, with one prominent new feature: allegations of public nuisance claims. The emergence of

[6]   *Id.* at 520.

public nuisance theories undergirding the new mass tort cases is a testament to the resourcefulness, creativity, and spirit of renewal characterizing the plaintiffs' mass tort litigation bar. Undeterred by the failure of public nuisance in past mass tort litigation, the plaintiffs' bar nonetheless resuscitated the public nuisance theory to apply in the new mass tort cases.

The public nuisance theory, at least, seemed tailormade for holding bad actor defendants accountable for creating and maintaining public nuisances affecting the public and communities. The task of the mass tort plaintiffs' bar, then, was to convince courts that public nuisance was not only a viable theory for addressing mass tort harms, but a just vehicle for remediation. The defense bar, initially blindsided by invocation of a relatively obscure, expansive, and vaguely defined concept, reacted with predictable opposition and disapproval.

Public nuisance became the new frontier in mass tort litigation in the twenty-first century, inspiring a debate that currently continues. As the mass tort attorneys continue to pursue public nuisance claims, attorneys, judges, institutional reform organizations, and academic scholars aligned in support or opposition to the new public nuisance theory.

11.1 THE PUBLIC NUISANCE DEBATE: ATTORNEYS, ALLIES, AND INSTITUTIONS

Defense attorneys and law firms involved in the twenty-first century public nuisance cases have been especially vocal in criticizing the emergence of a public nuisance theory used against their clients. Apart from litigation filings, defense attorneys have advanced their critical views in various media outlets, including website postings, client newsletters, litigation updates, and law review articles. The plaintiffs' bar, on the contrary, has remained unusually quiet in publicizing its support for the new use of public nuisance, apart from states' attorney generals' public releases of accomplishments in settling these cases.

In 2012, the defense-oriented Washington D.C. law firm Jones Day posted a critical commentary about the emerging public nuisance cases involving lead paint, firearms, MTBE, and climate change.[7] Surveying the negative judicial rulings in these cases, the author suggested that the recent rulings had "tarnished the aura of public nuisance as the 'tort du jour' invoked to entice the judiciary to take on public health and environmental problems allegedly not

---

[7] Traci L. Lovitt, Insights, Cooling Off Public Nuisance Claims (Oct. 2021), available at www .jonesday.com/en/insights/2012/cooling-off-public-nuisance-claims. Jones Day identified that it represented companies sued for public nuisance because of alleged harms from tobacco, firearms, lead paint, and climate change.

adequately redressed by elected officials and government programs."[8] Jones Day predicted that the vague standards for invoking and applying a public nuisance claim, coupled with the prospect of massive remedies, would likely "keep the theory alluring to advocacy organizations and government bodies."[9]

Remarking on the federal and Oklahoma state opioid litigation, a Texas defense attorney surveyed the ramifications of judicial support for public nuisance claims in mass tort cases.[10] Commentators, he noted, observed mounting pressure on the judiciary to expand the public nuisance doctrine beyond its historically narrow boundaries, in favor of governmental entities seeking relief. But, because public nuisance had no real standards, courts struggled to determine if traditional product liability or tort defenses applied to these claims. The fear was that attorneys would "distort public nuisance theory into an unrecognizable, catch-all cause of action that could be molded to fit the next mass-tort litigation."[11]

The new judicial endorsement of public nuisance theories could expose a variety of industries to new liabilities: oil, gas, and energy companies for their contributions to climate change, fast food companies for their role in causing obesity, smart phone manufacturers for inducing a need for increased emergency services due to driver accidents caused by cell phone distraction, and e-cigarette manufacturers for causing a vaping epidemic among youth.[12]

The defense attorney noted that a liberal interpretation of public nuisance law would leave defendants vulnerable to open-ended liability for any act or omission that caused injury or annoyance, without regard to the availability of other tort remedies. Moreover, the liberal interpretation of public nuisance would incentivize plaintiffs' attorneys to file mass tort products class actions as public nuisance lawsuits, to bypass traditional products liability defenses.[13] Courts' ruling in public nuisance litigation might create judge-made regulations that usurped the role of legislative bodies in determining what activities a state would or encourage, or not.

Victor E. Schwartz and his collaborators of the Public Policy Group in the law firm Shook, Hardy, and Bacon L.L.P, authored the most extensive

---

8   *Id.*
9   *Id.*
10 Brandon Winchester, Insights, Are Public Nuisance Claims the Next Super Torts? (Aug. 16, 2021), available at shjlawfirm.com/2021/08/16/are-public-nuisance-claims-the-next-super-torts.
11 *Id.* citing Victor E. Schwartz, Phil Goldberg & Corey Schaecher, Game Over? Why Recent State Supreme Court Decisions Should End the Attempted expansion of Public Nuisance Law, 62 Okla. L. Rev. 630, 631 (2010).
12 Winchester, *supra* note 10.
13 *Id.*

defense-oriented critique of the twentieth century public nuisance doctrine in a series of articles.[14] Schwartz's comprehensive critique of the emerging nuisance doctrine in 2006 captured the range of arguments against plaintiffs' innovative deployment of public nuisance law in the mass tort arena. In ensuing years, few new arguments would augment this initial appraisal. Many of Schwartz's objections derived from judicial decisions where courts declined to expand public nuisance doctrine or issued cautionary warnings about the negative consequences of novel uses of public nuisance law. Schwartz's critique embraced three broad categories of concern: (1) technical traditional tort issues, (2) broad conceptual problems, and (3) problematic policy implications.

Schwartz noted that in the first wave of public nuisance litigation most courts rejected plaintiffs' expansive invocation of the doctrine because public nuisance theory always targeted how properties or products were used, not manufactured.[15] Products liability law had well-defined boundaries, such as requiring that the harm be caused by a defective product.[16] By filing claims under a public nuisance theory, personal injury plaintiffs' attorneys hoped to expand liability for harm cause by products, while avoiding product liability rules such as design defect, statute of limitations, and the rule against recovery for economic loss.[17] "The reason personal injury lawyers have been lured by the elixir of public nuisance theory is because, if successful, it acts as a 'super tort.'"[18]

The novel invocation of public nuisance law in contemporary mass tort cases challenged the boundaries of traditional tort law in several ways. For

---

[14] *See generally* Victor E. Schwartz, Rendering Justice in Key Areas of Tort Law in the Next Decade, 40 Sw. L. Rev. 378 (2021); Victor E. Schwartz, Phil Goldberg & Christopher E. Appel, Deep Pocket Jurisprudence: Where Tort Law Should Draw the Line, 70 Okla. L. Rev. 359 (2018); Victor E. Schwartz & Christopher Appel, Government Regulation and Private Litigation: The Law Should Enhance Harmony, Not War, 23 B.U. Pub. Int. L.J. 185 (2014); Victor E. Schwartz, Phil Goldberg & Christopher E. Appel, Does the Judiciary Have the Tools for Regulating Greenhouse Gas Emissions, 46 Val. U.L. Rev. 69 (2012); Victor E. Schwartz, Phil Goldberg & Corey Schaecher, Why Trial Courts Have Been Quick to Cool "Global Warming" Suits, 77 Tenn. L. Rev. 803 (2010); Victor E. Schwartz, et al., Game Over?, *supra* note 11; Victor E. Schwartz, Phil Goldberg & Christopher E. Appel, Can Governments Impose a New Torts Duty to Prevent External Risks? The "No-Fault" Theories Behind Today's High-Stakes Government Recoupment Suits, 44 Wake Forest L. Rev. 923 (2009); Victor E. Schwartz and Phil Goldberg, The Law of Public Nuisance: Maintaining Rational Boundaries on a Rational Tort, 45 Washburn L. Rev. 541 (2006).

[15] Schwartz, et al., The Law of Public Nuisance, *id.* at 543.

[16] *Id.* at 552, 579.

[17] *Id.*

[18] *Id.*

example, public nuisance injury conventionally involved a misuse of real property. Some courts had stretched public nuisance law to encompass conduct that conflicted with a public right to health, safety, peace: the – comfort of a general community. But courts consistently held that cases involving communal injury were distinguishable from personal injury claims in product-based suits. Personal injury lawyers pursuing products claims under the guise of public nuisance tried to blur this distinction in the new mass tort litigation.[19]

Schwartz explained that public nuisance theory involved specific types of conduct in order for the conduct to be actionable.[20] Courts defined four types of such conduct: (1) unlawful, intentional acts, (2) lawful conduct involving conflicting uses of property, (3) lawful conduct, not involving land use that leads to unintended consequences, and (4) otherwise tortious conduct. The first two categories would fall within public nuisance theory, but the third would not; lawful conduct without the traditional connection to land would not constitute a public nuisance. The fourth category had been limited to assertions of an underlying negligence theory, but courts declined to find a public nuisance predicated on an underlying negligence theory.[21] In addition, states and local governments could define specific activities as a public nuisance through legislation, regulations, or ordinances. When a field of conduct was well regulated, conduct that might be categorized as unreasonable under common law might become non-tortious; the legislature or regulatory body by statute had determined such conduct was socially acceptable and reasonable.[22]

Novel public nuisance theories also challenged traditional elements of a tort claim by eviscerating the requirement of defendant's control over the instrumentality of the nuisance. Courts rejected liability in cases where there was an attenuated connection between a public's alleged harm and the defendant's control of its products once the product left the defendant's control. Moreover, if defendants exercised no control over the instrumentality, then a remedy directed against that defendant was of little use.[23] Numerous courts concluded that furnishing a product – chemicals, asbestos, guns, lead paint – was different from having control over the instrumentality.[24]

---

[19] *Id.* at 563.
[20] *Id.* at 564, noting that historically the public nuisance offense required was comparable to quasi-criminal activity.
[21] *Id.* at 565–66.
[22] *Id.* at 566.
[23] *Id.* at 567.
[24] *Id.*

Schwartz further observed that the plaintiffs' novel invocation of public nuisance evaded the traditional tort requirements of proximate causation and remoteness. In his view, analysis of proximate causation in a public nuisance claim should be the same as claims for traditional negligence: that a defendant whose conduct allegedly created a public nuisance had to reasonably foresee the consequence of its conduct. And those consequences could not be so remote from the conduct as to render a defendant's liability unfair and unreasonable.[25]

In the causation analysis, third party acts were intervening events that might cut off the chain of proximate causation; this was a key reason why courts failed to hold firearms and lead paint manufacturers liable under a public nuisance theory.[26] Schwartz suggested that a central reason why personal injury attorneys were so attracted to public nuisance was because they could not establish proximate causation under products liability law; public nuisance provided attorneys with a workaround solution to this problem.[27]

Schwartz noted broad conceptual problems with expanding the scope of public nuisance law. Part of the problem was that public nuisance theory was often defined by what it was not, rather than what it was. "This 'I know it when I see it' test leaves significant amount of wriggle room in the margins, as well as an opportunity for some courts, as in products liability cases, to move the tort far afield from the tort's intended use."[28]

Plaintiffs' attorneys were moving public nuisance far outside its traditional boundaries and using it to sue product manufacturers to circumvent the well-defined principles of products liability law.[29] The attorneys' efforts to expand public nuisance law was disconcerting because it would not only change the character of public nuisance law, but would undermine products liability law, as well. Courts repeatedly had stated that public nuisance law should not provide an end-run around the fundamental principles of products liability law.[30]

Moreover, governmental entities using public nuisance litigation to seek monetary damages violated the well-established rule that public nuisance remedies did not include damages. The public municipal recovery rule prohibited governments from seeking to recoup the costs of performance of

[25] *Id.* at 569.
[26] *Id.*
[27] *Id.* at 570.
[28] *Id.* at 561.
[29] *Id.* at 541.
[30] *Id.* at 580, citing cases.

ordinary municipal services. The entire public was to bear the costs of police, government abatement programs, and other services, and not by an alleged individual tortfeasor.[31]

Schwartz further objected to the novel use of public nuisance law based on public policy concerns. First, the new public nuisance doctrine upset the underlying principles of traditional products liability law that balanced the interests of consumers, manufacturers, and suppliers. These principles facilitated the public's recovery, and incentivized manufacturers to exercise due care in producing their products.[32] The new public nuisance doctrine would "devour" products liability law. Allowing a product-based case to be brought as a public nuisance claim "would unwisely and irreparably distort the fundamental principles and public policy goals of product liability."[33]

Second, a danger of using the new public nuisance doctrine against product manufacturers would empower courts to use their injunctive powers to mandate product redesign and regulate business methods.[34] Chief among this concern was the proper allocation of regulatory behavior on manufacturing defendants. Thus, commenting on the experience of environmental litigation, courts had ruled that regulating the manufacture of lawful products was the province of the legislature, not the judiciary.[35]

Third, approval of the new public nuisance theories would affect attorney conduct. Thus, the attractiveness of public nuisance claims would incentivize states' attorney generals and personal injury lawyers to convert the tort of public nuisance into a cutting-edge legal theory and to use it in modern twenty-first century mass tort litigations.[36] It would incentivize personal injury lawyers, in the name of industry reform, to offer their services to governmental entities on a contingency fee basis. Schwartz suggested that when the government used private contingency fee lawyers in public nuisance litigation, this practice improperly combined the private monetary motivations of private attorneys with government police power.[37]

Schwartz's seminal public nuisance article in 2006 provided the doctrinal framework for objections to the emerging public nuisance theory. With the advent of second wave of public nuisance litigation and the approval by some courts of public nuisance claims allied defense organizations weighed into the

---

[31] *Id.* at 570.
[32] *Id.* at 578.
[33] *Id.* at 579.
[34] *Id.* at 581.
[35] *Id.* at 549.
[36] *Id.* at 541.
[37] *Id.* at 582.

debate to characterize the new public nuisance mass tort litigation as constituting an alarming evolution of nuisance law. These critiques largely focused
on the same concerns Schwartz identified in 2006.

In 2019 the U.S. Chamber of Commerce's Institute for Legal Reform issued
a substantial monograph colorfully entitled *Waking the Litigation Monster:
The Misuse of Public Nuisance.*[38] The report sounded the same themes as
Schwartz: that traditionally public nuisance usually was connected to a defendant's use of land, that the only common law remedies were suits to enjoying
or abate the nuisance, and that individuals could only recover if their injury
differed from the injury suffered by the public.[39]

In cases where courts approved the new public nuisance claims for products cases, the courts had not held to historic tort law standards. The U.S.
Chamber of Commerce traced the advent of a new public nuisance theory
to the *Restatement (Second) of Torts* provisions, which constituted less of a
restatement and "more of a purposeful departure from prior precedent."[40]
The adoption of the *Restatement (Second)* broadened public nuisance to
embrace any interference with a public right so long as the interference could
be said to be unreasonable and allowed individuals to pursue an injunction
or abatement. Although the Reporters designed the *Restatement* provisions to
assist in environmental litigation, their flexible principles "[were] designed to
invite mischief."[41]

The plaintiffs' bar, including private attorneys working on behalf of governmental entities, had attempted to expand tort law beyond its traditional
boundaries to endow courts with increasing power to determine public policy.
The expansion of public nuisance doctrine embodied an especially potent
weapon for use by governmental entities and the contingency fee attorneys
representing them.[42] Plaintiffs' attorneys, in the second wave lawsuits, argued
that the traditional constraints of tort law should not apply to public nuisance
lawsuits because of their unique ability to bring representative claims on
behalf of constituents.[43]

Mass tort lawyers used public nuisance law to evade the requirements of
traditional tort doctrine in several ways. They attempted an end-run around

---

[38] U.S. Chamber of Commerce, Institute for Legal Reform, Waking the Litigation Monster:
The Misuse of Public Nuisance (Mar. 2019).

[39] *Id.* at 1.

[40] *Id.* at 7.

[41] *Id.* at 708, citing Donald Gifford, Public Nuisance as a Mass Products Liability Tort, 71 U.
Cin. L. Rev. 741, 808–09 (2003).

[42] *Id.* at 25.

[43] *Id.* at 26.

the requirement of interference with or violation of a public right as conventionally construed.[44] Plaintiffs avoided stating a claim for vindication of a recognized right and were able to seek large damages awards as a substitute for traditional governmental remedies of injunctions and abatement without having to prove causation as required in conventional tort law.[45] The attorneys avoided damages' limitations by using abatement recoveries, or forced settlements as substitutes for traditional remedies.[46]

The Chamber concluded that courts should decline plaintiffs' invitations to substitute their judgment for the political branches of government, and that public nuisance law was not needed where the executive and legislative branches had already balanced competing interests in designing and enacting regulatory schemes.[47] To the extent that a legislature created a comprehensive regulatory scheme directed at particular types of localized conduct, courts should be chary of interfering with the balance of interests the legislature accomplished.[48] Courts should continue to defer to the policy-making role of the executive and legislative branches in addressing local problems "and not allow public nuisance law to devour the law of tort."[49]

A Federalist Society contributor, advocating that the Supreme Court grant certiorari to consider judicial approval of the new public nuisance doctrine, opined that the cases represented a novel expansion of public nuisance law that needed to be controlled because it so far departed from the usual course of judicial proceedings as to call for an exercise of the Court's supervisory power.[50] Viewing the landscape of second wave public nuisance cases, the author suggested that there was a growing trend of cases that attempted to create a "backdoor to traditional standards of the Rule of Law through the novel or retroactive liability schemes that dispense with notions of causation, traceability, and overall fairness."[51]

The second wave public nuisance cases represented a basic distortion of the meaning of common law public nuisance "so as to render it unrecognizable...":

---

[44] *Id.* at 26–27.
[45] *Id.* at 1–2, 28–29.
[46] *Id.* at 27–28.
[47] *Id.* at 2, 31–33.
[48] *Id.* at 31.
[49] *Id.* at 35.
[50] Donald J. Cochan, The Federalist Society, Commentary, Is Public Nuisance Doctrine Becoming an Exception to the Rule of Law (Sept. 17, 2018), available at fedsoc.org/commentary/fedsoc-blog/is-public-nuisance-doctrine-becoming-an-exception-to-the-rule-of-law?
[51] *Id.*

Our better-enlightened present selves cannot impose retroactive liability judging the lesser-informed individuals and unknowingly harmful acts of earlier years. Fundamental to liberal legal order is a belief that we do not punish people decades later for doing things that, at the time of their acts, were lawful and done only without knowing but also without the ability to know their actions could be harmful. The law does not allow a mutation of tort law to serve the preferences of a better-informed future society that has developed new expectations (because it knows things that were not known in the past) and now wishes someone could be made to pay.[52]

The American Tort Reform Association issued a series of white papers in 2020 decrying the incipient trend among courts to approve public nuisance claims, characterizing these as completely an unprincipled and far departure from any longstanding liability law.[53] The public nuisance lawsuits were attempts to subject businesses to liability over societal problems regardless of fault, how the harm was developed or caused, or whether the elements of a traditional tort claim were satisfied.

The second-generation public nuisance litigation addressing opioids, vaping, climate change, and environmental cleanups, all sought to generate massive liability over complex crises despite a lack of factual or legal grounding for targeting certain industries. Experience demonstrated that public nuisance lawsuits by contingency fee attorneys would not solve complex social problems and any funds received in these lawsuits would be diverted to other governmental purposes.[54] Major public crises demanded attention and resolution by elected officials and government leaders, "but the continued wave of contingency-fee litigation by state and local governments was the wrong approach. It won't help victims or solve crisis, and instead creates lasting problems for the civil justice system."[55]

ATRA subjected trial attorneys to caustic criticism, suggesting that they search for a crisis people want solved and then look to represent a state or local government to sue on behalf of a community without having to abide by class action rules. The lawyers agree to work for free, to be paid only from the money the lawsuits generated. Public nuisance lawsuits were enticing for

---

[52] *Id.*

[53] American Tort Reform Association, The Plaintiffs' Lawyer Question for the Holy Grail: The Public Nuisance "Super Tort," (Apr. 14, 2020), available at www.atra.org/white_paper/public-nuisance-super-tort; *see also* American Tort Reform Association, The Alarming Evolution of Public Nuisance (Apr. 28, 2020), available at https://atra.org/the-alarming-evolution-of-public-nuisance; American Tort Reform Association, Public Nuisance Expansion and Litigation: Lawyers Pitch Potential Public Nuisance Lawsuits to Government Officials and Others Hoping to be Hired on a Contingency Fee Basis (Apr. 28, 2020), available at https://atra.org/issue/pub lic-nuisance-expansion-and-litigation-laywers-pitch-public-nuisance-lawsuits-to-government-officials-and-others-hoping-to-be-hired-on-a-contingency-fee-basis.

[54] *Id.* White Paper, The Plaintiff's Lawyer, at 13.

[55] *Id.*

elected officials who could inform constituents they were attempting to resolve a local, national, or international problem that would not cost the taxpayer anything. Moreover, plaintiffs' attorneys and government entities that pursued public nuisance lawsuits gambled that local elected judges would want to be seen as attempting to solve a community problem and obtain recoveries, despite traditional tort law. Trial lawyers gambled that targeted businesses would "buckle under the pressure of the media and litigation onslaught and settle the claims just to end the nightmare, regardless of truth or justice."[56]

Writing for the Heritage Foundation, John G. Malcolm, in a 2021 report, observed that using public nuisance law to solve the opioid crisis set a dangerous precedent.[57] Reiterating the many objections to the expansion of public nuisance law, Malcolm opined that the real culprits of the opioid crisis were the actors who fueled the problem by committing criminal acts in over-prescribing opioids when they were contraindicated, outside the scope of legitimate medical practice. Manufacturers that deliberately misbranded drugs or bribed physicians to overprescribe drugs were criminally liable. "But laying the blame at the feet of companies that followed applicable laws and produced and dispensed a legitimate and highly regulated product [was] not just a mistake. It [set] a dangerous precedent."[58]

Malcolm introduced politics into the discussion over expansion of public nuisance doctrine. For Malcolm, trial lawyers had for some time assertively acted to expand public nuisance law for such products as vaccines, "with most aggressive efforts involving the use of public nuisance as an ideological weapon against industries related to climate change and firearms."[59] Echoing ATRA's cynical view of plaintiffs' attorneys, Malcolm contended that the end goal of lawyers pushing public nuisance litigation seemed to be to pad the pockets of trial lawyers and cause product manufacturers and distributors to stop selling legal products that millions of law-abiding people used legitimately.[60]

But beyond profit-seeking, Malcolm suggested that trial lawyers were ideologically motivated to accomplish an expansion of public nuisance law. In March 2023, Malcolm noted that a consumer protection group, the Alliance for Consumers, sent a letter to Republican governors warning of attempts by

---

[56] *Id.* at 1.
[57] John Malcolm, The Heritage Foundation, Report, Using Public Nuisance Law to "Solve" the Opioid Crisis Sets a Dangerous Precedent (Dec. 20, 2021), available at heritage.org/crime-and-justice/report/using-public-nuisance-law-to-solve-the-opioid-crisis-sets-a-dangerous-precedent.
[58] *Id.*
[59] *Id.*
[60] John Malcolm, The Heritage Foundation, Commentary Courts, 2 New GOP State Attorneys General Stand Up to Trial Lawyers (Mar. 27, 2023), available at heritage.org/courts/commentary/2-new-gop-state-attorneys-general-stand-up-to-trial-lawyers.

left-leaning lawyers to use public nuisance litigation as a backdoor way to out-law guns "and otherwise push a liberal agenda through the courts to achieve goals they could not achieve through the legislative process." The new Iowa and Kansas attorney generals had terminated their contractual relationships with the plaintiffs' megafirm Morgan & Morgan. For Malcolm, the law firm Morgan & Morgan served as a "salient example of the alliance of left-wing trial lawyers and those pushing public nuisance litigation." The law firm sent 99 percent of its donations to Democrats and had played a major role to expand the public nuisance claims in the opioid litigation.[61]

Malcolm recommended that the two states' attorney generals who fired Morgan & Morgan could persuade some of their more "recalcitrant peers" to rethink how the new, expanded public nuisance law could be used to advance a left-wing agenda. And, perhaps, these states' attorney generals could be per-suaded to reconsider their relationship with these trial lawyers "who pocket exorbitant fees," because the trial lawyers then turned around and used their earnings to defeat the people who hired them.[62]

11.2 THE PUBLIC NUISANCE DEBATE: THE JUDICIARY

The judiciary has reacted with mixed responses to attorney initiatives to expand public nuisance claims asserted in twenty-first century mass tort litiga-tion. Courts almost universally declined to allow public nuisance claims to advance beyond pleading stages in the first wave of litigation involving asbes-tos, lead paint, and firearms. Courts continued to permit public nuisance claims to proceed in environmental pollution cases, provided the underlying facts and law fit comfortably in the traditional injury-to-property paradigm. With the advent of a second wave of public nuisance claims that plaintiffs' attorneys advanced in the opioid, e-cigarette, and climate litigation, some courts resisted the assertion of public nuisance claims relying on jurispru-dence that courts established in the first wave cases. However, other courts now embraced the new public nuisance theories, paving way to application of public nuisance claims in future mass tort litigation.

Courts that have resisted and rejected trial lawyers' advocacy of an expanded public nuisance theory typically resolve these claims at the pleading stage. In the debate surrounding expansion of public nuisance jurisprudence in

---

[61] *Id.* Morgan & Morgan represented cities and states in the opioid litigation and served on a steering committee in the MDL.

[62] *Id.* Malcolm contended the trial lawyers pocketed a disproportionate share of any funds recov-ered in the public nuisance litigation, which rightfully ought to go to the claimants and public that had been harmed.

twenty-first century mass torts, courts rejecting these claims have articulated three comprehensive grounds: (1) technical rulings concerning the elements of the claim or standard tort defenses, (2) reliance on broad constitutional principles, and (3) public policy concerns.

The most frequent rationales courts have expounded to reject public nuisance claims at the pleading stage reflect a narrow understanding of specific elements of proof of traditional tort claims and defenses. Thus, courts have repudiated public nuisance claims where plaintiffs have failed to establish an injury to a public right entitling them to relief. Relying on historical nuisance jurisprudence concerned with injuries arising out of interference with property rights, courts rejected plaintiff's modern vague, amorphous invocations of injuries to health, safety, and welfare.

Courts have held that plaintiffs' public nuisance claims failed where plaintiffs could not establish the requisite proximate cause of the nuisance, or that the injury was so remote from the defendants' conduct as to render it unfair to hold defendants accountable for their conduct in manufacturing or distributing their products. This was especially true where intervening events broke the chain of manufacture and distribution to end users resulting in some alleged harm, as in the lead paint, firearms, and opioid litigation. Courts repeatedly refused to allow public nuisance claims to proceed where the facts indicated that the defendant lacked control over the instrumentality of the nuisance once the product left defendant's control. Some courts, in rejecting expansive public nuisance claims, were sympathetic to the learned intermediary defense.

As a commentator has noted, courts have been reluctant to allow plaintiffs' lawyers to exploit public nuisance claims to avoid causation and traceability requirements. "When the defendants are small contributors to ubiquitous contamination springing from myriad sources, such as lead or greenhouse gas emissions, they are neither identifiable nor substantial creators of the alleged nuisance, not [sic] do they control the nuisance, nor can they abate it."[63]

Courts rejected public nuisance claims based on pleaded remedies. Thus, courts have repeatedly indicated that a public nuisance claim will not support a request for compensatory damages; the only remedies available are an injunction or abatement. Courts invoked the economic loss rule to bar recovery of monetary damages. Likewise, courts found that the municipal recovery doctrine bars recovery of costs and expenses that normally are borne by a community's citizenry for ordinary health, safety, and welfare services. Courts engaged in highly technical and factually specific constructions of plaintiffs'

---

[63] Lovitt, *supra* note 7.

pleading of a special injury to entitle individuals to damages, resulting in conflicting and confounding holdings.

Some courts have considered broader constitutional principles in evaluating whether to permit expanded public nuisance claims. These arguments include federal preemption, statutory displacement, primary jurisdiction, separation of powers, standing, Eleventh Amendment and Commerce Clause doctrines. In considering federal preemption, displacement, and primary jurisdiction arguments courts engaged in highly technical factual and legal statutory construction exercises to conclude whether public nuisance actions violate constitutional principles.

Although courts expansively have discussed these constitutionally based doctrines, few public nuisance claims have been rejected on these grounds. Courts have been most sympathetic to separation of powers arguments, where defendants successfully have convinced courts that endorsement of public nuisance claims would invade the proper jurisdiction and law-making role of the executive and legislative branches of government.

In evaluating the viability of public nuisance claims many courts have relied on broad articulations of public policy that weigh against expansion of traditional public nuisance law. Courts have resisted endorsing new approaches to nuisance that essentially convert ordinary personal injury or products liability cases into public nuisance claims, thereby evading the stricter, specific requirements of well-developed tort law. In the often colorful rhetorical language courts have suggested that if permitted, the new expansive public nuisance law would devour existing tort doctrines.

Courts have been unwilling to impose liability on and punish manufacturers for lawful conduct, especially where defendants have complied with applicable regulatory law. Courts have also refused to extend public nuisance claims that would disrupt the determinations of executive and legislative branches, in regulating conduct, that have carefully balanced the interests of all stakeholders. Courts have repudiated public nuisance claims which would impermissibly place the judiciary in the role of a regulator.

While many courts resisted expansions of public nuisance doctrine in the first wave of twenty-first century mass tort cases, some federal and state courts have allowed public nuisance claims to proceed in second wave litigation concerning lead paint, opioids, firearms, and e-cigarettes. In permitting these claims to proceed to trial, courts have embraced more flexible rationales supporting public nuisance as a viable cause of action to address societal harms. These courts have provided counterarguments to the contrary judicial holdings regarding public nuisance.

Courts permitting public nuisance claims have indicated that the definition of a public right embraces societal harm to the public's health, safety, and welfare. These courts have rejected the contrary narrow view that public nuisance must be based on some interference with the enjoyment of property. The *Restatement (Second)* definition of a public nuisance, courts have concluded, supports this more expansive view of public rights. After the 1979 publication of the *Restatement (Second)*, courts expanded the list of public rights embraced by public nuisance, including violations of the public's health, safety, and welfare. Thus, some courts became comfortable in concluding that the manufacture and distribution of products such as lead paint, MTBEs, PCBs, firearms, opioids, and e-cigarettes interfered with communities' health, safety, and welfare.

Moreover, some courts determined that the public nuisance claims asserted in these second wave cases were not personal injury or product liability lawsuits; the harms were not personal injury or product defect claims. Rather, the public nuisance harm was the defendants' conduct in creating and maintaining the public nuisance by their marketing and distribution activities. Thus, the argument that public nuisance would substitute for and devour the stricter requirements of traditional tort liability was fallacious. Consequently, the imposition of conventional tort requirements such as proximate causation and remoteness played no role in assessing a public nuisance claim. Likewise, the economic loss rule, a conventional bar to damages in ordinary tort cases, had no application.

Courts recognizing public nuisance claims allowed for injunctive, abatement, and damages relief. These courts concluded that the prohibition of damages under the municipal recovery rule played no part in cases where the public nuisance harm imposed extraordinary expenses on governmental entities to address burgeoning police, welfare, and social service costs of the crises precipitated by widespread use of opioids, e-cigarettes, and firearms. In such public nuisance litigation, the defendants should be held accountable and bear the costs of abating and remedying the public nuisance they created and maintained by their conduct. Moreover, if a jury found that the defendants created and maintained a public nuisance, the jury or court could order defendants to pay into an abatement fund.

The courts upholding the viability of public nuisance claims made short shrift of the various constitutionally based arguments. In virtually all cases courts concluded that neither express nor implied preemption or displacement doctrine precluded state courts from adjudicating the public nuisance claim under state statutory or common law. Similarly, federal and state courts permitting public nuisance claims rejected primary jurisdiction arguments, finding delegated judicial authority to resolve the public nuisance claims. In almost all cases, courts have upheld the standing of governmental entities as well as individuals to pursue public nuisance claims.

Nor did these courts find separation of powers issues, determining that courts retained the authority to decide those public nuisance claims that did not invade the jurisdiction of the executive or legislative branches. This was especially true where state legislatures specifically enacted public nuisance statutes comprehensively addressing defendants' conduct, such as the states' newly enacted firearms public nuisance laws.

Courts endorsing public nuisance claims rejected judicial decisions eschewing expanded public nuisance doctrine based on public policy concerns, especially subversion of traditional tort law. Thus, courts have pointed out that rather than vitiating tort law, the experience of the common law has always been to reflect changed circumstances. And public policy objections to public nuisance claims, based on the invasion of legislative prerogatives, held little sway where state legislatures acted to create tailored public nuisance statutes. Instead, public policy supported the recognition of public nuisance claims and remedies where defendants' conduct created and maintained a public nuisance that harmed the public in its enjoyment of health, safety, and welfare.

11.3 THE PUBLIC NUISANCE DEBATE: THE ACADEMIC SCHOLARS

The emergence of a new public nuisance model in the twenty-first century mass tort litigation has engaged the attention of academic scholars. Almost all scholarly commentary has been critical of an expansive notion of public nuisance to address modern harms and has disapproved of judicial decisions recognizing such claims.[64] The scholars' analyses embody many of the same prosaic criticisms in judicial decisions and practitioner commentaries, albeit in a much more nuanced, elevated exposition. Although the scholars have examined contemporary public nuisance law through different framing perspectives, most have reached the same conclusion that it represents an illegitimate and dysfunctional development in modern jurisprudence.[65]

---

[64] *See generally* Donald G. Gifford, Public Nuisance as a Mass Products Liability Tort, 71 U. Cin. L. Rev. 741 (2003).

[65] Thomas W. Merrill, The New Public Nuisance: Illegitimate and Dysfunctional, 132 Yale F. 985 (2023).

11.4 KENDRICK: IN PRAISE OF MODERN PUBLIC NUISANCE LAW

In this sea of disapproval, Professor Leslie Kendrick has contributed a positive appraisal of the new public nuisance law as a second-best solution to address the societal harms to public.[66] In contrast to numerous critics, Kendrick proposes that the new public nuisance law can be understood coherently with traditional tort law. In addition, "public nuisance law is an object lesson in the common law's balance of stability and evolution, across time and within varying regulatory contexts."[67]

Kendrick provides a useful roadmap to the landscape of public nuisance critiques. Surveying judicial decisions and academic commentary, she opines that criticism of public nuisance falls into three categories: traditionalist, formalist, and institutionalist. In support of the expanded application of public nuisance law, Kendrick addresses each of these objections and concludes that the perils of the modern doctrine "are easily overstated and its promise often overlooked."[68]

Kendrick defines the critics' traditionalist objections as arguing that public nuisance law never was intended to address modern societal problems such as the opioid crisis. Thus, traditionalists argue that public nuisance law is bounded by types of problems covered at some earlier time. In this regard, the traditionalist critique resembles an originalist view of public nuisance.[69]

In response to the traditionalist critique Kendrick counters that it is not enough to honor tradition for tradition's sake. She contends that the "tradition" of public nuisance law has a lengthy, diffused historical lineage and, at any rate, has evolved over time consistent with the nature of common law. Moreover, from a traditionalist perspective, public nuisance law historically has addressed societal problems such as harmful products.[70]

Kendrick defines the formalist approach to legal analysis as one that takes legal rules seriously, adopts an internal viewpoint, and prioritizes principles, consistency, and conceptual coherence.[71] She observes that formalist approaches to the new public nuisance law evaluate it in relation to

---

[66] Leslie Kendrick, The Perils and Promise of Public Nuisance, 132 Yale L. J. 702 (2023).

[67] *Id.* at 702.

[68] *Id.*

[69] *Id.* at 736.

[70] *Id.* at 702.

[71] *Id.* at 741. *See* Richard A. Epstein, The Private Law Connections to Public Nuisance Law: Some Realism About Today's Intellectual Nominalism, 17 J. L. Econ. Pol'y 282, 313. (2022). Kendrick notes that "formalism" is often used pejoratively and that a good deal of public nuisance scholarship disregards formalist critiques, because of disinterest with the doctrine.

conventional tort principles. In this regard, she catalogues the oft-repeated negative labels attached to the new doctrine: that public nuisance law is "impenetrable, 'amorphous and protean,' a 'grab bag or dust bin,' a creature that 'like the Hydra,' must be rein[ed] in,' or a 'monster that would devour in one gulp the entire of tort law of tort.'"[72]

After surveying the particulars of tort doctrines, Kendrick concludes that from a formalist perspective, modern public nuisance law doctrinally accords with tort law better than the critics contend. She believes that the *Restatement (Second)* set forth a proper standard when it defined a public nuisance as an unreasonable interference requiring either the activity that was intentional or unreasonable, or that was unintentional or otherwise tortious. Public nuisance law is consistent with tort law when it recognizes the black letter principle that one might have duties if one's reasonable conduct generates later-arising unreasonable risks.

Kendrick contends that the new public nuisance doctrine fits well within general tort principles.[73] These basic principles include (1) broad, relational public rights, (2) liability for original non-tortious conduct, and (3) recognition that responsibility and control are not (and never have been) coextensive. In this model, states and municipalities may pursue lawsuits for invasions of the public's inherent common rights and large-scale infringements of individual rights to health, safety, and welfare. Plaintiffs may seek abatement of defendants' activities for the public, and damages for individual injuries, in remediating the public nuisance.[74]

The institutional critique, Kendrick explains, embraces two themes. First, public nuisance is unnecessary because other actors are better suited and entrusted with addressing policy questions. Second, public nuisance disrupts the proper channels for assessing and resolving risks to public interest. This critique comprises an array of jurisprudential doctrines including legislative delegation, separation of powers, federalism and the administrative state, primary jurisdiction, federal preemption, agency costs, regulatory failures, and fraud and noncompliance.[75]

Kendrick concedes that while public nuisance law raises issues relating to institutional design and competence, scholars and commentators have amply documented the frequent failure of institutions to protect the public interests the institutions are charged with guarding. From an institutional perspective,

[72] *Id.* at 742.
[73] *Id.* at 766.
[74] *Id.*
[75] *Id.* at 762–787.

then, modern public nuisance law functions as a response to situations where regulatory mechanisms have failed or underperformed.[76] "Therefore, the question is not just what damage public nuisance might cause, but what damage might occur, or go unaddressed, in its absence."[77] Public nuisance, then, "should be considered part of a larger arsenal of tools to accomplish goals in the public interest … it has proved most useful in cases where more standards regulatory tools have failed or been exploited."[78]

Kendrick's core argument in support of the public nuisance doctrine reframes the debate, conceptualizing public nuisance as a means to enforce duties that we owe to one another by virtue of our status as public members. Thus, each has a duty to take reasonable care to address the risk one may be impose on another, and if one fails to do so, then the law can require one to fix or abate it.[79] An actor in the public arena owes reasonable steps toward mitigating risks from its conduct. If the actor fails and causes a public injury, this may rightly be addressed through damages.[80]

Kendrick endorses the concept of abatement funds, which she approves as a means to apportion responsibility among co-defendants.[81] In addition, to avoid the problem of governments shifting settlement funds to general purposes, she would require that public nuisance settlements funds or damage awards be earmarked to serve the public purposes for which they were obtained. And she recommends that governments make transparent contingency fee agreements with private attorneys assisting in the litigation.[82]

Kendrick generally concludes that while it is possible to reconcile public nuisance law within contemporary tort law, more could be done to safeguard its application in institutional contexts. The point, she argues, is not to dismiss public nuisance out of hand, but to address specific problems on a case-by-case basis.[83] Public nuisance, Kendrick suggests, is not a first-best solution to infringements of public rights. As a second-best solution, it might not be ideal, but it can alleviate risks or harms to public interests and require actors to internalize the costs of their activities.

Kendrick ends with a virtual paean to the common law. "Public nuisance demonstrates how the common law and law generally, evolves to address perceived failures; in so evolving, it creates, and sometimes recreates, its own

[76] *Id.* at 702.
[77] *Id.* at 778.
[78] *Id.* at 786.
[79] *Id.* at 787.
[80] *Id.*
[81] *Id.* at 788.
[82] *Id.* at 789–90.
[83] *Id.* at 788–89.

boundaries."[84] Public nuisance law has existed for centuries and remains a part of legal institutions, "Just as much as some of the more familiar parts."[85] As a common law doctrine public nuisance has evolved over time and can, in the future, address public policy considerations as they arise.

11.5 RESPONSE TO KENDRICK: PUBLIC NUISANCE AS ILLEGITIMATE AND DYSFUNCTIONAL

Professor Thomas W. Merrill responds to Kendrick's endorsement of the new public nuisance law as the second-best solution for addressing the communal harm of the twenty-first century. Noting that public nuisance law has a long history, he suggests it evolved from a criminal offense to a means for prosecutors to abate objectionable enterprises and finally "morphed" into a third phenomenon: the new public nuisance law.[86]

Merrill offers legitimacy objections to the new public law, and a functional critique of Kendrick's second-best solution.[87] He argues that the new public law is illegitimate and dysfunctional, whether viewed from a perspective of the rule of law or democratic theory. And he doubts that Kendrick's second-best appreciation of the new public nuisance law is the best response to the twenty-first century mass harms.

According to Merrill, the new public nuisance law has four features: (1) encompassing an extraordinarily broad definition, (2) vesting prosecutors and courts with inherent authority to determine what is and is not a right common to the public, (3) inspiring prosecutors to seek large damages for interferences with public rights, rather than abatement or injunctions, and (4) retaining private law firms under contingency fee contracts, which perform most of the legal work and targets deep-pocket defendants.[88]

Merrill contends that the new public law violates the rule of law and is inconsistent with the "basic norms of democratic government." In discussing the reasons why the new public law fails the rule of law, Merrill defaults to arguments that resonate in Kendrick's traditionalist category. Thus, Merrill suggests that a foundational element of the rule of law is that legal duties be sufficiently predictable to those whom the duties apply. Public nuisance law historically was concerned with defined activities that legislatures instructed prosecutors and courts to shut down, such as impediments blocking public

---

[84] *Id.* at 791.
[85] *Id.*
[86] Merrill, *supra* note 65, at 985.
[87] *Id.* at 986.
[88] *Id.* at 985–86.

highways or waterways, or conduct offending prevailing morals, such as gambling or houses of prostitution. But the new public nuisance law does not rest on any conventional notion or legislative determination of what constitutes a public nuisance. Instead, the new public law rests on the proposition that courts have an inherent authority to determine what is a public nuisance.[89]

The essential problem with the new public law had its genesis in the 1979 *Restatement (Second) of Torts*, which defined public nuisance so broadly and amorphously as to provide little information or guidance to a potential defendant to predict what constituted a public nuisance. And, ensuing state public nuisance laws were no better, vaguely defining public nuisance to consist of anything that tended to annoy the community, or that injured or endangered the public health, safety, or welfare. Although some state legislatures attempted to engraft traditional elements of tort law onto the new public nuisance, for the most part, the new public nuisance law had not yet settled on a consistent understanding of the elements of a claim.[90]

Merrill further objects that the new public law violates norms of democratic government. His democratic critique resonates in Kendrick's category of institutional challenges. Thus, Merrill notes the common law tradition consists of rules and standards courts derive from prior judicial decisions; courts have inherent authority to announce rules to resolve disputes if the case is governed by common law. But when a contested issue of social policy comes before a court, the ultimate authoritative source must be the controlling text enacted by a majority of the people. When an administrative agency resolves a contested issue of social policy, the agency's action can be traced to the delegated authority from the legislative branch.[91]

Under the norm of democratic governance, according to Merrill, disagreements over public policy must be resolved through voting and elections of governmental bodies; the public interest should then be determined through the process of deliberation and compromise by public institutions that are accountable to the people. The political branches of government are better suited to evaluate questions of public policy and have means to consider competing interests, through legislative hearings and notice-and-comment rulemaking. Through these deliberative processes legislatures accomplish public policy manifested in constitutions, statutes, and administrative actions pursuant to the delegated authority. Courts, in contrast, are constituted to decide disputes between adverse parties and are poor instrumentalities for

[89] *Id.* at 988.
[90] *Id.* at 988–90.
[91] *Id.* at 994.

sifting through conflicting ideas about what constitutes the public interest. Courts, then, are duty bound to say what the law is, and not to make it up.[92]

Finally, Merrill criticizes Kendrick's second-best justification, characterizing her approach as arguing that the new public nuisance law is better than nothing.[93] He suggests that her argument is based on the deterrent effect of significant ex post facto damage awards. But Merrill questions whether such damage awards will effectively serve to deter the conduct that society wants to dissuade or prevent. Using the opioid crisis as an example, he suggests that a better solution than public nuisance damages would be carefully designed reforms to establish an improved system of controls on the distribution of the drugs, going forward. "Transferring large sums of money from deep-pocketed pharmaceutical companies and pharmacy chains to state and local jurisdictions may gratify an impulse to punish someone for the present calamity. But it is unlikely to generate the type of improved system of controls needed to do better. Legislative action to establish a better system of oversight, supplemented by administrative agencies' adequate resources to enforce the legislative mandate, is a far more promising course of action."[94]

Lastly, Merrill contends that Kendrick fails to account for what he calls the political economy of the new public nuisance law. In this regard, he argues that the most startling feature of the new public nuisance law is its objective to seek damages, a departure from traditional public nuisance law. This objective has engendered joint ventures between public prosecutors and private personal injury law firms, in which in the nuisance litigation the public entity brings an action in the name of the people, but private attorneys accomplish most of the labor, working on contingency fee bases.[95]

The prospect of recovering massive damages has distorted incentives for public officials such as state attorney generals, who are elected politicians. "The new public nuisance presents a tempting way to score points with the electorate – that is, by blaming large corporations for major social problems and then taking them to task. It also provides a key donor group – personal injury lawyers – who contribute heavily to state AG election campaigns and stand to reap huge fee awards if public nuisance suits yield major settlements."[96]

Merrill suggests that there are several reasons to be concerned about the potential for underdeterrence and overdeterrence. Thus, the new model is

---

[92] *Id.* at 994–95.
[93] *Id.* at 998.
[94] *Id.* at 1002.
[95] *Id.* at 1004–05.
[96] *Id.* at 1008. *See also* Martin H. Redish, Private Contingent Fee Lawyers and Public Power: Constitutional and Political Implications, 18 Sup. Ct. Econ. Rev. 77 (2010).

based on who can pay the most money in damages, and not on which actor is most in need of deterrence. In contrast, imposing liability on an industry for the remote consequences of its conduct, such as contributions to climate change, might drive up product costs for ordinary consumers.[97]

11.6 THE LAW AND ECONOMICS CRITIQUES OF THE NEW PUBLIC NUISANCE LAW

Kendrick correctly notes that several scholars commenting on the new public law eschew formalist approaches to tort law. This is certainly true for the cohort of law and economics scholars who are largely disinterested in formalist critiques, but instead view the new public law through an economics lens.

Professor Keith N. Hylton proposes an economic justification and model for public and private nuisance doctrines that illustrates shared, common grounds.[98] According to Hylton, nuisance doctrine has a proper role where non-negligent actors do not fully internalize the social costs of their activity. The imposition of a strict liability nuisance regime, then, is permissible where a defendant's activity constitutes an unreasonable invasion of a public right, for which the external costs exceed the external benefits, or the costs of the defendant's activity are not reciprocal to the external costs of other local activities.[99]

Hylton opines that public and private nuisance protect the same rights and, therefore, justify the imposition of a strict liability regime in certain cases. Under both doctrines, the law aims to discourage nuisance activities, and not protect specific types of victims. He suggests that the common law doctrine of public nuisance best serves the goals of administrative efficiency and operational deterrence where the law establishes an appropriate threshold of public nuisance harm.[100]

Hylton further notes that in some mass harm cases his model would be ineffective to regulate activity where a product has been removed from the market or banned for several years, such as with lead paint. In addition, some mass harm cases are not suited for resolution under a public nuisance theory where the identification of defendants and proof of causation is problematic, such as in firearms litigation. These types of public nuisance lawsuits are misguided because the cost-benefit analysis for the unreasonableness of the defendant's activity may not support application of a strict liability regime.

---

[97] *Id.* at 1007.
[98] Keith N. Hylton, The Economics of Public Nuisance Law and the New Enforcement Actions, 18 S. Ct. Econ. Rev. 43 (2010).
[99] *Id.* at 55.
[100] *Id.* at 62.

Professor George L. Priest has focused on the disutility of applying market share liability theory to twenty-first century public nuisance litigation.[101] Tracing the doctrinal history of market share liability developed in earlier mass tort litigation, Priest suggests that the goal of the doctrine is "to improve welfare by internalizing injury costs to the firms that generate those costs in contexts in which the identification of the specific injurer is impossible."[102]

Priests' analysis focuses on the economic dynamic of the cost-internalization function of tort liability and why market share liability fails to accomplish this end. Manufacturers pass along the costs of defective products to consumers, who in turn demand safer products and compensation for injuries. Market competition incentivizes manufacturers to create safer products. This dynamic fails where considerable time has elapsed between a product's manufacture and subsequent injury. In such instances, market share liability does provide meaningful information or incentives, because costs are passed along to a different population than consumers who originally purchased the product. The experience of the DES and lead paint litigation illustrates this problem.[103]

Priest doubts as to whether the market share doctrine achieves its purpose, especially in many historical mass tort contexts, and as applied to the new public nuisance litigation. Market share liability suffers several flaws: there are few contexts in which the doctrine can allocate the costs of injury among defendants, and application of the doctrine is unlikely to incentivize manufacturers to produce safer products. Moreover, product manufacturers who may be held liable under a market share theory will be unable to insure against damage verdicts ex ante. Market share liability makes the most sense in contexts where providing insurance for consumer injury is implausible and unworkable.[104]

Professor David A. Dana criticizes the ability of new public nuisance law to address emerging litigation over climate change; he suggests the doctrine is ill-suited to resolve a common resource management problem that essentially

---

[101] George L. Priest, Market Share Liability in Personal Injury and Public Nuisance Litigation: An Economic Analysis, 18 S. Ct. Econ. L. Rev. 109 (2010).

[102] *Id.* at 113.

[103] *Id.* at 132. Priest concludes that the effect of market share liability in many mass tort contexts is the "taxation of one set of consumers or shareholders to pay benefits to a different set of consumers." *Id. See also* Epstein, *supra* note 71, at 304 (2022) (discussing the problem of expanding public nuisance theory in lead paint litigation as a retroactive form in dealing with liability today for which the lead paint was used years before its perils were known; the most straightforward applicable law is the law of products liability).

[104] *Id.*

involves the tragedy of the commons. Climate change is best conceptualized as an overexploitation of a common problem.[105] Thus, global warming presents a large-scale problem not suited for localized litigation; it is best not conceived as a binary dispute between pollution producers and affected subjects. Courts are "ill-suited to craft sensible and effective remedies in global warming cases."[106] Echoing an institutional critique, Dana suggests that assignment of rights in the climate commons is a public policy question best consigned to the political and legislative task.

11.7 PUBLIC NUISANCE AS A MODERN BUSINESS TORT

Professor Catherine M. Sharkey has characterized the new public nuisance doctrine as a modern business tort, with some approval for this recharacterization.[107] Her focus is on the plaintiff bar's innovative use of public nuisance law to recover purely financial losses between non-contracting parties where the economic loss rule might otherwise bar recovery under negligence principles. When so appreciated, "public nuisance could emerge as the quintessential business tort of the twenty-first century."[108]

Sharkey traces the advent of public nuisance's end-run around the economic loss doctrine to the *Restatement (Third) of Torts: Liability for Economic Harm.* The *Restatement (Third)*, she explains, limited the context in which negligent infliction of economic loss is a viable claim between strangers. On the contrary, she notes that the *Restatement (Third)* recognized public nuisance law as an exception to the economic loss rule barring of negligence claims, "recognizing that '[t]he social and private costs of a public nuisance ... can be large,' and that therefore '[a]llowing certain classes of private parties a right of action can ... usefully deter repetition of the wrong.'"[109]

This exception, Sharkey suggests, opened the door to more robust use of public nuisance law to address and remedy twenty-first century public harms, because the economic loss rule does not apply as a bar to public nuisance

---

[105] David A. Dana, The Mismatch Between Public Nuisance Law and Global Warming, 18 S. Ct. Econ. Rev. 9 (2010); *see also* Henry N. Butler, A Defense of Common Law Environmentalism: The Discovery of Better Environmental Policy, 58 Case W. Res. L. Rev. 705 (2008).

[106] *Id.* at 22. *See also* Epstein, *supra* note 71, at 300 (2022) (concluding that "if there is to be any attack on global warming it has to be done through a coordinated national program, not by piecemeal state actions").

[107] Catherine M. Sharkey, Public Nuisance as Modern Business Tort: A New Unified Framework for Liability for Economic Harms, 70 DePaul L. Rev. 431 (2021).

[108] *Id.* at 432.

[109] *Id.* at 432–33, citing the *Restatement (Third) of Torts: Liab. for Econ. Harm* §§ 1, 7, 8 (A.L.I. 2022).

litigation or recovery.[110] Instead, plaintiffs' recovery for financial losses may be recovered in public nuisance actions through application of the special injury rule. Consequently, the exception fueled the plaintiff's strategy of using public nuisance law to accomplish an end run around the economic loss rule in negligence claims.[111]

Sharkey proposes to reconcile the tort of negligence with public nuisance special injury rule through an enforcement rationale.[112] In her approach she would reconceptualize the public nuisance special injury rule to deputize a subclass of impacted individuals or entities to sue to force the tortfeasor to internalize the social costs of its activities.[113] She argues that when the cost of physical or property damage is attenuated, the cost-internalization function of tort law is particularly important to deter defendants' excessively risky conduct that is likely to lead to significant financial losses.[114]

The public nuisance special injury rule should be reframed and guided to incentivize enforcement for injuries that are distinct in kind, to be used where particular parties suffer significant, concentrated losses, including financial losses.[115] This enforcement rationale supports the optimal deterrence goal of tort law, taking too account the potential problems of over- or underdeterrence.[116]

Sharkey's proposal to reconceptualize public nuisance law as a modern business tort is thought-provoking and recognizes a positive role for public nuisance doctrine in certain situations. It provides a pathway for governmental entities to recover for financial losses through an expansive reading of the special injury rule, which often denies recovery to plaintiffs who fail to carry the burden of demonstrating a distinct injury apart from the community injuries. But her interpretation of the *Restatement (Third)* as fueling twenty-first century public nuisance litigation seems in tension with the *Restatement (Third)*'s comment that public nuisance is not to be used in products cases.[117] While it may be possible to reconcile Sharkey's interpretation of the *Restatement (Third)*'s impact on public nuisance litigation strategy, if Sharkey is correct then it may be that what the *Restatement (Third)* giveth, it also taketh away.

---

[110] *Id.* at 432–33, 437–40.
[111] *Id.* at 464.
[112] *Id.*
[113] *Id.* at 433–34, 448–50.
[114] *Id.* at 434.
[115] *Id.* at 464.
[116] *Id.* at 443.
[117] *Restatement (Third)*, *supra* note 109, at § 8, cmt. g.

Conclusion

Against the backdrop of competing arguments concerning the new and controversial use of public nuisance doctrine in the mass tort litigation arena, this conclusion returns to consideration of one of the book's central arguments: that conceptualizing the new public nuisance debate as a binary choice between traditional tort and evolving common and statutory law is not useful. In the twenty-first century, the new public nuisance law is here to stay. Given some courts' embrace of the new doctrine as providing abatement fund remedies, undoubtedly many more states' attorney generals, public officials, and private trial lawyers will continue to allege public nuisance causes of action. Moreover, allegations of public nuisance claims may induce some defendants to settle massive community harms in the face of such claims.

The new public nuisance law is in nascent development and consequently is in flux. Until this new public law reaches some form of jurisprudential consensus, courts will continue to issue conflicting opinions concerning the role and legitimacy of public nuisance law in the mass tort arena. Attorneys on both sides of the docket will continue to vilify and praise the new public nuisance law in rhetorical terms, and scholars will scrutinize judicial decisions seeking coherence through various academic lens and interpretive frameworks.

Until the new public nuisance law gets sorted out, the legal landscape is expansive enough to embrace the current judicial common law approach to evolving law, along with new public nuisance statutory initiatives. Thus, the existing common law regime, coupled with carefully crafted statutory enactments reflecting public policy and grounded in democratic theory, provides a middle ground approach that accommodates both the historical role of common law development as well as institutional preferences for legislatively enacted public policy choices.

One's opinions and conclusions about the new public nuisance law largely will be driven by personal ideological preferences and jurisprudential

understandings of the role of law. Thus, those inclined to originalist, formalist, and institutional views will likely find the development of the new public
nuisance doctrine illegitimate, if not abhorrent. But advocates of the idea that
the law is not static nor has ever been so, will embrace the new public law as
the most recent manifestation of the brilliance of the common law to meet
changed societal circumstances.

The typology of public nuisance critiques as falling into categories of tra-
ditionist, formalist, and institutionalist challenges is apt. The additional contention that the new public nuisance law also offends the rule of law and
democratic theory merely re-label traditionalist and institutional critiques.
Each of these critical challenges sets forth sound objections. Proponents of
the new public nuisance doctrine, however, have countered with correspond-
ing arguments in support of the new public nuisance law.

The traditionalist argument posits that public nuisance law goes back centuries and always has been understood to apply to a very narrow universe of
cases largely sounding in invasions or interferences with the use and enjoyment of property. Public nuisance law does not embrace vague and amorphous, ill-defined notions of rights commonly held by the public, as urged
in the new public nuisance litigation. The essence of a rule of law regime is
that persons be able to know and understand, in advance, what the law is and
when it may hold a violator accountable for their actions. The rule-of-law
objection also encompasses the concept that policy-laden decisions affecting
people ought to be enacted and declared by duly elected bodies and not by
judge-made laws.

The critics contend that contemporary public nuisance lawsuits are vastly
different and widely expanded from the theory's original intent. Public nuisance law has evolved to such a degree that merely selling an everyday product can create unlimited liability. Suing product manufacturers in public
nuisance suits has marked a controversial shift in public nuisance litigation.
Critics argue that expanded notions of public nuisance have enabled plaintiffs
to sue defendants in products cases regardless of the defendant's degree of
culpability, actual causation, or the availability of traditional tort theories of
recovery. The rise of public nuisance suits by governmental entities represents
an attempted end-run around the public right requirement.

The new uses of public nuisance law have turned courts away from tort
law's historical limitations, including remedies. Traditionally, governmental entities bringing public nuisance suits were limited to injunctive and
abatement remedies. The new public nuisance settlements have resulted
in enormous judgments and settlements in billions of dollars to pay for the
costs of abatement funds. Critics further contend that public nuisance and

product liability must remain two distinct causes of action: collapsing the two risks losing the limiting principles necessary for the orderly development of the common law.

On the contrary, advocates of the public nuisance law point out that public nuisance law has hardly been static over the centuries, with ever-expanding examples of public nuisances well beyond simple property invasions. This has been especially true since the ALI publication of the *Restatement (Second) of Torts* in 1979, the definition of public nuisance ushered in the modern age of expanded notions of public nuisance. Most states in their statutory public nuisance statutes adopted the *Restatement (Second)* definition of public nuisance, along with the *Restatement's* illustrations and comments. In the contemporary era, courts have found the definition of public nuisance to include a common public right to health, safety, and welfare. Moreover, in many state jurisdictions that have adopted the *Restatement's* definition of public nuisance, courts have also resorted to the common law of public nuisance in aid of interpreting the intention of their statutes. Thus, state statutory public nuisance law has long been aided by common law concepts.

Supporters of the expansion of public nuisance law to regulate products and marketing contend that the new applications of public nuisance law serve as an important tool to address the social effects or externalities of large-scale commercial conduct. It has always been the role of common law to adapt to changing circumstances, and the advent of the era of mass tort products litigation affecting entire communities embodies just such a changed circumstance permitting judicial interpretation and development of public nuisance jurisprudence. The tort of public nuisance has evolved over decades and historically the state has exercised discretion to identify community rights to be protected.

Courts had the authority to balance competing interests to determine whether targeted activity unreasonably interfered with a public right. The fact that the law of public nuisance cannot be reduced to a set of discrete principles that produces right or wrong answers concerning the common law reasonableness standard is beside the point: the law of public nuisance may be broadly worded, but that does not mean that it is undiscoverable or unmanageable.

The formalist critics complain, chiefly, that advocates of the new public nuisance law deploy this theory to circumvent the array of conventional tort theories sounding in negligence, products liability, and a host of other conventional tort theories. The new public nuisance claims, the critics argue, are merely surrogates for conventional tort law. Having declaimed that public nuisance claims are really products litigation in disguise, these critics then argue that public nuisance claims fail because they cannot satisfy the elements of conventional tort claims or survive the array of conventional tort defenses.

However, the formalist critique of the new public nuisance law is overdetermined and based on a straw-man argument. Once the critics or courts recast a public nuisance claim as a surrogate conventional tort claim, it is then too easy to contend the public nuisance claim does not satisfy the elements of some other tort claim, or resist conventional tort defenses. Moreover, this critique seemingly ignores the fact that the public nuisance claim embraces a set of elements that are unique to public nuisance claims. The critics' quarrel, then, would seem to be with the elements of a new claim the critics do not appreciate.

The institutionalist arguments against the new public nuisance law encompass a wide array of arguments sounding broadly in democratic theory and the respective role of governmental branches. Thus, the critics contend that the new public nuisance law violates the separation-of-powers doctrine by entrusting inappropriate policy-making authority to the judiciary, violates the primary jurisdiction doctrine by permitting courts to adjudicate claims that are better suited for resolution by administrative agencies with appropriate expertise, and violates preemption doctrines by allowing state courts to adjudicate claims where Congress has enacted federal statutes to occupy the field. Critics further argue that the new public law fundamentally violates democratic theory by allocating policy-making authority to judges, when policies relating to public nuisance should be the result of legislation accomplished by duly elected representatives of the people.

The core objection to the expansion of public nuisance is that state and local governments have turned to the courts to manage public policy problems, which usurps the proper role of the political branches. Critics argue that public nuisance is an ill-suited vehicle for remedying public policy problems and that as an instrument for making social policy, public nuisance actions should be treated with judicial restraint.

The most pointed response to the democratic theory critique are the legislative enactments, such as the detailed public nuisance firearms statutes enacted in New York, New Jersey, California, and Delaware. Critics can hardly be heard to complain that public nuisance claims fail democratic norms because these claims do not reflect the political will of the people, through their elected representations, when statutes have been enacted legislatively to accomplish this purpose. Even an ardent critic of public nuisance law has argued that "The rule-of-law objection would be overcome if the state legislature were to enact a statute declaring the production and distribution of cigarettes is a public nuisance; or the production and distribution of fossil fuels is a public nuisance, or that the manufacture and distribution of opioid medicines is a public nuisance. But no reasonable legislature would enact any such statute."[1]

Notwithstanding the contention that no reasonable legislature would enact any such statute, this is precisely what New York, New Jersey, California, and Delaware have done regarding firearms. If upheld in the courts, these new public nuisance statutes will present a formidable tool in the litigation toolkit of states' attorney generals, private attorneys, and individuals. Critics of the expansion of public nuisance law can have no quarrel with recent developments in state public nuisance statutes that in some circumstances are intended to enable mass litigation involving harmful products. Such statutes embody the policy choices of state legislatures, exercising their role in codifying social policy.

* * *

What, then, will be the new directions for public nuisance law in the mass tort arena? One commentator has suggested that the current judicial support for public nuisance claims in recent litigation embraces a second-best solution to thinking about the controversial landscape of public nuisance law. Public nuisance law comes into play when an activity is allegedly infringing a public right that other forms of regulation have failed to prevent it. "It might not be ideal, but in some cases it manages to alleviate risks or harms to public interests and to require actors to internalize the public costs of their activities. When public nuisance is needed, courts should retain the discretion to identify its appropriate usage, just as they have for centuries."[2]

Clearly, a preferred approach to the developing public nuisance jurisprudence is the emergence of carefully tailored public nuisance statutes to address specific types of harms. The new firearms public nuisance statutes are in the vanguard of this development, and we will have to await judicial determination concerning the legitimacy of these statutes to regulate the conduct of industries causing widescale societal harm. The drafting and enactment of public nuisance statutes might be enhanced with the inclusion of some guardrails.

In cases where courts have approved public nuisance claims or allowed them to proceed to trial, courts have embraced abatement funds as a means for remediation, providing monetary compensation to municipalities to pay for the costs of various services and programs to address the nuisance. These nuisance abatement funds have become more sophisticated in their requirements, in some instances mandating payouts to state or local governments over several years.

---

[1] Thomas W. Merrill, The New Public Nuisance: Illegitimate and Dysfunctional, 132 Yale L.J. Form 985, 988 (2023).

[2] Leslie Kendrick, The Perils and Promise of Public Nuisance, 132 Yale L.J. 702, 790 (2023).

However, the history of the tobacco Master Settlement Agreement provides an object lesson in the perils of such fund distributions without judicial oversight or other regulation. In the years after MSA payouts it has been well-documented that several state governments diverted money from tobacco settlement payouts not to the problems needing remediation, but instead allocated the money to the states' common treasury funds. If nuisance abatement fund remedies are to become commonplace, then public nuisance statutes ought to include provisions specifying that money obtained by settlement or judgment be dedicated to addressing the problems created and maintained by the nuisance.

Public nuisance law could be enhanced by regulating the joint venture relationships between states' attorney generals, government officials, and private personal injury lawyers who together prosecute the new public nuisance litigation. These public and private joint ventures have been the subject of much criticism for incentivizing states' attorneys general and the private bar to bring these suits in the expectation of enormous financial settlements from the deep-pocket defendants. While it is difficult to formulate such regulation, transparency values might enhance public perception of such joint ventures.[3] Transparency, in this context, would consist of making public retention and contingency fee arrangements. But other constraints are needed.

The new public nuisance law could benefit from a more developed and consistent jurisprudence relating to the requirement that an individual plaintiff demonstrate a special injury that is distinct in kind from the group harm. As one commentator has rightly pointed out, judicial outcomes relating to the special injury requirement in public nuisance law are, in practice, inconsistent and defy principled justification.[4] Most of the second wave public nuisance litigation has focused on the communal harm and few of these cases have considered whether an individual encompassed by the group harm may recover monetary damages. In the few cases where an individual plaintiff has asserted a claim for monetary relief apart from the group, courts have been compelled to resort to a body of unclear, inconsistent case laws to make judgments concerning whether a particular claimant satisfied the special injury rule. No doubt this will become a more important issue as the new public nuisance law develops and clarification of the special injury doctrine is needed.

* * *

---

[3] *Id.* at 789.
[4] Catherine M. Sharkey, Public Nuisance as Modern Business Tort: A New Unified Framework for Liability for Economic Harms, 70 DePaul L. Rev. 431, 439, 458–59 (2021).

Another way to appreciate the development of the new public nuisance law in the twenty-first century is to recognize that it is very much a part of the historic arc of mass tort litigation from the 1970s into the twenty-first century. The history of mass tort litigation – driven chiefly by an innovative, creative, and persistent plaintiffs' personal injury bar – has been a story of constant flux, innovation, and pushing the boundaries of traditional law with new theories and remedies. And, predictably, every innovation has been met with the defense bar's concerted efforts and its allies to resist change, invoking many of the same arguments defense advocates now assert against the incursions of public nuisance doctrine.

It would do well to remember that at the beginning of the modern mass tort era, refinery workers suffering from asbestos-related disease had no other remedy for their injuries except to file a workman's compensation claim, a cumbersome bureaucratic process that most often resulted in limited relief to claimants. The sea-change in product liability law, which ushered in the modern era of mass tort litigation, was the American Law Institute's publication of the *Restatement of Torts* § 402A.[5]

Section 402A created an expansive provision of strict liability, reaching: "One who sells any product in a defective condition unreasonably dangerous to the user or consumer or to his property is subject to liability for physical harm thereby caused to the ultimate user or consumer."[6] It made the seller of a product liable to a user even if the seller exercised all possible care in the preparation and sale of the product. The strict liability rule was no longer limited to products for human consumption, such as food and drink, or products intended for bodily use.

Section 402A now extended liability for any product that was expected to reach an ultimate consumer, and therefore, applied to products as various as automobiles, tires, an airplane, grinding wheel, water heater, gas stove, power tool, riveting machines, or insecticides. In addition, § 402A applied even though the ultimate user might have acquired the product through one or more intermediate dealers.

The plaintiffs' bar realized that § 402A provided a fresh avenue for suing and holding accountable product manufacturers and distributors for their products that caused occupational harm to laborers, such as refinery workers exposed to asbestos. The promulgation of § 402A inspired the first individual lawsuit by a plaintiff's attorney against asbestos manufacturers. Although this plaintiff

---

[5]   Paul Brodeur, *Outrageous Misconduct: The Asbestos Industry on Trial*, 27–29 (Pantheon Books 1985).

[6]   *Restatement (Second) of Torts* § 402A.

lost this first trial, the attorney settled with several defendants. In the process, the attorney acquired new asbestos clients, and thus, the nascent asbestos mass tort litigation was born and evolved from this inauspicious beginning.[7]

Asbestos was the first seminal mass tort litigation, and it soon became apparent to attorneys that the scope and magnitude of asbestos victims lent itself to aggregate claims into class action litigation. The experience of asbestos litigation gave rise to attorneys' pursuit of aggregation not only in asbestos litigation, but in other emerging mass tort cases involving DES, Bendectin, Agent Orange, and the Dalkon Shield. As courts became overwhelmed with mass tort cases, controversy arose over aggregationist techniques and the ability of the class action rule to sustain such litigation.

Once the floodgates of mass tort litigation opened, the ensuing decades of mass tort litigation manifested an ebb-and-flow pattern of plaintiff victories, innovation by attorneys and the courts, defeats with plaintiffs' attorneys retreating, regrouping, and returning with new theories. The fifty-year arc of mass tort litigation evidenced a pattern of initial judicial resistance to new ideas, but gradual acceptance of innovative procedural approaches to resolving massive cases. And, at every new development in mass tort litigation, the defense bar united in criticism of the illegitimacy of evolving legal theories and remedies.

One can draw a through-line from the beginnings of asbestos mass tort litigation to the twenty-first century new mass tort public nuisance MDL litigation involving lead paint, opioids, firearms, and e-cigarettes. Indeed, many of the lead attorneys in the twenty-first century public nuisance cases honed their strategic litigation skills on their learned experience in litigating and settling mass tort litigation extending back to asbestos, tobacco cases, medical device, pharmaceutical, environmental pollution cases, among many other mass torts.

Perhaps the best analogue in the history of mass tort litigation for the twenty-first century emergence of public nuisance claims is illustrated by the advent and development of medical monitoring in mass tort litigation. A request for medical monitoring in a mass tort case products case did not appear on the litigation landscape until the mid-1990s. Medical monitoring reflected another innovative theory advanced by plaintiffs' attorneys, which had great intuitive appeal in mass tort cases involving latent injury, such as tobacco litigation, toxic exposures, lead paint injuries, and certain pharmaceutical harms.

The request for medical monitoring was so new that it constituted a question of first impression in state and federal courts. Plaintiffs' attorneys were uncertain how to plead a request for medical monitoring, and whether

7   Brodeur, at 36, 39.

medical monitoring constituted a claim or a remedy. Correlatively, courts did not know how to respond to requests for medical monitoring, also uncertain whether medical monitoring constituted an independent claim for relief or a request for a remedy.

The question whether medical monitoring was a claim or remedy had significance for pleading. Plaintiffs most often pleaded medical monitoring in class litigation and courts soon became enmeshed in a debate concerning an appropriate pleading in the class action context. If medical monitoring were a claim, it might be pleaded as a damage action to recover monetary funds, but if medical monitoring was a remedy, then it needed to be asserted under the equitable injunctive relief provision which generally prohibited monetary relief. In the uncertain new terrain of medical monitoring, attorneys pleaded either or both provisions.

The defense bar united against the new medical monitoring requests. Defense counsel convinced many courts that requests for medical monitoring damage class actions failed the rule's predominance requirement because of the individualized nature of each class members' particular medical histories and medical needs. The defense bar further convinced many courts that requests for medical monitoring were illegitimate as a form of injunctive relief, because attorneys could not use the injunctive class category to receive compensation and thereby accomplish an end-run around the stricter certification requirements of an actual damage class action.

Notwithstanding the formal class action constraints on pleading medical monitoring, many courts began to approve requests for medical monitoring. As medical monitoring evolved with growing acceptance by some courts, further doctrinal controversy developed concerning whether courts could approve medical monitoring for class claimants in absence of claimants suffering from any current physical injury. And, as courts struggled with medical monitoring, many courts created ever more exacting standards for court-supervised medical monitoring funds and programs which would not pay compensation directly to claimants.

The emerging jurisprudence surrounding the controversy over the new medical monitoring requests inspired many states, but not all, to enact statutory medical monitoring claims, with elements for establishment of the claim. The medical monitoring statutes lay to rest the issue whether medical monitoring was a claim; but in those jurisdictions failing to enact statutes, courts defaulted to a remedy conception of medical monitoring.

In ensuing decades from the mid-1990s, federal and state courts have resolved hundreds of medical monitoring requests in mass tort litigation and have been equally divided in approving or disapproving medical monitoring. In states with medical monitoring statutes, the frequent reason for judicial disapproval in state and federal court has been the plaintiff's failure to satisfy elements of the claim. In medical monitoring litigation pursued without an underlying statutory basis, medical monitoring has been approved or disapproved on an array of grounds, some based on class action rationales.

Medical monitoring is very much a part of the twenty-first century mass tort litigation landscape, and it is still very much in flux. The uncertain jurisprudential legitimacy of medical monitoring was manifested in the American Law Institute's attempt, in 2021, to codify some medical monitoring principles in the final work on the *Restatement (Third) of Torts*. In 2021, the ALI proposed a set of principles, entitled *Restatement (Third) of Torts: Concluding Provisions*.[8]

The *Restatement (Third)* did not deal with the concept of medical monitoring in the project's substantial scope and many discrete parts. Thus, one of the orphan subjects to be addressed in the concluding provisions was medical monitoring. The initial draft recommended that courts adopt medical monitoring as a stand-alone tort, but this proved highly controversial. Several commentators reacted negatively, pointing out whether medical monitoring was an independent tort, or an element of damages, had significant ramifications. In the light of much criticism, ALI Reporters revised their draft to suggest that courts be given flexibility to use "[w]hichever terminology a court uses or approach a court chooses that would allow asymptomatic claimants to recover medical monitoring expenses."

The revised draft allowed recovery for medical monitoring expenses, even absent present bodily harm. It permitted recovery of medical monitoring expenses whenever "an actor's tortious conduct has exposed a person to a significant risk of serious future harm." The proposal drew immediate negative reaction from the defense bar, questioning whether the ALI should endorse any rule permitting tort recovery in the absence of present physical injury. Commentators also expressed concern about the ability of medical monitoring claims to potentially provide for unlimited or unpredictable liability. In its nearly 100-year history, the ALI had not adopted a *Restatement* provision allowing recovery for asymptomatic claimants. Courts were divided on this point, and therefore, the topic of medical monitoring merited restraint.[9]

---

[8] Christopher E. Appel and Mark A. Behrens, American Law Institute Proposes Controversial Medical Monitoring Rule in Final Parts of Torts Restatement, 87 Defense Couns. J. No. 4 (Jan. 19, 2021); Press Release, American Tort Reform Association, American Law Institute Risks Overstepping Boundaries with Proposed Restatements (Feb. 24, 2022).

[9] Appel & Behrens, *id*. At its March 2, 2022, Council meeting, the Council discussed but did not vote on the revised draft of the section on medical monitoring. The Reporters were instructed to further revise the material for consideration at a future date.

The narrative arc of medical monitoring in the history of mass tort litigation provides a useful parallel to thinking about the emergence of the new public nuisance paradigm in the twenty-first century. Like medical monitoring in the twentieth century, public nuisance claims were hardly pleaded in mass tort cases until the first decades of the twenty-first century, and so courts and litigants were largely unfamiliar with public nuisance law.

Like medical monitoring, public nuisance claims were pioneered by the same innovative mass tort plaintiffs' attorneys with decades of experience in landmark mass tort litigation. Like medical monitoring, public nuisance claims presented novel and untested litigation concepts that neither defendants nor courts had encountered in earlier mass tort cases. Like medical monitoring, there was substantial uncertainty concerning how to plead and defend against the new public nuisance claims.

Like medial monitoring, public nuisance claims initially were pleaded broadly and amorphously. Like medical monitoring claims, public nuisance claims were greeted with a fusillade of defense objections ranging from the constitutional to the doctrinal to the institutional. Like medical monitoring, many courts explained that public nuisance claims in the twenty-first century mass tort litigation presented issues of first impression. Like medical monitoring, many states have and will continue to enact public nuisance statutes specifically addressed to societal problems encompassing communal harm to health, safety, and welfare.

Like medical monitoring, the defense bar and its allies rallied, and continue to rally, against judicial approval of the new public nuisance law. The defense bar and its allies raise many of the same objections cultivated in opposition to medical monitoring: the inchoateness of the concept, using public nuisance as an illegitimate end run around traditional tort law, using public nuisance law to seek compensatory damages historically barred by doctrine, and, like medical monitoring, the prospect of public nuisance law imposing indeterminate, unpredictable, and unlimited liability. Furthermore, defense interests have criticized and challenged judicial approval and structuring of medical monitoring funds; in the same fashion, critics now challenge those courts that have undertaken creation and supervision of public nuisance abatement funds.

It is, therefore, no surprise that the new public nuisance is the latest object of contentious debate in the mass tort legal landscape. But the fate of the new public nuisance law is likely to follow a similar trajectory to that of medical monitoring. From an initial position of confusion and perplexity, litigants and the courts will sort out public nuisance claims based on a combination of common law doctrine, statutory interpretation aided by common law doctrine, and statutory strict liability.

The defense bar, its allies, and academic fellow travelers will continue to argue against approval of the new public nuisance law grounded in traditional, formal, institutional, democratic, economic, and political grounds. But the new public nuisance law, much like medical monitoring, is here to stay. It is the new frontier of mass tort litigation, but it is here to stay. It will be a doctrine in continuous flux, revision, and refinement, but public nuisance is now a fixed feature in the mass tort firmament.

Index

Printed in the USA
CPSIA information can be obtained
at www.ICGtesting.com
LVHW021658050124
768120LV00005B/469